CAMBRIDGE LATIN AMERICAN STUDIES

EDITORS
DAVID JOSLIN   JOHN STREET
CLIFFORD T. SMITH

11

ALIENATION OF CHURCH WEALTH IN MEXICO
1856–1875

THE SERIES

ALIENATION OF CHURCH WEALTH IN MEXICO

SOCIAL AND ECONOMIC ASPECTS OF THE LIBERAL REVOLUTION 1856–1875

BY

JAN BAZANT

Professor in the Centre of Historical Studies
El Colegio de México

EDITED AND TRANSLATED BY

MICHAEL P. COSTELOE

Lecturer in the Department of Spanish and Portuguese in
the University of Bristol

CAMBRIDGE

AT THE UNIVERSITY PRESS

1971

Published by the Syndics of the Cambridge University Press
Bentley House, 200 Euston Road, London N.W. 1
American Branch: 32 East 57th Street, New York, N.Y. 10022

© Cambridge University Press 1971

ISBN: 0 521 07872 5

Printed in Great Britain
at the University Printing House, Cambridge
(Brooke Crutchley, University Printer)

TO THE MEMORY OF MY PARENTS

CONTENTS

vii

Contents

TABLES

EDITOR'S NOTE

This monograph was originally written in Spanish, and in view of the specialized nature of many of the ecclesiastical and legal terms used, I have written a version rather than a direct translation of the original. In some instances, where there is no clear equivalent to the Spanish, I have added explanatory footnotes. In deciding on the precise English terms to be used, and for general assistance and advice, I am much indebted to the general editors of the series, Dr. J. Street and Professor D. Joslin.

M.P.C.

PREFACE

This monograph concerns the nationalization and sale of the wealth of the Roman Catholic Church in Mexico from 1822 until the end of the nineteenth century. Some references are included to possessions which were already nationalized in earlier periods but were sold by later governments, and in some cases the civil authorities merely appropriated certain real estate and, instead of selling, found other ways to dispose of it. Ecclesiastical wealth consisted largely of property and capital and it was distributed among a variety of institutions. Included here are the possessions of the established Church, that is the regular and secular clergy, those of educational and charitable institutions affiliated to the Church, such as the brotherhoods, colleges, hospitals, and poor houses, and the capital belonging to *capellanías*. Real estate belonging to the civil corporations, for example municipalities and villages, are referred to when relevant to the main topic.

The nationalization and sale of these goods throughout Mexico is considered but particular reference is made to specific regions, namely the Federal District and the states of Puebla, Veracruz, San Luis Potosí, Michoacán and Jalisco. I have restricted my attention to these areas because of the enormous amount of material in the notarial archives. An exhaustive investigation of these sources would require many years and a number of scholars. The Federal District is included partly because the official reports of the various Ministers contain a great amount of information on the capital city. The first three of the abovementioned states were studied partly because of the existence of such publications as the *Guías de forasteros* of Mexico and of Puebla, the third volume of the *Historia de Veracruz* by Miguel Lerdo de Tejada, and certain works concerning San Luis Potosí, all of which provide detailed information on the society in those cities and states and thus facilitate an analysis of the nationalization and its implementation. Michoacán is of special interest because, unlike all the other states, the continuity of the liberal government was not broken in the years 1858–60. Jalisco is significant because of the importance of its capital city, Guadalajara. These six areas are perhaps sufficiently representative of the country as a whole. Moreover, their clerical possessions amounted to more than two-thirds of all Church wealth and the purchase of the nationalized property within them equalled two-thirds of the total for the entire nation. Finally, it must be noted that

Preface

a full investigation of all the notarial archives in the Federal District and the five states was not made. Only those considered to be most important were selected on the basis of the completeness of their records.

I became interested in this topic in 1957 during the centenary of the Mexican Constitution of 1857. The several works published on that occasion were almost exclusively concerned with the ideological, juridical and political aspects, and it seemed to me necessary that an economic and social study should be made of the historical process known in Mexico as the Reform. Only by so doing can such questions as the following be answered: Is it true that before the Reform the Church was exceptionally rich? Were the nationalization and sale of clerical property and capital a success, and in what sense, or were they a failure? Is it true, as has been affirmed, that the liberal measures favoured only a few, above all foreign speculators, and that the people as a whole were harmed? Is it true that the property and capital were disposed of at a fraction of their real value? Finally, is it true that the country's economy progressed in subsequent years, precisely as a result of the new 'social base'?

I considered going more deeply into the topic until in the years 1963–64 I collaborated on a history of Mexico's foreign debt for the Colegio de México. Through this study I became more familiar with the subject of Church wealth and the Reform because of the close connection between the public debt and the nationalization of Church wealth. The debt was sometimes funded by mortgaging clerical property and in part redeemed by its sale. Another reason for undertaking the study was that more than a century has now passed since the events which are described took place. Mexico is no different from other nations. In France also, as Georges Lefèbvre has pointed out, the study of the financial, economic and social aspects of the sale of Church wealth began at the end of the nineteenth century, a hundred years after the Revolution. Hence it seems time to take the first step in Mexico.

A number of problems arose affecting the form of the work. For example, after the liberal administration of 1856–57, with few exceptions, a large part of the country was in the control of a conservative government which annulled the Reform legislation. Then, from 1861–63, the liberals regained power and continued to carry out their earlier reforms. In some instances the consequences of the measures which affected clerical possessions in 1856–57 are discussed in the chapters dealing with those years, and in others, for the reasons given in each case, they are inserted in the chapters relating to the years 1861–63. Apart from these exceptions, it seemed preferable to make a chronological study. After the period 1856–

Preface

57, described in chapters 2 and 3, chapter 4 deals with the reactionary government of 1858–60, chapters 5 and 6 with the years 1861–63, and chapter 7 with the Empire and the victorious republic until the end of the nationalization.

Certain other points of presentation require explanation. In footnote citations the sign MS has been omitted, since, unless otherwise stated, all archival references are to manuscripts. All monetary references in the text, notes and appendices are to pesos. Until 1861 the peso was subdivided into eight reales, one real being equal to twelve granos, but these latter units have been omitted here. Hence where some additions appear to be inaccurate to the extent of one peso, this is due to the inclusion of the reales and later of the centavos in the total sum. In 1861 the decimal system (1 peso = 100 centavos) was established.

Mexico, 1970   J. B.

ACKNOWLEDGEMENTS

Grateful acknowledgement is made to the many scholars and the staff of archives and libraries in Mexico and the United States. I am particularly indebted to Victor L. Urquidi, President of El Colegio de Mexico, and to my colleagues in the Centre of Historical Studies; and to my friends Professor D. Joslin, Dr. M. P. Costeloe, Professor J. H. Elliott, Dr. F. Chevalier, Dr. R. J. Knowlton, Dr. C. A. Hale, Professor R. Potash, Dr. D. Brading and Dr. J. Street and, last but not least, to my wife, Emma, for constant words of encouragement.

J. B.

ABBREVIATIONS

AGN	Archivo General de la Nación
AHINAH	Archivo Histórico del Instituto Nacional de Antropología e Historia
ANG	Archivo de Notarías, Guadalajara
ANM	Archivo de Notarías, Mexico City
ANMor	Archivo de Notarías, Morelia
ANP	Archivo de Notarías, Puebla
ANSLP	Archivo de Notarías, San Luis Potosí
ANV	Archivo de Notarías, Veracruz
BSMGE	*Boletín de la Sociedad Mexicana de Geografía y Estadística*
JE	Justicia Eclesiástica, section of AGN
MD 1862	Memoria de Desamortización 1862
MH 1857	Memoria de Hacienda 1857
MH 1870	Memoria de Hacienda 1870
PBN	Papeles de Bienes Nacionales, section of AGN
RPP	Registro Público de la Propiedad

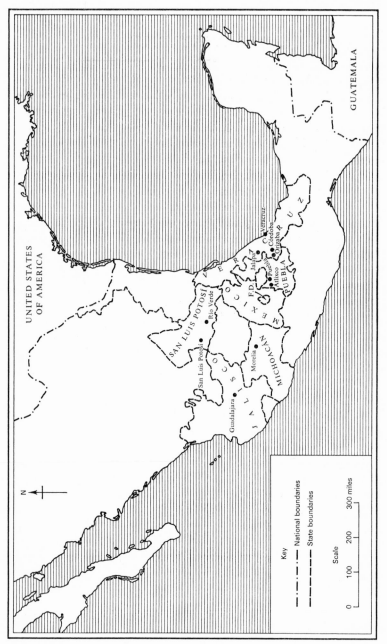

Mexico in 1857

INTRODUCTION

The confiscation of Church wealth, and its sale in one form or another, has usually occurred on those occasions in history in the anomalous situation of a rich Church existing side by side with an impoverished State. Often the poverty of the State was the result of a war which had left the national exchequer exhausted and in debt. Military expenditure reduced national wealth, as did the extravagant and profligate activities of monarchs. In contrast the life of most of the religious, in particular the regular orders was methodical and frugal. Moreover, ecclesiastical property enjoyed exemption from most civil taxes and there was a slow but continuous increase in legacies, inheritances and gifts to the Church. As the exchequer was impoverished the Church grew richer, and when this situation arose the State eventually began to seek an adequate justification to confiscate some or all of the clerical possessions.

The experience of some European countries which undertook the appropriation of Church wealth may be summarized as follows. In Spain the measure was the culmination of a prolonged struggle between the liberals and the conservatives. The former advocated the sale of the clerical possessions in order to redeem the national debt and at the same time to create a rural middle class which would afford them the social base they required. The opportunity to carry out this programme came in 1835 when the new liberal Prime Minister, Juan Alvárez Mendizábal, confiscated all Church properties and put them up for sale by public auction.[1] Nevertheless, the liberal programme was not realized: the very large amount of real estate which came on the market caused a fall in values and many properties were sold at extremely low prices; as a fiscal reform the nationalization failed. It was equally unsuccessful as a social reform, since both the wealthy liberals and the great landowners were able to outbid their poorer competitors in the auctions. The land was simply

---

[1] The information on Spain is taken from J. M. Sánchez, *Reform and reaction: the politico–religious background of the Spanish civil war* (Chapel Hill, University of North Carolina Press, 1964), pp. 13–29. In his *Contribución al estudio de la desamortización en España. La desamortización de Mendizábal en la provincia de Gerona* (Madrid, 1969), F. S. Segura shows that merchants were the main buyers in this part of Catalonia. In his most recent work, *Contribución al estudio de la desamortización en España. La desamortización de Mendizábal en la provincia de Madrid* (Madrid, 1969), the same author shows that the main beneficiaries of the sale of clerical goods in the province of Madrid were merchants, professional classes, landowners and aristocrats. These two detailed studies seem to prove the general thesis of J. M. Sánchez.

1

transferred to them and remained concentrated in the hands of a few owners. The existing landowners, until then sympathetic to the conservative Carlist cause, bought the clerical real estate. From then on, in order to protect their investments, they supported the liberals, for a Carlist victory would mean the return of the property to the Church. On the other hand, many of the most prominent of the liberal buyers became conservatives as a result of their acquisition of real estate. A new oligarchy of landowners arose from this fusion of liberals and Carlists.

In Castille the bourgeoisie and middle class were weak in comparison to the conservative elements such as the Church and the landowners, and economic development was retarded compared to France and England.

The conservatives regained power in Spain in 1844, and in the concordat of 1851 the Church accepted the disentailment as a fait accompli. The sales of ecclesiastical wealth were legalized and the concordat remained in force until 1931, with several interruptions. The first of these began in 1855 when the liberals returned to power and decreed the disentailment of the remaining clerical property.[1] Four years later the conservatives were again in control, and they signed an agreement with the Papacy in which Rome recognized the validity of the confiscations made in 1855–59. Faits accomplis prevailed.

The Spanish disentailment was inspired by what had happened during the French revolution as a result of the decision issued on 14 May 1790 by the constituent assembly to sell the goods which had been nationalized six months earlier. The sales began at the beginning of 1791,[2] and in the first two years involved mostly the possessions of the Church,[3] whereas in the critical years of 1793 and 1794 the properties of émigrés were sold. Some studies of these sales do not seem to make a clear distinction between the two phases in the process.[4] They refer to the nationalized goods without differentiating between those which originally belonged to the Church and those owned by the nobility. In the first phase the buyers of the clerical properties were above all the nobles and the bourgeoisie who had available cash or were government creditors seeking an investment.[5] The father of Balzac's famous character Eugénie Grandet, a frugal artisan,

[1] F. S. Segura, 'La desamortización de 1855', *Economía Financiera Española*, XIX–XX (Madrid, 1968).
[2] P. Bouthomnier, 'The role of the peasants in the revolution', in *Essays on the French revolution*, ed. T. A. Jackson (London, 1945), pp. 147–55.
[3] J. Jaurès, *Histoire socialiste de la révolution française* (Paris, 1927), vol. II, pp. 127–41.
[4] G. Lefèbvre, 'La vente des biens nationaux', reproduced in G. Lefèbvre, *Etudes sur la révolution française* (Paris, 1963), pp. 307–33.
[5] A. Latreille, *L'Eglise catholique et la révolution française* (Paris, 1946), vol. I, pp. 78–9.

used the money of his father-in-law, a wealthy merchant, to buy Church real estate. Until 1792 the sales seem to have benefited the same social groups as they were to do later in Spain, but the Jacobin revolution of 1793 brought about an unexpected change. It partly caused the sale of lands belonging to nobles who had emigrated, on terms which were possible for the peasants. Even though in that difficult time for the republic there were speculators among the buyers (who paid for the properties with the much depreciated *assignats*), there is no doubt that the rural population in general did benefit. For a brief period Robespierre gave the sales the character of an agrarian reform. Nevertheless, in the long term the result did not differ much from that in other countries, perhaps in part because many of the lands of those who emigrated were acquired by the émigrés themselves through intermediaries.[1]

The partial reforms of the Austrian emperor, Joseph II (1780–90), consisted mainly of the closing of almost half the monasteries and convents and the auction of their properties.[2] The product of the sales was given to the parishes, since at that time monks and nuns were looked on with much disfavour, whereas there was considerable sympathy for the parish priests. It seems that also in Austria (which included Bohemia, Moravia, Silesia and other provinces) there was wastage, speculation and some adverse social effects.[3]

Unlike in France, the English reform of the sixteenth century was not a popular movement or revolution but a measure imposed by the monarchy. As in other countries the confiscation and sale were accompanied by low prices, speculation and wastage.[4] The first historian to analyse those who acquired Church possessions in England was Alexandre Savine, of the University of Moscow.[5] His statistical table of the persons who obtained the monastic lands shows that the main beneficiaries were, among individuals, the nobles, courtiers, government employees and merchants.[6] Savine did not take into account, however, the fact that many of the original beneficiaries ceded, transferred or sold their claims to other

[1] Lefèbvre, 320.
[2] M. C. Goodwin, *The Papal conflict with Josephinism* (New York, 1938), pp. 50–3; on Bavaria, see A. S. Hanser, *Church and State in Bavaria, 1799–1806; an absolutist reform in the age of revolution* (dissertation of the University of Chicago, 1964), pp. 114–15.
[3] *Catholic Encyclopaedia*, 1913, vol. VIII, pp. 509–11.
[4] G. Constant, *The reformation in England* (London, 1934), vol. I, pp. 186–93.
[5] Author of *English monasteries on the eve of the dissolution* (Oxford, 1909). Also the first to study the sale of nationalized goods in France were foreigners, especially the Russian Loutchisky.
[6] Published in H. A. L. Fisher, *The history of England from the accession of Henry VII to the death of Henry VIII (1485–1547)*, vol. V of *The political history of England* (London, 1906), appendix II, pp. 499–501.

people. Current opinion, expressed by Dom David Knowles in *The religious orders in England*,[1] indicates that the final result of the transfer of Church real estate was that all the existing groups of landowners—both nobility and bourgeoisie—increased their holdings.[2] The favourable effect, direct and indirect, of the confiscation on the English economy has been noted many times, recently, for example, by J. U. Nef.[3] Although the English reform was not a social one, it does seem to have been a cause of economic progress.

The ideals of the Hussite revolution which broke out in Bohemia in 1419 were frustrated,[4] and the most important beneficiaries of the clerical possessions that were confiscated were the Hussite and Catholic nobles.[5] Some cities, especially Prague, benefited but the urban element was weaker in Bohemia than in western Europe and was therefore the first victim of the Counter Reformation of the sixteenth century. Later, in 1620, the protestant nobles were also defeated and their possessions appropriated. The Church, however, did not succeed in regaining the lands which had been confiscated two centuries earlier because part of them were in the hands of the Catholic nobility, and the emperor used the other part, consisting of property confiscated from the protestant nobles, to compensate those who had contributed to the military triumph of the Counter Reformation.[6]

A general picture emerges from the above examples: those who gained most from the nationalization of Church property were the great land-owners, whether they were noble or bourgeois, feudal or capitalist in origin. This result tended to consolidate the aristocracy in the political sphere. The different result in France—a democratic regime—was due to

[1] *The Tudor age*, vol. III (Cambridge, 1959), pp. 247–401.

[2] See also R. H. Tawney, 'The rise of the gentry', published in *Essays in economic history*, ed. E. M. Carus-Wilson (London, 1954), p. 173; G. M. Trevelyan, *Illustrated English social history* (London, 1954), vol. I, pp. 103–7; S. B. Liljegren, *The fall of the monasteries and social changes in England leading up to the great revolution* (Lund, 1924), pp. 109–11; L. Brentano, *Eine Geschichte der wirtschaftlichen Entwicklung Englands* (Jena, 1927), vol. II, pp. 23, 79, 83, 132–4; H. J. Habakkuk, 'The market for monastic property, 1593–1603', *The Economic History Review* (April 1958), pp. 62 ff.; G. W. O. Woodward, 'A speculation in monastic lands', *The English Historical Review* (October 1964), pp. 778–83.

[3] 'Prices and industrial capitalism in France and England, 1540–1640', published in *Essays in economic history*, ed. E. M. Carus-Wilson (London, 1954), p. 133.

[4] See the study in English by J. Kaminsky, 'Chiliasm and the Hussite revolution', published in the excellent collection edited by S. L. Thrupp, *Change in medieval society* (New York, 1964), pp. 249 ff.

[5] O. Odlozilik, *The Hussite king; Bohemia in European affairs, 1440–1471* (Rutgers University Press, 1965), p. 6.

[6] E. Denis, *La Bohême après la Montagne Blanche*, published in Czech as *Cechy po Bílé Hore* (Prague, 1904), vol. I, pp. 41, 245, 563.

the fact that not only the possessions of the clergy but also in part those of the nobility were nationalized.

The nationalization of Church property, which has had the most direct influence in modern times, including probably in Mexico, was motivated by a law issued in France on 2 November 1789. The aim of the measure was to enable the French crown to repay the debts it owed, mainly to foreign bankers. During the subsequent revolutionary and Napoleonic wars, this means of remedying national bankruptcy spread to Spain and later to its American colonies. Then on 26 December 1804 a royal decree was promulgated in New Spain, imposing a forced loan on all pious foundations. The purpose was to raise revenue with which to pay Spain's national debt. All the capital belonging to *capellanías*, or to the pious works of the regular orders, was ordered to be withdrawn from circulation and placed in the royal coffers.[1] This disguised disentailment was finally suspended shortly before the war of independence, by which time the Spanish crown had appropriated the enormous sum of over 12,000,000 pesos.

The fiscal condition of the new nation of Mexico after the long and damaging war of independence inevitably grew worse, and soon the possibility of nationalizing the wealth of the Church came to be considered. Thirty-five years of intermittent civil war were to pass, however, until the Lerdo law of 1856, and a further five years, until 1861, before the nationalization could be made effective throughout the country. This intervening period, from 1821 to 1861, saw the development of a struggle between the liberals, who by various means attempted to confiscate Church property and capital and to create a modern state, and their adversaries who, in spite of their declared intentions to the contrary, found themselves obliged to utilize Church wealth for their own financial needs. The liberals used the Church as a source of revenue in accordance with political conviction, whereas their opponents did the same in spite of it.

It may seem strange that both liberal and conservative governments should have sought to finance themselves with Church wealth. The explanation lies in the poverty of the country's resources. The traditional wealth of Mexico consisted of the mining of precious metals, but this industry had been almost ruined in the war of independence. Although

---

[1] A *capellanía*, similar to a chantry, was an ecclesiastical benefice consisting of a sum of money invested to yield an income which was paid to the beneficiary, known as the *capellán*: for a detailed description of this type of benefice, see R. J. Knowlton, 'Chaplaincies and the Mexican Reform', *Hispanic American Historical Review*, XLVIII (August 1968), 421–37; a pious work (*obra pía*) was a less precise benefice consisting of a fund or property the income from which was devoted to a pious work, usually designated by the founder.

the injection of British capital during the early years of the new republic did succeed in reviving it to some extent, nevertheless by the middle of the century new losses were being incurred, partly as a result of technical difficulties and the general political instability. The foreign companies sold their holdings to Mexican capitalists. Agriculture was also unprofitable, largely through the effects of the tithe and the lack of markets, which could only be opened up by the construction of railways, but the topography of the country presented seemingly insoluble problems to such development. Industry was created and sustained by conservative, protectionist policies; for example, the State prohibited the import of yarn and cloth, thereby sacrificing much-needed customs revenue, in order to stimulate the growth of a national textile industry.

The Mexican economy, therefore, could offer little to the national treasury. Frequent wars added to the progressive increase in expenditure, and it is obvious that the State would look with envy on the Church, which seemed to escape all the ill-effects of the deterioration in the national economy. Did the Church not possess untold riches accumulated from its activities as a bank and landowner? Did the churches not shine with the brilliance of silver and jewels? Were not the sacred images covered in gold and diamonds? Were the priests not wearing precious robes encrusted with pearls? Eyes were closed to the fact that such apparent luxury was an inherent part of the Roman Catholic worship and it was not known that at times the clerical coffers were empty.

This apparent wealth of the Church perhaps explains why monarchist, republican, conservative and liberal governments should all have considered nationalizing Church possessions in one form or another, but it does not account for the fact that these same governments did not choose to attack the group of merchants and financial speculators who might well have been better placed than the Church to provide funds for the national treasury. The reasons for this neglect of a potentially rich source of revenue are more profound and they lie in the social structure of Mexico at the time. The most respected social class was without doubt the rural landowners, the hacendados, some of whom were descendants of the viceregal nobility. The merchants were second in the social scale, and perhaps first in the economic scale, and in the absence of banks in the modern sense of the word, many made loans to commerce and to the civil authorities. Details of loans made to landowners will be given later. The rate of commercial interest fluctuated between 12% and 24% per annum, according to the circumstances, but the rate for loans to the government, which were always highly speculative, amounted to at least

24% per month. In contrast, the return on real estate, both urban and rural, was on average a mere 5% a year. Either because of the scarcity of good land, due to the configuration of the country, the lack of water and communications, or because of the greater security and social prestige afforded landowners, real estate was very highly valued.

Nevertheless, both investors and the professional classes, few of whom had much capital, aspired to become landowners, preferably hacendados, and thereby gain access to the highest group on the social pyramid. Of course, the number of large rural properties was limited. Some were to be found in the hands of the Church, which was gradually losing its strong position as in other countries. It was logical that the merchants, the holders of national debt bonds and the professional classes should seek to take advantage of the secular tendency against the Church. Furthermore, the hacendados themselves had little to lose and much to gain by a nationalization of Church property and capital. Such a measure would afford them the opportunity to redeem their debts to the Church at a favourable rate. It was relatively easy for some members of these groups to promote measures aimed at the confiscation of Church wealth whenever the national fiscal situation became critical. This often happened, as a result of the political instability and the lack of a financial policy which there had not been time to prepare. Yet it must be noted that only a section of each of these three groups were of liberal opinions. As in many other great historical movements the social classes were divided vertically, but it is precisely the presence of these vested interests which explains the inclination of both liberal- and conservative-orientated governments towards a nationalization, even though disguised, of Church wealth. Private interests, as well as fiscal needs, determined this pronounced tendency in most Mexican governments.

In 1850 there were 3,320 secular clergy, including 3,232 priests, and 88 lay brothers, the latter being distributed among the eight congregations of San Felipe Neri, a monastery of the order of San Camilo and the Jesuit Order. There were in addition 1,295 regulars distributed as follows: 1,043 in 144 monasteries which were responsible for thirty-two parishes and twenty-six missions; 252 in six Colleges of Propaganda Fide.[1] The total number of religious was therefore 4,615, which was approximately half the number recorded in the time of Humboldt and represented rather less than one per thousand souls in a country in which the population in 1839 is estimated to have been seven million, and in 1854–56 about

---

[1] M. Lerdo de Tejada, *Cuadro sinóptico de la república mexicana en 1856* (Mexico, 1856), pp. 80–2; figures taken from *Memoria de Justicia,* 1851.

eight million. This was clearly a low ratio in a country of such fervent religious observance as Mexico. If the secular clergy only are considered— they mostly administered the parishes—the ratio is even less, one per three thousand souls. Of course, there must be added to these numbers a further 1,484 nuns, 103 novices and 533 girls (pupils staying in convent schools and members of the lay population living in other convents). In 1850 these latter persons were housed in 58 convents, together with 1,266 servants. Therefore, totalling the nuns, novices, girls and the monks, the regular orders contained approximately 3,400 people, that is, more or less the same number as in the secular branch.

The economy of these two sectors within the Church differed con- siderably. The regular orders depended mainly on real estate and on capital invested by way of mortgage loans. In addition the majority of nuns brought to their respective communities a dowry of between 3,000 and 5,000 pesos, although this was rarely handed over in cash. It was usually paid by the parents who mortgaged a property to the convent for the amount of the dowry and thereafter paid a perpetual annual interest.

The monasteries also received varying amounts by way of alms and perquisites, although the revenue from these sources was much less than that yielded by their rural and urban properties and the interest on invested capital. In general the nuns only held urban real estate, and the nunneries, unlike the monasteries, were invariably situated in cities.

Among the secular clergy the bishops and canons lived mainly on the product of the tithe, first fruits and *aniversarios* (holidays to commemorate martyrs),[1] while the parish priests existed on the proceeds of parochial fees and masses.[2] Certain groups had special sources of income, for example the collegiate church of Guadalupe, which had twenty-five annual lotteries of 13,000 pesos each and a capital fund of 621,000 pesos owed to it by the government.[3] The secular clergy had comparatively little real estate, and the Church's building and other funds were usually supported by the properties owned by the cathedral and the parishes.[4] In 1856 the regular orders owned property in Mexico City valued at 11,065,768 pesos, and the secular clergy, to the value of 1,322,839 pesos.[5] The regular sector, although equal in numbers, was, at least in the capital, eight times richer in real estate than the secular.

---

[1] Ibid.
[2] J. M. L. Mora, *México y sus revoluciones* (2nd ed., Mexico, 1950), vol. 1, p. 109.
[3] Lerdo de Tejada, *Cuadro sinóptico*, 80–2.   [4] Ibid.
[5] *Noticia de las fincas pertenecientes a corporaciones civiles y eclesiásticas del distrito de México* (Mexico, 1856), pp. 30–3.

Introduction

The only published records which are reasonably abundant on the history of ecclesiastical property in Mexico from independence until the Reform are to be found in the reports of the Ministry of Justice and Ecclesiastical Affairs for the years 1825, 1826, 1827, 1828, 1832 and 1843. Reports were published in other years but they have no details on Church wealth and are usually restricted to information on the number of monks and nuns. During the early years of the republic the various Ministers fulfilled their obligation to keep the public informed, but for the year 1829 the report was not issued because of the civil war then in progress, and from 1830 to 1832 the conservative administration in power chose not to include them. In 1833 a liberal government gained control and more accounts were given, but the liberals were soon removed from power. Finally in 1843 Santa Anna, who, as will be shown later, was very interested in Church wealth, published the first account of the possessions of each of the convents and monasteries in the republic. It seems that subsequently the Reform government of 1856 intended to publish a similar report, for various sets of figures, referring only to monasteries, are to be found in the National Archive. More urgent business, however, probably the intervention of ecclesiastical property in the diocese of Puebla, prevented the publication.

As the riches of the regular orders were much more substantial than those of the secular clergy, and as statistical data are available for the years 1821–56 for the regulars, though not for the secular clergy, more attention has been given in this work to the wealth of the convents and monasteries.

In 1843 there were six regular orders in Mexico. The Augustinians, with twenty-one houses, were divided into two provinces, those of Mexico and Michoacán, and they were the richest of all the orders.[1] The Carmelites had sixteen monasteries in a single province. The Dominicans had twenty-six, divided into four provinces. The Mercedarians, although poor, had nineteen. The Order of San Diego, poorer still, had fourteen, and finally the Franciscans had fifty-one, divided into four provinces. Although the latter possessed little property, they did have a considerable amount of capital, but this was lower in value than the real estate of the other orders.

The nunneries were in most cases subject to the jurisdiction of the bishops. In 1843 the diocese of Mexico, which was the only archbishopric in the country at the time, contained nineteen convents, of which seventeen were in the capital and two in Querétaro.[2] In the bishopric of Puebla

[1] These figures are taken from *Memoria de Justicia*, 1844.
[2] Ibid.

9

there were ten, all situated in the city. Michoacán had six, located in various places throughout the diocese. Chiapas had one and Guadalajara seven, of which five were in the city itself. Finally, the Franciscans were in charge of eight others, located on the central pleateau, and the Dominicans two, one in the capital and the other in Oaxaca.

The nunneries were richer than the monasteries, even though they had to maintain almost double the number of persons. Often they served as a refuge for the daughters of wealthy families, and the dowry which each new entrant brought remained incorporated into the convent's property. One exception were the Capuchine nuns, who had neither real estate nor capital, living solely on the revenue received from charity. Other communities, known as *beaterios*, came under the supervision of the ecclesiastical authorities and they housed a number of women who belonged to no specific religious order.

Schools were usually dependent on the regular orders and those monasteries which were principally teaching institutions were known as colleges, headed by a rector.[1] For example, in the capital the Augustinians had in 1856 the college of San Pablo; the Carmelites the college of San Angel; the Dominicans the college of Porta Coeli; the Franciscans the college of Santiago Tlaltelolco; and the Mercedarians the college of Belem. Some nunneries were also devoted to education, as can be seen from the names of two, Enseñanza Antigua and Enseñanza Nueva.

In addition to education, the regular orders traditionally managed charitable organizations, for example the hospitals. Three of the orders, known as Hospitallers (*Hospitalarios*), were especially concerned, namely the Bethlehemites (*Hospitalarios de Belem*), the Order of San Juan de Dios, and the Hypolytes (*San Hipólito*). There were, of course, other hospitals with no clerical connections, for example in the capital there was the famous hospital of Jesus, founded and endowed by Hernán Cortés. The Hospitallers were suppressed in 1821 by the then liberal administration in Spain and the abolition was upheld in independent Mexico. The endowments which they had used to carry out their socially beneficial activities were nationalized. Details of their disposal are given in chapter 1.

Various other societies of pious laymen were connected with the Church. These were known as tertiary brothers and brotherhoods, depending on the degree to which they submitted to ecclesiastical discipline. Among the former those of San Francisco, affiliated to the regular order of the same name, were perhaps the best known. The brotherhoods, however, were of primary importance in Mexico. They

[1] Mora, *México y sus revoluciones*, I, 240.

were often formed for the purpose of venerating a sacred image or carrying out some special religious function, and over the years they had accumulated a large number of properties. When a brotherhood consisted of rich people it often carried out charitable work, for example the Biscayan merchants, associated in the brotherhood of Aranzazú, maintained the college of Biscayans. On the other hand, if the brotherhood was created by a trade guild, then its aim was usually to aid its own members with such costs as social security.

The classification of all these institutions and clerical endowments does not reveal the true function of the Church in the economy of Mexico. The tithe represented a high and fixed percentage of the gross yield from agriculture and as such was prejudicial to the economy of the country, but this levy was much reduced after its payment was made voluntary by the State in 1833. It is perhaps curious to note, in this connection, that the conservative governments after 1833 did not try to re-establish the tithes. Santa Anna reintroduced the obligatory nature of the monastic vows, which were also abolished in 1833, but he ignored the liberal tithe legislation. The reason for this was that the conservative administration in Mexico, and in other countries, tended to be a government of landowners, and they took advantage of the benefits ensuing from the liberal reform of 1833.

The Church was an important owner of both urban and rural real estate. The properties were usually rented to the lay population and the clergy merely collected the rents and had no concern in the management of their haciendas. The Church also had in its *juzgados de capellanías* a type of mortgage bank which made loans to urban and rural property owners at 5% and 6% annual interest.[1] This rate was, at the most, only half the amount demanded in mercantile loans but there are some indications that the large difference was perhaps only theoretical. For example, in 1847 one author alleged that the borrower would sign a contract for a loan of 50,000 pesos but in fact only received 40,000 pesos in cash, which thereby increased the real rate of interest from 6% to 8%.[2] The latter seems more likely but lack of evidence prevents any conclusive proof. As far as the hacendados were concerned, the interest paid to the Church was a fixed cost like the rent paid by a tenant. When making a loan the Church did not insist that the money should be used in a productive

[1] See M. P. Costeloe, *Church wealth in Mexico: A study of the 'juzgado de capellanías' in the archbishopric of Mexico, 1800–1856* (Cambridge, 1967).
[2] *Reflexiones sobre la ley de 17 de mayo del corriente año, que declara irredimible los capitales pertenecientes a corporaciones y obras pías; en respuesta al Monitor Republicano de 23 del mismo* (Mexico, 1847).

enterprise. In short the Church acted as an annuitant, and as it was not directly linked to actual production it was more vulnerable to liberal attacks. Hence it seemed easier to relieve the economy of the burden of the clerical debt.

Many attempts have been made to calculate the total value of Church wealth before the liberal reform. Enormous discrepancies exist in the many estimates and these are often to be explained by the political opinions of the author, the liberals tending to inflate, and the conservatives to deflate, their totals. The most famous estimate is that of the liberal theorist José María Luis Mora, who assessed the total riches of the Church at the end of 1832 to be almost 180,000,000 pesos.[1] This figure is clearly exaggerated on several counts. First, Mora capitalized the tithes, the parochial dues, first fruits and alms on the basis that they represented a 5% yield. All these were revenues which cannot be capitalized in this way since they were not the product of a capital. Secondly, Mora accepted as valid for 1832 the estimates made by Abad y Queipo for the year 1804, thus ignoring the fact that Church property and capital had decreased since that time. Thirdly, he included in his estimate the value of unproductive goods such as the convent and church buildings, jewels and works of art, and to these he attributed a value of 50,000,000 pesos. It may have seemed logical at the time to give such items a commercial value, but even so the total given is excessive, as the government discovered after 1861 when it found that many of the convent and monastery buildings were unsaleable. At the present day the same goods have no calculable value as they are now historical monuments or works of art.

Using only those productive possessions which were not dependent for their valuation on the political opinions of the writer, the total average annual value of the property of the regular orders, as given in Ministry reports between 1821 and 1856, was about 25,000,000 pesos. In addition, capital belonging to *capellanías* and pious works amounted to 15,000,000 pesos, the archbishopric of Mexico alone having just over 4,000,000 pesos' worth of these funds at the beginning of independence.[2] The remaining 10,000,000 pesos includes the value of the possessions of the secular clergy, the brotherhoods, schools and hospitals.

The total value of all the productive goods administered by the Church, and those institutions connected or affiliated to it, probably amounted before the Reform to approximately 50,000,000 pesos. This sum, however, must be considered as a minimum, for it is based on property details

[1] J. M. L. Mora, *Obras sueltas* (2nd ed., Mexico, 1963), p. 392.
[2] Costeloe, *Church wealth*, 87.

Introduction

produced by the clergy themselves and, as will be shown in later pages of this work, the ecclesiastical corporations frequently had in addition properties and funds which were not known to the government or at least were not revealed in the statistics of the report of the Ministry of Justice. It can be supposed that if these hidden assets were included, the total would increase by 10,000,000 pesos or perhaps even 20,000,000 pesos. The exact amount is unknown and impossible to ascertain. Finally, the value of unproductive assets, that is, the churches, convent and monastery buildings, may be estimated at 10,000,000 pesos, and the value of the gold, silver, jewels, works of art and other valuable objects at a further 10,000,000 pesos. In summary, therefore, the total value of the assets administered by the Church and its affiliated institutions was almost 100,000,000 pesos. It is reasonably certain that in the middle of the nineteenth century the total did not exceed this amount.[1]

These 100,000,000 pesos, as a maximum figure, represent a very large amount, but it is incorrect to believe that the Church, as has often been stated, owned half the national wealth. As will be indicated in chapter 7, although it is not possible to be precise, the proportion in the middle of the last century was much lower, being perhaps a fifth or a quarter. These estimates, both absolute and relative, modify the general impression held to date of the immensity of Church wealth in Mexico before the Reform.

[1] J. Sierra, *Juárez, su obra y su tiempo* (2nd ed., Mexico, 1948), p. 240.

CHAPTER I

NATIONALIZED GOODS AND CHURCH WEALTH, 1821–55

Mexico became independent in 1821 and problems were soon apparent. General Iturbide, leader of the independence government, inherited a fiscal deficit which he himself had unwittingly increased by reducing taxation and increasing costs to the level of 300,000 pesos a month.[1] Apart from this deficit on the current account, Mexico received as a viceregal legacy a national debt which in 1822 was estimated by the Minister of Hacienda at 76,000,000 pesos,[2] although this was later reduced to 45,000,000 pesos by the cancellation of certain fictitious items that had been included.[3]

Mexico also inherited from the viceroyalty a number of clerical possessions which had been nationalized during the colonial period; in particular there were those of the Inquisition, which had been abolished in 1813, re-established, and then permanently suppressed by the Spanish government in 1820. Its possessions, which devolved to the independent governments, were worth approximately 1,500,000 pesos.[4] More properties were received from the Pious Fund of the Californias, which had originally been established to maintain missions in those territories and had been administered by the Jesuits until their expulsion from New Spain in 1767. According to Mora the capital value of these goods amounted to 631,057 pesos.[5] Finally, others were received from various regular orders which had been suppressed, namely the Jesuits, the Benedictines, also known by the name of the monastery of Montserrat which was in fact a hospital, and the Hospitallers of Belem, San Juan de Dios and San Hipólito. The value of the properties from these sources, which were classified as 'temporalities', was calculated by Mora to be 3,513,000 pesos, although, as will be shown later, this figure is exaggerated.[6]

---

[1] M. Galván, *Colección de ordenes y decretos* (Mexico, 1829), vol. I, pp. 39–40.

[2] *Memoria de Hacienda, 1870* (hereinafter referred to as MH 1870), p. 45.

[3] *Memoria de Hacienda, 1823*, pp. 25–6.

[4] Mora, *México y sus revoluciones*, I, 338.

[5] Ibid., p. 339.   [6] Ibid., p. 340.

Nationalized goods and Church wealth, 1821–55

It was not surprising, therefore, that the newly independent government should seek to use these assets as security for a loan, in spite of the fact that the Church had been an effective supporter of the independence movement. After an unsuccessful attempt to raise a voluntary loan, Iturbide tried to use the nationalized properties to persuade financiers to make a loan to the government. He had been authorized to do this some two months after independence, on 26 November 1821, by the governing junta, which empowered him to seek one or more forced loans, imposing specific amounts on persons known to be wealthy, provided the latter had not voluntarily subscribed. These loans were to be for a term of six months, and repayment was guaranteed with the property of the Inquisition and the Pious Fund of the Californias. If the loans were not repaid within the stipulated term the government would immediately arrange to hold a public auction of these properties, and if obstacles to this arose the customs' revenue would be used for repayments.[1] As a further assurance the possessions of the Inquisition were specifically designated, for the institution was held in such disrespect that nobody had demanded its re-establishment.

The temporalities, that is the possessions of the Hospitallers and the Jesuits, were not included in the mortgage because there was some public support for their reintroduction into the country.[2] In spite of this, a few days later, on 8 December, a decree was issued ordering the management of the temporalities to be transferred to the city council.[3]

Hence when the forced loan was suspended on 16 March 1822 because of the hostility of those affected, it was also ordered that if the government did not receive sufficient funds from a loan of 1,500,000 pesos authorized on 2 January 1822,[4] the temporalities would be sold to the highest bidder. Offers for the real estate involved would be accepted on the basis of a reserve of two-thirds of the valuation price and capital funds could be redeemed at a 30% discount.[5] This discount of 30–33% was to form a precedent for the future. Ten days later the first auction was ordered to be held in fifteen days, if within the first eight days no money had been forthcoming from the loan.[6]

In fact none of the sales anticipated in the decrees took place. The

---

[1] Galván, *Colección*, I, 39–41.
[2] L. Alamán, *Historia de México desde los primeros movimientos que prepararon su independencia en el año de 1808 hasta la época presente* (4th ed., Mexico, 1942), vol. v, pp. 361–4.
[3] Ibid., p. 365. [4] Galván, *Colección*, I, 84.
[5] Ibid., II, 13. [6] Ibid., II, 18.

proposed auction of the Inquisition's property had already encountered difficulties, which probably involved partly the Church's opposition. A condition was inserted in the terms for the sale of the temporalities which gives cause to suspect that Iturbide was in fact threatening the sales solely to put pressure on the Church. Soon after the publication of the decree ordering the auction of the Inquisition's property, both the secular and regular branches of the clergy agreed to make the government a joint loan of 1,500,000 pesos, divided among the various ecclesiastical corporations.[1] Nevertheless, as can be deduced from the conservative historian Alamán's figures for the amount handed over by the metropolitan cathedral, the Church only succeeded in raising about one-fifth of the amount asked for by the government.[2] The sale of the temporalities was therefore ordered, although this was made conditional in case the cash was forthcoming from the Church. The government, however, does not seem to have had much success in its efforts to extract more funds.[3]

These various manoeuvres illustrate the tactics which were to be later employed by Santa Anna and Zuloaga. In spite of the fact that these governments were also elevated to power as a result of clerical support, they still employed the weapon of disentailment to obtain loans from the Church.

Although the Church no longer loaned much to the regency government, the properties of the temporalities were not offered for sale. The explanation lies, according to the ironic words of Alamán, in the lack of experience of those in power:

for in later times and in much more pressing circumstances—in 1847 during the United States' invasion—loans were easily obtained from the clergy, and the notes accepted by them with the mortgage of their property were negotiated at a considerable discount. Also, those same properties of the temporalities which were previously put up for sale and attracted no bids were appropriated without any problems of valuations or existing mortgages.[4]

In fact the properties were not sold in 1822, in part because of the reluctance of buyers, for whom the purchase of a former clerical property, even at only 67% of the valuation price, was probably still too costly.

The next opportunity for the sale of these former possessions of the Church came after Iturbide's fall from power. The new government, entitled the Supreme Executive Power, assumed office on 31 March 1823 and it had to deal with the national debt left by the imperial administration. This consisted mainly of paper money, which circulated at approxi-

---

[1] Alamán, *Historia*, v, 390, 484. [2] Ibid.
[3] Ibid., p. 489. [4] Ibid., pp. 489–90.

mately 20% of par value.[1] With the purpose of amortizing this and also the other public debts, the constituent congress decreed on 16 May 1823 —after a preliminary order of 29 April—that the property of the Inquisition and the temporalities should be sold in public auction.[2]

As in the previous decree a discount of exactly 30% (instead of one-third) was offered to purchasers of either the real estate or the capital funds. The capital in this instance consisted of loans secured by mortgages which the now abolished institutions had made to individuals or to civil or ecclesiastical corporations. The discount rate was only applicable to those purchases made within the first month of the publication of the decree. Apart from this there was the vague stipulation that 'in any case in which it may be considered convenient', time would be allowed to make payment. Finally, payment of half the sale price, equalling approximately one-third of the value of the property or capital, could be made in paper money or other credits of the national debt. In those cases where offers of the same amount were made, preference was to be given to the person paying at least half in cash and the remainder in paper money, perhaps because the current value of this was greater. In other words, 35% of the value of a property, or of the sum of a capital, was to be paid for in cash. The remaining 35% could be liquidated with 7% of the total, assuming that this part was paid in paper money. In round figures, therefore, the real estate and capital could be acquired at 42% of value, which represented a lower price than that fixed in the previous year.[3] In addition to details of the sale price, to which the earlier measure had been restricted, conditions of payment were now given and these made further concessions to possible buyers. It was therefore another step towards the realization of the sale of the former clerical properties. Indeed the atmosphere was propitious, for the influence of liberalism was beginning to be felt in the new government, particularly in the two Ministries concerned with Church wealth. These were, first, the Ministry of Hacienda, which had the responsibility for the sales; its Minister from 2 May 1823 was Francisco de Arrillaga, a Spanish merchant from Veracruz[4] and the second person from that state to hold the post after Antonio Medina, who had occupied it during the Empire. Secondly, there was the Ministry of Justice and Ecclesiastical Affairs, headed by another

[1] *Memoria de Hacienda*, 1823, p. 27; see also L. de Zavala, *Ensayo histórico de las revoluciones de México, desde 1808 hasta 1830* (vol. I, Paris, 1831; vol. II, New York, 1832), vol. I, p. 256.
[2] Galván, *Colección*, II, 118–21.
[3] The various credits had different values; those predating 1822 were circulating in 1828 at 5% of face value, whereas some of the later ones reached 50%: Zavala, *Ensayo histórico*, II, 54–5.   [4] Zavala, *Ensayo histórico*, I, 262.

person from Veracruz, Pablo de la Llave. Arrillaga's successor was José Ignacio Esteva, again a Veracruz merchant,[1] who was in office from 9 August 1824 until 4 March 1827, and subsequently from 8 March 1828 until 12 January 1829.[2] Finally, the decree ordered the issue, for the information of the public, of 'an exact and detailed account of all the properties and credits', and two accounts duly appeared on 28 May and 13 June 1823.[3]

According to the first of these the capital funds of the Inquisition, almost all invested by way of loans, amounted to 1,055,433 pesos, and in addition to this sum 345,627 pesos were owed in unpaid interest. There was also some urban property in the capital, apart from the Inquisition building itself, valued at 156,044 pesos. In total the assets of the Inquisition were valued at 1,577,104 pesos, although unpaid interest could not be considered as part of the capital. The Inquisition administered other funds: those of the brotherhood of San Pedro Mártir, valued at 153,347 pesos, and those of the Vergara estate, worth 169,651 pesos. If these latter two items were included, which for our purposes they are not, the total would rise to 1,880,103 pesos.

In the second account listing the temporalities, the urban and rural property of the Jesuits amounted to 536,675 pesos; those of the Montserrat monastery to 56,280 pesos; and those of the Hospitallers to 498,024 pesos: in total, a value of 1,090,979 pesos in real estate alone, for these organizations seem to have had no invested capital. This total, however, must be reduced by 565,431 pesos, comprising debts secured by the various properties to pious works, hospital patients, and to other institutions or individuals. It is not explained whether these debts also included unpaid interest or whether only the capital debt was indicated. Deducting this from the value of the real estate, the net worth of the temporalities was 525,548 pesos. Hence the figure of 3,500,000 pesos given by Mora for 1833 was clearly fictitious. The properties, worth more than 1,000,000 pesos, yielded 41,646 pesos per year in rents, equalling a return of only 3·8%, a figure which tends to reduce their real value.

In spite of the encouragement offered the buyers in the decree of 16 May 1823, lack of interest prevented any sales and the Minister of Hacienda was induced to suggest some six months later that buyers should

---

[1] Alamán, *Historia*, v, 746.   [2] MH 1870, pp. 1026–78.
[3] *Estado general que manifiesta todos los bienes y créditos que poseía el extinguido Tribunal de la Inquisición* (Mexico, 1823), based on the data of June 1820, and the *Estado de las fincas rústicas y urbanas respectivas a las temporalidades de los ex-jesuitas y ordenes hospitalarias y monacales suprimidos* (Mexico, 1823). These accounts are in the Colección Lafragua, Biblioteca Nacional, vol. 425.

be allowed to pay only a quarter of the price in cash instead of a half, or even that national debt credits might be accepted for the whole price.[1] Here the matter rested. The federal government, with its delicate balance between conservatives and liberals, did not urge the sales any further. Fortunately the nation's financial problem was resolved at this time, although only for four years, by the loan of 16,000,000 pesos contracted in London at the beginning of 1824 with Goldschmitt and Co. This was followed a few months later by another loan of the same amount from Barclay and Co.[2] Although Mexico in fact only received about 10,000,000 pesos from these two loans, this amount, together with the estimated 12,000,000 pesos of British capital invested in the mining industry, was sufficient to revive the stagnant economy and public finances.[3]

In 1828, however, civil war broke out. It is not surprising that the victorious liberal government of President Vicente Guerrero soon proposed to implement the 1823 decree. This was partly due to fiscal necessity and partly to liberal convictions, especially those of Lorenzo de Zavala, Minister of Hacienda since 18 April 1829. On 1 May he communicated his decision to hold the sales to the appropriate authorities in the city of Mexico. Two weeks later, on 16 May, the city authorities made a public announcement of the impending sales[4] and meanwhile two detailed reports on the goods to be offered were prepared.[5]

According to the two new accounts, drawn up in a similar form to the previous ones, the wealth of the Inquisition consisted of ten canonries, which were to be omitted because their revenue was considered to be fortuitous; mortgage loans to the nominal value of 908,222 pesos and unpaid interest of 461,872 pesos; and urban real estate to the sum of 210,529 pesos, including the Inquisition building valued at 112,232 pesos. In total the value was 1,580,623 pesos.

Except for the unpaid interest, the Inquisition's possessions were already worth less in 1829 than they had been in 1823. The unpaid interest was not properly part of the goods and, as is explained in the notes to the

---

[1] *Memoria de Hacienda, 1823*, p. 27.
[2] J. Bazant, *Historia de la deuda exterior de México (1823–1946)* (Mexico, 1968), pp. 24–32.
[3] Ibid., p. 40.
[4] M. Dublán y J. M. Lozano (eds.), *Legislación mexicana o colección completa de las disposiciones legislativas expedidas desde la independencia de la república* (Mexico, 1876–1912), vol. II, p. 108.
[5] *Estado de las fincas urbanas y rústicas respectivas a las temporalidades de los ex-jesuitas y Monacales suprimidos, con expresión de sus valores, gravámenes que reportan, y renta anual*, and the second, *Estado que manifiesta todos los bienes y créditos pertenecientes al extinguido Tribunal de la Inquisición de México, excluidos los correspondientes a los ramos que tenía sólo en administración, según se hallan en la presente fecha*. Both were published on 31 May, together with a public announcement that the first sale would be held on 11 June; Dublán y Lozano, II, 117–30.

account, several of the capital funds were lost as a result of excessive mortgages taken out on the properties used as security. The sum of 1,500,000 pesos is more or less in agreement with that given by Mora.[1]

The urban and rural property of the Benedictines and Jesuits produced an annual return of 8,281 pesos, which equalled a 3·5% yield on the capital of 239,530 pesos. This was much less than in 1823 and it implies that the management of the properties had been very poor. The report neglected to mention the value of the real estate and buildings belonging to the Hospitallers. In 1823 these had been assessed at about 500,000 pesos, and judging from other items they were probably worth less in 1829. Certainly the combined value of the wealth of the Inquisition and the temporalities did not amount to 2,000,000 pesos.

Just as these goods were offered for sale by the government, the country entered into a state of political ferment caused by the law expelling the Spanish population from Mexico which was issued on 20 May, a few days before the announcement of the first auction. Although this decree was not immediately implemented, and even its subsequent execution was only moderate,[2] there was nevertheless an obvious threat to the Spanish residents and their interests.

A Spanish attempt to invade the republic was soon expected, and on 27 July 1829 Barradas did indeed disembark near Tampico with a force of Spanish soldiers. Military costs suddenly increased and the sale of the temporalities finally took place, although probably only a small part was sold at the time, because after the Mexican defeat of the Spaniards on 11 September an increasingly reactionary opposition obliged Zavala to resign from the Ministry of Hacienda on 2 November. Finally, a successful counter-revolution gained power in the capital by the end of December.

The documentation concerning the sale of the temporalities survived in the archive of the Ministry of Hacienda. Rafael Mangino, Minister during Bustamante's conservative administration, published a summary of the sales in his annual report of 24 January 1831, corresponding to the fiscal year of 1830. No doubt he thought that by doing so he would discredit the previous government.[3] According to his summary, during the

---

[1] Mora, *México y sus revoluciones*, I, 339.

[2] R. Flores, *La contrarevolución en la independencia. Los españoles en la vida política, social y económica de México, 1804–1838* (Mexico, 1969), pp. 151 ff.

[3] After their victory two years later, the liberals took their revenge by publishing a report which included a list of lenders and details of loans ruinous for the public treasury contracted by the conservative government of Bustamante-Alamán: *Informe presentado al Exmo. Sr. Presidente de los Estados Unidos Mexicanos por el contador mayor, Jefe de la oficina de rezagos, Juan Antonio de Unzueta, en cumplimiento de la comisión que le confirió S.E. para que le manifieste el manejo y el estado que guardó la hacienda pública en los años de 1830, 1831, y 1832.*

last few months of the Guerrero-Zavala administration properties and capital to a value of 851,966 pesos were sold, that is between one-third and one-half of the total amount. The actual sale price, however, was 698,407 pesos, which means that they were sold at an 18% discount even though the standing law authorized up to 30%. Of this price the buyers paid only 213,966 pesos in cash, that is about 25% of the value, but the law had stipulated 35%. A further 101,179 pesos was left owing, to be paid in future instalments, although two years later the sum was still owing and it is not known if it ever was paid. In view of the generosity of governments towards their creditors, it was perhaps liquidated later with national debt credits. Finally, using various national debt bonds, known simply as credits, the buyers paid 383,260 pesos, which equals 45% of the value of the properties and substantially more than the 35% allowed for in the law. It is clear, therefore, that the sales were not conducted strictly within the terms of the ruling law.

As it is not known if the buyers paid their debt to the government it is impossible to calculate the true amount expended by them, and this is made even more difficult by the fact that different credits had different values. Assuming, for example, that the buyers acquired their credits at 10% of face value, that is paying about 40,000 pesos in cash, they received the real estate and capital for approximately 354,000 pesos, including the amount left owing. In other words, they obtained the goods for 42% of their value. However, they may well have paid the amount left owing with credits and therefore the purchase price drops to about one-third of valuation, for it is likely that they used the lowest valued credits. As the possession of a former Church property was disapproved of by public opinion, the buyers clearly viewed their purchases as any other investment, and as interest rates were high and the return on real estate low they were not prepared to pay more than a small part of the nominal value. In fact, assuming a yield on the properties of 5%, the buyers thus hoped to receive an annual return of 12–15% on their investment, taking into account the reduced purchase price.

Among more than a dozen buyers, Ignacio Adalid figured prominently in view of the amount he bought. He was a Mexican hacendado and probably an ancestor of Ignacio Torres Adalid, who was to be an important purchaser of ecclesiastical possessions in 1861. Others were Colonel Manuel Barrera, who was probably Mexican, and Felipe Neri del Barrio, an hacendado of Guatemalan origin and a man of liberal opinions, also to be a significant buyer in 1861. Of the others whom it is possible to identify there were José Espinosa, a Mexican hacendado, Estanislao Flores, a merchant and again prominent in 1861,[1] Dr. Juan de Dios Linares, a Mexican, and Lic. Mariano Domínguez, son of the *corregidor*, Miguel Domínguez. It is significant to note that no Spaniard or any other foreigner can be identified from the list of names. The Spaniards, who were reputedly richer in terms of actual cash than the Mexicans, were under pressure from the law ordering their expulsion and probably could not or did not want to buy.

The auctions of these Church properties and capital probably contributed to the decision of the conservatives to stage a military revolt against Guerrero, for it seemed that, having disposed of the temporalities, Zavala would proceed with the nationalization of clerical wealth. Their fear was justified in view of the disentailment project to be presented by Zavala in 1833. Yet although this may have been a cause of the reaction, the conservative government of Bustamante-Alamán did not cancel the sales that had already been effected, as is shown by the fact that at least two of the 1829 buyers, F. N. del Barrio and Manuel Barrera, loaned money to the conservative administration.[2] The liberals of 1833 likewise did not annul the deals made by financiers with the previous government. Faits accomplis have an extraordinary strength.

The 1829 sales have been dealt with in some detail because they illustrate on a lesser scale the operations of the years 1856–63, and the same problems then encountered were already present in miniature thirty years before.

It has been shown that in 1829 at most a half of the total possessions of the Inquisition and the temporalities were sold, and it can be assumed that the buyers chose the best of the properties. Those of the Hospitallers were less attractive and 'they were distributed with diverse titles in 1842 … [Santa Anna being president] among the government favourites, without excepting even the hospital buildings or those parts of them that were of some use'.[3] No information on these transactions comparable to that concerning 1829 has survived.

THE PIOUS FUND OF THE CALIFORNIAS

From the time of the expulsion of the Jesuits in 1767 this Fund was administered, together with the possessions of the Jesuits themselves, by the Temporalities Committee (*Junta de Temporalidades*). The viceregal

---

[1] *Memoria de las operaciones que han tenido lugar en la oficina especial de desamortización del distrito, desde el 7 de enero en que se abrió hasta el 5 de diciembre de 1861, en que cesaron sus labores, para continuarlas la Junta Superior de Hacienda* (Mexico, 1862) (cited hereinafter as MD 1862).
[2] Tables 1 and 20 f the *Informe* cited above, p. 20, n. 3.   [3] Alamán, *Historia*, v, 365.

authorities did not resist the temptation to make use of them, and thus in 1810 the hacienda of Arroyozarco was sold and a house in the capital belonging to the Fund was taken over for government offices.[1] By independence the assets were already reduced, but as the Fund was a private foundation its possessions were not offered for sale in 1823 or 1829.

Alamán was Minister of Foreign and Internal Affairs during the conservative government of 1830–32 and he was interested in the finances of the Fund. In his report to the chamber of deputies, which he presented on 12 February 1830, one month after taking office, he included a section on them with details up to 1827. According to his account[2] the capital of the Fund amounted to 560,400 pesos, but it was clearly impossible to collect several of the items incorporated in this sum, for example, 201,856 pesos owed by the Ministry of Hacienda, 162,618 pesos owed by the Merchant Guild, suppressed in the law of 16 October 1824, and 20,000 pesos owed by the government from the consolidation or forced loan imposed in 1804. The Fund did have various haciendas,[3] although Alamán did not give their value, and in the capital of the republic a large house, which was the property occupied rent free by the government offices. Several smaller houses were owned but the tenants did not pay rent or paid it directly to the government. The value of these is likewise not indicated. As a result of the low return on its investments the Fund owed the California missions 130,000 pesos.[4] A year later, in spite of Alamán's efforts, the finances had deteriorated even further and the missionaries were owed almost 200,000 pesos.[5] The Fund was obviously destined to disappear.

Through a government concession dated 17 January 1837 a national bank was established with the aim of amortizing, that is withdrawing, at par the copper money then circulating at a much reduced value,[6] but on 8 March this currency was officially devalued by half. A short time afterwards a decree of 15 April 1837 re-established the tobacco monopoly in all the republic, and the management committee of the bank was given the right to administer the tobacco revenue or, if it thought it convenient, to rent it out. Three days later the government ordered the remaining temporalities from the Jesuits and the Inquisition to be handed over to the bank. This proved to be the first step towards their eventual sale some five years later.

These actions referred to above can be explained by the ever increasing

---

[1] Ibid., v, 397.
[2] This is reproduced in L. Alamán, *Obras* (Mexico, 1942–48), vol. ix, p. 234.
[3] MH 1870, p. 11.　　　　　　　　　　[4] Alamán, *Obras*, ix, 220.
[5] Ibid., pp. 311–14.　　　　　　　　　[6] MH 1870, pp. 167–9.

military expenditure, related in the first place to the war with Texas and later to the brief war with France. The bank was empowered on 27 January 1838 to negotiate on its funds a loan of 6,000,000 pesos for 'the Texas war, the maintenance of national integrity and the defence of the coasts and frontiers of the republic'.[1] On 26 February it was authorized 'to supply the executive with any money it could', and on 22 June 'to negotiate, by mortgaging its own funds, an advance of 500,000 pesos'. Other loans followed to sustain the war against France, which finally ended on 9 March 1839 with Mexico agreeing to pay an indemnity of 600,000 pesos.[2]

Some weeks previously, on 1 February 1839, approval had been given to the contract between the amortization bank and the State whereby the former was to hold the tobacco monopoly for a period of five years.[3] Those contracting this agreement would control the cultivation of the plant and the manufacture and distribution of the product. The individuals involved were Benito Maqua, Cayetano Rubio, Francisco Rubio, Felipe Neri del Barrio, Manuel Escandón, and Miguel Bringas, all of whom were Mexicans.[4] One of them, F. N. del Barrio, has already been mentioned. Two of the others, Rubio and Escandón, were among the most important merchants, industrialists and financiers of the time, and del Barrio, Escandón and Bringas were to appear again as prominent buyers of ecclesiastical possessions in 1861. Rubio was to be content as a partner in a company which bought some of the goods.

The indemnity to be paid to France and intermittent civil strife made the acquisition of more money imperative and the government asked the bank to negotiate a loan, first on 18 February, then on 21 October 1839[5] and finally on 1 July 1841.[6] Eventually internal peace was re-established on 10 October 1841 by the new president, Santa Anna.

The State was in debt to the group of capitalists represented by the bank but it is very difficult to discover the amount of the certainly considerable sums involved. The financiers found in Santa Anna a man with whom they could reach agreement and they did so on 12 November when the government ordered the termination of the rental contract for the tobacco monopoly as from 1 January 1842.[7] Almost at the same time

---

[1] Ibid., pp. 181–3.   [2] Ibid., p. 192.   [3] Ibid., pp. 195–6.
[4] M. Payno, *México y sus cuestiones financieras con la Inglaterra, la España y la Francia* (Mexico, 1862), pp. 69 and 173.
[5] MH 1870, p. 196.   [6] Ibid., p. 214.
[7] The monopoly was hated by the people who wanted cheap tobacco and they protected the smugglers who were pursued by the army; see the novel by L. G. Inclán, *Astucia* (Mexico, 1946).

a law of 6 December 1841 ordered the liquidation of the national amortization bank.[1] On 5 February 1842 another law ordered the sale of the remaining properties of the temporalities, the value of which was to be calculated by capitalizing the return, estimated at 5%, and was to be paid in cash.[2] Alamán's words cited above refer to this sale. On 8 February the management of the Fund was returned to the government and on 24 October it was finally decreed that the capital, and urban and rural properties belonging to it, 'would be incorporated' into the national exchequer. The Ministry of Hacienda was to sell these assets 'for the capital which they represented at 6% of the annual return and the exchequer will recognize at an interest of 6% the total amount produced by these appropriations'. The tobacco monopoly was to be mortgaged to secure the payment of interest.[3] In other words the possessions of the Fund would not be confiscated but simply taken as a forced loan by the State, which would owe its value to the Fund.

This disguised nationalization was very characteristic of Santa Anna and it anticipates the measures adopted by him in 1847 and by Zuloaga in 1858. Conservative presidents did not confiscate Church wealth. They merely took properties or capital as forced loans and handed them over to their creditors. This explains the frequency of the laws which prohibited the Church from selling its possessions without the permission of the government. The first of these were issued by the liberal vice-president, Valentín Gómez Farías, in 1833 and 1834. The law of 20 November 1833 was clearly retroactive, for it suspended 'as illegal in their effects, until the decision of congress, all sales, transfers, investments and redemptions of goods and properties of the regular orders in the federal district made since independence'.[4] Then, in the circular of 24 January 1834, it was ordered that the rents of houses which had been sold in contravention of the decree of 20 November 1833 were to be paid into the government treasury.[5] There is at least one instance in which these decrees produced a protest by the clergy. It seems that the college of San Angel and the monastery del Santo Desierto, both of the Carmelite Order, had sold on credit several properties, with the result that, in obedience to the law, the buyers must pay the interest to the civil authorities. On 12 February 1834 the provincial of the Order requested the annulment of the decrees.[6]

---

[1] MH 1870, pp. 216–17.   [2] Dublán y Lozano, IV, 114.   [3] Ibid., IV, 301–2.
[4] L. G. Labastida, *Colección de leyes, decretos, reglamentos, circulares, órdenes y acuerdos relativos a la desamortización de los bienes de corporaciones civiles y religiosas y a la nacionalización de los que administraron las últimas* (Mexico, 1893), p. 111.   [5] Ibid., p. 112.
[6] *Exposición que el provincial del Carmen hizo al Supremo Gobierno sobre las ventas de fincas que celebraron algunos conventos de su orden* (Mexico, 1834).

Nationalized goods and Church wealth, 1821–55

Having removed Gómez Farías from power, President Santa Anna decided on 9 July of the same year that the sales should be subject to the decision of congress, but it appears that the latter body took no action on the matter.[1] The fact that the Carmelites had in 1843 almost the same number of properties as in 1832 indicates that they were unable to sell them. This was not the first occasion on which the Order had tried to dispose of its properties. In 1822 an unsuccessful attempt had been made to sell an hacienda in the state of San Luis Potosí for two-thirds of its value in order to be able to pay an amount allotted to the Order towards the loan to Iturbide.[2] Later, during the war with France, another decree was issued on 4 August 1838 which referred to the possessions of the regular orders.[3] Those of the secular clergy were not included as they were much less valuable. Furthermore the opinion was becoming widespread in the country that, while the secular clergy performed a useful task in society, a large part of the regular orders was superfluous.[4]

Soon after assuming power Santa Anna issued a circular on 13 October 1841, confirming the previous one of 1838. Another followed on 6 November which demanded that the regular orders should indicate whether they maintained primary schools on their premises in accordance with the law. On 5 January 1842 a decree was promulgated which declared that monks who entered the country without governmental permission would be treated like any other illegal foreign immigrant. On 27 June the regular orders were forbidden to sell their property and capital. Although the latter was not as important as their real estate, it was nonetheless substantial.

On 5 February 1843 the same prohibition was extended to the possessions of the brotherhoods, archconfraternities, pious works and other ecclesiastical institutions. On 1 July the possessions of the secular clergy, which were those under episcopal jurisdiction, were included, and finally on 31 August the sale of church ornaments was forbidden, the seller being declared a thief and the buyer an accomplice. The latter was without doubt the most stringent of all the decrees. In this way the whole of clerical wealth was included and the Church could do nothing except await an open or disguised nationalization.

At about the same time the amortization tax was established on 18

---

[1] Ibid. [2] Alamán, *Historia*, v, 484.

[3] *Memoria de Justicia*, January 1844: 'Noticia de los decretos y providencias dictadas por el Supremo Gobierno Provisional, en uso de la séptima de las bases acordadas en Tacubaya', section on ecclesiastical affairs, pp. 68–9.

[4] See for example the pamphlet by E. de Antuñano, *Economía política en México. Insurrección industrial. Documentos básicos para la historia de la industria moderna*, dated 23 October 1846.

August 1842. The Church would henceforth have to pay 15% of the value of every property or capital it acquired. Notaries were ordered not to issue purchase or mortgage deeds unless the tax had been paid.[1] The aim of the law was to hinder the future enrichment of the Church, but the measure could not be very effective for it was always possible to state prices in the deeds which were much lower than the real ones. Santa Anna, however, knew how to sweeten the pill. On 21 June 1843 he permitted the Jesuits to re-establish themselves in several states[2] and on 9 October of the same year he authorized the foundation of the congregation of the Sisters of Mercy.[3]

In spite of all these decrees, which seemed to herald the nationalization of Church wealth, Santa Anna limited himself basically to selling the remaining possessions of the temporalities and the Pious Fund of the Californias. No report on these operations was published during his administration, and after his fall from power in 1844 public opinion was against them and even the senate recommended that they be revised. The buyers defended themselves with two pamphlets.[4] The first, signed by Manuel Escandón and José Domingo Rascón, both representing buyers, alluded to the terms of sale; for example, the capitalization at 6%, instead of the usual 5% to determine the value of the property, was necessary in view of the low return from the haciendas. Whatever the validity of this argument, the capitalization at 6% did represent a reduction of 16·67% in the price. As for the terms of payment, a quarter of the value was accepted in national debt credits. The tobacco company had bought the properties, they claimed, because the government owed it money.

The buyers, however, had an eloquent adversary in Juan Rodríguez de San Miguel, who wrote several pamphlets on the matter and also mentioned it in the section on the Church in his almanac, *La república mexicana en 1846*. In spite of such opposition the buyers retained the properties, and Mexico was left with a debt to the Pious Fund of the Californias amounting to 1,207,671 pesos in capital alone.[5] The activities described above induced Juan José del Corral, former chief official in the Ministry of Hacienda, to complain as follows: 'Where are the millions of pesos of

---

[1] Dublan y Lozano, IV, 254.
[2] The circular prohibiting the entry of monks into the country was revoked on 15 September.
[3] *Memoria de Justicia, 1844*, pp. 68–9.
[4] *Observaciones que los actuales poseedores de los bienes que pertenecieron al fondo piadoso de Californias hacen a los señores diputados y senadores* (Mexico, 1845), and *Observaciones sobre los términos del decreto que el senado acaba de pasar sobre la revisión de los contratos en que se enagenaron dichos bienes* (Mexico, 1845).
[5] *Observaciones que los actuales . . .*, p. 27.

pre-independence credits, most of which are ecclesiastical in origin? They are in the pockets of the speculators. Where are the assets of the temporalities, of the Pious Fund of the Californias, of the hospitals? They have become the properties of the speculators.'[1] A subsequent statement by Corral that the speculators had also bought the best of the privately owned haciendas 'because landowners, not being able to borrow money at 5% or 6% annual interest, had to pay 48% at least, and hence could not keep their estates', does seem exaggerated. The hacendados (Corral only referred to these) seem to have been able to obtain credit on relatively easy terms from the *juzgado de capellanías*.[2]

The possessions of the Pious Fund of the Californias were distinct from those of the missions themselves. The latter were secularized by a decree of the liberal government, dated 17 August 1833,[3] and later appropriated by various persons.[4] Similarly the real estate, which in the colonial period maintained a hostel where Dominican missionaries lodged while in Mexico on their journey from Spain to the Philippines, was also different from the main Fund. It consisted of two haciendas called Chica and Grande, situated near Texcoco and valued at 100,000 pesos. These were confiscated by the authorities under the law of 4 July 1822,[5] an action which was not surprising in view of the fact that the owners were citizens of a hostile country, namely Spain. On 22 May 1827 they were confiscated by the state of Mexico and on 2 September by the federal government of Guerrero-Zavala, which rented them to the already mentioned F. N. del Barrio on 20 October, before the resignation of Zavala.[6] On 14 January 1836 the conservative administration authorized the Spanish Philippine missionaries to sell their goods. In response to this permission and to rid themselves of a tenant known for his liberal sympathies, the friars sold the properties to General José María Cervantes, who was an important owner of real estate in the capital.[7] Another Spanish friar, father Morán, appeared and asked for the sale to be declared void. The government agreed to pay compensation, which originated the so-called second Spanish convention, a branch of the country's foreign debt. The

[1] J. J. del Corral, *Breve reseña sobre el estado de la hacienda y del que se llama crédito público, o sea exposición de los males y ruina de la república, a que la han llevado y siguen conduciendo las maniobras de los agiotistas y de los malos empleados*, 28 October 1848, pp. 29–30.

[2] Costeloe, *Church wealth in Mexico*, passim.

[3] F. Bulnes, *Juárez y las revoluciones de Ayutla y de la Reforma* (Mexico, 1905), p. 88.

[4] H. H. Bancroft, *History of California* (San Francisco, 1886), vol. III, chapters 11, 12 and vol. IV, chapters 2, 7, 13, 15, 18, 23.

[5] Galván, II, 52.

[6] Payno, *México y sus cuestiones financieras...*, p. 188.

[7] Alamán, *Obras*, VII, 241.

government nevertheless accepted the sale as valid, perhaps in exchange for a loan of 50,000 pesos made by General Cervantes.[1]

THE CONSEQUENCES OF THE WAR WITH THE UNITED STATES

Fiscal difficulties even greater than those so far encountered arose in 1846 when Mexico was confronted with the United States army. President Mariano Paredes y Arrillaga was unable to raise more funds and he soon gave way at the beginning of August to Mariano Salas who appointed several liberals to important posts in his administration. Valentín Gómez Farías, his Minister of Hacienda from 28 August to 21 September, used these few weeks to put pressure on the Church in an attempt to raise the money needed for the war but he had no immediate success.[2]

He was followed as Minister by Antonio Haro y Tamariz, a liberal and a member of a family of industrialists in Puebla, and he began at the beginning of October to try a new tactic. He proposed a disentailment of ecclesiastical wealth which in many respects anticipated the 1856 Lerdo law.[3] Article 1 of his project stipulated:

the sale of the urban and rural property of the Church throughout the republic under the following terms: the buyers will be the tenants who occupy the properties or those persons to whom the latter have for this instance conceded their rights; the price will be calculated by capitalizing the rent at 5%; a guarantor of interest will be given by those who have provided one for the rent or lease; the recognizance of the sale price or the capital value of the property will be perpetual; buyers, nevertheless, will be able to redeem the capital.

The second article proposed that all prohibitions of the sale of Church properties be repealed, and the third, that the sellers should hand over the title deeds to the buyers.

This plan, however, did not resolve the fiscal difficulties for it was only proposed to oblige the seller and the buyer to pay the exchequer a fixed percentage in the three months following the attestation of the contract. In other words, probably six months would pass before the government saw an increase in its revenue as a result of the new law. The project, important as it was for the future, was in 1846 simply a theoretical exercise. As Haro could offer no immediate aid to the treasury he resigned on 13 November.

---

[1] Payno, *México y sus cuestiones financieras...*, p. 190.
[2] M. P. Costeloe, 'Church–State financial negotiations in Mexico during the American War, 1846–1847', *Revista de historia de América*, 60 (July–December 1965), 91–123.
[3] This project was discovered by Costeloe in the Archivo General de la Nación, section Justicia Eclesiástica (cited hereinafter as AGN, JE), vol. 151, fols. 212–13, and mentioned in the article referred to in note 2 above.

Meanwhile the situation was growing more critical day by day and the United States army was advancing southwards. Then President Salas resorted to a forced loan, mortgaging Church property. Like the State, the Church did not have funds in cash, and when the government ordered the clerical coffers opened they were found to be empty.[1] Unlike the State, the Church did have credit because it was able to guarantee it. Hence the government tried to force wealthy people to lend it money which was to be repaid with bills of exchange, underwritten by the Church, with a term of two years and secured by their possessions. The holders of these bills could even designate the properties or rents—these were in turn secured by a property—which they were entitled to appropriate if the ecclesiastical corporation involved did not pay the value of the bill. These were the details of the decree of 19 November 1846, in which the government attempted to obtain 2,000,000 pesos by allotting this amount in proportion among the rich men of the country.[2]

The Church resisted the proposed loan and finally agreed to endorse one of 850,000 pesos on condition that the previous decree was revoked.[3] Hence on 5 December another decree was published whereby the Church was to guarantee the above amount by means of an issue of bonds which the government would offer for sale to private citizens.[4] The bonds were probably sold at a considerable discount.

Valentín Gómez Farías took office as vice-president on 23 December in the midst of a rapidly deteriorating situation. The most urgent need was funds for Santa Anna who was in San Luis Potosí at the head of the army, where he was preparing for the campaign against the invader. On 11 January 1847 Gómez Farías decreed the nationalization and sale in public auction of clerical assets to the value of 15,000,000 pesos.[5] Certain goods were to be exempt, as follows:

those of hospitals, poor houses, houses of charity, schools and public education establishments of both sexes whose members were not bound by any monastic vow; *capellanías*, benefices and foundations to which entitlement was based on blood or ancestry; the sacred vessels, ornaments and other objects indispensable to worship; the possessions of nunneries to the extent of those needed to provide a dowry of 6,000 pesos per existing nun.

These exceptions were very reasonable, for grouped around the Church there were a number of institutions of recognized value in society, and the capital belonging to *capellanías* and part of that of the convents was

---

[1] W. H. Callcott, *Santa Anna* (Norman, 1936), p. 249.
[2] Dublán y Lozano, v, 211–16.   [3] Costeloe, 'Church–State...', p. 99.
[4] Dublán y Lozano, v, 235–6.   [5] Ibid., v, 246–8.

owned by private citizens and only administered by the Church. This reasoning also guided the liberal governments of 1858–62. As time was needed to determine in detail the value of the nationalized goods, the government ordered on 15 January the immediate 'occupation' of properties to an estimated value of 10,000,000 pesos.[1]

On his return to power Santa Anna repealed these decrees on 29 March[2] but not without first receiving on the previous day a promise from the Church that it would guarantee a loan of 1,500,000 pesos.[3] This is revealed in the congressional authorization to the executive, sanctioned on the same day, to obtain 20,000,000 pesos without recourse to forced loans and 'to negotiate contracts' with the ecclesiastical corporations. This procedure was emulated eleven years later by Zuloaga.

Further loans from the capitalists to the State followed in 1847, and like the previous ones they were secured with bonds, known afterwards as 'clerical bonds'. The clergy's complaint that the government 'had sold these bonds to many people at much reduced prices and the buyers had redeemed them at full face value from the Church'[4] is not entirely correct in view of the fact that the Church later succeeded in arranging several advantageous agreements with its creditors.[5] The negotiations with the State were not so favourable: for example, in return for a loan of 99,986 pesos the convent of Regina Coeli received 2,749 pesos in cash and the rest in treasury bonds, which at that time were circulating at 5% of par value, like other credits against the internal debt.[6]

In 1848, as a result of the treaty of Guadalupe Hidalgo, Mexico began to receive money in the form of the United States compensation, which was to amount to 12,000,000 pesos net. This unexpected revenue helped some way towards improving the nation's finances. With peace re-established the State no longer had such need of Church wealth.

The assumption of power for the last time by Santa Anna on 20 April 1853 was again accompanied by an increase in military expenditure. Faced with this situation, Antonio Haro y Tamariz, Minister of Hacienda, recalled his liberal past and suggested a loan of 17,000,000 pesos, using clerical property and capital as security. The money would be used to cover the budget deficit of 16,994,071 pesos.[7] The Church declared its

---

[1] Ibid., v, 248–52. [2] Ibid., v, 263.
[3] Costeloe, 'Church–State...', pp. 107–8.
[4] Reproduced by Costeloe in the above-cited article, p. 111.
[5] Costeloe, 'Church–State...', pp. 112 ff.
[6] J. Muriel, *Conventos de Monjas en la Nueva España* (Mexico, 1946), p. 55.
[7] MH 1870, pp. 398–408; W. H. Callcott, *Church and State in Mexico, 1822–1857* (Durham, 1926), pp. 161 ff.

opposition and Haro resigned on 5 August. The fiscal difficulties were then temporarily reduced by the sale to the United States, for the sum of 10,000,000 pesos, of a small territory known as the Mesilla. From this transaction Mexico received 7,000,000 pesos on 5 July 1854.[1] By this time the liberal revolt against Santa Anna was already under way.

CHURCH WEALTH FROM 1821 TO 1855

The tables to be found in the reports of the Ministry of Justice and Ecclesiastical Affairs only indicate the annual product of urban and rural properties and not their capital value. This can be calculated by capitalizing the rent at 5%, as was then customary. The result of these calculations and the corresponding amounts are shown in tables 1, 2 and 3. These figures reveal a surprising consistency. During the first twenty years of independence the amounts remain approximately stable, in spite of all difficulties which we have seen in previous pages. There was a slight drop in 1828 which perhaps can be explained by a decrease in the religious fervour of the population and which also seems to have been reflected in a decline in the yield from tithes and perhaps by the anti-Spanish campaign of that year. Subsequently the Church appears to have made a strong recovery during the conservative government of 1830–32. In 1843 the figures show considerable financial strength, indeed an increase, which thus reduces the importance of Santa Anna's anti-clerical measures.

The following comment may be made on the period beginning in 1848 and ending eight years later in 1856. As long as nobody attacked it and when there was a government which protected it, the Church gave signs of a notable capacity for recovery. The wounds suffered in 1846–47 were healed and clerical riches increased rather than diminished. It can be argued that this increase was nullified by a decline in the value of the peso but the few facts available on prices and salaries indicate that this factor did not basically change in comparison with the colonial period. Nevertheless, taking into account the slow economic progress of the country, ecclesiastical wealth probably did decline in relation to that of the nation. At any rate, Corral exaggerated when he wrote in 1848 that 'the best urban and rural properties of the religious corporations have passed into the hands of the speculators because, lacking cash to give in response to government appeals for help, the Church has given its properties as security, so that the speculators would lend money...'[2]

---

[1] MH 1870, pp. 421–3.   [2] Corral, *Breve reseña*, 29–30.

TABLE 1. *Assets of the monasteries, 1825–55 (pesos)*

Year	Real estate	Mortgages	Total
1825	5,089,840	2,243,354	7,353,194
1826	6,914,500	1,819,231	8,733,731
1827	6,746,440	1,962,145	8,708,585
1828	6,764,700	1,969,437	8,734,137
1832	6,191,900	1,825,093	8,016,993
1843	5,845,920	2,360,016	8,205,936
1855*	6,308,260	2,505,381	8,813,641

* The figures for 1855 are taken from AGN, JE, vol. 48, fols. 24–6. The Jesuits, re-established by Santa Anna, are omitted.

TABLE 2. *Assets of the convents, 1826–43 (pesos)*

Year	Real estate	Mortgages	Total
1826	11,322,220	4,698,424	16,020,644
1827	11,329,640	4,732,575	16,062,215
1828	10,971,640	3,072,861	14,044,501
1832	9,724,180	5,773,539	15,497,719
1843	12,516,400	5,514,132	18,030,532

TABLE 3. *Total assets of the regular orders, 1826–43 (pesos)*

Year	Total
1826	24,754,375
1827	24,770,600
1828	22,778,638
1832	23,514,712
1843	26,236,468

Corral's opinion that the Church had by then lost the best of its real estate holdings was widely held at the time. For example, José M. Pérez Hernández wrote in 1862 that the Carmelites had sold fourteen haciendas in 1849, mostly in the state of San Luis Potosí.[1] This statement was incorrect, for in 1843 the Carmelite Order had no such properties in that state, although it did have twenty haciendas in other parts of the country.[2] The revenue from two haciendas in San Luis Potosí had been used to finance the construction of the most beautiful church in the city but

[1] J. M. Pérez Hernández, *Estadística de la república mexicana* (Guadalajara, 1862), p. 205.
[2] *Memoria de Justicia*, 1844, table no. 6.

33

these had been disposed of earlier. On 20 February 1856 the Order still had nineteen haciendas throughout the country[1] but the only rural property it owned in the state of San Luis Potosí was an orchard which at the present day forms a municipal park. They had had this in 1843, but it was not then noted as it was considered part of the monastery premises.

Pérez Hernández probably followed a rumour, based in turn on a pamphlet published in 1834, in which the provincial of Carmen, no doubt impelled by the situation prevailing at the time, advised the sale of real estate and the investment of the proceeds in mortgages.[2] In part this recommendation was not implemented, as is shown by the following details: in 1832 the Carmelites had 19 rural and 243 urban properties;[3] in 1843, 20 and 239 respectively; and in 1856, 19 and 294 respectively. The latter 294 produced rather less than the 239 houses in 1843.

These figures given above, referring to real estate, show a marked stability, but those corresponding to capital invested in mortgages reveal a spectacular increase. In 1832 the Carmelites had 272,555 pesos in productive capital; in 1843, 646,664 pesos; and in 1856, 826,704 pesos. The same increase is to be found in the regional figures: for example, in San Luis Potosí, concurrent with a stagnation in urban dwellings, the capital increased in the same thirteen years between 1843 and 1856 from 2,600 to 48,000 pesos. The Carmelites thus fulfilled their proposal made in 1834 to increase their investments in loans but they did so without diminishing their real estate holdings. Hence by the time of the Reform they were richer than they had been at independence.

The impression that Church wealth suffered an irreparable blow in 1846–48 still seems to predominate today. One of the few works published in Mexico on this topic affirms that in Guadalajara the Augustinians sold from 1846 onwards all their properties in the city with the exception of the monastery building itself.[4] This is incorrect, for in 1856 alone at least twenty houses in the city belonging to the Order were disentailed.[5] From 1843 to 1856 the real estate holdings of this Augustinian monastery developed as follows: in 1843 there were three rural properties producing 2,000 pesos per year, sixty-one houses and capital funds of 6,740 pesos; in 1856 there was only one hacienda but this produced 1,800 pesos, almost

---

[1] AGN, JE, vol. 48, manuscript entitled *Estado general de los bienes y gravámenes que actualmente tiene la provincia de religiosos carmelitas descalzos de San Alberto en el año de 1856.*

[2] *Exposición que el provincial del Carmen...*, p. 9.

[3] Table from the *Memoria de Justicia*, 1833, reproduced by Mora, *México y sus revoluciones*, I, 437.

[4] R. Lancaster-Jones, 'Bienes del convento agustino en Guadalajara', *Historia Mexicana*, XIII (April–June 1964), 578 ff.

[5] *Memoria de Hacienda*, 1857, pp. 314–24.

as much as the three estates owned in 1843, fifty-eight houses and capital funds of 1,300 pesos, the latter producing a return of almost 10%.[1] The real estate thus shows a slight downward tendency.

If one looks at a more general picture of the Augustinian province of Michoacán (which included Guadalajara) the same downward tendency is revealed, even though the totals for 1856 are higher, due to the inclusion of the possessions of each individual monastery as well as those belonging to the province as a whole. In the entire country, however, the property and capital of the monasteries appear to have been worth more in 1856 than they had been twelve years earlier. The reduction in those of the Augustinians of Michoacán was compensated for by the rise in the holdings of the other regular orders.

It could be said that an increase in the goods and revenue did not necessarily signify prosperity, and here only an examination of specific cases can be illustrative. Certain ecclesiastical corporations did enjoy a surplus in their accounts, for example the Third Order of San Francisco and the Hospital de Terceros de San Francisco. These two institutions were affiliated as the hospital was founded by the tertiary brothers of San Francisco.[2]

The capital funds of the Third Order, amounting to 250,013 pesos, produced 11,763 pesos, which equals a yield of just less than 5%. 9,258 pesos of this amount was spent on feeding the prisoners in the jails and on various pious works. 2,478 pesos remained as a surplus which could be invested, spent on works of charity or in aid to the hospital. The balance sheet of the Hospital de Terceros indicates the various pious works, the object of each one being the maintenance of one or two beds in the hospital. It was thought that a capital of 3,000 pesos was needed to keep one patient (*capellanías* and dowries were also usually a minimum of 3,000 pesos each). The total amount of the capital funds is unknown—there is a page missing in the list—but by capitalizing at 5% the hospital's annual revenue the sum of 80,400 pesos is obtained. Nevertheless, the

---

[1] *Memoria de Justicia*, 1844, table no. 6, and *Estado que manifiesta el número de conventos, religiosos, novicios, curatos, cátedras, alumnos internos y externos, escuelas, niños, fincas rústicas y urbanas, sus productos, capitales activos y pasivos, limosnas y obvenciones de esta provincia de Agustinos de Michoacán*, dated Salamanca, 26 January 1856; AGN, JE, vol. 48.

[2] *Estado que detalla las rentas del Tercer Orden de Penitencia de Nuestro Padre San Francisco de México con expresión de capitales, sujetos o fincas que los reconocen, costos que el Tercer Orden tiene que erogar y utilidades que percibe de cada uno; Estado que detalla las rentas del Hospital de Terceros de Nuestro Padre San Francicso de México, con expresión de los capitales, sujetos o fincas que los reconocen; fundadores de cada obra pía y objetos para que están vinculados*: undated but a note has 1838 so that these manuscripts are from this year or earlier, AGN, Papeles de Bienes Nacionales (cited hereinafter as PBN), leg. 121.

hospital owed the same Third Order of San Francisco 37,388 pesos at 5% annual interest, that is 1,869 pesos. Deducting this amount from the annual revenue of 4,020 pesos, there is left a surplus of 2,150 pesos. Six patients[1] and four employees, that is ten people, had to live on this money,[2] and for that number it may have been sufficient. These figures are from before 1846. Later ones are not available.

The accounts of La Concepción, the richest convent in Mexico, show a surplus in the difficult year of 1848, judging by the profit and loss account for October. This was presented by the property administrator (*mayordomo*) on 3 November 1848.[3] 6,517 pesos were received from rents, and the toll office which levied tolls on certain roads paid 150 pesos, representing two months interest on a loan of 18,000 pesos made at 5% a year. After deduction of a rebate of 15 pesos the total income was 6,652 pesos and of this sum the administrator handed over to the convent accountant 5,577 pesos. This left 1,074 pesos from which the administrator deducted 322 pesos as his emolument, which equalled 5% of the revenue he collected, and the remaining 741 pesos he gave to the convent when he presented his accounts. The net profit, therefore, was more than 10%, which was an enviable amount for La Concepción had had to sell six houses valued at 126,000 pesos precisely in the two years 1847–48.[4]

Other nunneries were not so fortunate. The accounts of San Jerónimo for the thirteen months from 1 January 1852 to 31 January 1853 have survived. They were presented by the administrator, Lic. Pedro Verdugo, on his resignation from the post, and they show that the revenue was 51,983 pesos and expenditure 50,607 pesos.[5] This small surplus was achieved in spite of the fact that tenants paid in the same period of time only 35,946 pesos instead of 66,516 pesos, the latter amount including rent already owed. During the three years from 1848 to 1850 rents should have produced 140,602 pesos but in fact yielded only 96,316 pesos. What would have been the net profit if all the tenants had paid on time? The same delay is evident in the payment of interest. The capital '*de gruesa*', that is, belonging to the convent, should have produced in the same three years 55,035 pesos, but only 24,810 pesos were received, and the funds of the pious works administered by the convent should have

[1] J. Muriel, *Hospitales de la Nueva España* (Mexico, 1960), vol. II, p. 162.
[2] J. N. del Valle, *El viajero en México* (Mexico, 1859), p. 610.
[3] *Cuenta ordenada y relación jurada que yo, Jorge Madrigal, doy a las MRM abadesa y contadora del Sagrado Convento de la Purísima Concepción de lo cobrado de sus rentas en todo el mes de octubre de 1848 como su mayordomo o administrador que soy,* AGN, PBN, leg. 92, exp. 10.
[4] Muriel, *Conventos de Monjas*, 46.
[5] AGN, PBN, leg. 74, exp. 3.

produced a further 10,988 pesos, including interest already owed, but the borrowers paid only 7,759 pesos. The actual return on both real estate and capital was much less than the theoretical yield.

The habit of tenants and borrowers of falling behind with the payment of their rent and interest was not new. As early as 1826 the same practice was evident, as can be seen in the 'Noticia de los conventos del arzobispado de México. Año de 1826.'[1] It can be assumed that the delays increased as a result of the unstable conditions in the country.

The extent to which this above habit prevailed is indicated in the accounts of the nunnery Jesús María for 1850.[2] A calculation shows that the sixty annual rents amounted to 34,875 pesos, but this is only the theoretical amount and in practice much less was received. Tenants owed 34,400 pesos, equalling approximately the theoretical return on the sixty rents. In addition there was a sum of 355,300 pesos, divided between sixty capital funds, which consisted partly of redeemable loans owned by the convent and partly of loans from pious funds which were merely administered by it. At least a further 170,000 pesos, owed by the government, have not been included. The accumulated debt of borrowers amounted to 135,521 pesos, not including the government debt. The nunnery of Regina Coeli was in a similar or even worse situation in 1848–50.[3]

In some cases the accounts show a deficit, for example those of Santa Teresa la Nueva, one of the small nunneries in the capital. In 1853 its properties produced 9,000 pesos and its capital 1,240 pesos, a combined income of 10,240 pesos. 12,888 pesos were spent, however, leaving a deficit of 2,648 pesos. The convent expended the excessive sum of 2,400 pesos in repairs to one property.[4] No doubt if it had been more moderate in its expenditure the accounts could have been balanced, as were those of the other nunneries.

Finally there are the accounts of the Augustinian monastery in Guadala-

---

[1] Reproduced in *Boletín del Archivo General de la Nación*, no. 3 (1953), pp. 474–500.

[2] *Entrega que hace don José Garay en representación de la testamentaría de su padre al nuevo mayordomo, D. Carlos A. de Medina, de las fincas y demás posesiones pertenecientes al convento de Jesús María*, AGN, PBN, leg. 74.

[3] Archivo Histórico del Instituto Nacional de Antropología e Historia (cited hereinafter as AHINAH), vol. 74, Fondo Franciscano: *Libro de posesiones pertenecientes al Sagrado Convento de Sras. Religiosas de la Natividad de Nuestra Señora y Regina Coeli, cuyas cuentas corresponden al año de 1848. Y presenta su mayordomo administrador Vicente Pozo*, dated 15 March 1849. Volume 75 has the equivalent account corresponding to the year 1849, dated 21 March 1850. In volume 76 there is *Libro de censos y depósitos, pertenecientes al Sagrado Convento de Sras. Religiosas de la Natividad de Nuestra Señora y Regina Coeli, correspondiente al año de 1850*, dated 28 March 1851.

[4] AGN, PBN, leg. 74, exp. 2.

jara for the year 1846.[1] The monastery owned urban dwellings worth 58,440 pesos and rural properties to the value of 36,000 pesos (on the basis of capitalizing rent at 5%). Capital invested in loans amounted to 6,740 pesos, giving a total amount of 201,180 pesos which should have produced approximately 10,000 pesos a year. However, 64,000 pesos were owed to other corporations, including 12,000 pesos to the convent of Jesús María and in unpaid interest 4,921. This interest debt is taken from the already cited accounts of Jesús María. A further 13,000 pesos were owed to three priests and 6,000 pesos to two private citizens. In total the capital debt was 83,000 pesos. To service this would have cost the monastery at least 4,000 pesos a year. In fact it received in the twenty-nine months between May 1844 and October 1846 the sum of 28,356 pesos and spent in the same period 27,917 pesos on interest, ordinary and extraordinary taxes for the war, the maintenance of nineteen monks, the costs of worship, salaries of servants and repairs to property. In spite of the extraordinary war taxes a small surplus was achieved. In summary, the finances of the regular orders seem to have been healthy, especially in the difficult time from 1848 onwards. Any surplus could be invested to increase their holdings of property and capital. Furthermore, it was in part due to the reduction in the number of monks and nuns which had taken place since independence, as is shown in table 4.

Within a quarter of a century, and having been the same at the beginning of independence, the number of monks was reduced by half and the number of nuns only by a quarter. This reduction in the number of both perhaps reflects the diffusion of liberal ideas which was more rapid and more effective among men than among women. Another reason perhaps was that for an unmarried woman without relatives it was difficult to find any place other than a nunnery. Economic motives were probably not important for the standard of living of the nuns was maintained, judging by the number of servants, which only decreased substantially in 1849, perhaps as a result of the war with the United States. A division of the possessions of the regular orders in 1826 and in 1843 between the number of nuns and girls reveals that the capital corresponding to each one rose from 6,000 to 7,000 pesos. In 1825 the capital corresponding to each monk amounted to 3,700 pesos; in 1855 to approximately 8,800 pesos, that is more than double.

Nevertheless, it would be erroneous to deduce from this that the

---

[1] *Memoria de las alhajas, bienes y fincas rústicas y urbanas, capitales a rédito a favor y en contra de este colegio agustino de Guadalajara, y su actual estado en todo su interior y exterior, hecha en 24 de octubre de 1846*: this manuscript is in the possession of R. Lancaster-Jones who reproduced it in his aforementioned article.

TABLE 4. *Number of regular clergy in Mexico*

Year	Monks	Nuns	Girls	Servants
1825	1,987	—	—	—
1826	1,918	1,931	622	1,475
1827	1,679	1,968	760	1,553
1828	1,592	1,983	665	1,559
1829	1,518	1,905	820	1,758
1830	1,460	1,911	652	1,714
1832	1,363	1,847	696	1,546
1843	1,194	1,609	998	1,345
1849	1,127	1,541	740	879
1850	1,043	1,494	533	1,266

standard of living enjoyed by the monks increased, for this would have been reflected in the writings of the time. Rather it seems that the surplus was consumed in the increasing or more frequent extraordinary taxes, in forced loans and other analogous costs. If the number of nuns and monks had not diminished, the regular orders would have had to live on their capital. The reduction in numbers allowed them to achieve an increase. Only a more extensive and detailed study, however, could reveal if the economy of the regular orders in the years 1846 to 1855 was really healthy or if its apparent strength was only superficial.

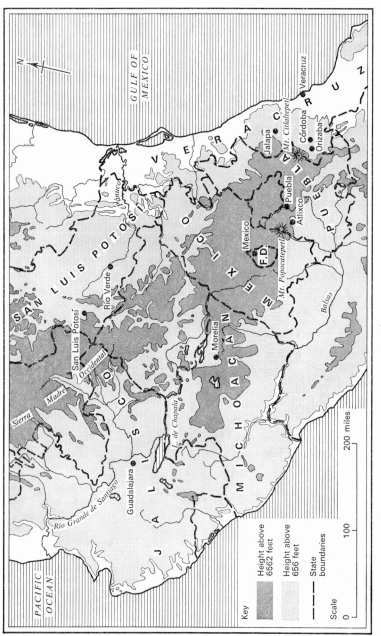

Central Mexico

Key

Height above 6562 feet

Height above 656 feet

State boundaries

Scale

0   100   200 miles

PUEBLA AND VERACRUZ. THE INTERVENTION AND THE DISENTAILMENT OF CHURCH WEALTH, 1856–57[1]

In the autumn of 1855, after their victory over Santa Anna and his supporters, the men of the Reform began to dictate various liberal laws,[2] but peace was still not brought to the country. The political panorama was overshadowed at the end of the year by the conservative revolt in the state of Puebla led by Antonio Haro y Tamariz, former Minister of Hacienda in the 1846 liberal administration and again under Santa Anna in 1853. The rebels succeeded in occupying the city of Puebla on 21 January 1856 and they established a military government, supported by forced loans levied on the clergy and local businessmen. Two months later the revolt was suppressed by the forces of the incumbent President Ignacio Comonfort.[3] During the two weeks that the siege of the city lasted the federal government incurred expenditure amounting to 439,908 pesos,[4] and in addition the military operations had caused considerable damage.

President Comonfort decided to obtain compensation for these costs and on 31 March he ordered the attachment of clerical possessions in the rich diocese of Puebla, which included not only the state of that name but also that of Veracruz and the territory of Tlaxcala.

---

[1] 'Intervention' is a legal term, meaning here attachment or embargo; the Spanish word is *intervención*. 'Disentailment' is used throughout in the sense of 'to take out of mortmain' (*mano muerta*); the Spanish word is *desamortización*.

[2] The first of these laws, known as the Juárez law, was issued on 22 November. It suppressed the judicial privileges enjoyed by the clergy.

[3] J. Bravo Ugarte, *Historia de México* (Mexico, 1944), vol. III, book 1, pp. 236–7.

[4] N. de Zamacois, *Historia de México desde sus tiempos más remotos hasta nuestros días* (Barcelona, 1876–82), vol. XIV, p. 191: according to Payno, *Memoria de Hacienda*, 1856, p. 13 (this *Memoria* covers the period from December 1855 to May 1856), the rebellion cost the government a total of 1,200,000 pesos.

THE ECONOMY AND SOCIETY OF PUEBLA

Puebla was an outstanding industrial city. In an age when the industrial revolution had scarcely made any impression in Mexico, the country's most important manufacture was textiles, particularly the cotton industry, and in this Puebla was unrivalled in the production of fabrics. During the years 1843–45 its share of the total national production of yarn and coarse cloth rose to 40–50%,[1] and although the city, with about 70,000 inhabitants, had only just over one-third of the population of the capital, its industry was more powerful. Puebla's share in the Mexican cotton industry does seem to have declined in the years 1843–53 but the city continued to be the foremost in the manufacture of yarn and fabrics.[2]

The Mexican spinning mills used modern machinery and they compared favourably in size with those in the United States.[3] Power was provided by water, mules and labour but, unlike the capital of the republic, there were no mills in Puebla dependent for their energy on human strength. Its industry was therefore more advanced.[4] The industrial revolution, which had won in the cotton mills, was still struggling in the middle of the nineteenth century against the competition of independent, individual weavers. Some of these had already been reduced to the level of domestic workers, buying their yarn on credit and delivering the finished product to the industrialists.

Puebla was foremost in prints and was ahead of other regions in the manufacture of shawls and woollen fabrics except cloth, which was the speciality of Querétaro.[5] Weaving was carried on in the city and in the surrounding districts in small domestic workshops. Puebla, however, was not limited to the textile industry, and in this city with its old industrial traditions the production of ceramics flourished,[6] and in 1857 there was a porcelain factory employing 100 workers, belonging to Joaquín Haro y Tamariz.[7]

[1] *Memorias de la Dirección General de Industria*, 1843–45; J. Bazant, 'Estudio sobre la productividad de la industria algodonera mexicana en 1843–1845', *Industria nacional y comercio exterior (1842–1851)* (Mexico, 1962), vol. vii, of the *Colección de documentos para la historia del comercio exterior*.

[2] The details for 1853 are reproduced in 'Estado de las fábricas de hilados y tejidos de algodón existentes en la república mexicana', *Memoria de Fomento*, 1857.

[3] Bazant, 'Estudio sobre la productividad...', p. 45.

[4] J. Bazant, 'Industria algodonera poblana de 1800–1843 en números', *Historia Mexicana*, xiv (July–September 1964), 138.

[5] *Memorias de la Dirección General de Industria*, 1843, 1844, tables.

[6] J. Bazant, 'Evolution of the textile industry of Puebla, 1544–1845', *Comparative studies in society and history*, vii (October 1964), 56–69.

[7] 'Estado que manifiesta las fábricas de loza y vidrio de que tiene conocimiento este ministerio, existentes en la república', *Memoria de Fomento*, 1857.

The crops harvested on the rich haciendas of Atlixco were taken to the mills in Puebla which made good use of the abundant hydraulic power available. It was precisely in these old flour mills, or beside them, that the best cotton mills were created.

As a result of these myriad activities, its geographical location and the well-organized coach service from Mexico–Puebla–Veracruz, the city became an important commercial centre. Industrialists usually had large businesses in which they sold all kinds of merchandise, including cloth and yarn of their own manufacture, to merchants and consumers and to the weavers. Others continued to operate the flour mills, since to be the owner of a large cotton business it was necessary to have inherited or bought a mill, and they were thus able to take advantage of the produce of their own haciendas or those which they rented from the Church. The bourgeoisie of Puebla, therefore, were able to integrate their activities vertically.

Reference has already been made to Antonio Haro y Tamariz, a descendant of a Puebla family of industrialists. His father was a merchant, a manager of a mill on his wife's behalf and a town councillor from 1802.[1] Two sons, Joaquín and Luis, had several cotton mills of their own, and some years later Luis rented the Constancia Mexicana,[2] the biggest mill in Puebla.[3] Both sons held public office, another brother chose a career in the Church and the fourth became a politician, first on the liberal and later on the conservative side.

Another prominent industrialist in Puebla was Cosme Furlong, the son of a refugee Irish Catholic, who had acquired several flour mills.[4] As was to be expected, three of his eight sons were presbyters; another, Patricio, fought for the liberal cause, and the remaining four became merchants and industrialists. Two of the latter held office in the state's liberal administration of 1848–53, and one of these, Cosme, transformed an inherited mill into a cotton business and established a business selling yarn and cloth.[5] He collaborated with the state governor, Mújica y Osorio, and on the resignation of the latter in 1853 he assumed the governorship under the Santa Anna administration.

Another prominent person in Puebla was Juan Tamborrel, who came from Orizaba. He manufactured woollen fabrics and owned a business

[1] H. Leicht, *Las calles de Puebla* (Puebla, 1934), pp. 185–6.
[2] *Memorias de la Dirección General de Industria* and the aforementioned *Memoria de Fomento*, tables.
[3] Leicht, 186.
[4] Ibid., pp. 164–9.
[5] J. N. del Valle, *Guía de forasteros de la capital de Puebla* (Puebla, 1852), p. 133.

selling imported cloth. He was a public official in 1861, the year of the liberal victory.[1]

The clearest case illustrating the union of commerce, industry and liberal politics was personified in Juan Mújica y Osorio. He was the son of a prominent Puebla merchant and he owned a large store, a business selling cloth and yarn, a textile factory and a mill.[2] He was governor of the state in 1843–53, after which he accepted a post in Santa Anna's government, only to be exiled from the capital in 1854. He returned to the governorship in 1857.

The most important manufacturer was Esteban de Antuñano, a native of Veracruz and son of a Spanish merchant. He opened a business in Puebla for the sale of cloth, and, motivated by the prohibition on the import of manufactured textiles, he later established the Constancia Mexicana, in a mill which he had bought. On behalf of his wife he owned several haciendas in the valley of Atlixco[3] and he also had cotton-producing lands in Veracruz. Although closely connected with Lucas Alamán, he was inclined towards liberalism and on 23 October 1846 he published a pamphlet in which he proposed 'the closure of the colleges teaching Latin for purposes of theology and jurisprudence...the abolition of monasteries and the reduction of nunneries, each individual thereby affected being given an adequate stipend; the formation with ecclesiastical funds of credit banks which would give priority to the encouragement of manufacturing skills and tropical agriculture...'[4] Antuñano unfortunately died a few months later and hence it cannot be known if he would have continued to hold such views.

In their political inclinations the Puebla bourgeoisie was similar to that of European countries, although such views were perhaps more noticeable on the limited regional scale than in the nation's capital where merchants and industrialists depended on a government which was often contrary to their interests. In Puebla, on the other hand, the bourgeoisie controlled the government. Nevertheless, as indicated above in the biographical references, the liberal sympathies of some of the bourgeoisie were not very intense. Perhaps the change of views of Antonio Haro y Tamariz is symptomatic. Clerical power had to impose itself sooner or later. The capture of Puebla in March 1856 perhaps symbolized the change.

Six years later, at the beginning of May 1862, the French army expected

---

[1] Ibid., p. 131; Leicht, p. 460.   [2] Leicht, 262–3; Valle, *Guía*, 130 ff.
[3] Leicht, 17; M. A. Quintana, *Estevan de Antuñano* (Mexico, 1957), vol. I, p. 11.
[4] E. de Antuñano, *Economía política en México* (Puebla, 1846).

to be welcomed with flowers in this 'the city most hostile to Juárez'.[1] Following their military triumph of 5 May the Mexican leaders received, instead of the congratulations of the Puebla bourgeoisie, a letter from the city's French colony in which they expressed their gratitude for the humane treatment afforded the French prisoners.[2]

Perhaps there were more profound causes of this change of outlook on the part of the Puebla bourgeoisie. As merchants they were supporters of free trade which then formed part of liberal doctrine, but as industrialists the same individuals were bound to the protectionism of the conservatives. The moment must have arrived, however, in which their investment in the cotton industry was worth more than that in imported merchandise. Such a situation existed already in 1850–55 when the capital invested in the cotton industry exceeded 2,000,000 pesos.[3] The principal merchants of Puebla had become industrialists.

On the other hand, foreigners had not by then penetrated the spinning industry and some were even restricted to weaving coarse cloth. In 1843 the most important manufacturer of the latter was the Spanish merchant Ciriaco Marrón.[4] Another foreign merchant was Edward Turnbull, an Englishman, who also owned a linen factory and a flour mill.[5] This, however, is an exception. The flour mills, and the great spinning factories connected to them, remained in the hands of the local people.[6] The foreigners were mainly involved in trade. Of the fifteen most important businesses in the city in 1852, six belonged to individuals with English, German or French surnames. The owners of the others had Spanish names, but it is only known in a few cases whether they were Spanish or Mexican. It seems that there were also many foreigners among the owners of general stores and other mercantile establishments. This foreign influence in the commerce of the city is not surprising as it was located on the main travel route used by foreigners from Veracruz to Mexico. Also, of course, the foreigners must have been supporters of the Reform since, with the exception of the Spaniards, they came from countries in which complete freedom of religion was already established. On the personal level the foreign merchants seem to have been on good terms with the Puebla industrialists and landowners and no conflict arose between them.

[1] V. Riva Palacio (ed.), *México a través de los siglos* (Mexico, n.d.), vol. v, pp. 533–6.
[2] Ibid., pp. 537–8.
[3] *Memoria de Fomento*, 1857, above-cited table.
[4] *Memoria de la Dirección General de Industria*, 1843, table no. 7.
[5] Valle, *Guía*, 131.   [6] Ibid.

CHURCH WEALTH IN PUEBLA

In order to carry out the decree of 31 March 1856 the Minister of Justice and Ecclesiastical Affairs, who was responsible for its implementation, asked for reports of the amount of property and capital affected by the intervention. On 24 June a list was sent from Puebla detailing the value of the holdings of each ecclesiastical corporation.[1] This includes only the real estate within the city and the capital invested in loans. According to the informant it was incomplete, as it did not contain the rural properties on the outskirts of the city, the valuations were inaccurate, the *capellanías* which were occupied were lacking and the regular orders could have concealed some of their holdings. On the other hand some of the figures given are very inflated, if compared with those of the 1843 report of the Minister of Justice and Ecclesiastical Affairs and the manuscript of 31 December 1855. For example, the monastery of San Agustín is said to have possessions to the value of 431,500 pesos, whereas in the Minister's report—there are no figures for 1855—the total is approximately 200,000 pesos. Such a discrepancy seems incredible. In contrast the monastery of Santo Domingo is assigned about 200,000 pesos, while according to the previous accounts it should have had between 400,000 and 450,000 pesos, if its rents were capitalized at 5%. In 1843 the latter was the method used for calculating the value. It is of course just possible that the Augustinian properties yielded a much lower return in that year and those of the Dominicans a much higher one.

Much more detailed information exists on the Church's possessions in other cities to be dealt with in this monograph. Every house belonging to each ecclesiastical corporation, with its location and value, is recorded and this, of course, greatly reduces the possibility of error. In the case of Puebla, however, this is the only available account and it is given in summary in table 5, on the assumption that the specific inaccuracies in each corporation are broadly compensated by the overall result.

In 1852 the city of Puebla consisted of 3,066 houses valued at 9,322,681 pesos,[2] and in the surrounding areas there were 49 rural properties worth 719,505 pesos, giving a total real estate valuation of 10,042,186 pesos. Therefore the Church, in this city known as the Rome of Mexico, owned approximately one-half of all the real estate. The decision of the government to impose an intervention on these goods is not surprising.

[1] AGN, JE, vol. 175, fols. 268 ff.   [2] Valle, *Guía*, 397.

TABLE 5. *Church real estate in Puebla, 1856*

Monastic property	807,030 pesos
Convent property	2,966,247 pesos
Total for regular clergy	3,773,277 pesos
Possessions of the secular clergy	732,462 pesos
Brotherhoods and similar organizations	305,606 pesos
Hospitals, poor houses and orphanages	189,285 pesos
Schools (incomplete because some are included in the figures pertaining to the convents)	61,846 pesos
Total value of Church real estate in Puebla	5,062,476 pesos

THE INTERVENTION

The words of the preamble to the decree of 31 March reflect the political passions that had been aroused: 'Public opinion accuses the clergy of Puebla of having fomented the war by all means available to them, and there is evidence to show that a considerable part of clerical wealth was invested in encouraging the uprising...'[1]

The question of the truth or falsehood of this statement belongs to political history, although according to the Mexican historian, Justo Sierra, the bishop of Puebla did refuse to be identified with the reaction.[2] Whatever the truth, the preamble revealed the reason for the intervention of Church wealth in the rich diocese of Puebla. The object was to compensate 'the republic for the costs it incurred in repressing the reaction which has ended in the city, the inhabitants of the said city for the damage and losses suffered by them during the war, subject to prior justification of claims, the widows, orphans and wounded who have been reduced to poverty in the state as a result of the same war'. This was followed by a flexible measure: 'the intervention decreed in article 1 will continue until, in the judgement of the government, peace and public order have been consolidated in the nation'. Neither the decree nor the regulations governing it, which were issued on the same day, seem to have been sufficient since the Church quickly protested, and on 9 April the government confiscated 13,000 pesos from the cathedral safe. The expulsion of the bishop in May frustrated an attempt at negotiation[3] and on 20 June

---

[1] Labastida, *Colección de leyes*, pp. XXXI–XXXVI.

[2] J. Sierra, *Evolución política de la república mexicana* (3rd ed., Mexico, 1950), p. 201.

[3] A. Carrión. *Historia de la ciudad de la Puebla de los Angeles* (Puebla, 1896–97), vol. II, p. 427.

another decree was promulgated. The introductory clause stated: 'The venerable clergy of the diocese of Puebla have refused to comply with the law of 31 March which ordered the intervention of their possessions; in view of this, the said possessions will be deposited with and administered by agents of the government.' The formation of a 'Receiver of intervened goods' (*Depositaria de bienes intervenidos*) was ordered in which the product of all clerical possessions in the diocese was to be placed. This would safeguard the goods and arrange the collection of any product from them in order to fulfil the aims of the law of 31 March. The new office was to be under the control of the Ministry of Justice and Ecclesiastical Affairs, not the Ministry of Hacienda which at this time was about to issue its law disentailing Church property.

This was therefore a confiscation of revenue by attaching its source. The opposition aroused by the decrees, which were certainly too general and vague, forced the government to define its aim. Hence on 16 August, when the disentailment law was already being implemented in Puebla, another decree was issued. This declared that 'respect for the Supreme Government and the principles of justice on which the law of 31 March was based, demand that the latter law be speedily effected'. It continued that 'clerical possessions in the diocese of Puebla to the value of 1,000,000 pesos were to be used for the purposes expressed in the law of 31 March'. This sum probably covered the costs and damage caused by the civil war. The new measure further ordered that the 'governor of the state would indicate to each ecclesiastical corporation the amount it must contribute, which was to be determined in relation to the size of its holdings'. Exceptions were allowed, for example the schools, hospitals, poor houses, orphanages and parishes known to be poor, and any amount already paid by a corporation towards its quota by 16 August would be taken into account. Once the sum had been paid the distraint of the goods would cease. On 2 September the levy was divided among the ecclesiastical corporations.[1]

Simultaneously with the intervention, Puebla faced the disentailment of 'corporate possessions', a term of wider meaning than ecclesiastical possessions, with the result that both measures were carried out side by side. The 'General Receiver of ecclesiastical possessions in Puebla' or, as it was also called, 'General Depositary of goods attached from the venerable clergy of Puebla', took charge of the administration of Church wealth in the diocese. Abundant records of its activities have survived and they include, among other things, accounts of income and expenditure in the states of Puebla and Veracruz. They also contain many

[1] Ibid., p. 449.

claims by private citizens for damage and losses incurred during the revolt.[1]

Here only those cases which concerned clerical property will be discussed. On 13 August 1856 the Puebla state governor resolved that, owing to their civil character, the hospitals of San Juan de Dios and San Roque were exempt from the intervention.[2] These hospitals were managed by the municipal authorities, but the possessions of the biggest and richest of the hospitals, San Pedro, were attached because it came under episcopal jurisdiction. In fact one of its administrators in 1852 was the canon J. A. Haro y Tamariz.[3] Then on 13 December the bishop of Puebla requested the Ministry of Justice to return the properties 'in order to meet hospital expenditure with the revenue they yielded'. This request was granted two days later because the hospital was a charitable institution and therefore exempt from the intervention in accordance with the decree of 16 August.

A different tactic was adopted for the rich monasteries and nunneries. The prior of the Augustinian monastery in Puebla made a similar request to the Minister of Justice on 8 October, in which he referred to an alleged verbal promise by the latter that the monastery would be left with all the revenue it had before the intervention.[4] In spite of this all the rents and interest were going to the Receiver's office, which apparently was giving nothing back to the monks for their expenditure. The office no doubt wanted to recover quickly the quota of 85,000 pesos which had been assigned to the monastery under the law of 16 August. This sum equals 8·5% of the 1,000,000 pesos which the government was seeking to extract from the Puebla clergy. When the government apportioned this amount among the ecclesiastical corporations it had been guided by the already quoted list of their possessions. According to this the holdings of the Augustinians amounted to approximately the same proportion, 8·5% of 5,000,000 pesos, equalling 425,000 pesos. The fact that the prior did not complain that the quota was too high could signify that the monastery's goods were about 430,000 pesos. The prior concluded by asking that they be excused payment of the quota in the same way as the monastery of La Merced, which was in fact poor, and the convent of La Soledad.

[1] For example, *El Gobernador del estado de Puebla consulta lo que deba hacerse en los casos de reclamaciones de daños y perjuicios ocasionados en la reacción; Resolución sobre los trámites que deben darse a las reclamaciones sobre indemnización de daños y perjuicios resentidos por los particulares en la última campaña de Puebla*, AGN, JE, vol. 176, fols. 239–53; the records are in AGN, JE, vols. 175–8.   [2] AGN, JE, vol. 176, fols. 54 ff.

[3] Valle, *Guía*, 205.   [4] AGN, JE, vol. 176, fols. 102 ff.

4

BDN

The Minister of Justice, Ezequiel Montes, referred the request to the governor of Puebla on 11 December 'for him to resolve as he thought convenient'. The latter's decision has not been found in the archive of the Ministry of Justice but, judging from what happened afterwards, if there was a decision it was negative. It seems that the monastery renewed its complaint, for on 4 June 1857 the Minister of Justice asked the governor to inform him of the amount which the Receiver was giving each month to the Augustinians out of the revenue of their own properties.[1] The office reported that to date nothing had been given as the monks had refused to present a budget of their costs, and that they were living on provisions furnished by merchants. The prior replied that he had presented the budget already on 22 January, by which time he must have certainly realized that his monastery would not be exempted from the intervention. He had also sent proof of the costs incurred during an average year and month. He concluded by saying that the monastery was currently living on charity. The Minister finally resolved that the Receiver should give the monastery a monthly amount in accordance with its budget. On 12 July 1857 the prior presented a new budget based on expenditure for the month of August 1856. This amounted to 2,062 pesos, rather more than 24,000 pesos a year, which was an excessive sum for a monastery housing only fourteen persons.[2] Although a considerable part of the money requested was intended for the reconstruction of the church, it remains probable that the prior had inflated the costs. Assuming that the holdings of the Augustinians totalled more than 400,000 pesos, this was scarcely enough to produce a return of 24,000 pesos. For the latter the capital needed would be 480,000 pesos, assuming a 5% yield. The revenue from the properties was therefore to be paid entirely to the monastery, the state receiving nothing. It is not known if the decision of the Minister was implemented.

Two important clauses in the law of 16 August have not yet been mentioned. These were that the state governor must demand the redemption of loans made by the clergy, for which the contractual term had expired, and also permit voluntary redemptions of those still current; and order the sale by public auction, subject to prior valuation, of the property and capital of those corporations which had not paid their quota by the end of the time designated for them to do so. Such sales were not to include the properties which were affected by the law of 25 June.[3]

The first of these measures meant the following: the mortgages given by the Church were for a stipulated term, usually between five and nine

[1] Ibid., pp. 359–69.   [2] Valle, *Guía*, 30.   [3] Labastida, xxxv.

50

years, after which the borrowers were theoretically obliged to repay the loan. In practice the Church was willing to grant extensions and to continue to collect the interest as if the loan was an annuity or perpetual contract. The consequence of this policy was that the great majority of loans were already due for repayment, as they had been contracted many years before. Therefore the government, under the terms of the law, could oblige borrowers to redeem the debts, repaying not the Church but the civil authorities. In those cases in which the term of the loans had not already expired the debtors were given the right to redeem them, again by paying the government and not the Church.

The second measure stated that the government would sell the real estate of those corporations which did not pay their quota on time, but the latter were unable to meet their quota without selling some of their properties, a course of action they did not want to adopt. They did not have the cash available because the tenants were paying their rent directly to the government and not into the clerical coffers. There were even printed forms for payment of rent, of which the following is an example: 'The General Treasury Receiver of goods attached from the venerable clergy of the diocese of Puebla certifies that the total monthly rent of the house located in...amounted to the sum of... and that the tenant...has paid the rent until...'[1] The tenants of clerical property had paid their rent to the Church until 31 March 1856 and thereafter to the State. The adjudication[2] instruments, which will be discussed in detail later, state that the buyers of these properties would pay interest to the Church as soon as the intervention had ended. For the moment only those houses which had not been assigned under the Lerdo law were to be sold. This provision was clearly intended to avoid conflict between the two laws.

It is evident that these measures ordering the redemption of debts and the sale of houses were confiscatory, unlike the Lerdo law of 25 June. Moreover they foreshadowed the nationalization of ecclesiastical property and capital which was to be decreed in July 1859. The available records indicate that few properties were sold and few debts redeemed. The country was not yet prepared for a confiscation of Church wealth. Some examples of sales that did take place are to be found in the National Archive.[3] In one case the Carmelite hacienda La Sabana was sold to

---

[1] For example, see the form appended to fol. 433 of the register of notary number 5 for 1856, dealing with the transfer of a house in accordance with the Lerdo law; Archivo de Notarías de Puebla (cited hereinafter as ANP).

[2] The word 'adjudication' is used throughout with reference to those properties which were assigned or awarded under the terms of the Lerdo law; the Spanish word is *adjudicación*.

[3] AGN, JE, vol. 176, fols. 269–77.

Manuel Howard, apparently in October 1856. This transaction was recorded in the 1857 report of the Minister of Hacienda, which should have contained only the sales made under the Lerdo law,[1] but in the archive document it was stated that the sale had been made in accordance with the decree of 16 August. The Minister's report indicated the price to have been 66,000 pesos but the information on the terms of payment is confused and it is only known that payment of 17,250 pesos was made in national debt bonds. It is not known how much was paid in cash nor the amount that was left owing.

The same Manuel Howard, using bonds worth 16,800 pesos, redeemed the mortgage debt of Ciriaco Marrón on the hacienda La Ciénaga, which had been assigned to him under the Lerdo law. The adjudication of this property was not recorded in the 1857 report, even though the redemption of the debt had been attested in October 1856.

In a third case Ramón Hacho, a merchant,[2] redeemed in October the sum of 5,510 pesos which was owed on the mortgage of an hacienda, probably to an ecclesiastical corporation. He paid half in cash and half in national debt bonds. The property was owned by a third person and it is likely that the debt was due. The decree of 16 August had not specified exactly who was to redeem such debts, and at least in this instance it was not the debtor but another person.

Clerical revenues continued to flow into the government coffers until 9 September 1857 when President Comonfort, following his new conservative policy, ordered the end of the intervention. The funds of the now liquidated Receiver's office were transferred to the revenue office.[3] Two months later, however, a reactionary plot was discovered in Puebla and the state's new governor, Miguel Cástulo Alatriste, a lawyer and fervent liberal, re-established the intervention on 11 November. This was finally abolished on 28 April 1858 by a decree of General Zuloaga.[4] He had assumed power in January of that year but delayed three months in revoking the measure, which was so bitterly opposed by the Church.

THE DISENTAILMENT

On 20 May 1856 Miguel Lerdo de Tejada became Minister of Hacienda, and he probably found in the Ministry's archive the project devised earlier by Haro y Tamariz, to which reference was made in chapter 1.

---

[1] *Memoria de Hacienda*, 1857 (cited hereinafter as MH 1857), p. 467.
[2] Valle, *Guía*, 131.   [3] Dublán y Lozano, VIII, 619.
[4] Riva Palacio, *México a través de los siglos*, V, 261; MH 1870, p. 479.

The result was the law of 25 June 1856, known as the Lerdo law. In an ironical quirk of fate it was to be Haro y Tamariz who opposed the new measure. Article 1 stipulated that 'the ownership of all urban and rural properties of civil and ecclesiastical corporations in the republic will be assigned to those persons who are renting them, for an amount corresponding to the rent at present paid, calculating this to be equal to a 6% annual interest'.[1] Article 3 defined the corporations as all religious communities of both sexes, brotherhoods and archconfraternities, congregations, parishes, councils, schools, and in general any establishment or foundation of a perpetual or indefinite character. The law thus affected not only the Church but also a multitude of civil, religious and private corporations.

The only payment required of the future owners was a tax on the transfer of ownership, equivalent to 5% of the capital value of the property and payable partly in cash and partly in national debt bonds (article 32). The capital value would be owed to the corporation as a redeemable mortgage on the property, the new owners being empowered to redeem at their convenience all or part of the debt (article 7). These two clauses imposed little on the tenant and yet at the same time they were not prejudicial to the ecclesiastical corporations which were to change from being the owners of real estate to being the mortgage creditors.

If the tenant did not claim the property within three months, any other person could do so, subject to his having previously denounced it (article 10). If there were no denouncers, and if the property had not been rented when the law was published, it would be auctioned (articles 5 and 10). This latter case must have been rather exceptional for the properties were usually rented. The clause on denouncers is to be explained as follows: in the majority of cases the tenant had spent years in the same house, for people were then not as mobile as nowadays, and he was accustomed, and at the same time attached to it, as a result of his expenditure on repairs and other costs. He must have felt some satisfaction that the Lerdo law obliged his corporate landlord to sell him the house which he had come to consider over the years as his own. The corporations rarely offered to sell their houses, but the wish to own a house is a legitimate aspiration of every man or family and the Lerdo law set out precisely to satisfy this desire. This probably explains the enthusiastic reception given the law by five daily newspapers in Mexico City: *Republicano*, *Monitor*, *Heraldo*, *Le Trait d'Union* and *Siglo Diez y Nueve*. Two others were opposed: *Patria* and *Sociedad*.[2] It must also be remembered, however,

---

Reproduced in MH 1857, documents, pp. 3–9.　　[2] *El Siglo Diez y Nueve*, 3 July 1856.

that the great majority of the population were believers in the Roman Catholic faith and they did not want to harm the Church. The possibility thus existed that if the tenant did not seek to transfer the house to himself, some stranger might do so, depriving him of the tenancy and evicting him from the place in which he had lived and perhaps worked, as was the case of many of the small workshops and businesses to be found in every city. Faced with this danger most tenants chose to claim the properties. When they did not do so and when there were no denouncers, as seems to have been more common than might be expected, the sale was effected by public auction.

In spite of its intention to convert the tenant or the citizen at large into a property owner, the law did not overlook the tenant as such. Most of the population lived in rented houses but a tenant was not necessarily poor. In fact many were rich men living in a rented property because the Church had refused to sell it. The tenant who was henceforth to be the owner of his house had to respect any existing subtenancies in the property for a period of three years (article 19). In those cases in which the tenant renounced his right to claim the house, which was then assigned to another person, he continued to enjoy protection for three years during which the new owner could not raise the rent (articles 19 and 20). This order was very important, in view of the widespread fear that the implementation of the law would lead to a sudden increase in rents.

Those persons who acquired a property under the law by adjudication or auction would be the legal owners in every respect. They could sell it freely and dispose of it in the same way as any other owner. Their only obligation to the previous proprietor, that is the civil or ecclesiastical corporation, was to pay interest equal to the amount of rent they were paying at the time of the disentailment (article 21). In other words, they had to pay the same amount as before, but now not as rent of a property but as interest on a capital invested in their own house. This form of transferring ownership was not new. For example, in 1833 the monastery of Carmen had sold several houses for hardly anything in cash. Instead the properties were mortgaged to the Order for almost their entire value.[1] The Church was therefore accustomed to these terms of payment.

The new owners had the right, although not the obligation, to redeem all or part of their mortgage debt at any time (article 7), thus enabling them to act according to their circumstances or convenience. The amount of the debt equalled the rent, now called interest, capitalized at 6%; for example, if the rent was 600 pesos a year the sale price and value of the

---

[1] *Exposición que el provincial del Carmen...*

mortgage was 10,000 pesos. The innovation introduced by Lerdo was the adoption of a percentage figure, to be used in calculating capital value, which was higher than the traditional 5%. Haro y Tamariz's earlier project had been based on the more usual 5%. Using this lower sum an annual rent of 600 pesos would give a capital value of 12,000 pesos. Lerdo therefore offered the tenants and the public the incentive of a 16·67% discount on the capital value of the properties.

At first sight this advantage seemed problematical since the new owner was henceforth responsible for the cost of repairs, whereas previously the tenant had only to pay his rent. Now he was faced with the rent-interest and the additional amount on repairs. This was misleading, however, for it seems that the Church spent very little on repairs, the tenant having to organize them himself. Perhaps this neglect by the clerical landlords offered a means of compensating for the generally low rents which they charged. Hence in many, if not the majority of cases, the tenant who became an owner obtained a real benefit under the Lerdo law.

The law did not confiscate Church property. It merely tried to change its form, and even the new arrangement that was envisaged was not unknown to the Church since its *juzgados de capellanías* operated as banks. There was now an attempt to broaden this existing clerical activity. The ecclesiastical capital would be guaranteed by mortgages, but in the case of a debtor who did not pay the corresponding interest the Church could no longer repossess the property. It could now only seek its sale in public auction (article 24).[1] Lerdo considered the rights of the former owners to be well secured, but here there is a weak point in the scheme. In future no corporation could be the owner of real estate (article 25). If any of the future buyers did not pay the interest the Church could no longer put pressure on them with the threat of eviction. Certainly every buyer would have to provide a guarantor (clause 17), but if the guarantor likewise failed to pay the Church could not take action against his property. These points perhaps go some way towards explaining clerical opposition to the Lerdo law.

The main aim was not financial, for apart from the 5% tax on the transfer of ownership the public treasure was to receive nothing. Its purpose was economic, in the sense that the disentailment would lead to an increase in the purchase and sale of property and thus to economic progress, and also the social aim was to create a strong class of property owners who would be adherents to the liberal regime. It will be seen later whether these aims were realized.

[1] MH 1857, p. 7 of the addenda.

Finally, the law concerned itself with technical details. All the transfers made under the terms of the law by adjudication or sale by auction were to be recorded by public instrument (article 27). Every week the notaries in the capital were to send the Minister of Hacienda an extract of all the instruments attested by them, together with a description of the property, the name of the corporation selling it, the sale price and the name of the purchaser (article 28). Notaries in the states were required to send the same information to the chief treasury official of the region who would forward it to the Minister (article 28). To ensure that all the notaries fulfilled this obligation, heavy penalties were threatened for those who failed to do so.

The possibility that the corporations might refuse to sell their properties or to sign the instruments of sale was also foreseen. In such cases the deed was to be attested in the name of the corporation by the senior political authority, or by a judge, on the basis of a rent to be determined by existing tenancy agreements or the most recent receipt that the tenant could provide (article 29).

As had been stipulated in article 28, quite detailed information on the progress of the disentailment was deposited in the Ministry of Hacienda. The notarial registers from which these extracts were taken have been preserved almost intact but the extracts themselves were probably destroyed after being reproduced in Lerdo's 1857 report. This was entitled: *Memoria presentada al Excmo. Sr. Presidente Sustituto de la república por el C. Miguel Lerdo de Tejada, dando cuenta de la marcha que han seguido los negocios de la hacienda pública, en el tiempo que tuvo a su cargo la secretaría de este ramo.* This report, to be quoted throughout this monograph, will henceforth be referred to as the 1857 report. It was signed on 10 February 1857, although the data concerning the disentailment, on pages 170–535 of the accompanying addenda, covers the period up to 31 December 1856. Document number 149 is headed as follows: 'General account of the urban and rural properties of the civil and ecclesiastical corporations,which have been assigned and sold in public auction, in accordance with the law of 25 June 1856, including details of their location, corporations to which they belong, value at which they were sold, and names of the buyers.' This occupies 365 of the 733 pages of the addenda to the report and it will be referred to here as the Account.

A comparison of this document with various notarial registers reveals that there are many typographical errors in Lerdo's report. These are not restricted to simple mistakes which perhaps make a surname unrecognizable or give an incorrect sale price. There are more serious faults: for example, the same adjudication is repeated on different pages, thereby increasing the number and total value of the transactions. On the other hand there are also omissions, although it is impossible to calculate whether these make up for the repetitions. The report therefore was carelessly printed, which contrasts with other official publications of the time in which the typographers usually took pride in their work. Nevertheless, taking into account the fact that the document contains details of more than 8,000 adjudications and auction sales, the number of errors is not excessive.

The Account begins with the Federal District and continues with the states, which are grouped in alphabetical order. The total value of disentailed property up to 31 December 1856 was 23,019,280 pesos. The first section on the Federal District is divided between adjudications and auction sales. In those of the states no such division is made, but an examination of the notarial registers shows that the adjudications are included almost exclusively. The delay in the provinces, as compared with the capital, caused in part by the slowness of communications, meant that the auctions took place in the states until 1857.

The information on Puebla is on pages 441–70 of the addenda. 705 adjudications are listed, with a value of 2,602,259 pesos. Most of the transactions concern sales in the towns of Huauchingo, Tlacotepec, Calpam and others. The properties involved belonged to municipalities, brotherhoods and parishes, and they were usually sold for less than 100 pesos each. The sales in the city of Puebla comprise the smallest number in terms of the total of adjudications, but they have the greatest value and it is to these we now turn.

The statistical data contains the name of the city, town or village, the location of the property with the name and number of the street, or the name of a rural property, the name of the selling corporation, the sale price and, finally, the name of the buyer. A number of facts are omitted, for example, whether the buyer was the tenant, a denouncer or a successful bidder, the annual rent, or if the sale price had been determined according to the law, and various other items.

Fortunately these omissions can be rectified by reference to the notarial registers. At this time there were ten notaries in the city of Puebla and for the purposes of this study the registers of number 5, pertaining to the notary Gregorio Sandoval, were selected for examination, both because of the high number of transactions recorded in them and because of the orderly manner in which they were drawn up.

In the registers for the years 1856 and 1857—the details for the second year are not in the 1857 report—it is first evident that all the disentailment instruments of ecclesiastical property and capital were signed by the prefect, Antonio M. de Zamacona, or another government representative. The opposition of the Church was monolithic. The same cannot be said of the civil corporations, particularly those controlled by the municipal authorities; for example the poor house, represented by its administrator, sold an hacienda. The corporations controlled by the Church refused to obey the law. The registers have attached to them the proofs of payment of taxes, of rent (the forms cited above at p. 51, issued by the Receiver) and the 5% tax on the sale price. The latter was paid partly in cash and partly in bonds prescribed in the Lerdo law.

The disentailment instruments for 1856 are divided into two types, which correspond to the two different forms of disentailment undertaken in Puebla during that year, namely the adjudications and the conventional sales. After promulgating the law on 25 June, Lerdo also thought of the possibility that the corporation and tenant might agree on a price which was lower than that arrived at by capitalizing the rent at 6%, and various other cases that could arise. Consequently he issued on 30 July a series of regulations in which articles 10–12 established the so-called 'conventional sales' as follows:[1] 'If the tenant renounces his right to adjudication in order to make a conventional purchase of the property, the corporation may sell it to him for the price and conditions stipulated.' No special permission from the civil authority was required by the Church for such a transaction. If the purchase price was as a result lower, the sales tax would nonetheless be paid as if the adjudication had been made on the basis of the capital value as calculated under the law. It was also stated that, subject to prior government permission, the Church could negotiate conventional sales of properties which were not rented. Finally, if the tenants renounced their right to the property, the Church could sell it to another person.

The so-called conventional sales in Puebla were rather different. It has already been stated that all the disentailment instruments in the city were signed by a government representative, including those of conventional sales. The difference between the adjudication and the conventional sales consisted of the price, for whereas the former was the result of the capitalization of the rent at 6%, that of the latter was less. The Puebla authorities interpreted the regulations governing the law in their own way.

This curious division of the disentailment operations is not to be found in the 1857 report, which only sought to register the adjudications and

---

[1] MH 1857, pp. 14–20.

auction sales made in accordance with the law of 25 June. Nevertheless it has already been shown that this report included at least one transaction made under the intervention decree and furthermore, many conventional sales which did not keep strictly to the law. There were no auction sales in Puebla in 1856 or at least none were recorded in the notarial register mentioned above. On the other hand the report did not reproduce all the transactions. An attempt has been made here to locate each instrument in the pages corresponding to the state of Puebla with the aim of showing whether they are complete or not, as well as the presence or absence of errors.

Normally several transactions from the notarial registers are reproduced together, one below the other, and afterwards the sales registered by the other notaries are detailed until it is again the turn of notary number 5. Hence it seems that the notaries fulfilled their obligation to send periodically the details of the instruments and these were being placed in the archive of the Ministry to be published later more or less in the order in which they were received. Two tables have been compiled which contain all the sales recorded in 1856 by notary number 5. The first of these refers to the adjudications and the second to the conventional sales. They form appendices I and II. Of the fifty-one adjudications only one does not appear in the Minister's report and of the eighteen conventional sales, one is likewise missing. On the other hand, without needing to consult the registers, repetitions of a number of sales shown in the 1857 report can easily be proved because the data, from the location of the property to the name of the buyer, is exactly the same. The totals in this report are mere approximations rather than exact amounts.

The adjudications began in Puebla on 23 July, scarcely a month after the promulgation of the law. They continued through August and they ended at the beginning of October. The tenants hastened to become owners, and all except one of the fifty-one adjudications which took place concerned tenants of houses. Three of them were the main tenant, article 4 of the law stating that if there were several tenants the right of adjudication belonged to the one who paid the highest rent, or if the same rent was paid, to the person with the longest occupation of the property. There was only one case in which a subtenant was assigned a house in accordance with article 10 of the law, the tenant having renounced his right to do so.

In every case the sale price was calculated by capitalizing the rent at 6%, and the amount of rent was checked with receipts furnished by the Receiver's office. The law was carried out and this indeed seemed the easiest course of action in view of the short time available and the great amount of work in which the notaries must have been involved.

The 'conventional sales' were rather more complicated. About half the buyers were tenants, although the exact number is not known because in several instances their status was not recorded. In four cases the buyers were not the tenants. In two of these cases a property was requested because the tenant had renounced his right to it, and in the remaining two because the house was unoccupied. The general feature of all these sales was the price, which amounted to two-thirds of the cadastral value. When tenants were involved they indicated the rent they were paying, but the capital value represented by these rents was rather higher than the cadastral value, which is always shown in the instrument. The prospective buyers argued that they were not prepared to acquire the properties at a price estimated by capitalizing the rent. For example, on 9 October a merchant declared that he was paying a rent double the previous amount and it was because of this that he had not claimed the house, for the price would have been 18,000 pesos. Furthermore he himself had made improvements to the value of 2,000 pesos. Article 10 of the regulations governing the law was in his favour and based on this he asked for a conventional sale, offering to pay 11,000 pesos, which was slightly more than two-thirds of the cadastral valuation of 16,000 pesos. The offer was accepted, and again in accordance with the law, a much higher sales tax, corresponding to 18,000 pesos, was paid. On 11 October another individual, apparently the tenant, stated that he did not wish adjudication because the house required expensive repairs. He offered 5,350 pesos, approximately two-thirds of the cadastral value of 8,000 pesos. In the end he bought it for 6,000 pesos but the sales tax was assessed at 5% of 9,600 pesos, which was the figure obtained by capitalizing the rent. As time was needed to negotiate a conventional sale, this type of operation was begun before notary number 5 in the middle of September and ended a month later.

On the basis of the examples given above it is reasonable to ask why, if it was possible to achieve on request a reduction of one-third on the legal price, all the tenants did not ask for a conventional sale instead of adjudication; and secondly, who were the persons who obtained the conventional sales. Fortunately a list exists, intended to be complete, of 136 conventional sales confirmed by the government of Puebla up to the end of October 1856. The federal government may have suspected some irregularity, although the exact form of the disentailment can have been of no direct concern to the treasury since its revenue was the same in both cases. Nevertheless the state government was asked to provide an account of conventional sales effected in 1856. A reply, together with the abovementioned list, was sent at the end of March.[1] The list contains the sales registered by the notary number 5 and by all the others, but even so it is incomplete because several transactions recorded by him are not included. Moreover many sales noted on the list are not in the 1857 report, for reasons which it is impossible to ascertain. The margin of error in this case seems considerable.

The 136 conventional sales amounted to a total value of 698,438 pesos. Less then half of this sum corresponded to the sixty-two sales effected as a result of the tenant's renouncement or through the house being vacant. More than half, 373,097 pesos, referred to seventy-four purchases made by former tenants. This proportion is about the same as that found on a lesser scale in the registers of notary number 5. In the case of the former tenants the list mentioned the capitalization of rents at 6% which gave a total of 596,388 pesos. Therefore the buyers had achieved a total discount of 223,291 pesos, which is more than a third of the value of the properties if this is calculated on the basis of the rents.

Judging from the size of their purchases several government officials and merchants, in particular foreigners, were prominent. It is not known whether the ordinary and current tenants requested a conventional sale, but if they did so they met with refusal; thus most disentailments were effected by way of adjudications. The majority of tenants seem to have been quick to have the houses assigned to themselves because, among other possible reasons, with the passage of time an increasing percentage of the sales tax had to be paid in cash and a correspondingly smaller part in bonds (article 32 of the law). Nevertheless, one or two months after the publication of the regulations governing the law, an influential group thought of interpreting article 10 to their own benefit. Conventional sales of the Puebla type have not been found in other cities. With this exception the disentailment followed the terms of the Lerdo law.

It does not follow from this, however, that all the well-to-do people or government officials made their purchases by conventional sales, nor that all the buyers were merchants or persons of influence. For example, the large Carmelite haciendas in the state of Puebla were disentailed, above all by merchants and officials but at the legal price. In 1843 the four Carmelite estates at Atlixco produced 7,230 pesos a year which, capitalized at 6%, gives a valuation of 120,500 pesos. In 1856 they were assigned for 110,176 pesos. Again in 1843, which is the last date for which

[1] AGN, JE, vol. 176, fols. 275, 276.

there are figures, the Carmelites' sole hacienda in Tehuacán produced 3,000 pesos, giving a capital value of 50,000 pesos. In 1856 this was disentailed for 60,000 pesos. Clearly the haciendas retained their value.

In order to discover whether the city of Puebla was perhaps an exception in the state as a whole, the register for 1856 of the only notary in Atlixco was examined. Situated at the foot of the volcano Popocatepetl, this town was the centre of a rich agricultural region where the regular orders and private individuals had farms. In 1856 the sales of rural estates and ranches were almost all attested before notaries in the state capital, and the register of Atlixco therefore contains, with a few exceptions, adjudications of only local urban houses. The register shows that those to whom adjudications were made were, in almost every case, the tenants, and that the price was equal to the rent capitalized at 6%. The details are given in appendix III.

Lerdo resigned on 3 January 1857, before completing the disentailment. His last circular was sent to the state governors on 2 January and in this he observed that

there were states in which the majority of corporate owned properties were still not disentailed. Whatever the reason for this, no further time to fulfil the law can be allowed and therefore, in order that the measure be concluded, the president has ordered the sale by auction by the District authorities of all such remaining properties in the states and territories...[1]

Apparently Puebla was one of those states, as the following examples indicate. In 1843 the Augustinians had seventy-five houses in the city of Puebla but sales of only twenty-seven of these were recorded in the 1857 report. Only eleven of the fifty houses, and three of the five haciendas belonging to the Dominicans, were disentailed and likewise only four of the twenty-one houses owned by the Carmelites in 1843 were sold. The Mercedarians had forty-two houses and eight of these were affected. In Atlixco seven of the thirteen Augustinian houses were sold, one of the eleven Carmelite and two of the fourteen Mercedarian. On the other hand, as described above, all four Carmelite haciendas in Atlixco and the one in Tehuacán were sold. Clearly the haciendas attracted greater interest. The number of instances were nevertheless too few to be able to draw a general conclusion but the price of an hacienda was equal to about five or ten houses.

Taking into account the fact that the 1857 report is incomplete, we may infer that the number of houses sold was higher than that stated in it, but to ascertain the exact amount every register of all the notaries

[1] MH 1857, p. 165.

would have to be examined. On the other hand it is possible that the number of houses owned by the regular orders diminished between 1843 and 1856, but this is unlikely in view of the overall increase in their holdings during these years. For whatever reason, the disentailment in Puebla remained incomplete.

The circular of 2 January appears to have been counter-productive and it was followed by another on 29 July by the new Minister of Hacienda, José María Iglesias. He mentioned the difficulties which residents in the states faced if they wanted to participate in the sales held in the capital and he therefore revoked the previous circular. In future the sales would take place in the states as before, but interested parties could complain directly to the Ministry if it was found that the state authorities were being obstructive.[1]

In fact during the first part of the year no transaction was recorded before notary number 5. It is not known whether any Puebla residents did go to the capital to bid for properties in their state because in such cases the purchases would have been formalized before a notary in Mexico City, and since no case of this kind has been found in the notarial registers in the capital it can be assumed that they were very rare.

The first transaction of 1857 attested before the notary number 5 took place on 16 July, before the issue of the circular of the 29th of that month. Although the earlier circular of 2 January referred only to auction sales and not adjudications, it seems that the whole process of disentailment had come to a halt. This first transaction was a conventional purchase made by the tenant for one-third of the value of the house. The second was a normal adjudication requested by the tenant and the third, on 1 August, an adjudication requested by a denouncer, not the tenant. The transactions increased in September and above all in October, the final one being at the beginning of November. In all there were twenty-three adjudications, mostly involving tenants, and only three 'conventional sales' (appendix IV).

Although there were few 'conventional sales' in Puebla in 1857, many auction sales were held. The rules for these had been established in the regulations governing the Lerdo law. The price was to be calculated on the basis of the value declared for tax purposes, which of course was less than the capitalization of the rent at 6%. In other cases the price was fixed by valuation. Bids of two-thirds of the value were to be admitted.[2]

In Puebla the procedure was as follows. Interested parties, who were never the tenants, presented a certificate from the Receiver's office which

---

[1] Labastida, 64.   [2] MH 1857, p. 18 of the addenda.

stated that the house was neither assigned nor sold and they offered two-thirds of the fiscal value or of the valuation price. The offer was accepted because other persons refrained from competing, and the auction was thus a mere formality as the price obtained was similar to those of the conventional sales. The price was invariably two-thirds of whichever valuation was used. The supposition that the auction was simply a formal procedure is confirmed by the printed forms provided for each one that was held. These contain the following words:

the sale was announced of the house no...street...belonging to...valued at...for which D...offered and there being no other higher bid, the property was sold to the said Sr...who presented a security guaranteed by D...and therefore you should provide him with the corresponding instrument which the interested party and the guarantor of the bid must sign...

According to the law successful bidders were to present a bond, usually signed by a merchant or a person of repute. Indeed when the latter were themselves bidding the merchants acted as their guarantors, thus giving the impression that it was a business deal between friends. For the less well-known it was perhaps more difficult to find a bond, and this might explain the frequency with which the same names appear in the auctions. In this way one person was able to acquire several houses. The only actual payment consisted of the sales tax, and there was a good chance of making a profit since the purchase price was only two-thirds of the fiscal value, and even less if the value was based on the rent.

Almost all the auctions recorded by notary number 5 were held during October 1857, particularly those in which more than one property was offered for sale. There were in all twenty-four auctions but the number of properties sold was higher because several auctions offered more than one house. For the most part the buyers in 1857 were the same persons as in 1856, and in this sense the sales effected in 1857 were a continuation of those made in the previous year (Appendix v).

The notarial register at Atlixco for 1857 has also been examined. This shows that there were many adjudications of houses during the year, and three of haciendas or ranches. On 29 July the hacienda San Agustín, belonging to the monastery of the same name, was assigned for 41,666 pesos to a Spanish citizen who had been the tenant for forty-one years. The price was calculated by capitalizing the rent of 2,500 pesos at 6%.[1] On 30 July the ranch of Tlapala, owned by the monastery of Carmen, was disentailed by a nephew of the tenant, which was obviously a family arrangement. The price was calculated as in the previous case.[2] Finally on

---

[1] Atlixco register, 1857, fol. 121, ANP.   [2] Ibid., fols. 128 ff.

14 October an hacienda belonging to the parish of Atlixco was sold in auction to a merchant who 'after competing with two other persons, made the best bid'. This is the only case of a genuine auction that has been found and the purchase price was 10% higher than the valuation.[1]

Sales in Puebla in 1857 were not as numerous as in the previous year, as is confirmed by the indexes to the registers of the other notaries. Taking both years together, however, it is certain that the Lerdo law was for the most part carried out during the eighteen months of its effective life. The majority of the real estate owned by the Church passed into private hands.

THE BUYERS OF CORPORATE PROPERTY IN PUEBLA

The great value of the 1857 report consists of the list of more than 300 names of people to whom corporate possessions in the city of Puebla were adjudicated. These persons represent a cross-section of Puebla society, although perhaps somewhat inaccurately because not all the citizens of Puebla acquired corporate property. For example there were no buyers from the Haro y Tamariz family, at least in 1856. This does not necessarily imply their hostility to the disentailment, although in this particular family it did exist, but perhaps may simply mean that this family lived already in their own houses and hence had no need to adjudicate them.

Although the names in the Minister's report may not provide a complete picture of Puebla society, they do give an approximate idea of the social groups which acquired an interest in the success of the Lerdo law and the Reform in general. Such groups would defend the liberal cause in the future, especially after the reactionary coup by Zuloaga in January 1858 which led to their being forced to return the disentailed properties to the Church. If the group of buyers was significant both in number and status, then the cause of the Reform was won in Puebla.

In an attempt to ascertain if the above was the case an alphabetical list has been made of all the buyers in the city of Puebla. This shows that the great majority bought only one house, from which it can be concluded that they were the tenants of corporation-owned houses. Moreover, again in most cases, the value of a property did not reach 10,000 pesos, the more usual figure being around 5,000 pesos.

A further attempt was then made to identify the economic and social position of each person on the basis of their profession or occupation.

[1] Ibid., fol. 289.

Several works were useful in this task, particularly the *Guía de forasteros de Puebla* of 1852, and other publications, for example the *Gran almanaque Mexicano* (1868) by Eugenio Maillefert, various *Guías de forasteros* of Mexico City, the reports of the *Dirección General de Industria* and other similar ones and, finally, the notarial records.

It has been possible, using these sources, to identify the profession or occupation of about half of the buyers, and for less than a half the nationality was discovered, something which is much more difficult to ascertain. Those whose nationality is known were mostly Mexicans, and among them almost all the occupations or professions are represented. It can be concluded from this that the liberal regime did succeed in its attempt to interest the nation in the reforms and that Lerdo was right to impugn the statement that the disentailment only served to enrich a few individuals.[1]

The occupation and nationality of the other half of the buyers are not known. The *Guía de forasteros* registered almost all the small trading establishments and the people who owned them, but it omitted the most numerous of all, namely the weavers. Perhaps some of the latter were among the buyers, which would give the disentailment an even more popular character. This, however, must be pure hypothesis. The fact that so many persons cannot be found in the *Guía de forasteros* may in part be explained by the book's date of publication, 1851, which of course was several years before the Lerdo law, and by other analogous reasons.

With the object of studying the transactions which were carried out in other parts of the state of Puebla, a list was compiled of thirty people who bought properties of a minimum value of 1,000 pesos. This sum was chosen to eliminate the host of purchases worth less than 100 pesos made in different towns and villages in the state, which also incidentally confirm the vested interest which at least some of the rural population were to have in the Reform. It was again possible to identify almost half the buyers—merchants and public officials—but the occupation of the majority remains unknown. They were probably local people, particularly in Atlixco where most of the transactions took place.

Thus if an analysis is restricted to those who bought properties worth, for example, 10,000 pesos or more, a picture of the ruling social group can be obtained, for using the *Guía de forasteros* and other publications it is easier to identify the rich than the poor and the well-known than the unknown. The result is an alphabetical list of the buyers in the state of Puebla, each person or family having acquired property worth at least 10,000 pesos. All the individuals with the same surname, whom it seemed

[1] MH 1857, p. 10.

reasonable to conclude were from the same family, have been grouped together. This list therefore forms appendix VI. In place of more than 300 people, only seventy-four families or individuals remain, and they bought real estate to the total value of 1,460,368 pesos. Nothing is known about fifteen of these people, buyers of 202,432 pesos' worth of property and this leaves fifty-nine whose occupation or profession is known and whose newly acquired holdings were worth 1,257,935 pesos. This total is divisible as follows: 850,276 pesos or 67% was acquired by thirty-eight merchants and industrialists; the remaining 33% by different categories of Mexicans. Within this general division 322,699 pesos or 26% was obtained by sixteen public officials, especially lawyers; 46,850 pesos by three persons who were public officials and merchants at the same time; and finally, 38,109 pesos by a priest and an existing property owner.

Twenty-eight people whose occupation and nationality are not known have likewise been eliminated from this list of seventy-four and the property which they purchased was worth 436,690 pesos. This leaves forty-six people whose adjudications had a value of 1,023,677 pesos. Eight of these were foreign merchants who paid 260,767 pesos, equalling 26% of the total and thirty-six were Mexicans, of whom eighteen were merchants and eighteen officials and diverse occupations. They disentailed the remaining 74%, worth 762,909 pesos.

Of course these can only be mere approximations, since in the first place the 1857 report is incomplete, even when further amounts based on the list of conventional sales are added to the list of seventy-four persons. Secondly, the transactions of 1857 are missing, but as these mostly seem to involve the same people as in the previous year, it can be concluded that the figures are reasonably representative of the dominant group in Puebla interested in the Reform, perhaps in part through their being involved as a result of the adjudications which they had obtained. This group consisted mostly of Mexican merchants, industrialists and liberal officials.

These characteristics are even more prominent if, from the list of seventy-four, the thirteen persons or families with minimum purchases of 25,000 pesos are chosen. The total expended by these thirteen amounts, in round figures, to 500,000 pesos, more than 33% of the total of 1,460,368 pesos. Four foreigners are outstanding because of the size of their purchases. There are several apparently Mexican merchants, three professional families from Puebla and one from elsewhere, all of whom were renowned for their devotion to the liberal cause. If one considers that among the citizens of Puebla only Haro y Tamariz was prominent on the conservative side, while for the liberals there was Alatriste, Isunza, Romero Vargas and Zamacona, to name only a few, the conclusion must be that people with a university level education, who usually came from the urban middle class, had a marked preference for the liberal programme. This perhaps would help to explain the strength of the liberal movement and, in the final analysis, its victory.

SOCIAL AND ECONOMIC PANORAMA OF VERACRUZ

The state and port of Veracruz occupied a very special place in the life of the country. Veracruz had been for three hundred years almost the only point of contact between Europe and New Spain. Its economy turned on trade, imported merchandise being received by sea and then dispatched to Puebla and Mexico City, and it shipped the goods from the interior, especially precious metals. Due to their position as the sole intermediaries, the Spanish merchants in the port were the best informed on recent events in Europe. Some idea of their level of culture can be derived from the fact that in 1810, when the war of independence began, Veracruz was one of only four cities in New Spain to have a printing press, the others being Mexico, Puebla and Guadalajara.

Because of its strategic importance the city was surrounded by fortifications. The fortress of San Juan de Ulúa, which was situated on a small island off the coast, was the key to the port, just as this was itself the key to the country. After the winning of independence in 1821 this privileged position became a cause of decline, for every power that wanted to attack Mexico made the port the target for its cannons. For example, in the 1847 war between Mexico and the United States, between four and five hundred of its inhabitants died and 6,700 cannon balls 'made the fortunes of many Veracruz residents disappear'.[1] In 1844 Cumplido in his *Noveno calendario* lamented that

a city which through its mercantile activity and riches could in other times merit the name of Tyre of America, today is in the lowest state of decline. Its trade, which in 1802 amounted to the enormous sum of 82,047,000 pesos, is now insignificant; its population which in 1804 was more than 20,000, including the garrison, now is scarcely 7,000 persons of all classes. Veracruz is the town in the republic which has suffered most calamities in these recent times.[2]

[1] M. Rivera Cambas, *Historia antigua y moderna de Jalapa y de las revoluciones en el estado de Veracruz* (Mexico, 1870), vol. III, pp. 872–4.
[2] Cited in M. B. Trens, *Historia de la h ciudad de Veracruz y de su ayuntamiento* (Mexico, 1955), pp. 92–3.

This lament seems to be confirmed by official statistics.[1] The people of Veracruz, especially the merchants, paid a high price for their privileged position.

Nevertheless the innate energy of its inhabitants brought a revival and by 1856 its population already amounted to almost 10,000.[2] Certainly, considering that the state of the same name was calculated in 1856 to have a population of 339,000 inhabitants,[3] Veracruz was one of the smallest state capitals in the republic. What was important in the port, however, was the quality of its residents. After 1847 many new buildings were erected, for example the customs house, treasury office, theatre, market and wharf, and the former monastery of Belem (ex-hospital of the Bethlehemites) was converted into the best hospital in the country.[4] Veracruz still retained its key position in the relations between Mexico and the Western world, for even when the frontier with the United States was moved much closer to the heart of Mexico as a result of the loss of the enormous territory of Texas during the 1847 war, there were still no railways which could transport goods from the north. Hence trade with the United States continued to be conducted by sea. It was logical that the inventions which were revolutionizing life in Europe and North America should arrive first at Veracruz. In 1851 the telegraph was constructed between Veracruz and Mexico, five years after the opening of the one connecting New York and Washington. Within a short time it began to be extended from the capital to Querétaro and beyond. The president of the line at Veracruz was Hermenegildo Viya who, in addition to his business interests in the port, owned a large store in the capital which specialized in the sale of chocolate.[5] As a means of communication the telegraph was a substitute for the railways which had been delayed in Mexico because of the country's topography. Meanwhile travel by stage coach was improved and in 1850 daily services were inaugurated from Veracruz to Guadalajara passing through the capital, the whole journey taking nine days.[6] Eventually the first railway in Mexico was laid at Veracruz and by 1857 almost twenty kilometres were in use. Gas lighting already existed in 1855 and the city's educational system was equally advanced; the municipality maintained free primary schools and also a

[1] M. Lerdo de Tejada, *Apuntes históricos de la h. ciudad de Veracruz* (1st ed., Mexico, 1857; 2nd ed., Mexico, 1945), vol. II, pp. 206–8; *Estadística del estado libre y soberano de Veracruz* (Jalapa, 1831), pp. 71–2.

[2] A. García y Cubas, *Noticias geográficas y estadísticas de la república mexicana* (Mexico, 1857).

[3] Ibid.

[4] Lerdo de Tejada, *Apuntes históricos*, 591–601.

[5] Valle, *El viajero en México*, 203, 339; the correct orthography is Viya.

[6] Lerdo de Tejada, *Apuntes históricos*, 591–601.

secondary school called the Veracruz Institute. The city was affected every year by yellow fever, and with the aim of modernizing and making it more healthy to live in Lerdo proposed the demolition of the fortifications and the San Juan de Ulúa fortress, or at least their conversion to civil use, a project which was advanced for its time.[1]

The port had close connections with three cities in the state, Jalapa, Córdoba and Orizaba, all of which were situated outside the yellow fever area and which were therefore places in which rich Veracruz residents spent part of the year and also owned properties and businesses. In 1856 Jalapa was an important market town of 10,000 inhabitants[2] and, due to its abundant water supply, the site of four textile factories.[3] Orizaba had a population of 15,000[4] and with greater hydraulic power available it had the biggest cotton mill in the country, using more than 11,000 spindles.[5] Córdoba had 6,000 inhabitants and it was the centre of a rich agricultural area which then specialized in the production of tobacco.[6]

The importance of the state of Veracruz in the country's economy was due not only to geographical factors but also to the human element. Perhaps tempered in part by their incessant struggle against the climate, which at times stimulated and at others depressed them, the citizens of Veracruz showed an uncommon spirit of enterprise and interest in economic, financial and fiscal matters. It is a fact of some significance that natives of Veracruz provided fourteen Ministers of Hacienda in the period 1821–56, including José Ignacio Esteva, father and son, Antonio Garay, an industrialist and speculator in the capital, and Miguel Lerdo de Tejada, and this list does not include Arillaga, a Spaniard resident in the port.[7]

In 1855 there were two hundred and fifty Mexican and foreign firms in the port, although which of the two categories was in the majority is unknown.[8] Fifty-eight of these were 'large businesses', according to the records for 1850. In addition, in 1851 there were thirty-nine commission brokers whose names are unknown. Finally in 1850 there were six property management offices.[9] In the valuable third volume of his history of Veracruz, Lerdo copied the entire census of houses, including the number of each, in progressive order, not by street, the name of the owner, the value of the property and also the name of its administrator.[10] On the

---

[1] Ibid.
[2] *Diccionario universal de historia y geografía* (Mexico, 1853–56), appendix, vol. II, 1856.
[3] *Memoria de Fomento*, 1857, table.   [4] *Diccionario universal*, appendix 3, 1856.
[5] *Memoria de Fomento*, 1857, table.   [6] *Diccionario universal*, appendix, vol. I, 1855.
[7] Lerdo de Tejada, *Apuntes históricos*, vol. III (1858), p. 118; there is no second edition of this volume which contains unique material for a social and economic study of Veracruz.
[8] Ibid., pp. 48, 59–61.   [9] Ibid., pp. 57, 62.   [10] Ibid., pp. 155–81.

basis of this information an alphabetical list of the latter has been compiled. Sometimes the merchants noted were not involved in the administration of real estate and in other cases the administrators had no connection with trade. Eugenio Maillefert's *Gran almanaque mexicano y directorio del comercio de la república mexicana para el año de 1869*, in which the information seems to be from 1867, has been used to complete the picture.[1] Clearly these facts can only be applied to 1857 with some caution, although change in that time was slower than it is today.

The census of all the houses in the port has also been used to compile an alphabetical list of the 369 private property owners, excluding the corporations. Together with the list of administrators, the number of houses and their value have been calculated, and an attempt has been made to find the nationality and occupation of each owner. The same third volume also contains the names of all municipal, state and federal officials.[2] Aided by all this information, a picture of the groups directing Veracruz society has been drawn up.

A large majority of the owners, as well as of the administrators, owned or managed between one and three houses, and from this it is reasonable to conclude that there was a numerous middle class. Nevertheless, as always a smaller number of men owned or managed most of the properties. According to the classification of Veracruz residents by occupation there were 114 proprietors, that is people who were not mainly devoted to trade or any other specific activity but who lived on the revenue from their properties.[3] Of course there may have been rural property owners among these, but there are unlikely to have been many because few ranches and haciendas were near the port, owing to the climate and soil. Consequently many of the 114 individuals were mainly owners of urban property in the city of Veracruz. In the list which has been compiled there are about a dozen individuals or families who were neither merchants, property owners nor government officials but who possessed substantial real estate holdings. The richest were the three members of the Barbadillo family with thirty-six houses valued at 129,400 pesos. Others had less and a simple calculation of the return on property indicates that even the largest proprietors could not exist exclusively on rents. They must also have lived on income from their rural holdings or perhaps from some business interest. Clearly among so many names of owners there are many merchants, property administrators and government employees.

Among the Veracruz merchants who have already been mentioned was

[1] The section on Veracruz is on pp. 308–11.
[2] Lerdo de Tejada, *Apuntes históricos*, III, 75–8.   [3] Ibid , p. 45.

Viya, with a business in Mexico and another in Veracruz, operating as the firm Viya Brothers. This business, apart from owning six houses worth 91,600 pesos, administered a further thirteen valued at 134,500 pesos. Of course this type of management was a subsidiary activity, considering the fact that an administrator could earn perhaps 5% of the revenue he collected or the rent, which equalled 6% of the capital value of the property. The firm's ownership of six houses, which were all quite expensive by Veracruz standards, each being worth an average of 15,000 pesos, seems to accord with the economic and social position of the Viya family, who also owned the most important telegraph line in the republic. The Paso y Troncoso and the Muriel families were two others who achieved local prominence as merchants and national importance through their business transactions with the federal government. Pedro del Paso y Troncoso was a store owner, the most active administrator, managing seventy houses worth 528,660 pesos and, together with his relatives, an owner of substantial real estate. Furthermore in 1855 he had bonds of the 'first Spanish convention' to the value of 158,000 pesos. This convention between Mexico and Spain had recognized the old claims of Spanish citizens against Mexico, and Paso y Troncoso had acquired one of these, presumably at a low price.[1] Longinos Benito Muriel had a store in Mexico and a flour mill,[2] and in Veracruz he was a merchant, the manager of twenty-eight houses worth 171,600 pesos and, with his family, owned real estate worth more than 100,000 pesos. Finally, the business firm of Muriel Brothers owned in 1855 credits from the same Spanish convention to a value of 36,000 pesos.[3] These involved a great number of small amounts for which the government of New Spain became indebted during the years 1811–20 to the tobacco growers in the region of Orizaba and Córdoba. This area was in fact the only place in which it was permitted to grow tobacco which the growers sold to the government. The original creditors were Mexican farmers, and after buying the credits the Muriel Brothers' firm was probably able to have them included in the international agreement.

Another group of Veracruz residents belonging to the ruling social elite were those who had shops in the port and at the same time cotton mills in Jalapa, for example Sáyago, de la Serna and Manuel García Teruel, who was born in Jalapa and later lived in Puebla.[4] In 1857 they owned three of the four textile factories then in Jalapa.[5] Their real estate holdings

---

[1] Payno, *México y sus cuestiones financieras*, 173.   [2] Valle, *El viajero en México*, 203, 333.

[3] Payno, *México y sus cuestiones financieras*, 174–8.

[4] See his will made in 1865 in Puebla before notary number 5, fols. 251 ff., ANP.

[5] *Memoria de Fomento*, 1857, table.

in the port were not as substantial as those of the first social group mentioned, but two of them, Bernardo Sáyago and García Teruel, did have many properties in Jalapa, which were mortgaged to the Church.[1]

In the cities of Orizaba and Córdoba there was an interesting group of three Frenchmen: Auguste Legrand, who had come to the country as a partner of Lucas Alamán in the textile factory of Cocolapam in Orizaba,[2] Carlos Saulnier, a textile engineer who had arrived in 1831 to instruct Mexicans in the 'mechanical skills' and who in 1841 was the owner of a textile factory in Orizaba with 125 looms and 200 workers;[3] and Juan Bautista Sisos (Sissos), who was the representative in Córdoba of Nicanor Béistegui in the tobacco transaction with Manning and Mackintosh, that is he was the person responsible for dealing with the growers on behalf of the concessionaries holding the monopoly.[4]

Córdoba and Orizaba, especially the former, were the birthplaces of liberal lawyers, for example Ignacio de la Llave, several times governor of the state,[5] and the young Francisco Hernández y Hernández and José María Mena, subsequently governors in 1868–72 and 1875–77 respectively. In the port of Veracruz the talented inhabitants dedicated themselves to trade, but in Córdoba they were more interested in the professions, leaving trade to the foreigners.

Finally there was a group of Veracruz citizens among whom were José Ignacio Esteva, merchant and administrator of eight houses worth 347,530 pesos, José Gutiérrez Zamora, also a merchant and administrator of thirty-seven houses worth 146,500 pesos, and Joaquín Muñoz y Muñoz, merchant and administrator of twenty-three houses valued at 132,200 pesos. These men were not industrialists nor important owners of urban real estate in the port, but on the other hand they were involved in politics. Esteva was Minister of Hacienda in 1851, Muñoz y Muñoz was governor of the state in 1835–38 and 1841–44, and José Gutiérrez Zamora was closely connected with his brother Manuel, who had given up trade

[1] *Estado demostrativo de los capitales, propiedades y otros fondos pertenecientes al clero en el departamento de Jalapa, formado en cumplimiento del supremo decreto de 31 de marzo próximo pasado,* 1856, AGN, JE, vol. 175, fol. 107.

[2] J. C. Valadés. *Alamán. Estadista e historiador* (Mexico, 1938), p. 392.

[3] *Informes y cuentas del banco de Avío,* 1 January 1832, reproduced in L. Chávez-Orozco (ed.), *El banco de Avío y el fomento de la industria nacional* (Mexico, 1966), p. 109; *Semanario de la industria mexicana* (Mexico, 1842), p. 80.

[4] Manning and Mackintosh correspondence, 1851, Latin American Collection, University of Texas.

[5] E. M. de los Ríos, *Liberales ilustres mexicanos de la Reforma y la intervención* (Mexico, 1890), p. 89.

to enter politics and became governor precisely during the years of the Reform, 1857–61.[1]

The Spanish merchants in Veracruz were prominent for their liberal sympathies even at the end of the colonial period[2] and liberal sentiments inherited from the Spaniards found easy expression in 1833 during the vice-presidency of Valentín Gómez Farías. On 30 November of that year the state congress approved a decree which ordered the secularization of all the regular orders, except that of San Francisco which enjoyed universal respect, and the nationalization of their possessions which were to be used for education and the public good.[3] The project was not implemented because of the reactionary coup d'état of Santa Anna in April 1834.

There were four monasteries in the port: Dominican, Franciscan, Mercedarian and Augustinian. There were no nunneries, possibly because of the tropical climate. The numbers of monks in the monasteries were as follows: in 1826 there were at least ten[4]—eight without the Augustinians whose number was not indicated; in 1843 eight;[5] in 1850 five;[6] and in 1856 only four, that is one in each.[7] The monasteries, like the houses which they owned, were badly damaged during the bombardment of 1847 but unlike private and public buildings they were not reconstructed or repaired, so that by 1856 they were in danger of collapse.[8] The number of priests was even lower: in 1849 there were six, which was a very small number for a population of much more than ten thousand if the neighbouring villages without parishes are included, and in 1856 the number seems to have dropped to only four.[9]

The rather unbelieving character of the people of Veracruz was reflected in the attitude of the local clergy. Lerdo described the priests as 'restricted to the exercise of their tranquil ministry, not interfering under any circumstances in the political questions which have disturbed the country'.[10] Consequently when the civil war broke out at the beginning of 1858, Veracruz accepted without difficulty the constitutional government.

[1] F. González de Cossío, *Xalapa. Breve reseña histórica* (Mexico, 1957), list of the governors on p. 445.
[2] Alamán, *Historia*, iii, 407.
[3] *Sesión del honorable congreso de Veracruz, en que se discutió y aprobó el decreto que declara de la pertenencia del estado algunos conventos y sus propiedades* (Veracruz, 1833), p. 37.
[4] *Memoria de Justicia*, 1826.
[5] Ibid., 1844.
[6] Ibid., 1851.
[7] Lerdo de Tejada, *Apuntes históricos*, iii, 78.
[8] Ibid., pp. 32–3.
[9] Ibid., pp. 45, 78.
[10] Ibid., ii, 600.

TABLE 6. *Church real estate in Veracruz, 1856*

Nature of the corporation	No. of houses	Value (pesos)
Secular clergy (parish, its possessions managed by José Ignacio Esteva)	18	40,000
Regular clergy		
Monasteries in Veracruz	43	141,200
Nunneries of Puebla (goods managed by P. del Paso y Troncoso)	22	155,300
Total for regular clergy	65	296,500
Third Order of San Francisco	10	28,300
Brotherhoods (there were ten; the possessions of the richest, that of Santísimo, were managed by Esteva)	59	156,060
Capellanías and pious works (there were ten of the latter, the richest being that of Misericordia, managed by P. del Paso y Troncoso)	38	269,860
Total real estate of ecclesiastical corporations	190	790,720

CORPORATE PROPERTIES

The municipality owned thirty-three properties, including those of the former Bethlehemite monastery, valued at 235,800 pesos. Another civil corporation was the Charity Junta (*Junta de Caridad*), which managed two hospitals and which consisted of representatives of the town council and a lay brother of the Third Order of San Francisco.[1] The people of Veracruz did not permit Church interference in public welfare. The Charity Junta had houses worth 243,900 pesos[2] and so, in total, the civil corporations in the port owned ninety-three houses with a value of 502,800 pesos.[3]

Ecclesiastical possessions can be classified as in table 6.[4] The most interesting fact to emerge from this table is the poverty of the monasteries which even in their own city were poorer than the Puebla nunneries, which only had a fraction of their possessions in the port.

The relative wealth of the civil corporations was characteristic of

[1] Ibid., III, 119–20. [2] Ibid., p. 14, and the census on pp. 155 ff. [3] MH 1857, p. 490.
[4] Lerdo de Tejada, *Apuntes históricos*, III, 14, and the aforementioned census.

Veracruz, for whereas in Puebla and, as will be seen later, in Mexico, their real estate holdings were minimal compared to those of the Church, in Veracruz they amounted to five-eighths of the latter. Finally, taking into account the fact that individuals owned 793 houses worth 3,996,000 pesos, out of a total of 1,076 properties worth 5,289,520 it can be concluded that, unlike the situation in Puebla, the Church held only 16% of the total value of urban real estate.

The existence of considerable properties in the port owned by the Puebla nunneries is due to the fact that the state of Veracruz was part of the Puebla diocese. In the view of the ecclesiastical authorities in Puebla, Veracruz was a province in which they held its best real estate. This is evident from the fact that the Puebla nunneries had only half the number of properties owned by the local monasteries but their total value was greater. Consequently when the federal government wanted to punish the Puebla clergy with the intervention decree of 31 March 1856, it extended its scope over the whole diocese. Nevertheless the government cannot have hoped to derive much by way of indemnity from the clerical possessions in Veracruz, for their value hardly amounted to 800,000 pesos, compared to the five millions which the Church possessed in the capital of the see.

In accordance with this law the Minister of Justice asked the Veracruz state government for details of ecclesiastical possessions, not only real estate but also capital, that is mortgage loans on which the interest was in future to be paid into the federal treasury, together with the rent from property. As a result of this request statistics are available of these possessions in the port of Veracruz, Orizaba, Córdoba and Jalapa. The information concerning Veracruz will be presented in chapter 4, when the nationalization of ecclesiastical capital, decreed in 1859, is discussed.

The details on Orizaba are divided into real estate and capital for each corporation.[1] Here only the real estate will be discussed and the capital funds reserved for the corresponding chapter. The corporation owning most real estate was the oratory of San Felipe Neri, a congregation of secular clergy with property valued at 62,700 pesos. The nuns of San Felipe Neri lived under the supervision of the latter and their houses were worth 4,000 pesos, giving a total of 66,700. The only monastery in Orizaba was of the Carmelites and they had properties worth 37,000 pesos, which made them almost as poor as their colleagues in Veracruz.

---

[1] *Estado que manifiesta las cantidades por los diversos ramos pertenecientes a los bienes eclesiásticos, formado con arreglo al artículo 8 de la parte reglamentaria del superior decreto de 31 de marzo de 1856*, AGN, JE, vol. 175, fols. 176–7.

Other ecclesiastical possessions in Orizaba were as follows: properties belonging to the Puebla convent of Santa Teresa worth 5,500 pesos; those of the tithe collection district of the Puebla see, 5,000 pesos; those of the Third Order of San Francisco, 8,400 pesos; those of *capellanías*, 12,600 pesos; and the remainder, to a value of 93,515 pesos, belonged to the brotherhoods. An estimate of the total value of Church property in Orizaba amounts to 228,715 pesos.

The facts given in the 1857 report indicate that houses owned by the municipality were worth about 50,000 pesos, including the possessions of the San Juan de Dios hospital.

The list of Church possessions in Córdoba does not make this division between real estate and capital and therefore it is impossible to separate the two.[1] The total of both is calculated to have been 200,000 pesos. To ascertain the approximate value of the real estate in the city the corresponding adjudications noted in the 1857 report must be added up, although this information cannot of course be exact, in the first place because some houses were possibly sold for less than they were worth, and secondly, because the disentailment probably did not end in 1856. These figures have been completed with others from a later list, dated 1862.[2] According to this clerical real estate in Córdoba was worth about 50,000 pesos or less than a quarter of the total goods.

The only corporation in Córdoba worthy of mention for its real estate holdings was the Girls' School, which owned the hacienda of Omealco. According to the 1856 list this property produced no rent because it was involved in legal proceedings and therefore the value attributed to it was nil.[3] Nevertheless it was disentailed for 16,666 pesos, which equals a rent of 1,000 per year. The details of this transaction are known due to the register of the Córdoba notary, Sebastián Palma.[4] On 10 July 1856 Esteban Ambiel, a French resident of Orizaba, advised the rector of the school that, as the tenant, he was seeking to have the property assigned to himself. Ambiel owed the school money for rent, but on the other hand he had carried out repairs which were not accredited to him. As no agreement could be reached between them the school rented the hacienda to

---

[1] *Estado que manifiesta las fincas, capitales y fondos eclesiásticos de esta ciudad y villas de Huatusco y Coscomatepec, con arreglo a lo dispuesto en el artículo 2 del decreto del supremo gobierno de 31 del próximo pasado y de conformidad con su 5a. y 9a. de la parte reglamentaria del mismo*, 3 May 1856, AGN, JE, vol. 175, fols. 141–8.

[2] *Noticia de los capitales pertenecientes a bienes eclesiásticos y otras corporaciones, que han sido redimidos por las personas que se expresan, así como las adjudicaciones, sacadas de los únicos datos que en la actualidad existen*, Córdoba, 26 June 1862, AGN, PBN, leg. 734.

[3] AGN, JE, vol. 175, fols. 141–8.

[4] Fols. 166–80; this register is in the possession of the Córdoba notary Savador D. Zamudio.

another person, but Ambiel refused to vacate the property, with the result that the new tenant had to start legal action against him. This he did and at the same time he presented himself in competition with the Frenchman for the adjudication. The judge in Córdoba, M. Antuñez, awarded the property to Ambiel on 25 July for a price of 16,666 pesos, which equalled a rent of 1,000 capitalized at 6%, and he further resolved that the school should pay Ambiel a small amount in settlement of the disputed accounts between them, for it owed him more for improvements, repairs and costs than he owed in rent. As the school refused to sign the deed the political chief, R. Ceballos, did so on 4 August. The sales tax of 833 pesos was paid two days later. This school also had bad luck with other properties, as will be seen in chapter 6. The other corporations had even less real estate. The solitary monastery in Córdoba, that of San Diego, had none but it did have capital which in 1843 was calculated to amount to 11,475 pesos.[1] The details in the 1857 report indicate that the town council of Córdoba did have substantial holdings but printing errors make an exact calculation of these impossible. Certainly they were worth more than 50,000 pesos, perhaps more than the Church properties.

The information relating to Jalapa once again divides the Church goods between real estate and capital.[2] Ecclesiastical properties in the city are calculated to have been worth 58,000 pesos, and indeed those of the Franciscan monastery alone amounted to 19,000 pesos. This contradicts the reports of the Ministry of Justice which state that the monastery had no real estate and only capital, although this situation would have been more in accord with the traditional poverty of the Order. Nevertheless the 1856 list details each house and its number in progressive order— houses were identified by number, not by the name of the street—and it is therefore difficult to doubt the accuracy of the account, in spite of the earlier statement by the Ministry of Justice. It may well be that in the accounts which were sent to the Minister of Justice and on which his reports were based, the friars concealed the existence of the properties. A typical institution in Jalapa was the Beaterio, which was a girls' school directed by Franciscan nuns. This owned only one house and at least in real estate it was therefore poorer than the school in Córdoba. The rest of the 58,000 pesos' worth of Church properties belonged almost entirely to brotherhoods.

Civil corporations, particularly the city council, were also rich proprie-

[1] *Memoria de Justicia,* 1844, table 6.
[2] *Estado demostrativo de los capitales, propiedades y otros fondos pertenecientes al clero en el departamento de Jalapa, formado en cumplimiento del supremo decreto de 31 de marzo próximo pasado,* Jalapa, May 1856, AGN, JE, vol. 175, fol. 107.

tors in Jalapa. The two hospitals, San Juan de Dios and the women's hospital, had between them houses valued at 35,000 pesos, if the rents are capitalized at 5%.[1] Other holdings which were used to maintain the council have to be added, and in total these civil properties were probably not much less than those of the Church.

The Church real estate in these four cities, which were virtually the only ones in the state of Veracruz, was worth an approximate total value of 1,100,000 pesos, which was only a fifth of the clerical property in the city of Puebla alone. There were no rich ecclesiastical haciendas in Veracruz like those in the state of Puebla. Secondly, the properties of the civil corporations in Veracruz were worth at least 650,000 pesos, approximately 60% of the Church holdings, although the municipal properties in Orizaba, Córdoba and Jalapa may have been greater than those indicated.

The relative poverty of the Church in Veracruz and the wealth of its civil corporations were almost certainly related to the liberal mentality so characteristic of that region.

THE DISENTAILMENT IN THE STATE OF VERACRUZ

The notarial registers for the port of Veracruz do not seem to have survived. They may have been destroyed by the hot and humid climate or by the bombardments so frequent in the history of the town, or perhaps for some other reasons. The oldest one that has been found dates from 1868 and it contains some references to the sales made in 1856 and in 1859.[2] The gaps in the available information have been filled in to some extent by the third volume of Lerdo's *Historia de Veracruz* which contains a complete account of the disentailment operations, entitled as follows: 'Note. Of the 283 houses belonging to civil and ecclesiastical corporations indicated in the preceding list, 262 were transferred by the month of April 1857, in accordance with the law of 25 June 1856, and in this order.'[3] This is, in fact, the same list to be found in the 1857 report but it is here more complete as it continues to April 1857. The difference, however, is small for there were probably only eleven transactions which took place at the beginning of the year and were placed at the end of the list. With few exceptions the transactions follow the same order in both publications, no doubt the chronological order. Naturally the Minister's report, in the section on the State of Veracruz, intercalates the details on Córdoba,

---

[1] *Diccionario universal*, appendix, vol. II, 1856.

[2] Register of notaries José María Bello and Marcos María Castellanos, in the possession of Veracruz notary Leandro Rivero.

[3] Lerdo de Tejada, *Apuntes históricos*, III, 182–9.

Orizaba, Jalapa and other towns in the state. These were also probably placed in the order in which the Treasury Office in Veracruz received the information, or in that which the Minister of Hacienda in the capital was given from the port.

A comparison and collation of both documents have made possible a reasonably exact appreciation of the type and number of errors in the 1857 report. The most frequent mistake is in the names of the buyers, which are incorrect due to printing errors, and those of foreigners are misspelt more frequently than those with Spanish surnames. In the latter the paternal surname is not always used or merely appears as an initial, for example M. Gutiérrez Zamora becomes M. G. Zamora, which can easily lead to confusion. The comparison of the 1857 report with the third volume of Lerdo's work, which is almost free of errors, indicates that the frequency of the mistake in the names of the buyers is not less than 5% of the total number of names. Mistakes in amounts, that is sale prices, are less frequent. It has been possible to correct, although not entirely, the information in the 1857 report on the city of Veracruz. Some few mistakes have been found in the Lerdo work, in particular in one case the same sale is twice repeated, and this can easily be seen because in the 1857 report details are given of the houses, their numbers, former owners, sale price and buyers. Finally, including one or two doubtful cases, the total value of sales amounted to about 10,000 pesos less than 1,388,792, which was the sum given by Lerdo. The figure is therefore 1,378,792, revealing an error of less than 1%. The number of properties sold also seems to have been added up incorrectly, the total being 269, not 262 as stated.

In summary, 269 of the 283 houses belonging to civil and ecclesiastical corporations were sold in 1856, including eleven cases of disentailment which took place at the beginning of 1857. Unlike Puebla, the disentailment in Veracruz was almost completed in 1856, which was no doubt due to the absence of a clerical opposition in the port and the effort which both the authorities and the local people made to carry out the law. All the real estate of all the corporations was sold, with one curious exception, namely the fifteen houses of the pious work, Misericordia, valued at 110,400 pesos.[1] For reasons unknown these houses were respected and one can only speculate whether the motive for this was sufficiently strong to protect them in 1857 and 1858–61 when it must have been very difficult, above all in Veracruz, to escape at least some of the effects of nationalization.

In spite of the fact that fifteen houses worth 110,400 pesos were not

---

[1] Ibid., p. 14; there is a difference in addition of one house.

disentailed, the total sum yielded by those which were sold exceeded the value of the 283 houses of all the corporations, which was 1,294,320 pesos.[1] This rise is because most of the houses were sold for more than the price shown in the census or land register. The comparison which has been made for several corporations between the sale price according to the Lerdo law and the value given in the census, can be seen in table 7.

TABLE 7. *Sale price and census value of houses sold in Veracruz, 1856–57*

Name of the corporation	No. of houses	Sale price (pesos)	Value according to census (pesos)
Hospital and Charity Junta	58	323,835	238,000
Municipality (incomplete)	21	118,080	88,400
Parish (incomplete)	14	33,040	28,700
Pious work, Gil	4	57,200	44,700
Archconfraternity of Rosario	9	37,185	32,300
Archconfraternity of Santísimo (one missing)	19	66,443	45,930
	125	635,787	478,030

Lerdo states that in making the property register in Veracruz in 1851 all the rents were capitalized at 6%, but 35% of the total was deducted to allow for empty houses and the costs of repairs and administration. He thought the deduction excessive for normal times.[2] Thus to achieve the figure obtained by capitalizing rents at 6%, that is the price anticipated by the Lerdo law, the value given in the census has to be multiplied by approximately 1·5. The 478,000 pesos then become 717,000, which was the sum at which the houses should have been assigned, not the 635,787 which in fact was realized. The difference in the two totals is probably explained by some houses not being assigned to the tenants or denouncers. Some may have been sold by means of a conventional sale or auction, in which case, as indicated in Puebla, prices were lower. At any rate many corporation-owned properties as important as those of the Charity Junta achieved a considerably higher than valuation price, which seems to show careful management.

In contrast, the case of the regular orders is completely the converse. Five houses belonging to San Agustín, valued in the census at 19,100 pesos,

[1] Ibid., p. 15.
[2] Ibid., p. 13. Lerdo's statement could be checked if the 1856 register could be found—rents of the properties must have been noted in it.

were sold for 14,635; six houses of Santo Domingo, valued at 30,300, were sold for 22,840; three of La Merced, valued at 9,400, were disentailed for 5,272; all the eight houses of Santa Teresa of Puebla, worth 73,100, were sold for 60,562 pesos. These houses belonging to the regular orders were perhaps in such a poor condition that they were sold or auctioned for only approximately half the value which they had according to the Lerdo law.

A list has been compiled from these sources of all the 133 buyers of the corporate properties in the city of Veracruz. The great majority of them acquired one or two houses, from which it can be concluded by the example of Puebla that most were tenants who made the purchase by way of an adjudication or a conventional sale.

The available information on Veracruz society has made it possible to identify most of the buyers. As was to be expected, many were merchants and some of these members of the council, magistrates and aldermen. These were public offices for which merchants were especially suited, both in Europe and in Mexico. The nationality of some of the merchants is known and others can be assumed to be foreigners as their surnames are not Spanish. In the majority of cases, however, it is not known if the specific merchant was Mexican or Spanish. This list confirms what happened in Puebla; the disentailment succeeded in attracting a considerable sector of the population. In order to make the list more compact it has been reduced to those persons who each made purchases of 6,000 pesos or more. The result is given in appendix VII.

Measured by the amount which each group bought, the merchants are more important in Veracruz than in Puebla and the officials less so. The percentages have not been calculated because the information given in the 1857 report and in Lerdo's work is by no means completely exact. This is illustrated in a case noted in the notarial register for 1868.[1] In 1856 Rafael Gutiérrez Zamora, the municipal treasurer and probably another brother of the governor, formed with two other persons an association to disentail corporate properties. This is the only example of such an association found in the state. The new company then acquired seven houses for 55,680 pesos, which was a quite high price if compared with the values shown in the municipal land register. On 10 October 1859 the houses were redeemed at the same price and in 1868, after the final triumph of the republic, the association was dissolved and the houses distributed, Gutiérrez Zamora receiving about half of them. In the 1857 report and in Lerdo's history neither the company nor its partners appear as the buyers. Instead other persons are named and they were probably the com-

[1] Register of J. M. Bello and M. M. Castellanos, 1868, 15 December, fol. 437.

pany's representatives. Similar cases, which have been found often in the places studied, reduce the exactness of the tables given in appendices VI, VII and XVI.

Fortunately the complete registers of the Orizaba notary seem to have been preserved. The disentailment instruments are almost all in the second volume for 1856 and an extract of most of them is given in appendix VIII. The properties which were sold belonged above all to the brotherhoods, the councils, the San Juan de Dios hospital and the Carmen monastery. For the most part the buyers seem to have been tenants who obtained the houses at a price calculated by capitalizing the rent at 6%. As in the case of Veracruz the details of these transactions were intercalated in the 1857 report among those corresponding to other towns in the state. Various transactions noted in the notarial register were not recorded in the report. The opposite was also true, some being in the report but not in the register at Orizaba. An addition of all the sales, including those missing in the register and the report and also twenty others made in 1857,[1] reveals that in Orizaba and surrounding areas corporate properties to the value of about 100,000 pesos were sold. There may have been more, considering that in auctions properties were sold for an amount much lower than the valuation price. Hence in Orizaba perhaps almost a half of the corporate houses were sold. The fact that all the instruments were signed by the political chief, Francisco Talavera, and not the seller indicates that the Church opposed the sales.

An example of a sale was the auction held on 22 November 1856 in which a ranch belonging to the San Juan de Dios hospital was sold for 20,500 to Carlos Saulnier, who had the abovementioned political chief as his guarantor.[2] Saulnier also acquired agricultural equipment and livestock on the same property for 2,000 pesos.[3] Nearby this ranch he bought a flour mill, which was the most valuable of the Carmen monastery's properties, for 20,416 pesos.[4] Adding these purchases to those made by Saulnier at the same time in Veracruz and Puebla, his total amounts to about 80,000 pesos. It is interesting to note how a person was able to integrate his interests along the Veracruz–Puebla route.

As the information for Orizaba for the years 1856–57 is incomplete, whereas reasonably full details are available for the later years of 1861–62,[5] the transfer of clerical property and its social implications in the town will be discussed in chapter 6.

---

[1] 1857 register, Orizaba, vols. I, II, in Biblioteca de la Universidad Veracruzana, Jalapa.
[2] 1856 register, Orizaba, vol. II, fol. 429, deed no. 155; MH 1857, p. 510.
[3] Ibid., 1856 register, Orizaba.   [4] This is not recorded in the register; MH 1857, p. 511.
[5] *Noticia de las fincas y capitales del clero, enajenados en esta ciudad*, undated, AGN, PBN, leg. 734.

The facts on Córdoba given in the 1857 report seem to be incomplete and confused but fortunately, due to the already quoted list of 1862, it has been possible to analyse the transactions involving clerical property and capital. The results of this analysis will be given in chapter 6.

The notarial registers in Jalapa have survived in perfect order. There is one volume for 1856 and another for 1857, and then a special volume which details 130 adjudications made in 1856 for amounts not exceeding 1,000 pesos each. Finally the volume for 1857 has an appended section of fifty-three pages which records twenty-four disentailments of a value of less than 1,000 pesos each. Of the eleven instruments from 1856 in the main volume and of the four from the first part of the volume for the next year, extracts have been made which are given in appendix IX. As in Orizaba all the deeds were signed by the political chief but, unlike in that city, it appears that there were more denouncers and auction buyers than persons obtaining adjudications on the grounds of tenancy rights. In the same way as the tenants the denouncers were assigned houses at a price calculated by capitalizing the rent at 6%, but the buyers in auctions paid only two-thirds of the valuation price. In only one case was an individual assigned a house as a tenant, and another as a denouncer. The first fifty of the 130 transactions for an amount of less than 1,000 pesos were examined, and without exception all the buyers were tenants. These latter cases concerned rural lands belonging to the different brotherhoods, and their value varied between 10 and 1,000 pesos. Among the sale prices sums of 16 and 33 pesos, corresponding to an annual rent of one or two pesos, were quite common. Clearly [on a smaller scale the tenants hastened to carry out the law.

As in the case of Orizaba, not all the instruments in Jalapa for the year 1856 were recorded in the 1857 report and vice versa. According to the incomplete data given, nearly one hundred persons bought properties for 43,369 pesos, which was only a small part of the total value of real estate owned by the civil and ecclesiastical corporations, estimated above at about 100,000 pesos. Ten of the hundred buyers acquired properties to the value of 33,682, which equals three-quarters of the total. Only two of these have been identified beyond doubt; one was a printer and school-master and the other a Veracruz merchant. Even on this much reduced scale the interest in the Reform programme shown by the middle class and the merchants is demonstrated. The restricted example of Jalapa confirms the results obtained from Puebla, in the sense that the merchants, trades-men and professional classes were bound to the destiny of the liberal party, which no doubt helped it to win the civil war of 1858–60.

CHAPTER 3

THE DISENTAILMENT IN MEXICO, SAN LUIS POTOSÍ, MICHOACÁN AND JALISCO, 1856–57

THE CITY OF MEXICO: ECONOMIC AND SOCIAL LIFE

In 1856 the population of the district of Mexico, now the Federal District, was calculated to be 230,000, and that of the city itself 200,000.[1] At first sight the republic's capital seemed similar to Puebla and Veracruz, although of course on a bigger scale. There were several dozen large stores, some of which were involved in trade in general while others specialized in the buying and selling of a particular merchandise.[2] The speciality might be groceries or textiles or it could be a specific foodstuff such as sugar. There were also several finance houses. In an age when there were no banks, some individuals or companies made loans to merchants and the *juzgado de capellanías*, the Church's own banking organization, had little interest in these private transactions.

Among the main businessmen were the following: Pío Bermejillo, Spanish financier and hacendado;[3] J. B. Jecker, Swiss, and an important shareholder in the Taxco mines and the Mineral Catorce in San Luis Potosí, as well as the principal owner of a finance company, with particular connections to French residents in Mexico;[4] Nathaniel Davidson, British, financier and representative of the Rothschild firm, and in addition owner of the biggest iron foundry in the country costing 87,771 pesos and providing work for 113 workers and employees;[5] Isidoro de la Torre, Spanish, financier, owner of a store selling the sugar produced on the haciendas, including his own, situated south of the capital, owner of a flour mill and finally, manufacturer of fine porcelain;[6] Juan Goríbar, Mexican, sugar merchant and hacendado, well-known for his work for charity;[7]

---

[1] A. García Cubas, *Noticias geográficas y estadísticas de la república mexicana* (Mexico, 1854), 27 pp.

[2] M. Galván Rivera, *Guía de forasteros en la ciudad de México para el año de 1854* (Mexico, 1854), pp. 287 ff.; Valle, *El viajero en México*, pp. 200 ff.   [3] Zamacois, XIV, 619.

[4] E. Turlington, *Mexico and her foreign creditors* (New York, 1930), p. 117.

[5] *Memoria de Fomento*, 1857, corresponding table.   [6] Zamacois, XIV, 619.

[7] Galván Rivera, *Guía*, 344.

the brothers Miguel and Leandro Mosso, Mexicans, merchants and hacendados;[1] Archibald Hope, British, selling in his store the woollen fabrics produced in his own mill, San Ildefonso;[2] Francisco de Paula Portilla, Mexican, and a financier;[3] Gregorio Mier y Terán, Spanish, financier and hacendado, linked to the cause of independence since the time of Iturbide.[4] Almost all these names will be encountered again during the course of this work.

It would nonetheless be a mistake to believe that all the most important businessmen were foreigners. The following were Mexican: Cayetano Rubio, already referred to in chapter 1, and to be mentioned throughout, owner of one of the largest cotton mills called Hércules, situated in Querétaro, and of another in Tlalpam, near the capital.[5] Like the others Rubio also owned haciendas.[6] Next, although no less important than the above, was the firm of Martínez del Río Brothers, operating a finance house and a store selling cottons made in their own mill Miraflores, situated in Tlalmanalco in the valley of Mexico.[7] Not all the members of this family, which was originally Spanish, were involved in trade, for example José Pablo Martínez was at one time perhaps the most famous doctor in the capital.[8] Eustaquio Barrón, son of a Spanish merchant, was British consul in Tepic. He was associated there with a person of British origin, William Forbes, who was the consul for the United States. They were joint owners of the cotton mill Jauja, in the same city.[9] Juan Antonio Béistegui, also the owner of a cotton mill, Colmena, located near the capital, belonged to a family famous in the mining world.[10] Genaro Béistegui was lessee of the national mint which in those days was let by the government, and in association with Manual Escandón, Nicanor Béistegui bought the company called Real del Monte, which was the biggest silver producer.[11] Manuel Escandón, born in Orizaba and his brother Antonio, who came from Puebla, were the best-known of the businessmen of the time,[12] particularly Manuel who was described by

[1] Zamacois, xiv, 619.
[2] *Memoria de Fomento*, 1857, table.
[3] F. Mejía, *Memorias* (Mexico, 1958), p. 54.
[4] *Diccionario Porrúa de historia, biografía y geografía de México* (Mexico, 1964).
[5] *Memoria de Fomento*, 1857, table.
[6] *Representación que hacen al congreso constituyente varios dueños de propiedades territoriales contra algunos artículos de los proyectos fundamentales que se discuten actualmente* (Mexico, 1856).
[7] *Memoria de Fomento*, 1857, table.
[8] *Diccionario Porrúa.*
[9] *Memoria de Fomento*, 1857, table.
[10] Ibid.
[11] MH 1857, p. 28 and *Diccionario Porrúa.*
[12] *Diccionario Porrúa.*

Payno in his novel *Los bandidos del Río Frio* as a financial wizard, able to derive profit even from adversity. Together with the others on this list Escandón had a textile factory, at first the Escoba in Jalisco[1] and later, the biggest of them all, Cocolapam, which with its 11,000 spindles was a giant of Mexican industry.[2] Perhaps Escandón's greatest merit was in the encouragement he gave to modern means of transport. About 1849–50 he established the first coach company,[3] and some years later he was the joint owner with Gregorio Mier y Terán of the railway from Mexico to the town of Guadalupe, which was a section in the Mexico–Veracruz line. This branch, Mexico–Guadalupe, was inaugurated on 4 June 1857 'having been blessed on that day, and the trains running from then on, powered by a beautiful and luxurious locomotive'.[4] Vicente Escandón was another member of this family.

Another group of businessmen, distinct from these merchants, was the brokers who were the intermediaries in every type of mercantile transaction, not only in the buying and selling of real estate but also, for example, of foodstuffs, and they were involved in what would nowadays be called banking and stock exchange dealings. Their honorarium was on a commission basis determined by a schedule.[5] In a way similar to the notaries the word of the brokers was respected in judgements or in difficulties which arose between contracting parties.[6] According to their regulations and schedule, issued on 13 July 1854, the title of 'broker' required the holder to have Mexican citizenship, which he must retain as long as he was in the profession.[7] Few foreigners were naturalized Mexicans, as can be seen from the 1930–31 report of the Ministry of Foreign Affairs which contains a complete list of those who, since independence, adopted Mexican citizenship.[8] Hence it can be concluded that the majority of brokers were Mexican by birth. This is confirmed in the list of them given in the *Guía de forasteros* for 1854[9] and that of 1859.[10] In this latter year there were more than one hundred in the capital, a higher number than five years previously. Of course Mexican citizenship alone did not

[1] *Memoria de la Dirección General de Industria*, 1844, table 5.
[2] *Memoria de Fomento*, 1857, table.
[3] P. Macedo, *La evolución mercantil. Comunicaciones y obras públicas. La hacienda pública. Tres monografías que dan idea de una parte de la evolución económica de México* (Mexico, 1905), p. 194.
[4] Valle, *El viajero en México*, 341.
[5] Ibid., pp. 210–18.
[6] Lerdo de Tejada, *Apuntes históricos*, III, 62.
[7] E. Maillefert, *Gran almanaque mexicano y directorio del comercio de la república mexicana para el año de 1869* (Mexico, 1869), pp. 70–86.
[8] *Memoria de Relaciones Exteriores de 1930–31*, vol. I, pp. 899–1344.
[9] Galván Rivera, *Guía*, 172–8.
[10] Valle, *Guía*, 203–10.

qualify a person to be trained as a broker. Five years' business experience and an unblemished moral conduct were also required.[1]

The most renowned merchants, some of whom had already retired from active trading, were members of the *Lonja de Mexico*.[2] The Lonja was a social club to which the principal merchants of the city belonged, and membership of it was both an honour and a sign of wealth. Acceptance by existing members was not the only entry requirement, for aspiring candidates had to acquire a share worth, it may be supposed, a substantial amount in view of the exclusive character of the club. In 1859 there were forty-six member-owners who, according to the statutes, could sell or give away their shares, but the club reserved the right to buy them at the market price. There was also a category of members known as subscribers who were recommended by the full members and could use the club's facilities, especially its reading room, in return for a monthly fee. In 1859 there were 110 of these subscribers. All games of chance were forbidden on the premises, and 'any lack of moderation and courtesy among the members while in the club was considered an offence to the establishment' and would be punished.

All the members were prominent merchants, industrialists, miners and bankers, united by their affiliation to an exclusive group. In 1859 the following were among the members: Eustaquio Barrón, Nicanor and Isidro Béistegui, N. Davidson, Manuel, Antonio and Vicente Escandón, Juan Goríbar, Gregorio Martínez del Río, Gregorio Mier y Terán, Cayetano Rubio and Isidoro de la Torre. There were both Mexicans and foreigners in the Lonja. The social élite had an international character.

Nevertheless some merchants could not, or did not want to, belong to the Lonja. Felipe Neri del Barrio y Larrazábal, who has already been mentioned in chapter 1, was prominent among the rich people on whom the forced loan of 19 November 1846 was levied.[3] He was also a member of the so-called Junta Superior of the school of painting and sculpture, the Academia Nacional de San Carlos.[4] Some members of the Lonja and other persons interested in art also held this honorary post. Barrio was a partner of Martínez del Río in the cotton mill Miraflores,[5] and he owned the sugar producing hacienda Temixco, which was near Cuernavaca.[6] His office was in the first block of San Francisco street—at the present day,

---

[1] Maillefert, 70–86.
[2] Valle, *El viajero en México*, 191 ff.
[3] The list was reproduced in Dublán y Lozano, v, 214–16.
[4] Valle, *El viajero en México*, 371–2.
[5] *Memoria de la Dirección General de Industria*, 1844, table 5.
[6] Alamán, *Obras*, xii, 441.

Madero where the House of Tiles now stands—and Barrón, the Béisteguis and the Escandón brothers also had offices there.

Barrio was of Guatemalan origin and at first he was of liberal sympathies, apparently being a friend of Valentín Gómez Farías.[1] He married Rafaela Rengel y Fagoaga, marchioness of El Apartado and a member of the famous Fagoaga mining family,[2] and perhaps this had some influence on him for he was later connected with members of the conservative government. His evolution was similar to that of José María Gutiérrez Estrada, who was at first praised by Mora because of his liberal ideas but who later became a proponent of monarchy.[3] The Lonja, composed as it was of the bourgeoisie, perhaps did not have much to attract Barrio, even though several of its members were richer than he was. Perhaps social position interested him more than money.

The structure of the economically dominant group so far described seems basically the same as that of Puebla and Veracruz. There were numerous merchants who owned stores, and many were foreigners, particularly French, German, British, United States and Spanish. Mexican merchants had acquired or inherited haciendas, which in a country of aristocratic traditions gave them a social standing almost equal to that of the descendants of the colonial nobility, who for their part had bought the former Jesuit haciendas with the profits from the silver mines.[4] In the years covered by this study the numerous members of these old, noble families still retained their wealth, but with few exceptions they were now retired from active economic life. Hence little or no mention will be made of them.

The foreign merchants were involved, apart from their trading interests, in industry and mining. Few were still great landowners, partly because they preferred to use their capital in more productive enterprises and partly because the nation did not wish to see the rural areas invaded by foreigners. The decree of 12 March 1828 which prohibited the acquisition of rural properties by foreigners—by implication they could acquire urban property[5]—was annulled on 11 March 1842.[6] This new law authorized that 'foreigners, domiciled and resident in the republic, may acquire and possess urban and rural property by purchase, adjudication, denouncement or by any other title established by the law'. It was confirmed

[1] On one occasion Gómez Farías asked him for a loan of 500 pesos: Callcott, *Church and State*, 123.
[2] R. Ortega y Pérez Gallardo, *Historia genealógica de las familias más antiguas de México* (Mexico, 1908–10), part 1, vol. 1.
[3] *Diccionario Porrúa*.
[4] Alamán, *Obras*, I, 101–2.
[5] Dublán y Lozano, II, 64.
[6] Ibid., IV, 130.

in almost the same words on 1 February 1856, shortly before the promulgation of the Lerdo law.[1] Until the 1842 law it was generally only Spaniards who acquired haciendas in Mexico, for they usually married Mexican women and their children, some of whom continued in trade, were Mexican.

As we have seen, Mexican merchant-hacendados showed a preference for haciendas of a commercial type, which at the time were the sugar plantations which combined the cultivation of the cane with the refining of sugar. As in Puebla, and it seems also in Veracruz, many merchants became, in the shelter of protectionist policies, manufacturers of cotton yarn and fabrics and thus succeeded in diversifying their activities and increasing their sources of profit. Most of the cotton industry in the capital, in Puebla and in Veracruz, belonged to Mexicans.[2]

Nevertheless neither trade, industry, mining, agriculture nor transport was the most important business activity of the principal merchants in the capital. Such activities as these were secondary to the financial operations undertaken with the government. It can be assumed that the merchants in Puebla and Veracruz also loaned money to their local government but this was economically insignificant in comparison with the federal government and small compared with the private fortunes of the citizens of Puebla and Veracruz. The modest finances of these state governments were relatively well-organized because the bourgeoisie were the governors and the most important and uncertain expenditure, namely the army and military costs, was nil. In contrast, the federal government had to manage an enormous budget of between 10,000,000 and 20,000,000 pesos a year, and moreover, no bourgeois became president of the republic. The great merchants had to renounce political power, but they achieved instead financial power over the government.

Loans to the federal government basically consisted of handing over an amount in bonds of the national debt, which the government accepted at face value. For example, a person would lend 100,000 pesos at 6% and he would give 10,000 of this in cash and the rest in national debt credits. At the end of the year the lender should therefore receive 106,000 pesos. At the beginning of independence these national debt bonds could be acquired in the market at a price of between 5% and 50% of their par value, but in later years the price became more uniform. Assuming that the lender bought them for an average of 10% of face value, he thus disbursed in the transaction 19,000 pesos. As one year later he should receive

[1] Ibid., VIII, 950.
[2] See the lists in *Memorias de la Dirección General de Industria* and the *Memoria de Fomento*, 1857.

106,000, the real annual interest on the loan amounted to more than 400% a year, or 36% a month. In mercantile loans, interest rates varied between 12% and 24% a year or between 1% and 2% a month. Obviously the interest was proportional to the risk, for lenders rarely received the contracted amount and they then had to enter into difficult negotiations with the government in order to save their capital and earn a profit. Here reference will only be made to those who succeeded in these deals, not to those who lost their fortunes.

It can well be imagined that these transactions, which in time became known as speculation, were universally condemned, just as usury has always been. Canon law permitted an annual interest of only 6%, and to achieve more the rate had to be disguised in some way. It was natural, although illogical, to criticize the speculators, for their activity was essentially no different to that of the person who risked his capital in a mining venture, hoping to recover at least ten times the amount invested. Yet few were more respected than the wealthy miners.

In the first chapter, the company renting the tobacco monopoly and the form in which the partners recovered their credit were mentioned. The remainder of the debt was acquired in 1843 by the firm Martínez del Río Brothers. These credits were sold 'in the same way as those of the widows' and employees' fund except they fetched a higher price because of the allocated amounts designated for their repayment and the high social standing of those people who had large amounts of them in their possession'.[1] The firm Martínez del Río went to the Supreme Court in an attempt to collect the debt and on 28 October 1846 the justices found in the company's favour. Consequently on 11 November the Minister of Hacienda, Haro y Tamariz, accepted the claim. This was one case in which a liberal government favoured a firm known for its conservative connections. In order finally to be able to collect the debt, the firm became a British company and that country's representative concluded with the Mexican Minister a treaty, called a convention, by which Mexico promised to pay the sum outstanding. This debt, which thus acquired an international character, amounted in 1852 to about 3·5 million pesos.[2]

The tobacco monopoly continued independent of the bonds which were the object of this English convention. On 18 August 1848 the then liberal government rented the monopoly to two conservatives, Manuel Escandón and Miguel Bringas—the same partners already referred to in chapter 1 in connection with the amortization bank of 1839 (p. 24)— and to the British company of Manning and Mackintosh, which was

---

[1] Payno, *México y sus cuestiones financieras*, 73 ff.   [2] MH 1870, p. 378.

known for its tenancy of the mints and its loans to the government.[1] On 20 April 1854 Santa Anna rented the tobacco revenue to Cayetano Rubio and Manuel Lizardi in a way very onerous to the treasury.[2] Lizardi was a merchant and a financial agent of Mexico in London. The opposition against this monopoly contributed to the unity of the people in their revolt against the dictatorship of Santa Anna. The victorious liberal regime which followed declared on 21 January 1856 the freedom of sowing, cultivation, refining and trading of tobacco, and one week later it proclaimed an amnesty for those sentenced for involvement in contraband tobacco.[3]

Cayetano Rubio was the owner, among other things, of the bonds of the second Spanish convention, which was the second financial agreement between the Spanish Minister and Mexico. These were derived from the credits of Padre Morán, also mentioned in chapter 1. In 1852 this debt amounted to approximately 1,000,000 pesos.[4] Other transactions involving Rubio were the renting by a liberal government, in exchange for a loan, of the mints in San Luis Potosí and the Mineral Catorce on 7 September 1857.[5] On 29 October 1842 this same capitalist had bought from Santa Anna's government the salt mines of Peñón Blanco for 304,166 pesos. The terms were as follows: the tenant was to be compensated with 164,837 pesos for loans made to the government before the sale, 5,000 pesos of the price was to be paid to the government in cash and the rest, 134,439 pesos, in national debt bonds. Twenty years later, on 9 July 1862, the liberal government under the pressure of circumstances ratified the transaction.[6]

Success in the cotton industry also necessitated some influence in government circles. The enormous variation in the cotton harvest in Mexico meant that the mills sometimes had to be provided with imported cotton, and to acquire this an import permit was needed. This partly explains why the cotton manufacturers were Mexicans belonging to the same social group which has already been described.

These men, linked to the conservative regime in power from 1830 to 1855 with only a few interruptions, seem to refute the usual thesis of the economically and technologically retrograde character of the conservatives. Nobody is surprised that the liberal leader, Lorenzo Zavala, was in

[1] Payno, *México y sus cuestiones financieras*, 74.
[2] G. Prieto, *Lecciones elementales de economía política* (2nd ed., Mexico, 1876), pp. 698–9.
[3] Dublán y Lozano, VIII, 30, 137.
[4] MH 1870, p. 378; Payno, *México y sus cuestiones financieras*, 205.
[5] MH 1870, p. 748.
[6] Ibid., pp. 582–3.

his youth engaged in agriculture and trade, and later in the mining industry in Taxco and investment in real estate in Texas.[1] Nevertheless a man
of even greater entrepreneurial activity than Zavala was the main leader
of the conservative movement, Lucas Alamán. In his autobiography
Alamán candidly admitted that while in Paris he had bought various
objects with the purpose of selling them in Mexico; one of the few deals,
it seems, which had gone well for him throughout his life.[2] His merits in
the encouragement of mining and industry are beyond doubt, although he
personally failed in the mining and industrial ventures which he undertook. Even worse was his experience with his hacienda Trojes near
Celaya, and it was this which perhaps was to make him speak with nos-
talgia in 1830 of agriculture in Texas, where the farmer enjoyed 'freedom
from tithes and the other burdens to which Mexico is subjected'.[3]

ECCLESIASTICAL POSSESSIONS IN THE CAPITAL

Some days after the regulations governing the disentailment law were
issued, Lerdo signed a circular, dated 9 August 1856, to all the governors
of states and territories in the republic. In this they were asked to publish
as quickly as possible a complete list of the real estate owned by corporations. There was a twofold aim: first to avoid concealment of assets by
the corporations, and secondly, to inform those members of the public
who were likely to be interested in the measure. The result, as far as the
capital was concerned, was the 'Account of the properties belonging to
civil and ecclesiastical corporations in the District of Mexico', which was
a publication of forty-four pages.

The account has an entry for each corporation and, within it, details
of each house, with the street, number and taxable value. At the end of
each entry the properties and values are totalled. Although in some cases
there are errors, particularly in the values and the additions, these are only
minimal discrepancies and almost all of them are corrected in the table of
errors included on the last page of the book. In synthesis, corporate
properties in the city of Mexico can be classified as in table 8.

The following details can be given of some of the categories noted.
The colleges included the seminary which was not dependent on the
monasteries but on the archbishopric, and several schools of a civil
character, especially the college of San Ignacio and the college of San
Ildefonso, which had as rector Sebastián Lerdo de Tejada, brother of the

---

[1] *Diccionario Porrúa.*   [2] Alamán, *Obras*, XII, 19 ff.
[3] Cited in Valadés, *Alamán*, 273.

TABLE 8. *Value of corporate properties in the city of Mexico, 1856*

Corporation	No. of properties	Value (in pesos)
20 nunneries	1,024	9,758,123
11 monasteries, including San Camilo, 3 of La Merced, 2 of Carmen, and the goods of 3 provinces	193	1,307,645
Colleges (partly of the regular orders)	122	809,836
Congregations and brotherhoods	157	1,231,984
Hospitals	96	1,067,076
Pious works	57	376,287
Secular clergy (memorials and cathedral building fund, collegiate church of Guadalupe, S. Felipe Neri, *juzgado de capellanías*, parishes)	169	1,322,839
Various (University, Third Order, School of Agriculture, Sisters of Mercy, orphanage and poor house, and 12 houses belonging to council without a corresponding value)	95	711,170
Total	1,913	16,584,960[1]

Minister of Hacienda and a future president of the country. Among the brotherhoods the richest was the Archicofradía del Santísimo en Catedral, with houses valued at 320,828 pesos. The revenue from these, apart from that yielded by invested capital, was used for the dowries of orphans who wanted to enter the convent, to maintain a school for poor girls and other charitable works, as well as the normal religious functions. Its members were from the wealthy people in the capital.[2] The silversmiths' corporation is included in the brotherhoods. It owned twelve buildings worth 124,000 pesos, and it seems to have been the only one to have acquired a civil character before the Reform. In fact it did preserve some religious traditions, particularly the worship of an image of the Virgin, made by the silversmiths and weighing nearly 2,000 ounces. The members also gave aid to the poor.[3] The richest of the hospitals was that of San Andrés, which depended on the archbishopric and had fifty-one houses worth 552,101 pesos, and the hospital of Jesus, founded by Cortés and a civil corporation with twenty-four houses, worth 309,909 pesos.

[1] This account was based on the valuation of 1836-38, reproduced by J. L. Cossío, *Avalúo de los terrenos de la ciudad, publicado en la Memoria del Ayuntamiento de 1830, y de las casas de la misma, practicado en 1836 al decretarse la contribución predial* (Mexico, 1937).

[2] J. M. Marroqui, *La ciudad de México* (Mexico, 1900-3), vol. III, pp. 442-7.

[3] Ibid., pp. 448-50.

The category of 'various' includes several civil corporations and also a religious one like the Sisters of Mercy, who owned seven buildings valued at 83,120 pesos. In some cases it is very difficult to decide if an institution was civil or ecclesiastic—the latter includes organizations of a religious inspiration or controlled by the Church—but it is certain that the real estate of the civil bodies, at least in the capital, represented only a very small percentage of the total. Considering that there were about 4,000 houses in the capital,[1] it can be concluded that the Church possessed at least half of all the real estate.

THE DISENTAILMENT

The law of 25 June 1856, which caused the greatest transfer of property in Mexico during the nineteenth century, had been prepared by the already mentioned decree of 1 February of that year. This decree foresaw that foreigners could acquire both the urban and rural real estate. Certainly their number does not appear to have been great; in 1855 there were in the country 5,141 Spaniards, 2,048 French, 615 British, 581 Germans, 444 United States citizens, and 405 others, giving a total of 9,234.[2] The proportion of Spaniards, who in 1821 had been almost the only foreigners in Mexico, had dropped to just over one-half of the total, while of the rest the French amounted to just over one-half. The importance of the Spaniards, however, did not correspond to their number, for their supremacy had been ceded to the French and the British, especially the latter, in matters of large-scale business.

It seems nonetheless that the real number of foreigners resident in the country was higher. The figures given above only include those who had been issued with the so-called safe-conduct pass by the Ministry of Foreign Affairs in 1855, a document which had to be authenticated each year. Not all did this, and so Lerdo de Tejada calculated their total number to be 25,000, including families.[3] As the total population of the republic was about 8,000,000, the number of foreigners, even using the higher figure, was insignificant. Yet this handful of foreigners had a powerful influence on the nation's trade. The decree of 1 February 1856 was inspired by the liberal spirit of the Reform but in its final results, as will be seen in due course, a handful of foreigners acquired a large part of the urban real estate.

[1] Pérez Hernández, 250 ff. ;Lerdo de Tejada on page 80 of his *Cuadro sinóptico* estimated the number at 5,000. [2] Lerdo de Tejada, *Cuadro sinóptico*, 29.
[3] Ibid.

The Lerdo law also originated from the same liberal doctrine and it was proposed to disentail the real estate of both the ecclesiastical and the civil corporations, particularly the municipalities and the indigenous communities. Hostility to the Church, however, far from being satiated by the decree of intervention of the ecclesiastical possessions in Puebla, issued on 31 March 1856, continued very much alive. This is indicated by the decree of 26 April 1856, derogating the obligatory nature of the monastic vows, which had been re-established two years earlier by Santa Anna, and by the law of 7 June of the same year which suppressed the Jesuits, also re-established by Santa Anna.[1] In this increasingly hostile anti-clerical atmosphere, the Lerdo law was put into effect in the capital of the republic on 28 June 1856.[2]

The majority of the ecclesiastical corporations in the city decided to boycott the law and this of course was not entirely unexpected. In fact such an attitude had already been anticipated in article 29, which stated that the instruments of sale would be executed by a government representative in those cases in which the corporations refused to transfer their real estate. Article 16 of the corresponding regulations, issued on 30 July, was even more specific and declared that the political authority would sign the deeds in the name of the corporation.[3] This is what happened in most of the sales of clerical property that were made; for example, every one of the numerous instruments executed before the notary, Francisco Pérez de León, was signed by Ignacio Ramírez and other judges, but none by an ecclesiastical community. The same thing happened before the other notaries in the capital. Usually an examination of the indexes to the notarial registers is sufficient to illustrate this, for these indicate the type of transaction, location of the property, corporation owner, name of buyer and the seller, which in this case was of course the government. Details of conventional sales will be given later.

Articles 14 and 15 of the regulations anticipated another form of Church opposition.[4] The corporation should give to the buyer the title deeds of the disentailed property and the certificate showing whether there were mortgages on it. The latter was issued by the Mortgage Office, which was the forerunner of the present day Public Register of Property. If the Church refused to hand over these documents, the new buyers would have no obligation to pay interest to the clerical corporation formerly owning the house. This was clearly a serious threat to the Church. Nevertheless it seems that in most cases the corporations acted as if the Lerdo law

[1] Dublán y Lozano, VIII, 154, 189.   [2] MH 1857, p. 13 of the addenda.
[3] Ibid., p. 17 of the addenda.   [4] Ibid.

did not exist, and they did not hand over the title deeds. The consequences of this will be described later.

Within a few weeks an alleged conspiracy was discovered in the Franciscan monastery, and in view of the excitement resulting from the law this was not surprising. On 16 September 1856 the government re-acted in an attempt to punish the Church by closing down the monastery. This did not own any real estate except for the monastery building but the latter was the most central and extensive, and consequently the most valuable, property in the city. It covered a large part of the block which at the present day is bordered by the streets of Madero, Bolívar, Carranza and San Juan de Letrán, and is now divided into four blocks. The property included not only the church, chapels and buildings but also a garden and a cemetery. In common with the liberals of the French revolution, Mexican liberals were greatly annoyed by the existence of these enormous properties which hindered the movement of traffic and the development of cities. Then on 16 September the Minister for Development, Manuel Siliceo, ordered the construction of a new street crossing the area, thus splitting the property into two parts. This measure was to some extent justified by the fact that the property, which was originally small, had gradually encompassed the neighbouring houses.[1] On the same day Ezequiel Montes, Minister of Justice, decreed the suppression of the monastery, the nationalization of its possessions and their sale by the Ministry of Development.[2] Work was immediately begun on the opening of the new street. These decrees contradicted the Lerdo law which excep-ted the monastery and convent buildings from the disentailment (article 8) and this no doubt explains in part why these measures were not signed by the Minister of Hacienda. The decrees in fact represented something new, for as a result of them the capital of the republic had its first fore-warning of the confiscation to be decreed in Veracruz in 1859 and imple-mented in Mexico in 1861.

It was in this atmosphere of political and religious agitation that the Minister of Hacienda proceeded to apply the disentailment law. By 31 December 1856 real estate to the value of 13,029,115 pesos had been dis-entailed in the District of Mexico. In this total there were 2,092 adjudi-cations worth 8,905,134 pesos and 570 auction sales for 4,123,981 pesos.[3] Unlike the information referring to the states, the details for the District of Mexico are divided between the adjudication and the auction sales, which according to the law had to be held in the last three months of the

[1] *Memoria de Hacienda*, 1873–74, addenda, p. 129   [2] Dublán y Lozano, VIII, 243–4.
[3] MH 1857, addenda, pp. 170–289.

year, since three months, July, August and September, were allowed for the adjudications.

More than two-thirds of the total value of the disentailments consisted of adjudications. The registers of the notary Francisco Pérez de León for the year 1856 have been examined in order to discover to what extent the law was carried out. These registers, the biggest of any notary for that year, are in three volumes, the first covering the period to 26 September, the second from this date to the end of the year, and the third containing the respective files—requests, receipts etc.—although this is incomplete. In fact F. Pérez de León arranged the greatest number of disentailment transactions. He executed 601 instruments for almost 5,000,000 pesos.[1] The proportion of his work was later indicated in the 1872–73 report of the Minister of Hacienda, which described the activities of the city's thirty-five notaries who in 1856–65 executed 3,549 instruments for a total value of 33,800,000 pesos. Pérez de León's registers reveal that all the adjudicators were the sole or the main tenants and that the sale price was calculated by capitalizing the rent at 6% (see appendix x). An examination of some of the other notarial records showed that those of Pérez de León may be taken as typical.

The value of the houses varied greatly, as did the economic and social status of the tenant. In 1856 many prominent people were tenants, and as such they were assigned the houses in which they lived or conducted their business. One of the richest men in the capital, Nathaniel Davidson, had his office in 3 Don Juan Manuel Street, and the property belonged to the convent of La Encarnación. It was disentailed for 25,000 pesos, which was more than the valuation of 21,100 given in the previously cited Account.[2] Another case involved the president of the republic, Ignacio Comonfort, who was one of two tenants of a house belonging to the convent of La Concepción. This was valued, according to the Account, at 15,500 pesos. Both tenants paid a monthly rent of 62·5 pesos,[3] and Comonfort was assigned the house for 22,500 pesos, which was a little less than the rent capitalized at 6%.[4] Even the Minister of Hacienda set a good example by disentailing number 5 in the elegant street Empedradillo, where he was the tenant. This house belonged to the Hospital of Jesus, and although it was valued at 23,333 pesos the adjudication price was 33,333, probably because this was the figure arrived at by capitalizing the 2,000 pesos annual rent at 6%.[5] These examples illustrate that not only

[1] *Memoria de Hacienda*, 1872–73, document no. 17.
[2] MH 1857, addenda, p. 212.   [3] AHINAH, vol. II, no. 61, no. 13, fol. 6.
[4] MH 1857, addenda, p. 197.   [5] Ibid., p. 175.

the poor tenants, who were in the majority but are difficult to identify, but also the rich or well-known, carried out the law. The disentailment, which was not a confiscation, was looked on as an inescapable fact, and moreover as the only way of acquiring one's own house. Therefore, far from being embarrassed at having been assigned a house, prominent liberals carried out the law publicly in order to guide the rest of the people.

Usually a person or family were assigned only one house, in which they were the tenants, although there are some cases in which a single individual acquired two or three. Such a person might rent several properties, one for his home, another for business premises and another for his relatives. This was quite normal, unlike the extreme case in which one person was the tenant of seventeen properties, all belonging to the same institution. Probably the proprietor in the latter example considered it more convenient to deal with one individual and therefore allowed the tenant to let the houses on his own account. The case was referred to Lerdo, who decided on 9 September that in accordance with the law the tenant had the right to claim all the houses.[1] In spite of this favourable decision, the tenant does not appear as the adjudicator in the detailed list contained in the 1857 report. Lerdo also resolved a similar case on 10 September. Occupation of a room did not confer the right of adjudication, that is, a person who had the right to live in some of the rooms of a house but who did not have a tenancy or subtenancy contract could not claim the house for himself.[2] These were extreme cases, however, for usually when a person claimed several properties—the most seems to have been a single case of twelve—it can be assumed that the adjudicator was a denouncer. As we have seen in the case of Puebla, there were few cases of denouncement because the tenants hastened to acquire the properties for themselves, either through a desire to own their own house or through fear of being deprived of their tenancy by a denouncer.

Various requests for clarification on the interpretation of article 8 of the law were made. This excepted from the disentailment

the buildings devoted directly or immediately to the service or purpose of the corporations, even though an integral part of them might be let as, for example, the monasteries, nunneries, episcopal and municipal palaces, colleges, hospitals, poor houses, markets, houses of correction and public welfare. As a part of each one of the said buildings there may be included in this exception an adjoining house which is inhabited through tenure of an office by those who serve the object of the institution, for example the houses of parish priests and convent chaplains.

[1] Ibid., p. 37; Dublán y Lozano, VIII, 240.
[2] MH 1857, addenda, p. 38; Dublán y Lozano, VIII, 241.

Soon after the start of the disentailment the Minister of Hacienda resolved on 6 September that the *casas colecturías*, which were the warehouses used by the Church for the storage and sale of the tithe produce, should be excepted from the law.[1] Perhaps encouraged by this decision and trusting in the veneration accorded to the image of the Virgin, the collegiate church of Guadalupe asked on 4 October that its houses, in which the canons, prebends and members of the chapter lived, should also be excepted. Lerdo replied on the 21st of the same month that only one house, adjacent to the building and used for the purposes of the corporation, could be granted exemption.[2] No doubt the canons, who were not monks and who apparently lived in houses set apart from the basilica, did suffer from the consequences of the law, unlike the regular orders who of course all resided within the monastery or convent building. It is possible that the canons adjudicated the houses in which they lived, which was the solution advised by Lerdo. If this did happen then they remained in their homes and the collegiate church in effect retained its property.

An interesting case occurred in Morelia, which was the capital of the state of Michoacán. The San Juan de Dios hospital, managed by the bishopric, had several houses adjacent to it, and these were to be used according to a projected scheme as an infirmary for women and by the Sisters of Mercy. The cathedral chapter naturally requested that the properties should be excepted from the disentailment. It was a dubious case, for article 8 only mentioned one house and moreover the properties were not yet being used for their stated purpose. It might have seemed that there was here an attempt to evade the law. Nevertheless, perhaps seeking to be benevolent towards the Sisters of Mercy, who were universally respected, Lerdo approved the request on 14 October, with the single condition that the houses must be occupied, in the manner requested, within three months.[3]

A very important part of article 8 came at the end: 'of the properties belonging to councils, the buildings, public lands and ground used exclusively for the service of public in the towns to which they belong, are also excepted'. These words are connected with the future possession of the goods of the indigenous communities. This aspect, however, is part of the history of the agrarian problem in Mexico and will not be dealt with in this monograph.

Apart from the exceptions mentioned above, the disentailment law covered all real estate holdings. In particular it included the valuable

---

[1] MH 1857, addenda, p. 32; Dublán y Lozano, VIII, 240.
[2] MH 1857, addenda, p. 64.   [3] Ibid., p. 95.

sugar producing haciendas with their sugar refining plants, located to the south of the capital in the districts of Cuernavaca and Cuautla. Details of one of these will be given later. Irrigation canals, which were sometimes quite large, often crossed common land owned by the municipality or by the village. On 20 October Lerdo resolved that in such cases the land should be assigned to the owners of the sugar plantations, a decision which no doubt conferred considerable benefits on them.[1] The few corporately owned sugar plantations were disentailed, as were the refining mills. The adjudication of one of these was registered in Guanajuato. It did not belong to the Church, which avoided involvement in mining or metallurgical enterprises, but to the Charity Junta.[2]

In Puebla the adjudications included the so-called conventional sales. In Mexico City the registers of the notary, F. Pérez de León, contain none of these transactions nor any examples of authentic sales by agreement, which presume the acceptance by the Church of the Lerdo law. Only one instance of a voluntary sale was found in the other notarial registers of the capital. This involved three houses owned by the Carmelites 'del Desierto' —a different group from those 'de San Angel'—and, following renouncement of adjudication by the tenants, the properties were bought by someone else.[3] Details of some conventional sales are to be found in other sources. Among these the sale by the Carmelite monastery of their orchard in San Angel, near the city of Mexico, might be mentioned. At that time many convents and monasteries had adjoining gardens, not only those outside the cities but also sometimes those within urban areas. The most famous case was the garden of the Franciscan monastery in the capital. Originally the friars used this to produce fruit for their own consumption and as a kind of rural retreat, but by 1856 some parts of the extensive area covered by the garden were already let. The tenant was the Frenchman Constancio Tonel who had a plant nursery there,[4] and he was assigned the property for 24,000 pesos.[5] As the Franciscans did not have real estate apart from the monastery buildings, the garden and a part of the buildings were the only property they lost in the disentailment.

The Carmelite garden in San Angel was the biggest in the District of Mexico, the wall around it stretching for more than a league and the total area being more than a square kilometre.[6] After the disentailment was

---

[1] Ibid., p. 63. [2] Ibid., p. 127.
[3] 1856 register of José María Natera, 23 September, Archivo de Notarías de México (cited hereinafter as ANM).
[4] J. L. Cossío, *Guía retrospectiva de la ciudad de México* (Mexico, 1941); AHINAH, vol. II, no. 61.
[5] MH 1857, addenda, p. 171. [6] Cossío, *Guía*, 75.

initiated the Carmelites decided to sell part of it. To do so they sought permission from the government since apparently the garden was not let (article 11 of the regulations). Their request was granted on 8 July and eighteen plots were offered for sale, two of which were sold on 8 August.[1] As was usual the buyer did not pay in cash but mortgaged the two lots at 6% a year for nine years. The term could be extended and also the buyer had the right to redeem the mortgage at any time. Following their policy of adapting to the circumstances, the Carmelites were able to save their garden, or at least a part of it, from the disentailment. The sales mentioned above are not included in the 1857 report.

The sales that were registered in the report concern the properties belonging to the Poor House, which was one of the most important institutions of public welfare, aiding in 1864 some 500 persons of both sexes and all ages.[2] In 1859 the management committee consisted of the president of the republic and of well-known figures such as the banker Manuel Lizardi, former Minister of Hacienda, Ignacio Trigueros, Juan Goríbar and E. Mackintosh, of the British banking firm of Manning and Mackintosh, and several clerics.[3] In 1856 its main properties were thirteen houses worth 811,415 pesos, which produced an annual return of only 10,608 pesos, implying, if the figure is correct, that the management was scarcely efficient.[4] In the Account the institution is noted as having only six houses, four of which were valued at 33,185 pesos. No valuation is given for the other two, but even so this much lower figure must cast some doubt on the accuracy of the previously cited sum of 811,415 pesos.

The appearance of the Lerdo law caused the corporations to think of selling their real estate to those persons whom they could trust, thereby in effect preserving their holdings in their control. This manoeuvre was only successful on a few occasions, however, for the following reason: the law gave prior right of adjudication to the tenant, who was usually a person with no connection to the corporate owner, and therefore the tenant claimed the property for himself precisely in order to ensure that unknown individuals did not acquire it. The conventional sales of the Poor House property seem to have been made to persons who were not the tenants and they were approved by Lerdo on 20 September.[5] Six of these sales can be located in the 1857 report. The one involving the highest amount was for 33,333 pesos, which corresponds to the capitalization at

---

[1] *Testimonio de las escrituras otorgadas por el R. P. Rector del Colegio de Carmelitas de San Angel a favor de D. Tomás Orozco, de los lotes que de la huerta del mismo colegio le vendió en 1856*, MSS in the Latin American Collection, University of Texas.
[2] Cossío, *Guía*, 169.   [3] Valle, *El viajero en México*, 592.
[4] Ibid., p. 591.   [5] Labastida, 103.

6% of an annual rent of 2,000 pesos.[1] It is not known if the sales of the rest of the properties could not be carried out because of difficulties with the tenants.

Another institution which tried to convert its real estate holdings into capital by means of conventional sales was the Franciscan college of Santiago Tlaltelolco, which owned eight properties valued at 70,803 pesos.[2] On 17 September 1856 the college sold a house at 7 Coliseo to Manuel Ruíz, who was the main tenant. The price was 46,000 pesos, with a mortgage at 6% a year; in other words, under the same terms as the disentailment, the tenant paying nothing of the capital value but only the interest. The house had been valued at 25,308 pesos.[3] Ruíz later sold it for 42,000 pesos to Miguel Bringas, a Mexican capitalist with conservative views. Another tenant had to be paid 4,000 pesos to persuade him not to seek adjudication. This type of cost frequently ensued from the Lerdo law. On the same day the college sold to Manuel Gargollo the property housing the coach terminal, and the price for this was 22,525 pesos with a mortgage at 6%.[4] Gargollo was an important owner of credits from the first Spanish convention, a capitalist connected with the conservatives and proprietor of the coach company. The monthly rent which he was paying for the property was 108 pesos, so that the sale price equalled approximately the capitalization of the rent at 6%. The house had been valued at 22,525 pesos.

The college was not always able to sell its houses to persons of its choice and number 5 Coliseo was assigned to the tenant José María Iglesias, a prominent liberal, 'against the opposition of the college'. The institution naturally preferred to sell to conservatives, thus reducing difficulties to a minimum.[5] The house had been valued at 13,870 pesos but the adjudication price was much higher, at 24,300 pesos, a sum which was probably based on the rent. All three of these transactions were recorded in the 1857 report.[6]

The most interesting case of a voluntary sale concerns the monastery of La Merced. The history of the case is as follows:[7] in 1809 the convent of La Concepción, the richest of all the nunneries, lent La Merced the sum of 60,000 pesos to be used in the purchase of the ranches of Mejicapa,

---

[1] MH 1857, addenda, pp. 171, 187, 193; the same house, for 33,333 pesos, is twice repeated in the *Memoria*; also a property noted as belonging to the Poor House was in fact owned by the convent of Santa Teresa la Nueva.

[2] *Noticia de las fincas pertenecientes a corporaciones civiles y eclesiásticas del distrito de México* (Mexico, 1856), p. 21.   [3] AHINAH, vol. II, no. 61, 127, fol. 35.

[4] Ibid.   [5] Ibid.

[6] MH 1857, addenda, pp. 171, 201, 228.   [7] AGN, PBN, leg. 1523, exp. 8, fols. 1–15.

Nueva Holanda and La Merced. Strange though it may seem the regular orders demanded guarantors from one another and in this instance La Concepción accepted as guarantor the Spaniard Gabriel Yermo, one of the wealthiest men in New Spain. It turned out that they could not have made a better choice, for when La Merced did not honour the debt, Yermo paid the amount owing. With the deterioration of the situation and the ever increasing danger of a nationalization of clerical goods, Yermo's estate, through his descendants, the main one of whom was probably M. Yermo who in 1859 had a sugar store,[1] started judicial proceedings against the La Merced. By then the debt amounted to more than 100,000 pesos, including the accumulated interest of more than twenty years. Finally, on 5 May 1856 Yermo's lawyer and the monastery came to a settlement for the sum of 50,000 pesos and the latter immediately decided to sell several houses to meet the debt. On 11 June seven houses were auctioned which fetched a price of 39,810 pesos—the manuscript incorrectly states 40,810. This price was approximately the same as the valuation put on the houses by the Account, but the monastery was to receive only 29,810 pesos in cash, for some buyers were unable to pay the whole amount. The ranches were sold, 'mortgaged' to their tenants; in other words the buyers did not actually have to hand over any of the purchase price.

On the basis of these facts, the prior of La Merced then asked the Minister of Justice on 21 June for permission to sell the houses, and this was conceded four days later, the same day as the Lerdo law was issued. The sales had already been made, and they could not be cancelled because they preceded the promulgation of the law. Money was still needed, however, to complete the 50,000 pesos owed to Yermo, and so on 9 July the prior asked permission to sell more houses. This was again granted and a further fifteen were sold. Such a number could not pass unnoticed and notes were exchanged between the Ministers of Justice and Hacienda. Eventually on 20 December Lerdo annulled the second series of sales, alleging an abuse of the law on the part of the monastery and conceding the tenants the right of adjudication.[2]

Lerdo did not know that some of the houses sold before the publication of his law were nonetheless disentailed. Two were assigned to their tenants, thus frustrating the sale and depriving the monastery of 11,000 pesos of the amount it expected to receive. These adjudications were illegal because, in law, the monastery was no longer the owner of the

[1] Valle, *El viajero en México*, 292.
[2] The decision is reproduced in the MH 1857, p. 152.

houses. In spite of this the adjudications were maintained until 27 December when the prior informed the Minister of Justice of all these circumstances that have been related, and they almost certainly continued until the annulment by Zuloaga in January 1858 of all the adjudications.

Three houses from the second series of sales, which had been cancelled by Lerdo, were assigned to their tenants, in particular to one who for ten years had been conducting a lawsuit against the monastery over improvements and the entry fine. The other houses were sold for a price lower than that given in the Account, because of the risk of an adjudication or denouncement, and the terms of payment were much more unfavourable to the monastery. Thus from the sale of the fifteen houses the corporation received only 16,500 pesos in cash, which, added to the product of the sale of the seven houses, amounted to 35,200 pesos. 4,700 pesos were deducted to cover costs, with the result that Yermo was paid only 30,686 pesos. Hence the guarantor succeeded in recovering only half of his original credit.

These circumstances caused the prior on 27 December to ask the Minister of Justice to intercede with his colleague in the Ministry of Hacienda to persuade him to approve the second series of sales. Four days later Ezequiel Montes forwarded the petition to his colleague with the request 'that he should resolve as he saw fit'. Here the file ends. Lerdo resigned at the beginning of January and his successors paid no attention to the matter. Were the sales really cancelled or not?

In his decision of 20 December Lerdo had conceded the right of adjudication to the tenants, but in his already quoted communication, dated a week later, the prior wrote that the houses had been sold to the tenants, except when the latter had renounced their rights under the law, in which case the monastery paid them what they had spent on improvements.

This affirmation that the second sale had been made at least in part to the tenants seems to be confirmed by an examination of the buyers. Two of them, both lawyers, were living in 1854 in the same house that they bought two years later.[1] It does seem, therefore, that they were tenants of La Merced and if this is so, then the sales were not cancelled. As for the other two houses in the second sale, it is known that the sales were still recognized two years later for, as they had been sold voluntarily by the monastery, they were not affected by the derogation of the Lerdo law in 1858.[2] Finally, only the four adjudications which frustrated the

[1] Galván Rivera, *Guía*, 143 ff.
[2] AGN, PBN, leg. 1523, exp. 8, fols. 1–7; this expediente will be referred to throughout this work.

planned sales were noted in the 1857 report. Neither the remaining sales to the buyers chosen by the monastery nor the adjudications of the same houses to other people are mentioned. All this permits the conclusion that the sales subsisted because they were in essence authentic conventional sales to the tenants. In the few cases in which the tenants were not the same as the buyers, the former were assigned the properties.

Would the monastery pay Yermo the balance of the 1857 debt? It is doubtful for, as will be shown later, the disentailment of 1856 upset the economic situation of the regular orders, and two years later, in 1858, the position was even more difficult. Of course Yermo could have gone to the length of attaching some of the remaining houses of La Merced in order to collect the balance, but it had few left as a result of the disentailment.

Contrary to what one might suppose, several monasteries in the capital, in particular the Carmelites, Franciscans and Mercedarians, tried to seek salvation by submitting, although indirectly, to the Lerdo law. However, the nunneries in the capital, almost all of which came under the episcopal jurisdiction, did not, as far as is known, adopt the policy of conventional sales. Therefore, it cannot now be maintained that the opposition of the Church to the law was monolithic, for whereas the secular clergy were indeed hostile, some of the regular orders accepted it.

Almost one-third of the total value of the disentailment in the District of Mexico in 1856 came from auction sales. Separated from the adjudications, these auctions were noted in the 1857 report on pages 266–89 of the addenda. The title of this section indicates that they were held from 3 October to 31 December 1856. The Lerdo law conceded tenants a term of three months to claim their rights. At the end of this time, about 1 October, the properties were to be sold by public auction.

The details of these auctions are reproduced in the same form as the adjudications, except that, due to lack of space, instead of the name of the corporation, that of the guarantor is put at the side of the successful bidder. In most cases the corporations owning the houses which were sold have been identified. Sometimes the houses are grouped by corporation, which leads to the conclusion that all the properties of each were sold in one auction, but in other instances the houses are grouped according to the buyers, from which it seems that a person bought houses of different corporations in several successive auctions. Finally, in some examples a buyer acquired several houses of one corporation; in other words, he specialized in a particular convent or monastery.

Unlike the list of adjudications in which the buyers constantly change, the same names tend to recur in the auctions, with the result that in 319 sales ten persons bought houses worth 2,408,994 pesos, almost 60% of the total value of the auctions. Eight of the ten were Mexican liberals. Another interesting point is that a particular bidder almost always had the same guarantor. As in the case of Puebla, it seems that the bidder and the guarantor were associates in this or some other business.

For information on the auctions, the following registers of Fr. Pérez de León were examined in detail: volume II for 1856, beginning the 27 September and concluding at the end of December; the two registers for 1857, the first having 610 pages and ending on 9 January, and the second, beginning on page 611 and terminating at the end of the year on page 1172. The month of January 1857 ends on page 830, in volume II, and it is full of the sales made to Manuel Morales Puente. These auctions took place at the end of the previous year—they are almost all noted in the 1857 report—but the execution of the deeds was delayed, no doubt because of legal procedure such as the payment of the sales tax, and of course the time and work involved in writing them all down. One can well imagine that at that time the government offices and the notaries were working day and night.

Appendix XI contains an extract of the register for 1856, with twenty-four auction sales. This number was thought sufficient as an example, for subsequent sales were based on the same formula. There was indeed no time for variations, as several hundred auctions had to be recorded in the books in the shortest possible time. For example, fourteen of the instruments included in the sample given as appendix XI were dated 3 December, and six the 18th of the same month. All twenty related to the transactions made in favour of Francisco Schiafino, and with the exception of the first, all were noted in the 1857 report. In fact the classification of the first transaction is debatable for it concerns a subtenant who subrogated the tenant's rights, and hence it was more like an adjudication, although again it is not listed in the 1857 report's section on adjudications.

In the twenty-three remaining cases, the successful bidder was neither the tenant nor the subtenant. The auctions were held in accordance with article 10 of the law, which stipulated public sales when the property was not claimed by the tenant, subtenant or denouncer. In only one case was an auction held to comply with article 5, which ordered the public sale of a house which was not let, and this seems to prove the hypothesis that, with a few exceptions, all the houses were rented.

As had happened in Puebla, bidders did not compete against one another. Usually only one person made an offer and he was sold the property at that price. It seems reasonably certain that the buyers had come to a tacit arrangement among themselves not to compete against each other, if not a specific agreement over the sharing out of the houses that had not been claimed. Furthermore, there was simply no time for real auctions. The average prices realized were approximately two-thirds of the value, according to the valuation given in the instruments or in the Account.

The 1857 report shows that Francisco Schiafino always had Nicolás Gómez as his guarantor in the auctions, but in the deeds other names appear in that capacity, for example José de la Luz Moreno, Balbontín or M. Caballero de Carranza, a Puebla merchant. It seems that the security was a routine formality and that bidders perhaps even bought on behalf of their guarantors. Sometimes the same guarantor acted for different bidders, for example C. Butterfield, who provided security for Marcelino Sánchez, one of the ten major bidders, and also for various other people.

This impression that the bidders were representing a consortium is confirmed in the case of Manuel Morales Puente, the most active of all the buyers. In 150 transactions he acquired houses worth 986,997 pesos, which equalled almost a quarter of the total value of all the auction sales in the district of Mexico. According to the 1857 report his guarantors were always the same two individuals, I. Loperena and C. Rubio. These men were in effect his partners and the text in every instrument of sale was repeated in almost exactly the same words:

> ...the sale resulted in purchase by Don Manuel Morales Puente, representative of a limited company...Señor Morales Puente...expressly declares that in the name of this company, there is reserved the right of designation of houses to each partner, to the persons also in this capacity, Don Cayetano Rubio and Don Ignacio Loperena and the said Morales Puente, at whose disposition the properties remain; it must be noted that until the distribution or designation of the properties is made, all those bought by the company will be considered to belong to it alone, with no individual having particular claims, for each partner will have the special individual right when his property is designated to him, for all of which it is henceforth established that it will be sufficient to place the corresponding note in the original draft and in the respective attestation...[1]

The designation or distribution mentioned in the deed took place on 16 March 1857 before the same notary, after all the auctions had ended.[2] The company, M. Morales Puente, was dissolved on this date and the houses were distributed as shown in table 9 (each house was noted with its address and former owner).

[1] F. Pérez de León, 1856 register, vol. II, fols. 692–7, ANM.
[2] 1857 register, vol. II, fols. 890 ff.

TABLE 9. *Distribution of houses owned by Morales Puente, 1857*

Name of buyer	No. of houses	Value (pesos)
Ignacio Loperena	69	461,716
Cayetano Rubio	12	30,601
Ignacio Muñoz Campuzano	26	116,666
Ramón Larrainzar	32	143,641
M. Morales Puente	36	182,197
	175	934,821[1]

The guarantors were also noted. They were merchants or proprietors and they had to guarantee the payment of monthly interest by the buyers. Their names indicate that they were relatives of the partners, except in the case of M. Morales Puente who, as a lawyer and public official, probably did not have any merchant among his relatives.

It may be asked why it was necessary or convenient to form a company to buy ecclesiastical goods. The date of the formation of this one has not been discovered, but it can be assumed that it was organized specifically for this purpose. Why did each of the partners not bid on his own account? In the first place, time was short for it was near the end of the year, and Lerdo was determined to end the disentailment, whatever the cost. Even though the men of the Reform would have preferred every house to be assigned to its tenant, and that real estate should be fragmented so that a strong middle class was created, it seemed a lesser evil to them that a large part of the property should pass into the hands of a few individuals rather than remain in the possession of the Church. It was clearly easier to carry out a large transaction through the means of a company. Secondly, the transaction required considerable funds. If one takes into account that, under article 32 of the law, after the term of three months had passed, the 5% tax on the value of the disentailed houses had to be paid entirely in cash, and under article 33 that all auction and other costs had to be paid by the buyer, then the purchase of almost 1,000,000 pesos' worth of real estate required disbursement of at least 50,000 pesos. Such a large sum could only be provided by a merchant or capitalist, but never by a professional person, who, on the other hand, might have some influence in official circles, which in turn might be important, given the time factor. These therefore are the reasons for the association of a bidder and a group of capitalists.

[1] For reasons unknown this total is less than the sum of the auctions registered in the *Memoria de Hacienda* in the name of Morales Puente.

The capitalists probably calculated as follows: they were buying at a reduced price, which to some extent compensated for the risk that a political change would lead to the annulment of the sales; secondly, in 1856 the liberals seemed firmly in control of power and therefore the risk appeared small. Furthermore, in the case of some capitalists who were previously connected to conservative governments, it seemed convenient to establish relations with the liberal administration. The buyers were offered the prospect of personal enrichment, but they accepted in turn a risk to their persons. Considerable courage was needed in view of the attacks which the Church fulminated against the buyers, especially the liberals.

The tenants who refrained from having the houses in which they lived assigned to themselves, thus allowing strangers to buy them and running the risk of being deprived of their tenancies, did so for other motives. They probably thought that the liberal government would not last long, and that the conservatives would return the houses to the corporations, which would perhaps reward them for their loyalty. Between a third and a half of the tenants, if we consider also those houses which were not disentailed, seem to have held this view, and this perhaps explains in part the tenacity and cruelty of the three years' war. In due course it will be seen who was right and who was wrong in their calculations. For the moment it is sufficient to say that the auction sales were of a speculative nature.

Unlike the case of Puebla, an almost complete list is available of the buyers of clerical property in the Federal District in 1861. This list will be analysed in chapter 5, and therefore it is not necessary to give here the details of the buyers in the capital, based on the incomplete facts available for 1856.

It has already been seen that in Puebla the disentailment of 1856 was very incomplete. In general the states were dilatory in comparison to the metropolis, except in a few cases, for example Veracruz, where almost all the ecclesiastical properties were sold in 1856. In the capital the disentailment in that year was reasonably complete. In the city alone, not including the District, approximately 900 urban houses were assigned and a further 600 were auctioned. There were 570 auctions but in some more than one house was sold. In total, therefore, between 1,500 and 1,600 houses were disentailed, approximately four-fifths or five-sixths of 1,900, which was the maximum number affected by the law. The same proportion is seen in a comparison of the total price of the disentailment in 1856. This was 13,000,000 pesos, and the value of the corporate real estate was between

16,000,000 and 17,000,000 pesos, according to the Account. The disentailment would be even more complete if the many houses that were sold at less than their worth were taken into account.

This can be proved by the following examples: 28 houses belonging to the monastery of San Agustín, valued at 268,880 pesos, were disentailed for 166,557 pesos, a fall of 38%; six belonging to the Third Order of Carmen, valued at 32,000 pesos, were sold for 21,502 pesos, a fall of 33%; eighteen owned by the San Andrés hospital, valued at 225,505 pesos, were disentailed for 158,701 pesos, a drop of 30%; six belonging to the Terceros hospital, valued at 48,150 pesos, were sold for 29,460 pesos, 39% less; eight belonging to the University, valued at 113,800 pesos, were sold for 84,200 pesos, 27% less; twelve of the silversmiths' guild, valued at 124,000 pesos, were sold for 89,873 pesos, 28% less; and twelve owned by the Carmelites del Desierto, valued at 148,320 pesos, were sold—some in 1856 and others in 1861—for 103,562 pesos, a fall of 31%. These valuation figures were taken from the 1856 Account, and the sale prices, with the one exception noted, from the 1857 report. Since 1823 the price of clerical properties sold on a wholesale basis by the government had shown a fall of one-third. The possession of these ecclesiastical properties was not a sign of social prestige and so the buyers, who had to have an acute mercantile sense like any other investor, insisted that the properties were sold to them at a low price, thus making their return equal to that received from other comparable types of investment.

The basic data from instruments of sale for January 1857 were reproduced in the 1857 report and there were only a few sales in February and almost none in the rest of the year.

Either because of the inhabitants' greater enthusiasm for liberal ideas or because of better government organization, or for both reasons, the disentailment in the nation's capital was to a large extent completed in 1856.

IMMEDIATE RESULT OF THE DISENTAILMENT

Under the Lerdo law a transfer of property was effected in the course of a few months on such a huge scale that repercussions on the economy and society of the country were inevitable. In the first place, as the law conceded the right of property to many diverse persons, for example tenants, subtenants, strangers or denouncers, conflicts between these parties soon arose. The following case provides an illustration of this: Agustín Arrangoiz, apparently tenant at an annual rent of 20,000 pesos of a sugar plantation near Cuautla belonging to the Dominicans, was assigned it for

333,333 pesos. This was the highest price given in the 1857 report. Another person, however, denounced the property and the adjudicator protested. In response to the latter the Minister of Hacienda decided on 15 October 1856 that the denouncement could not be admitted.[1] The denouncer persisted with his claim and one week later Lerdo wrote to the governor of the state of Mexico, who then had jurisdiction over the districts of Cuernavaca and Cuautla, pointing out that he had only restated the principle that a denouncement of a property which had been properly assigned under the law could not be admitted. The denouncer could seek to have his rights determined by the respective courts.[2] Two days later Lerdo issued a further clarification that 'only a general ruling had been given, so that in those cases where the courts found that an adjudication of a property had been made in conformity with the law, it should not be assigned thereafter to a denouncer'.[3] In such cases where conflict arose Lerdo left the solution of them to the courts and, given the traditional slow pace at which these worked, a multitude of impending litigation and expense for the adjudicators ensued.

In one of the few cases concerning a house which had not been let, two denouncements were made simultaneously, although one of them was through a representative, and others followed later. Lerdo resolved that the house should be divided between the first two denouncers.[4]

Another difficulty which arose was between the new owners and the tenants. In the case of an adjudication the former could have previously been the tenants, and the latter the sub- or secondary tenants. When the new owners were the successful buyers in auctions, the tenants were as before. Some buyers, seeking to increase the rents, demanded that the tenants vacated the houses on the grounds that they were going to occupy them themselves. They did this without giving the notice of forty days and without guaranteeing that they would not rent them for a further four years, both of which were legal requirements to be observed for vacating privately owned houses. Then on 25 January 1857 the Minister of Hacienda ordered that article 19 of the disentailment law must be obeyed. This conceded tenants a term of three years from the promulgation of the law during which the tenancy contract could not be modified.[5]

The new owners also faced problems. The number of houses sold by auction in the District of Mexico amounted to at least a third of the total

[1] MH 1857, p. 61.
[2] Ibid., p. 99.
[3] Ibid., p. 102.
[4] Ibid., p. 120.
[5] *Circular manuscrita*, Biblioteca Nacional, Colección Lafragua, vol. 120.

and the buyers were confronted with tenants, many of whom had renounced their rights to adjudication in obedience to the dictates of the Church. Such people could have had little love for their new liberal landlords, and they certainly had no wish to pay rent to individuals who in their eyes were not the legal owners. They had to act with caution, however, for article 19 of the law did give the new proprietors the right 'to ask that the property be vacated on other grounds, in accordance with existing law'. In some parts of the country, for example Guadalajara, the tenants refused to pay their rent to the denouncers or auction buyers, and when they could not avoid doing so they preferred to move house, leaving their former dwelling empty. This caused a fall in the value of the property.[1] It is possible that these tenants were secretly paying their rent to the former corporate owner.

When the new owners were not the ex-tenants but buyers in auction or denouncers, difficulties arose with the tenants who probably felt that the houses would soon be returned to the corporations. If at times, or even frequently, the landlords did not receive the rent, they in turn did not pay interest to the former corporate owner. The corporations had refused to give the buyers the original title deeds. Consequently the buyers refused to pay interest, an action which they were entitled to adopt under article 15 of the regulations governing the law. On 13 January 1857 the administrator of the convent of San Bernardo sent the archbishop an account which showed that the institution's revenue from property and capital amounted to 400 to 500 pesos a month before the introduction of the Lerdo law. After this, income was reduced by two-thirds because buyers were not paying the interest that they owed. The administrator admitted that he had not handed over the deeds to the buyers because they could destroy them, and if a political change did occur—presumably this was the thinking behind the administrator's reasoning—the convent would require them to prove ownership.[2] Another almost identical case was that of the convent of Santa Teresa la Nueva. According to information dated 11 August 1857 almost all of its properties had been auctioned, and as the new owners were not paying interest, the current revenue did not cover half of the amount needed even to feed the nuns.[3] This might well be something of an exaggeration. The convent of Regina also reported that many court cases had arisen as a consequence of the law.[4] Curiously these complaints came from the

---

[1] L. Pérez Verdía, *Historia particular del estado de Jalisco, desde los primeros tiempos de que hay noticia hasta nuestros días* (Guadalajara, 1952), vol. II, p. 518.
[2] AGN, PBN, leg. 74, exp. 51.   [3] Ibid., leg. 1711, exp. unmarked, dated May 1859.
    Ibid., leg. 74, exp. 34.

nunneries. The monasteries, which were independent of the see and hence more conciliatory, probably had fewer difficulties.

As about half of the population were opposed to the Lerdo law, a fact of which the Church was well aware, the immediate results were rather chaotic. Many tenants did not pay rents, buyers did not pay interest and the corporations could not meet their commitments. In this sense the economy was paralysed. It was clear that this state of affairs could not last indefinitely and that it would have to be resolved one way or the other.

As for the alienation of the properties, it has often been stated that the Lerdo law had an adverse social effect. To cite one typical view:

the number of real property owners did not increase; some speculators took advantage of the law to make immoral deals; some rich people increased their fortunes and no poor person remedied his poverty...and the movement noted in the capital and in other cities through the repair of some houses cannot even be considered as scant compensation for the difficulties which that measure brought on the government...[1]

Certainly many hacendados did increase their holdings, and in this respect it is interesting to note that as far as is known none of the numerous conservative landowners made any protest against the Lerdo law. In contrast, many of the most important hacendados in the country, who lived in the capital, did protest on 10 July against agrarian reform projects which were being discussed in congress but which were not approved.[2] This opposition was supported a short time afterwards by landowners in the states of Michoacán and Puebla, in which rich haciendas were characteristic.[3] The protests were signed by hacendados of both political persuasions.

Even though the purchases through auctions seem to have been speculative business ventures undertaken by a limited number of persons, there is no doubt that the great majority of adjudications were made by tenants, most of whom, like the people as a whole, were poor. Lerdo was right to say, as he did on resigning his post as Minister of Hacienda, that his law had created more then 9,000 new property owners.[4] Although many of these were later to lose their houses as a result of subsequent events, the fact remains that in the short term real estate, which until then

[1] A. de la Portilla, *México en 1856 y 1857. Gobierno del General Comonfort* (New York, 1858), p. 70.

[2] *Representación que hacen varios dueños de propiedades territoriales...*

[3] *Representaciones que hacen al congreso constituyente varios dueños de fincas rústicas y urbanas, en Michoacán, Guanajuato, Guerrero y Puebla, secundando la que los propietarios, residentes en la capital de la república, dirigieron al mismo congreso el 10 de julio del presente año, contra algunos artículos de los proyectos de leyes fundamentales que se están discutiendo* (Mexico, 1856); this was signed only by hacendados from Puebla and Michoacán.

[4] MH 1857, p. 10.

had been concentrated in the hands of a few corporations, was fragmented, even if not in the proportion sought by the men of the Reform. A peaceful and stable situation was required for the full implementation of the Lerdo law, but this was denied the Minister of Hacienda.

SAN LUIS POTOSÍ: ITS ECONOMY, SOCIETY AND ECCLESIASTICAL POSSESSIONS

After studying the capital of the republic, the industrial city of Puebla, which was also the centre of an agricultural area, and the mainly mercantile city of Veracruz, we now turn to the mining town of San Luis Potosí. Although the silver mines near the city, which had made it rich and famous in colonial times, had been in decline since the eighteenth century, other mining districts in the state of San Luis Potosí, especially the Mineral Catorce, were replacing those of past renown. Hence in the middle of the last century, the state with approximately 400,000 inhabitants was still predominantly concerned with the mining industry. The capital city had 33,581 inhabitants and it was the political and commercial centre of the region.[1] The western part of the state was semi-desert and typical of the northern areas of the country, but one part to the east was well known for its agriculture. The centre of this was Río Verde, with 4,000 inhabitants.[2]

Unlike Mexico, Puebla and Veracruz, there is no business directory available for San Luis Potosí for the years preceding the Reform. All that is known is that in 1853 there were three businesses selling cloth, employing ten people; four grocery stores with seventeen employees; and about six dozen smaller shops.[3] The name and nationality of the traders are not known. For 1868 facts are available in the already cited *Almanaque* by Maillefert. At that time there were fourteen stores and many shops, drapers, groceries and others. Several of the owners had German or English surnames.[4] As for industry, there were in 1853 several dozen small textile workshops, which specialized in shawls, and one tobacco factory, which employed 350 men and 400 women. There were also five registered brokers—their number, like that of the notaries, was limited

---

[1] *Diccionario universal*, appendix 3, 1856.
[2] Ibid.
[3] 'Noticia que manifiesta las profesiones, industria y ocupación de los habitantes de la ciudad de San Luis Potosí', *Boletín de la Sociedad Mexicana de Geografía y Estadística* (cited hereinafter as *BSMGE*), vol. VII, pp. 288 ff.; dated 1859 but the information is from 1853.
[4] Maillefert, 304–5; it also has a small section on Río Verde, which seems to have been much more important then than now.

by regulations—and six mine owners. Finally there were twenty-three lawyers, or in round figures one per thousand of the inhabitants, which was a very high ratio. It can be concluded that most of them lacked any remunerative work and this might explain in part their liberal inclinations. There were forty-three regulars who lived on the substantial ecclesiastical goods.[1] The contrast between the professional class and the friars speaks for itself.

On the other hand, abundant information is available on the haciendas and the mines in the state. One source, for 1853, gives the name of the hacendados and the speciality of each agricultural enterprise.[2] Most of the 194 haciendas and ranches in the state were cattle and cereal producers but about a dozen, particularly in the district of Río Verde, were devoted to sugar cane production, which was, as in other parts of the country, a sign of the commercialization of agriculture. This is confirmed by the data for 1868 when there were seven sugar cane mills in the state, six of which were powered by water, and eighty-nine small cane mills, moved by animal traction. There were also three flour mills, two of which were operated by hydraulic power.[3]

The 1868–69 data on the mining industry gives the names of the mine owners, or the financial backers, who were the speculators financing the mining operations, and the owners of the smelting haciendas, metallurgical enterprises which extracted the silver from the ore.[4] Judging by the number of the latter—there were thirty—the size of each one must have been relatively small.

Both lists permit a reconstruction of the economic and social activity of three outstanding Mexican families in the state, Verástegui, Gordoa and Bustamante, all of whom were related to one another through marriage. The Verástegui had above all sugar haciendas in the Río Verde region. The most renowned member of the family, Paulo, who was a lawyer, had in addition to his own hacienda the tenancy of the only ecclesiastical one in the state, Ojo de Agua de Solano. The Bustamantes were also hacendados. It is not known whether these families had businesses in the state capital prior to the Reform, as did their colleagues in the cities of Mexico and Puebla. The Gordoa family were involved in mining and the cited list mentions Crescencio María and Antonio Gordoa

[1] 'Noticia que manifiesta las profesiones...', *BSMGE*, vol. VII, pp. 288 ff.
[2] 'Noticia de las haciendas y ranchos que existen en el estado de San Luis Potosí, con expresión del dueño, giro principal de la finca y municipalidad en que está situada. Año de 1853', *BSMGE*, vol. VII, 1859.
[3] *Memoria del gobierno de estado de San Luis Potosí*, 1868–69, table 15.
[4] Ibid., table 13.

as mine owners or financial backers. They also had at least one hacienda, of 'livestock and cane'.

From what has been said previously, the liberal connections of these three families of hacendados, mine owners and lawyers are not unusual. C. M. Gordoa was state governor in 1857;[1] Pablo Gordoa was a deputy in 1862.[2] Pilar Bustamante was an elected deputy in 1857;[3] Francisco Bustamante was deputy in 1862 and governor in 1877, and Juan Bustamante was governor in 1867. Finally, Jose María and Paulo (Pablo) Verástegui were deputies in 1862.

There is an official list made by the Treasury Office of the amount and structure of ecclesiastical property in the state of San Luis Potosí in 1856, and this contains for each corporation the houses, their location and value.[4] The list is intended to be complete but as usual it can be proved that there are omissions in it. It is possible on the other hand that it contains some houses which in 1856 were no longer owned by the corporations.

Table 10 has been compiled from this list. For a better understanding of the table, the following needs to be explained: the four monasteries were all in the state capital, as were almost all their properties, with the exception of the Augustinian, which owned one hacienda. The brotherhoods were richer than the monasteries but here not only those in the capital but also those in other cities, towns and villages in the state, are included. Comparing only the ones in the city of San Luis Potosí, their properties were less than those of the monasteries. Most of the properties were urban, particularly those in the state capital. In the item referring to municipalities, all the municipal properties in the cities, towns and villages are included. Public buildings in the capital have been omitted, although they were included by mistake in the official list. As the actual monastery buildings were not entered, nor should public buildings be added.

385 houses, valued at 286,429 pesos, out of the total indicated in the table, were in the city of San Luis Potosí. Were the corporations, almost all of which were clerical, rich compared with the private citizens? There

---

[1] R. del Castillo, *Cuadro sinóptico del estado de San Luis Potosí, con varios datos históricos, geográficos, estadísticos y administrativos* (San Luis Potosí, 1878).

[2] F. Buenrostro, *Historia del primero y segundo congresos constitucionales de la república mexicana* (Mexico, 1874–82), vol. II, p. 151.

[3] Ibid., I, 44.

[4] 'Noticia que forma esta oficina de las fincas urbanas y rústicas pertenecientes a corporaciones civiles y eclesiásticos, existentes en todo el estado, hasta el día 5 de julio próximo pasado que se publicó en esta capital la ley de desamortización', dated 18 September 1856 and reproduced in J. Betancourt, *San Luis Potosí, sus plazas y calles* (San Luis Potosí, 1921), pp. 319–46.

TABLE 10. *Church real estate in San Luis Potosí, 1856*

Corporation	No. of properties	Value (in pesos)
Monasteries (S. Francisco, Merced, Carmen, A. Agustín)	166	130,232
Parishes (different throughout the state)	32	23,274
Pious works	17	20,774
Third Order of San Francisco and of La Merced	13	10,312
Brotherhoods (nine, the richest being that of Nuestro Amo)	210	133,558
Colleges (the Guadalupano Josefino and the Beaterio)	33	64,704
San Juan de Dios Hospital (originally of the order of San Juan)	19	13,840
Municipalities	32	60,540
Totals	522	457,234

are two conflicting accounts of the total value of all real estate in the capital. According to the first, property had been calculated in 1844–45 to be worth 2,246,840 pesos, a figure arrived at by capitalizing the rents at 5%.[1] According to the second for the year 1847, the census valuation was 1,771,160 pesos.[2] Perhaps this latter value was obtained on the basis of the first, with a deduction of 25%, as happened in Veracruz where the subtraction was 35%. Whatever it was, ecclesiastical property in the state capital was only a small part of the total real estate. Unlike Mexico and Puebla, the Church in San Luis Potosí, as in Veracruz, was rather poor.

The Carmen monastery had sold its haciendas, and this left as the most valuable clerical property in the whole of the state a single hacienda, which was owned by the Augustinians. It was valued at 36,000 pesos, which at 5% corresponds to a rent of 1,800 a year, although in 1843 and in 1855 the rent was in fact 2,300, which gives a value of 46,000.[3]

[1] Betancourt, 303.

[2] 'Noticia que comprende el valor de fincas urbanas y rústicas, el de las cuotas asignadas a los establecimientos industriales, sueldos y salarios, profesiones y ejercicios lucrativos, objetos de lujo y giros mercantiles: las cantidades recaudadas por cada uno de los ramos expresados: los honorarios y demás gastos de recaudación, y el producto líquido que resultó a favor del estado en el año próximo pasado de 1847', *BSMGE*, vol. VII, 1859.

[3] *Memoria de Justicia*, 1844; AGN, JE, vol. 48, table 4.

THE DISENTAILMENT IN SAN LUIS POTOSÍ (1856–57)

The Lerdo law came into force in San Luis Potosí on 5 July 1856. Although the government published the list of properties on 18 September, the disentailment transactions began in July. The result of them is to be found in the 1857 report.[1] The number of adjudications was 221 and their value 147,851 pesos. Thus in 1856 about a third of the corporate real estate in the state was disentailed. Most of the adjudications were, as usual, small sales of municipal lands, and common lands of the towns and villages. A few were for 1,000 pesos or more, and there were only three for more than 10,000 pesos each, but the latter amounted to 72,083 pesos which was 48·7% of the total. Included in them there was one transaction for 50,000 pesos, but this represented more than one-third of the total. There is no doubt that the disentailment in 1856 was very incomplete.

Three public notaries were then practising in the state capital,[2] and the registers of two of them, Isidro Calvillo (1856–96) and Ignacio López Portillo (1856–77) have survived complete. Those of the former have been examined in detail. The great majority of the ecclesiastical corporations, not the municipal, refused to sell, so that the deeds were signed by justices of the peace and later by the prefects of the district. The adjudications, which are almost all reproduced in the 1857 report, began in July with the municipal lands (common lands) which were sold to their tenants. Only small amounts resulting from the capitalization of rent at 6% were involved. These are followed by the adjudications of houses to their tenants; for example, a house belonging to the girls' school of San Nicolás (el Beaterio) was sold to the German citizen E. Kreutzmann (noted as Krenzman in the 1857 report). He had his 'establishment' in the house, although it is not known if this was trading or industrial, and he paid 600 pesos a year in rent. The purchase price was 10,000 pesos, which for a house in San Luis Potosí was expensive. Three-quarters of the 5% tax were paid in cash, and the remainder in bonds, in accordance with the law. Details can be seen in appendix XII.

What is particularly interesting in I. Calvillo's register are the conventional sales made of property belonging to the Augustinian monastery. The Augustinian province of Michoacán, to which the San Luis Potosí community was affiliated, adopted a policy of voluntary sales of its holdings. At first some difficulties were experienced, as several of the other regular orders found, because of the monastery garden. This was very extensive, covering a large part of the six blocks connected into one

[1] MH 1857, addenda, pp. 472–81.   [2] *BSMGE*, vol. VII, 1859.

property owned by the Augustinians.[1] In 1856 it was rented by a doctor at 50 pesos a year, a quite modest sum. In fact the monks were not interested in entering into a business deal over it, for all they required was someone who would cultivate the trees and look after the security of the monastery. After the Lerdo law the state governor proposed the opening of a street through the garden and the prior consented to this. The new street would leave part of the garden separated from the building and the prior wanted to sell this section, divided into five plots. The doctor, however, asked for adjudication and this was granted to him by the judge. The prior then claimed that the doctor had renounced his right to adjudication verbally and before witnesses, and on 28 October, he asked the Minister of Justice, Ezequiel Montes, to recognize the monastery's right to sell that part of the garden. Montes referred the matter to his colleague, Lerdo, who resolved on 8 November that the prior could go to the courts, which was of course a slow and costly procedure.[2] The monastery preferred to negotiate and a year later an agreement was reached under which the doctor desisted from his claims to adjudication in exchange for two of the plots in the garden, which were now of no interest to the monastery since it had retained the parts adjacent to the cells. The three remaining plots were sold a short time afterwards.[3]

Apparently the Augustinians had no difficulty with the conventional sale of their other properties. The aforementioned hacienda was sold on 22 September to the tenant, Paulo Verástegui, for 50,000 pesos, which was the sum calculated by capitalizing the rent at 4·6%. It was a high price, especially taking into account the fact that the hacienda was not a sugar plantation.[4] Perhaps the property suited the buyer because of its location, since it was near to others he owned in the same region.

The Augustinians were equally fortunate in selling their urban houses, which in September and October 1856 were bought by the tenants under article 10 of the regulations governing the law. In the instruments of sale it is explained that the monastery was obliged to sell because 'the province was severely encumbered as a result of costly litigation...monthly loans which were being made to the Supreme Government, and a debt owed to Sr. don Cayetano Gómez', a capitalist from Morelia to whom further

[1] See the plan of the city in 1847, reproduced in P. F. Velázquez, *Historia de San Luis Potosí* (Mexico, 1947), vol. III, p. 242.

[2] MH 1857, addenda, pp. 108–11.

[3] 1857 register of I. Calvillo, fols. 150, 153, and that of 1858, fol. 78, Archivo de Notarías de San Luis Potosí (cited hereinafter as ANSLP).

[4] Register of Manuel Arriola, ANSLP, according to information from Rafael Montejano y Aguiñaga.

reference will be made shortly, or simply because of 'the circumstances of the time'. Hence, according to the instruments, the monastery sold its houses, now in poor condition, at a low price. At the same time, however, a separate, secret agreement was signed in which the buyer 'declares that, although in the said deeds of sale, the sale price is given as paid, this is not so. Instead he accepts the price as a mortgage loan, with the obligation to execute the respective instrument, when the Pope approves the sales and the disentailment law is not revoked. Should the contrary happen, he will return the property...' For the monastery the advantages of this arrangement are obvious. Moreover the prices which the Augustinians achieved were much higher than the fiscal valuation. Perhaps in order to have to pay less tax, they must have returned a lower value for their houses. In fact it is odd that the thirty houses belonging to San Francisco (in San Luis Potosí the latter did have real estate) were valued at 25,700 pesos, the thirty-six of Carmen at 26,600, the sixty-seven of La Merced at 33,490 and yet the thirty of San Agustín were worth only 5,625. Subsequently, unlike San Agustín, the houses of the other corporations, particularly those of Carmen, San Francisco, the hospital and the brotherhood of Animas were disentailed for a price lower than the fiscal valuation. One exception were those of La Merced, which realized their full valuation price. The conventional sales are given in appendix XIII.

The delay in the disentailment meant that this was continued strongly in 1857, especially in the months March to May, when a great number of transactions were recorded in the notarial register. Almost all were auction sales, which followed this formula: '...the Prefect, several interested parties being present, allowed five minutes for bidding, and after several offers, the final one was made by Sr... for...' The competition does not seem to have been very keen judging by the price, which was almost always two-thirds of the fiscal valuation. The bidders were more or less the same people who had bought in 1856 and who were to buy in 1859–61. As the information for these latter years is more complete, the nature of the buyers will be discussed in chapter 6. The sales can be seen in detail in appendix XIV.

Finally, the adjudications of property owned above all by the brotherhoods in Río Verde have been consulted. These are all reproduced in the 1857 report. Only at the end of 1856 were there any adjudications as a result of a denouncement, and several auctions for larger amounts.[1]

---

[1] *Registro en que constan las adjudicaciones que se han verificado en este distrito de las fincas de corporaciones civiles y eclesiásticos, desde el 29 septiembre último hasta el 16 de noviembre de 1856,* parish archive of Río Verde, microfilm in the library of the University of San Luis Potosí.

THE DISENTAILMENT IN MICHOACÁN

The beautiful state of Michoacán, with 600,000 inhabitants, was known for its agricultural, forestry and mining wealth.[1] Its wheat haciendas, situated in a temperate zone in the northern part of the state, were the best in the country. The owners were well aware of their interests and together with their colleagues in the state of Puebla they joined the hacendados living in Mexico City in a protest against an agrarian reform project, which was being discussed at the time in the national congress.[2] At the end of July 1856 the best-known landowners were Cayetano Gómez, Juan Campero Calderón, Agustín Luna, Ignacio Alva, Francisco and Norberto Páramo, J. R. Patiño, G. de Carrasquedo, and I. Muñoz Campuzano. It was a characteristic feature of Michoacán, unlike the other states so far described, that at least three of the local hacendados were active as leaders in the liberal movement. These were the brilliant Melchor Ocampo, owner of the hacienda Pomoca, near Maravatío; Epitacio Huerta, who left his work on his hacienda Tunguitiro, near Coeneo, to direct military operations against the dictatorship of Santa Anna;[3] and finally, Porfirio García de León. Of course, these three men were not the only landowners in the national liberal movement, but what made them outstanding was the fact that they were real farmers, who lived for at least part of the time on their estates, whereas the others were city men who used their haciendas only as a secondary activity.

Morelia, the state capital with 33,000 inhabitants,[4] was the mercantile centre but perhaps because of the distance from Mexico City to the east and from Guadalajara to the west, and the lack of direct access to the sea, there were scarcely any merchants in it who were not Mexican or Spaniards.[5] One of the few firms which, judging by its name, Macouzet and Co., was foreign, certainly existed in 1858.[6] This absence of foreigners perhaps meant that the commercial atmosphere was more national. Some merchants, for example Félix Alva, fought for the liberal cause.[7]

It was also perhaps due to such factors as the above that Michoacán at

[1] J. G. Romero, *Noticias para formar la estadística del obispado de Michoacán* (Mexico, 1862), p. 39.
[2] *Representaciones que hacen al congreso constituyente...*, cited in chapter 2.
[3] J. Bravo Ugarte, *Historia sucinta de Michoacán* (Mexico, 1964), vol. III, p. 96.
[4] Romero, *Noticias*, 36.
[5] Maillefert, 297–9.
[6] On 19 January 1859 a loan from this firm to D. García de Carrasquedo was confirmed; register of M. Valdovinos, fol. 257, Archivo de Notarías de Morelia (cited hereinafter as ANMor).
[7] Bravo Ugarte, *Historia de Michoacán*, III, 340.

that time had no textile factory, although one of its citizens, Cayetano Gómez—the same person that the Augustinians in San Luis Potosí indicated as the creditor of the Augustinian province of Michoacán—did own the cotton mill, San Cayetano, in the federal territory of Colima.[1] Originally Gómez was the main merchant in Morelia.[2]

No complete account of Church wealth in Michoacán on the eve of the Reform is available.[3] There are only a few figures on the monastic possessions. There were five monasteries in Morelia: a Franciscan; one of the Order of San Diego (members of this were also called the 'reformed of San Francisco'); an Augustinian; one of Carmen; and one of La Merced. Only a Dominican was lacking. The richest was the Augustinian, which in 1856, in addition to numerous haciendas and ranches, owned twenty-nine houses in the state capital.[4] The Carmelites had thirty-eight very poor houses in Morelia,[5] the Mercedarians had eighteen, which were likewise not very productive, and the Orders of San Diego and San Francisco had no real estate. The transactions noted in the 1857 report indicate that the nuns of Santa Catarina had several properties. Contrary to what might be expected in view of Morelia's magnificent cathedral, the bishopric does not seem to have been rich in property holdings. Among the civil corporations the poor house and the council each owned one hacienda. The Augustinians therefore possessed about half of the corporately owned real estate in the state of Michoacán.

According to the 1857 report, property to the value of 935,481 pesos was disentailed in the state in 1856.[6] The disentailment must have been reasonably complete, as all the houses belonging to San Agustín and La Merced were sold. In fact it seems that the latter monastery sold more houses than it owned. This can be explained partly by some possessions having been concealed, and partly because a house could have out-

---

[1] *Memoria de la Dirección General de Industria,* table 3; at that time Colima was in the department of Michoacán.

[2] *Segunda exposición que el comercio de la capital del departamento de Morelia hace al soberano congreso, manifestándole la justicia y necesidad de derogar la ley de 26 de noviembre de 1839 que aumentó los derechos de consumo a los efectos extranjeros en las aduanas interiores* (Mexico, 1840).

[3] The details in *Diccionario universal,* vol. v, 1854, pp. 365–70, and Romero, *Noticias,* do not seem exact or complete.

[4] AGN, JE, vol. 48, table 4 and a special table, *Estado que manifiesta el número de conventos, religiosos, novicios, curatos, cátedras, alumnos internos y externos, escuelas, niños, fincas rústicas y urbanas, sus productos, capitales activos y pasivos, limosnas y obvenciones de esta provincia de agustinos de Michoacán,* dated 26 January 1856.

[5] AGN, ibid., and a special table, *Estado general de los bienes y gravámenes que actualmente tiene la provincia de religiosos carmelitas descalzos de San Alberto en el año de 1856,* dated 20 February 1856.

[6] MH 1857, addenda, pp. 413–25.

buildings, which were sometimes considered separately. Two properties belonging to San Diego were also sold, although according to the official list this monastery did not have any. The houses of El Carmen do not appear in the 1857 report, but an examination of the notarial registers reveals that some were indeed adjudicated.

The register of the notary Manuel Valdovinos for the year 1856–57 begins precisely with the instruments relating to El Carmen. The first transaction was as follows:[1] José D. Navarro, tenant of a house owned by the monastery, wrote on 8 August that he had gone to see the prior with the purpose of seeking an adjudication by agreement. The prior told him that all the houses were already sold, and moreover that anyone who bought property under the Lerdo law would be automatically excommunicated. Navarro therefore asked the judge to assign the house to him. This was granted but eventually the tenant decided against it when he learned that he would have to pay a tax. He was poor and, as he stated in a second letter written by another person, he did not know how to sign his name.

After this the register continues with several adjudications of Carmelite houses and on 25 September the sale of the Augustinian holdings began. The Augustinian province of Michoacán, which comprised monasteries in the state of that name, and in the states of Jalisco, Guanajuato, Querétaro, Zacatecas, Durango and San Luis Potosí, adopted from the beginning a conciliatory attitude towards the Lerdo law. News of the law reached Morelia on 2 July, which was the day on which the capital's newspapers arrived, and it was put in force on the 5th of the month. In those three days the Augustinians took steps to sell some properties. Thus on 7 July they sold an hacienda in Cuitzeo for 40,000 pesos, before the law had been published in the town. The price was by means of a mortgage at 5%, which meant that nothing was paid in cash. Suspecting an attempt to evade the law, the state government annulled the sale. Then the lawyer Teófilo García de Carrasquedo, son of the buyer, asked Lerdo to approve the transaction since his father, Isidro, was the tenant of the hacienda. His father had been secretary of the state government in 1846.[2] Lerdo granted this request on 16 August.[3] This is the first transaction recorded in the list for Michoacán in the 1857 report. The list was almost certainly printed in chronological order.

---

[1] Fols. 8 ff.

[2] J. Rodríguez de San Miguel, *La república mexicana en 1846, o sea directorio general de los supremos poderes, y de las principales autoridades, corporaciones y oficinas de la nación* (Mexico, 1845).

[3] MH 1857, pp. 24, 26, 69.

The monastery did not always want to sell its property to its long-standing tenants. Four persons, tenants for many years of various lands on an hacienda in the state of Guanajuato, complained that a new tenant had appeared on 14 July, apparently a priest, who now was seeking to deprive them of their rights, alleging that the Augustinian province had rented the same lands to him on 12 April before the notary Valdovinos. The register for 1856–57 begins on 8 July and the previous one ends with December 1855. The one corresponding to the intervening period, from January–June, is missing and therefore it cannot be ascertained if the alleged contract really existed. In Lerdo's opinion the law was so clear that any decision by him was superfluous,[1] but in spite of this, or perhaps because of this, the matter was still pending at the end of 1856, judging from the omission of all the contending parties from the buyers listed in the 1857 report.

It seems that the conciliatory attitude of the Augustinians earned a certain benevolence from Lerdo. The monastery in Morelia decided to give a part of their garden—which was not let—to the town council for nothing. The latter wanted to open two streets through it and on 2 September Lerdo responded by approving the sale of the rest of the garden.[2] Perhaps because of this the following conventional sales were conducted without difficulty. On 25 September the province sold the hacienda Taretan[3] for 200,000 pesos to its tenant, Cayetano Gómez.[4] According to the instrument, a contract promising sale already existed between Gómez and the province, possibly as a result of the loan he made to it. The creditor demanded that the contract be fulfilled, and when the Lerdo law was promulgated he asked the government for permission to buy, although such approval was unnecessary under the regulations governing the law. The rent of the hacienda is not indicated nor is the way in which the price was determined, but the terms of payment are given; the buyer was to pay nothing in cash but he would mortgage the property for the 200,000 pesos at 5% annual interest, payable twice a year, as if it was rent. The mortgage was redeemable at any time. The hacienda also had previous mortgages on it, but the amount of these had not been decided when the transaction was concluded. The buyer would probably accept responsibility for these. One important stipulation was as follows: if the government should again permit the clergy to own real estate, Gómez

---

[1] Ibid., pp. 65–6.

[2] Ibid., p. 74.

[3] The provinces had goods apart from those belonging to the monasteries under their jurisdiction.

[4] 1856–1857 register, ANMor, fols. 45 ff.; MH 1857, addenda, p. 415.

would return the hacienda and continue as before as the tenant. The deed was signed by the prior of the Cuitzeo monastery in the name of the Augustinian province.

Two days earlier, on 23 September, the provincial had authorized the Morelia monastery to sell its holdings, on condition that the sales were for the true value and not according to a capitalization of the rent at 6%. This was perhaps partly because the monastery let its properties for an amount less than they were really worth.[1] No instrument of sale indicated the rent that was paid for any property, and in this respect the transactions undertaken in Morelia differ from those recorded by the notaries in the states already investigated.

The four conventional sales made from 1 to 3 October,[2] which include one effected by the bishopric, apparently following the example of the Augustinians, were in all probability made to the tenants, because to sell them a house did not need special permission from the government. On the other hand the seven subsequent transactions, all on 4 October, were certainly not to tenants because each has attached a special permit from the state government to sell the house 'as the tenant had renounced his rights'.[3] Most of the buyers of these houses were professional people and liberal merchants, and this was to be expected, as to obtain permission for such a transaction, some access to government circles was probably necessary. The next case is of interest because it concerns a large rural property. On 4 October San Agustín sold an hacienda for 24,000 pesos to the merchant and landowner Agustín Luna.[4] Payment was to be made as follows: 16,000 on a redeemable mortgage at 5% and 8,000 in annual sums of 2,000. The buyer had permission to purchase because the tenant had renounced his rights, and he agreed to respect the tenancy. When the latter contract had terminated, Luna would receive the hacienda. After this there are details of seven conventional sales of the Augustinian houses in Morelia, all being made with the previous renunciation of the tenants. Two other transactions will be mentioned here because they concern haciendas: on 4 October the same Augustinian monastery sold an hacienda for 31,000 pesos to the merchant Manuel Cárdenas. 30,000 of this was by redeemable mortgage at 5% and the buyer was to settle the remaining 1,000 in three payments to be made in 1857. The latter 1,000 had already been paid by 22 October, according to a note in the margin of the

---

[1] The authorization is inserted in the same register (1856–1857) between later deeds.
[2] Fols. 53 to 58, 1856–1857 register, ANMor.
[3] Fols. 63–70, ibid.
[4] Fol. 73, ibid.; *Representaciones que hacen al congreso constituyente...*; Maillefert, 298.

register.[1] There is no special permission attached and so it can be assumed that the buyer was the tenant. The second case, dated 8 October, is similar:[2] the monastery sold an hacienda for 37,000 pesos to the landowner J. Campero Calderón (called in the 1857 report J. C. Calderón, pp. 414–15 of the addenda, and moreover the sale was recorded twice in error). Of the 37,000, all but 1,000, to be paid in cash the next year, was on the usual mortgage basis. Nevertheless the buyer made the required cash payment of 24 October. He also seems to have been the tenant. Almost all these transactions appear in the 1857 report.

There were scarcely any cases of disentailment in 1857 recorded by the notary Valdovinos. The disentailment had been more or less completed in 1856.

JALISCO

The state of this name is the most western of those studied in this book. Partly because of the distance from Mexico City and partly through the proximity to the Pacific, the capital, Guadalajara, enjoyed since early colonial times a very special place, to the extent that in several respects it was independent of the central authorities. Its importance is revealed by the fact that in 1810 it was one of the four cities in New Spain which had a printing press. In 1854–56 the state had approximately 800,000 inhabitants and the capital about 70,000, or almost as many as Puebla.[3] The short distance between Guadalajara and the maritime ports gave the city a more cosmopolitan character than, for example, Morelia and San Luis Potosí. In 1867 there were among its merchants a number of persons with English, French or German surnames, although Mexicans and Spaniards predominated.[4] Agriculture and industry were the most outstanding of the economic activities. To the east of the state there were rich haciendas typical of the region called El Bajío, and some of these belonged to the Church. In 1856 there were five cotton mills: Jauja, belonging to Barrón, Forbes and Co.; Prosperidad Jalisciense, owned by the Guadalajara merchant José Palomar, who also had the paper mill El Batán; Experiencia and Escoba, belonging to Olazagarre, Prieto and Co.; and finally Bellavista, which belonged to Juan Antonio Aguirre.[5] About 1880 Experiencia was

[1] Fol. 92, 1856–1857 register, ANMor.
[2] Fol. 105, ibid.
[3] *Diccionario universal*, IV, 1854; L. Banda, *Estadística de Jalisco, formada con vista de los mejores datos oficiales y noticias ministradas por sujetos idóneos, en los años de 1854 a 1863* (Guadalajara, 1873); L. González y González, 'La situación social de Jalisco en vísperas de la Reforma', in *La Reforma en Jalisco y el Bajío* (Guadalajara, 1959).
[4] Maillefert, 292–4.
[5] *Memoria de Fomento*, 1857.

in the hands of F. Martínez Negrete, who was a member of the firm of the same name.[1] The industries which arose during the conservative regime of Santa Anna would indicate that the manufacturers in Jalisco were also Mexicans. Unlike Morelia, the liberal movement and government in Guadalajara were directed by lawyers such as Ogazón, his nephew Vallarta[2] and the Camarena family.

Details are available only of those ecclesiastical properties which belonged to the monastic orders in the state of Jalisco. The monastery or college of San Agustín of Guadalajara had an hacienda valued at 36,000 pesos (calculated by capitalizing rent at 5%), and fifty-eight houses worth 186,000 pesos;[3] the Carmelites had one hacienda valued at 66,000 and twenty-two houses worth 28,000;[4] the Dominicans sixty-five houses at 80,000; the Franciscans eight houses at 10,000; and the Mercedarians thirty-one very poor houses at 10,000.[5] Hence the monastic orders in Jalisco had only two haciendas, which was a very small proportion of their total number in the state.

Four nunneries had 419 houses valued at 800,000 pesos and mortgages to the extent of 333,000 pesos,[6] compared with which the capital of the monasteries was insignificant. The Capuchines, who had no property, formed the fifth convent. Together the regular orders in Guadalajara, even though richer than those of Morelia, had real estate worth approximately 1·2 million pesos, or less than one-third of the amount held by those in Puebla. This is quite significant, bearing in mind that the Guadalajara population almost equalled that of Puebla. The wealth of the other sectors of the Church is not known. According to the 1857 report, only five haciendas were disentailed in Jalisco in 1856, including one owned by the Casa de Misericordia (Hospicio de Cabañas), which was a charitable institution administered by the bishop.[7] It is possible that the haciendas were not all sold in 1856 or perhaps some transactions of that year were omitted in the 1857 report which states that in Jalisco real estate to the value of 820,554 pesos was disentailed in 1856. This amount represents only a small part of total clerical wealth in the state, for in 1865–66 purchases of nationalized goods worth 2,000,000 pesos were presented for revision. The delay in the disentailment is revealed by the example of the

[1] E. Busto, *Estadística de la república mexicana* (Mexico, 1880), vol. I, table 2.
[2] M. González Navarro (ed.), *Vallarta en la Reforma* (Mexico, 1956), pp. xxiv, ix.
[3] AGN, JE, vol. 48, *Estado*, 26 January 1856.
[4] AGN, ibid., *Estado*, 20 February 1856.
[5] Table of 1856 made for a *Memoria de Justicia*; AGN, JE, vol. 48, fols. 24–6.
[6] *Memoria de Justicia*, 1844, table 7.
[7] 1856 register of Juan Riestra, Archivo de Notarías de Guadalajara (cited hereinafter as ANG), fol. 306.

Augustinian monastery which owned fifty-eight houses, only twenty of which were sold in 1856.

Nevertheless, the fact that the disentailment was not completed cannot be explained by Church hostility to the Lerdo law. The notarial registers in Guadalajara which have been consulted indicate more the contrary. In that of the notary Ramón Barbosa for 1856, the first disentailment deeds to be examined concerned municipal property—these were signed by the Receiver, A. Camarena. Next, seven documents were read in which the different monasteries in the city sold houses to various people during September and October.[1] These are followed by transactions of sales of the Augustinian houses. No case of an adjudication or of an auction was found in the register. Only conventional sales are recorded and signed by representatives of the monastic orders. The same thing is to be noted in the register of Juan Riestra for 1856, from which twenty-seven conventional sales concerning three haciendas and twenty-four houses in Guadalajara were examined in detail. These were owned by monasteries and convents, a hospital, the Cabañas poor house, the office of vacant *capellanías* and pious works, and a school.[2] Among the monasteries San Agustín was predominant, although it must not be forgotten that this was a teaching community. The details can be seen in appendix xv, although some aspects may be singled out here. The three most costly properties were haciendas and all were sold to their tenants. One of the latter was Pedro J. Prieto, possibly a partner in the industrial firm of Olazagarre, Prieto and Co., and another the lawyer Jesús Camarena. In respect of the latter, Pedro and Merced Camarena appear as the buyers in the register, but in the 1857 report Jesús Camarena is noted. It may be that they were his children. As for the sale prices, only the valuation of the Carmen hacienda is known. This was valued at 66,000 pesos (rent capitalized at 5%) but it was sold for 95,000, equalling a rent of only 3·5%. The price of the houses varied between 5,000 and 10,000 pesos but there were several cheaper and several more expensive. All the buyers were tenants and many of them were merchants, although this does not necessarily mean that there was a greater proportion of merchants among the buyers in Guadalajara than in the other cities already studied. It may simply mean that the Guadalajara notaries never forgot to write after the name of the buyer the words 'of this city and business'. By implication almost all the merchants were Mexicans, for when any foreigner was noted in the registers he always had to show his safe conduct pass.

The sales by the Augustinian monastery as usual offer several interesting

---

[1] Fols. 202–91.   [2] Fols. 302–420.

examples. The monastery owned a number of houses in the most central part of the city, which were rented to merchants who conducted their business from them. The tenants began to prepare to acquire their house and shop—some probably lived above the shops. In some instances the tenants agreed with the monastery to liquidate the purchase price with merchandise, an arrangement no doubt also convenient to the friars. For example, Sra. M. de Pacheco bought her property for 3,600 pesos, recognizing this sum as a mortgage which was to return a 5% annual interest. The value of each payment on account was to be a maximum of 20% of the capital, prior notice of six months being given. Finally, at least a year must elapse before a further payment could be demanded.

As in Morelia, but unlike the other cities in which the notarial registers have been consulted, those in Guadalajara do not indicate the rent paid by the tenants. Also as in Morelia, the buyers' debts in the Jalisco capital were at 5% annual interest. From this it can be concluded that the sale price was calculated by capitalizing the rent at 5%; in other words, the buyers would continue paying the corporation the same amount as before, but now as interest, not as rent. The capitalization at 5% gave the Church the opportunity to obtain higher prices than those that would have been realized in strict conformity with the Lerdo law. Why, however, were the tenants prepared to purchase at a higher price, when they could have claimed the house at 6% in accordance with the law? Was it simply to avoid complications? One possible partial explanation has been suggested by a local historian: the capitalization at 6% ordered by the Lerdo law was unjust, according to the writer, because many mortgages had been contracted at 3% a year. Hence the law reduced the price of the properties by half.[1] If there is any truth in this affirmation, then it would partly explain the purchases, as the tenants still acquired the houses at a discount, although not as large as that offered by Lerdo. It appears that the Church in Guadalajara was at that time more liberal than in other parts of the country[2] but even if this was not the case a conciliatory and reasonable attitude could and did produce benefits for it. Whatever the truth of the matter, the monasteries, especially the Augustinian, and all the other ecclesiastical corporations in Guadalajara, did not wait in 1856 for the tenants to be assigned the houses. Instead they were sold to them at a higher price than that guaranteed by the law. The register for 1856 of the notary Luis Gonzaga Arreola also contains only conventional sales and no adjudication of clerical goods. This is unique in the whole country—not

---

[1] L. Pérez Verdía, *Historia particular del estado de Jalisco*, II, 518.
[2] Bravo Ugarte, *Historia de México*, III, book I, 284.

forgetting the limited number of registers examined—in that all the disentailment transactions in 1856 were by means of conventional or voluntary sales by the ecclesiastical corporations. This applied not only to the regular clergy but also to the secular branch.

It has been shown that in 1856 only a small part of clerical properties in Jalisco were disentailed or sold. The disentailment continued in 1857 but now not in the form of conventional sales but by denouncements and auctions. In the register of Jesús Durán for 1857—no transactions were noted by him in 1856—twelve adjudication instruments resulting from denouncement or auction were examined.[1] These examples all took place in the last three months of the year and most of the assigned properties belonged to the regular orders. Needless to say the deeds were not signed by the clergy but by the civil authorities. The price was usually two-thirds of the value of the property. The surnames indicate that all the adjudicators were Mexican or Spanish. Two were lawyers, presumably Mexican. In at least one case a person denounced several houses and later distributed them to other people,[2] although unlike in Mexico City companies were not formed for the purpose of the auctions, perhaps because of the relatively small number of transactions involved.

THE COUNTRY AS A WHOLE

The six federal entities which have been studied form only a minority of the country, both in number and in the area they comprise. Nevertheless the picture changes if the distribution of Church wealth in the different states of the republic is taken into account. When the government imposed a forced loan of 2,000,000 pesos on the Church on 19 November 1846, this sum was allotted in proportion to the archbishopric of Mexico and the five sees of Puebla, Guadalajara, Michoacán, Oaxaca and Durango. The amount assigned to each diocese was at the same time distributed between the different states or parts of them.[3] The bishoprics of Yucatan, Chiapas, Monterrey, Sonora and California, that is the south-east, with its special features, were not included, and nor was the unpopulated and poor northern area of the country. These distant regions will not be referred to in this work. It can be assumed that the government, through the Ministry of Justice and Ecclesiastical Affairs, had a more or less exact idea of Church wealth, and that therefore the proportions made by the law were in general terms correct.

[1] 1857 register of Jesús Durán, ANG, fols. 9–55.
[2] 1861 register of Jesús Durán, ANG, fol. 24, 28 February where the auction of 31 August 1857 is mentioned. [3] Dublán y Lozano, v, 214.

The allotted amounts were as follows: to the Federal District, 800,000 pesos; state of Puebla, 250,000; Veracruz, 158,000 (of this, 8,000 pertained to the archbishopric of Mexico); San Luis Potosí, 42,000 (30,000 for that part belonging to the diocese of Michoacán, 10,000 for that of Guadalajara and 2,000 to the archbishopric); Michoacán, 60,000; Jalisco, 135,000. The total amounted to 1,445,000, almost three-quarters of the 2,000,000 pesos demanded by the government. If the peripheral regions are now included, ecclesiastical possessions in the six federal entities probably amounted to two-thirds of all Church wealth in Mexico. This was of course in 1846 but it can be assumed with reasonable certainty that no radical changes had occurred in ten years.

It must now be asked if the property and capital disentailed in 1856 also corresponded to two-thirds of the value of all the transactions in the republic. An addition of the figures given in the 1857 report—13,000,000 pesos approximately, for the district of Mexico; 2,600,000 for Puebla; 1,700,000 for Veracruz; 150,000 for San Luis Potosí; 950,000 for Michoacán; and more than 820,000 for Jalisco—gives a total of 19,200,000, or four-fifths of the overall total of 23,000,000 pesos, including Yucatan. It must be remembered, however, that the disentailment included the properties of civil corporations which in some regions, for example Veracruz, were quite substantial. The main cause of the difference in proportions, however, was the varying pace of the disentailment in the different federal entities. Whereas in Veracruz and Michoacán the disentailment was fairly complete in 1856, and in the nation's capital most of the corporate properties were disentailed, on the other hand in Puebla and San Luis Potosí certainly only a small part were sold.

These disproportions are most evident in the figures relating to Querétaro. In 1846 this state was assigned 40,000 pesos, about the same as San Luis Potosí. In 1856 properties were disentailed in Querétaro for 251,809 pesos, but of this amount only 83,333 corresponded to Church real estate (sale of an hacienda owned by El Carmen). Almost all the rest was from the sale in plots of the hacienda La Esperanza, which belonged to the municipality. It can be supposed that the disentailment in Querétaro was accelerated in the following year, as happened in Puebla and San Luis Potosí.

The hypothesis that the clerical possessions in the six federal entities studied in this work formed two-thirds of all Church property and capital, appears to be confirmed by the figures given in the revision of the nationalization operations, which was carried out during the imperial administration in 1865–66.[1] The total Church wealth nationalized, including real estate and capital, amounted to 62,000,000 pesos. Of this sum, approximately 19,750,000 pertained to the Federal District; 10,650,000 to Puebla; 2,300,000 to Veracruz; 1,000,000 to San Luis Potosí; 4,600,000 to Michoacán; and 4,600,000 to Jalisco: a total therefore of 42,900,000 pesos, which equals a little over two-thirds of the 62,000,000. This latter sum includes the sales of clerical possessions in the states of Yucatan, Campeche and Nuevo León, but it omits those of Chiapas, Chihuahua, Guerrero, Sonora, Tabasco and Tamaulipas. The proportion of two-thirds therefore is approximately correct.

The six federal entities comprise the greater part of Church property and capital and of the nationalization transactions, and moreover they can be considered as regions representative of the country. The city of Mexico was the financial, political and intellectual capital of the republic and as such it was imitated everywhere. Puebla was the country's industrial centre and it included the agricultural district of Atlixco. The port of Veracruz was the most important trading centre, together with mercantile and industrial cities like Jalapa, Orizaba and Córdoba. San Luis Potosí can be taken as an example of a mining state, and the northern part of Michoacán as typical of the agricultural region extending between Querétaro and Guadalajara, which is known as the Bajío. Several states representative of the different economic activities have therefore been used, and they also illustrate the geographical regions of the country: Mexico and Puebla—the centre; Veracruz—the tropical east; San Luis Potosí—the semi desert, mining north; Michoacán and Jalisco—the temperate and agricultural west. Hence together the five states and the federal district may be considered characteristic of the country. On the basis of what happened in them, one can reasonably generalize about the entire republic.

This claim is also confirmed by an analysis of the adjudications for more than 10,000 pesos each, which were made in 1856 in the twenty-two states, territories and federal district. The information relating to the states not included in this work has been taken from the figures given in the 1857 report and this is basically the same as that described for the federal district and the states of Puebla, Veracruz, San Luis Potosí, Michoacán and Jalisco. This impression is confirmed even more if a list of fifty buyers of 25,000 pesos or more each is compiled from the report.[2]

[1] 'Operaciones presentadas a revisión al llamado imperio, hasta marzo de 1866', *Memoria de Hacienda*, 1873, document 19.

[2] J. Bazant, 'La desamortización de los bienes corporativos de 1856', *Historia Mexicana*, XVI, no. 2 (October–December 1966).

This list, which also includes the states of Guanajuato, Mexico, Querétaro, Oaxaca, Colima and Zacatecas, reveals that most buyers were, in descending order of importance, merchants, public officials, and hacendados; and that they were, in the majority of cases, Mexicans. Hence what we have seen in detail in the cities of Mexico, Puebla, Veracruz, San Luis Potosí, Morelia and Guadalajara is confirmed. It is also likely that the majority of smaller buyers were throughout the country the tenants and general public, as was the case in the five cities.[1]

If this was so, then one may conclude that the great number of persons who refused to buy ecclesiastical possessions in 1856–57, thus making way for denouncements and auction sales, certainly explains the ease with which Zuloaga's reactionary government was established in January 1858. At the same time, however, the fact that the majority of tenants did indeed carry out the disentailment and that many merchants and professional people, who were the most progressive elements in society, expedited the auctions, perhaps explains the final victory of liberal arms some three years later.

[1] This was the case in the city of Oaxaca. See C. R. Berry, 'The fiction and fact of the Reform: the case of the central district of Oaxaca, 1856–67', *The Americas*, XXVI (January 1970), no. 3, 277–90.

CHAPTER 4

THE CIVIL WAR, 1858–60

The efforts of the liberals culminated in the publication of the constitution of 5 February 1857, which embodied the ideals and aims formulated during the previous two decades. The disentailment, however, was not destined to endure in the form of the Lerdo law. The first signs of a change were noticed after the resignation of Lerdo, which was interpreted as a defeat for the radical group.[1] A subtle movement in public opinion was particularly revealed in the petition sent to President Comonfort on 17 February 1857. This was signed by many well-known people and they asked that the monastery of San Francisco, which had been closed since September of the previous year, should be reopened.[2] In Mexico, as in other parts of the world, Saint Francis and the monastic order which he founded inspired respect even among those who were not fervent believers. Two days later Comonfort issued a decree, signed by the Minister of Justice, José María Iglesias, re-establishing the monastery 'in that part of the building designated by the Minister for Development'. This was an allusion to the new street which had recently been opened through the property.[3] The monastery remained basically intact and the monks returned.

ANNULMENT OF THE LERDO LAW

The country needed a breathing space to digest the huge transfer of property caused by the disentailment and to permit the realignment of political forces. Thus the conservative newspaper, El Tiempo, acknowledged on 6 August 1857 that in spite of having been 'the origin of ruin for countless families', the Lerdo law was a fait accompli and should be sanctioned through a concordat with the Pope. But the voice of reason was not to prevail. The reactionary groups were not satisfied with the conservative approach lately adopted by Comonfort. They resorted to military revolt, as a result of which General Félix Zuloaga assumed the

[1] Report of the Committee of Mexican Bondholders (29 April 1861, London); A. de la Portilla, México en 1856 y 1857, 144.
[2] Riva Palacio, México a través de los siglos, v, 223.
[3] Dublán y Lozano, viii, 419.

presidency on 23 January 1858, and the civil war between the liberals and conservatives began. As the first act of his government Zuloaga declared null and void the law of 25 June 1856, although not before receiving a promise from the Church that it would lend him 1,500,000 pesos.[1]

The decree of 28 January revoked the disentailment law and its regulations in respect of the ecclesiastical corporations. All disentailment transactions were void and from that moment the Church regained complete ownership of its disentailed properties.[2] The corresponding regulations were issued on 1 March.[3] According to article 2, the corporations could collect the rents directly from the tenants or lessees (most of whom, as we have seen, had acquired their property under the Lerdo law). Article 5 stated that every adjudicator or buyer at auction was 'obliged to hand over to the respective community or corporation the title deeds which he had received from it, together with the certificate of adjudication or auction which had been issued'. To make sure that the latter was fulfilled, the decree threatened fines and imprisonment 'maintaining the detention until that which is herein stipulated is carried out' (article 6). No doubt it was not worthwhile for anyone to suffer this punishment. Since in many cases, however, the corporations had not handed over the title deeds to the adjudicators or successful bidders, the latter could not return them. On the other hand the regulations, which were certainly formulated in agreement with the wishes of the Church, tried to be just to the tenants who had taken advantage of the disentailment. For example it was ordered that 'the cost of any repair or maintenance work on the houses will be credited to their adjudicators or buyers, subject to prior justification of it' (article 11). As many adjudicators had carried out improvements to the houses, a thing they had previously been unwilling to do as tenants, it was just that the corporations should take them into consideration. Moreover, it was of course in the Church's interest for the future to be on good terms with the thousands of tenants. Another sign of good-will concerned the rural properties, which were to be returned after the harvest (article 14). As was to be expected, those people who were tenants of urban or rural property when the Lerdo law was promulgated were given the right to continue their tenancy under the terms in force before the law. Those who had been deprived of their tenancy as a result of the law could reassume it (article 25).

The decree, therefore, was limited to an attempt to erase the year and

---

[1] The minutes of the metropolitan chapter are given in Riva Palacio, *México a través de los siglos*, V, 308.   [2] Labastida, 214.   [3] Ibid.

a half which passed between the promulgation and the annulment of the Lerdo law. The Church did not attempt to punish the adjudicators who had acquired the houses, sometimes against their own conscience. To make any distinction would have needed an investigation of every case, and in rejecting this the Church showed considerable political acumen, for the possibility was open to it of attracting the support of many indifferent or hesitant people. The Church and the conservative party realized that they had to govern a nation which was in part anti-clerical. Only one punishment was imposed: those tenants who had allowed the term for adjudication to pass in order to be able to buy the house afterwards in an auction lost their rights to the tenancy, and the corporations were authorized to seek new occupants (article 26). Clearly the intention was to penalize those who had given signs that they wanted to speculate with the clerical properties. The number of persons of this type, however, seems to have been very small, for the tenants who wanted to acquire the property almost always had it assigned to themselves.

The government also committed itself to return to the buyers the sales tax. Those who had paid in bonds and certificates would have these returned immediately (article 9), but the government did not have the money to return the part that had been paid in cash which, taking the country as a whole, certainly amounted to more than 1,000,000 pesos.[1] The government promised to repay this with the issue of a bond (article 10).

The decree included in the ecclesiastical possessions that were to be returned the properties belonging to charitable institutions, such as hospitals, orphanages, poor houses 'and other establishments of this nature' (article 27), which included the brotherhoods and schools. The properties of the purely civil corporations, like the city and village councils, were not referred to in the decree or its regulations. A later measure, namely a decree of the reactionary government dated 9 May 1860, shows that the disentailment of municipal and communal properties was not affected. It declared that the civil corporations could own real estate, which they had been forbidden to do by the Lerdo law. Hence the sales made under the latter remained valid, and only the fraudulent or illegal disentailment transactions would be annulled.[2] All these operations therefore would have to be revised, but the conservative government did not now have time to do this. The conservatives were not motivated by an interest in municipal properties but by fiscal necessity. The decree ordered

[1] In 1856 alone the amount was 675,000 pesos; MH 1857, p. 535.
[2] MH 1870, p, 516; Colección Lafragua, vol. 120.

the buyers to redeem their mortgage debt within three months, paying the government in cash one-third of the price of the property.

Article 3 of the regulations, dated 1 March, ordered the notaries who had executed the deeds of adjudication or auction to proceed within fifteen days to write in the register, in the margin of each instrument which was not cancelled by the interested party, the following note: 'As a result of the provisions of the law of 28 January of the present year, this adjudication or sale is null and void; and the property to which it refers continues in the ownership and possession of the respective corporation or community.' Article 4 imposed heavy penalties on those notaries who refused to carry out this order, and the punishment was sufficiently severe to persuade them to obey.

It seems that few people went to the notaries to cancel the instruments personally, for the margins of the registers are filled with annotations, which are almost illegible. All the registers in the capital which have been examined contain the note stipulated by the decree. In Puebla, which during the civil war suffered the same fate as Mexico City, the notary Gregorio Sandoval anticipated the regulations of 1 March. As early as 12 February he made an entry after the final certificate in his 1857 register, cancelling all the instruments of adjudication and the conventional sales: 'By virtue of the circular which immediately follows...all instruments of adjudication, conventional and auction sales of property belonging to the venerable clergy, executed in respect of the law of 25 June 1856, are cancelled and null and void.'[1] The circular which he referred to was sent on 10 February by the Prefect of Puebla and it requested that, apart from the cancellation, the notaries should remit 'the names of the adjudicators and auction buyers, the ownership of the properties, and the date of the instruments'.[2] Finally, one example proves that article 4 of the regulations which also ordered an inspection of the notarial registers was implemented: 'This register was examined for the purposes expressed in the regulations of the law of 28 January. Puebla, 12 May 1858.' This was signed by two persons commissioned by the Puebla prefecture.

Although the port of Veracruz remained throughout in the control of the constitutional government, the conservative army was able to advance quite close to the city. In the spring of 1858 the conservatives occupied the towns of Orizaba, Córdoba and Jalapa, with the result that the disentailment deeds were cancelled in Orizaba—each one individually—

[1] 1856 register of Gregorio Sandoval, ANP, fol. 567.
[2] Ibid.

on 4 May, in Córdoba on 6 May and in Jalapa on 11 May. These places remained occupied, with one interruption, until August 1860.[1]

On the other hand, events in San Luis Potosí were more turbulent. The conservatives gained power there on 21 January 1858 by means of a military uprising,[2] and the disentailment instruments were cancelled between 22 and 30 March, at least in the register which was consulted. On 30 June of the same year the liberal army entered the state capital, but already by 12 September the conservatives were again in possession. On 3 April 1859 the liberals re-entered the city, on 24 November the conservatives, and on 30 April 1860 the liberals, this time for good.

The registers in San Luis Potosí and in the other cities, however, do not contain annotations by the liberals cancelling the annulments ordered by Zuloaga. Apparently the liberals thought that their decrees repealing everything enacted by Zuloaga and afterwards by Miramón were sufficient and there was no need to add notes in the margin of the registers.

Like the city of Veracruz, Morelia remained in the hands of the constitutionalists during the civil war, with the exception of a few days.[3] Therefore the registers in Morelia have no cancellations added. In Guadalajara, however, the disentailment instruments were annulled in 1858.

For some time the conservative government did not know what to do about one sort of disentailment operation, the conventional sales. On 28 June, four months after the promulgation of the regulations relating to the cancellation of the Lerdo law, Zuloaga declared null and void all the sales of clerical properties, including the conventional sales.[4] He had reasons for wanting to see the Church real estate kept intact. His decree must have caused considerable discontent among the many buyers who had bought their houses by mutual agreement with the ecclesiastical authorities. Even though the Church may have been prevailed upon to sell by the Lerdo law, the transactions were voluntary from the legal point of view. It may also be supposed that as the corporations had been able in some cases to sell to persons in their confidence, many of these buyers must have been supporters of the conservative regime. Indeed, the Church itself may have thought it convenient to maintain the validity of the sales, for sometimes a high price, secured by a mortgage, had been achieved. Finally it was a matter of indifference to Zuloaga, who was concerned with preserving clerical possessions, which he wanted to use as a guarantee for loans, whether the goods were in real estate or capital,

---

[1] González de Cossío, *Xalapa*, 236–8.   [2] Velázquez, *Historia de San Luis Potosí*, III, 286.
[3] Bravo Ugarte, *Historia de Michoacán*, III, 105.
[4] MH 1870, p. 481.

although the former was preferable. Thus five months later, on 6 December, the government resolved that 'all conventional sales of urban and rural properties contracted freely and deliberately by the ecclesiastical corporations before or after the law of 25 June 1856 are valid'.[1]

It seems that the law of 28 June annulling the sales was not taken seriously. This can be seen in the following example: in September 1856 the monastery of La Merced had sold two houses to its agent José María Salas. This transaction was one of the many effected by the monastery which were described in the previous chapter. It was not indicated whether the buyer was the tenant. The purchase price was 8,000 pesos, of which Salas paid 1,000 and owed the remainder. It was therefore a typical conventional sale, and it remained valid after 28 June, judging from a note, dated 24 July, in which the Prefect of La Merced decided to reduce Salas's debt to 4,000 pesos because 3,000 were owed to him for his remuneration.[2] In other words no notice was taken of the decree. Clearly, if a corporation had sold a house to a person of its own choosing there was no point in repudiating the transaction. It was no doubt because it was ineffectual that Zuloaga revoked the decree.

In San Luis Potosí the sales which the Augustinians had made in 1857 of five plots in the monastery garden were not cancelled, as is indicated by the absence of any annotations in the notarial register.[3] Fifteen other conventional sales by the monastery were nevertheless annulled on 5 January 1859 as the result of a private agreement from October 1856.

The decree of 28 January did not of course refer to the so-called conventional sales made in Puebla, for which the approval of the ecclesiastical corporations had not been obtained. These had been in essence a modification of the adjudications and as such they were all annulled.

The effect of the repeal of the Lerdo law on daily life was immediate. On the next day, 29 January 1858, the archbishop sent a circular to the corporations in which he asked for information on the following: the rent paid by the tenant before the adjudication, the sale price and the date of adjudication; how much the adjudicator had paid to the corporation in respect of interest on the capital (as we have seen, some paid and some did not); and if the house had been returned in the same condition as it was when sold. The circular ended by warning the corporations not to make any arrangements with adjudicators or buyers without having prior permission to do so. In reply to this circular, the corporations began to

---

[1] Decree of 6 December 1858, Colección Lafragua, vol. 120.
[2] AGN, PBN, leg. 1523, exp. 8, fols. 1–7.
[3] 1857 register of I. Calvillo, ANSLP, fols. 78, 150, 153.

inform the archbishop of their problems and their communications were entered in a notebook ninety-six pages in length.[1] This begins with 6 February and contains copies of 302 replies from the various monasteries, nunneries, hospitals, parishes, schools and brotherhoods. The fact that the two latter institutions were included, although not mentioned in the decree or regulations on the return of the properties, shows that they were covered by the law. Most of the copies are undated, but from notes in the margin it can be concluded that the last were written in April. It is not known whether a later notebook was compiled but it would be rather more likely that the problems and difficulties were encountered at the beginning. In the same way it is not known whether all the replies were copied in the notebook, although if this was the case then very few of the corporations obeyed the archbishop's order. If they had all done so and sent the detailed data on every one of the adjudicated or auctioned properties, the result would not have fitted into the notebook. The reports were not always detailed, however: for example, the wealthy archcon-fraternity of Aranzazú briefly answered that all its houses had been re-turned in good order except one, which was in ruins.[2]

The great majority of the cases recorded concern problems which arose when the decree of annulment was applied. The return of the adjudicated or auctioned properties was enforced throughout the terri-tory controlled by the conservatives and it could only be avoided by fleeing from the area. There were two ways of returning them: the liberals simply handed over the titles, when they had them, and began to pay rent again to the corporation; the conservatives asked to be forgiven for having adjudicated the house. The French diplomatic representative reported on 20 February that 'the amount of clerical possessions returned is already considerable. The newspapers are filled with letters from adjudicators whose intention is evidently to repent in an honourable and public manner. The spontaneous return is made by those who were forced by the circumstances to buy, so that they would not be deprived of their houses.'[3]

Several foreign merchants went so far as to protest against Zuloaga's law. In Puebla Edward Turnbull, a British citizen, even dared to register formally his protest on 24 March and, not being content with this, he made the notary write at the same time in the margin of the adjudication

[1] AHINAH, vol. II, no. 61.
[2] Ibid., fol. 41.
[3] These reports, useful for the years 1858–60 when Mexico was isolated from the world, were reproduced in L. Díaz (ed.), *Versión francesa de México. Informes diplomáticos* (Mexico, 1963–67); the quotation is from vol. II, 1858–61, p. 2.

instrument, 'compelled and enforced by the law of 28.1.1858 . . . the certified copy of this deed is returned to the proprietary corporation . . .'[1] This note was signed by Turnbull himself.[2] Encouraged by the latter, Manuel Lara, a United States citizen, also registered a protest with a notary on 6 April.[3] Curiously no Frenchman seems to have made a similar gesture of dissent, in spite of the fact that there were many among the buyers in Puebla. The explanation lies partly in the policies of the different nations for whereas, for example, the U.S. government sympathized with the liberal administration in Veracruz, the French representative had told his fellow citizens in the country from the very beginning that his government would not support the validity of the adjudications and that the whole affair was entirely at their own risk.[4] To some extent foreigners in general enjoyed in one sense a privileged position because they were considered to have no connection with revolutions and their consequences. Hence they could afford the luxury of protesting against certain government measures without the risk of imprisonment, although possibly exposing themselves to general hostility or personal revenge.

It appears that the problem which recurred most frequently when a property was returned involved the repairs and improvements made by adjudicators. These must have been frequent, considering that a critic, hostile to the Lerdo law, admitted that one favourable outcome of it was 'the activity noticed in the capital and other cities in repairing some houses', although he did not neglect to add that this 'could not be considered even slight compensation for the difficulties which that measure caused the government'.[5] Such cases are common both in the notebook and the documents preserved in the National Archive. Usually after haggling for a varying length of time, everything was settled amicably.[6]

Other cases are more interesting in their consequences, particularly those in which the tenants, obeying the mandates of the Church or their conscience, refused to claim adjudication of the house, permitting another person to do so. In many such instances they had lost the tenancy which they now reclaimed in accordance with the regulations of 1 March. These matters were registered in the notebook[7] and also in the large files housed

[1] Notary 5, 1858, ANP, fol. 29. [2] Ibid., 1856, fol. 211.

[3] Ibid., 1858, fol. 40.

[4] Díaz, *Versión francesa*, I, 304–5, II, 103.

[5] Portilla, *México en 1856 y 1857*, 70.

[6] R. J. Knowlton described one such case in 'Some practical effects of clerical opposition to the Mexican Reform, 1856–1860', *Hispanic American Historical Review*, XLV, 2 (May 1965), 252.

[7] For example, document no. 126, fol. 35, relating to a tenant of a house belonging to the Augustinian monastery.

in the National Archive. In the first one Sra. Rayón, apparently a devout believer, had lost her longstanding tenancy of a house owned by the convent of Santa Teresa la Antigua because she had not wanted to have the house assigned.[1] At the beginning of March she asked the archbishop to reinstate her as the tenant, but the efforts of the convent administrator to make the adjudicator vacate the house were unsuccessful. The administrator was Antonio María Salonio, a lawyer and former governor of the state of Veracruz, and the adjudicator was a government official. When Salonio reported the situation to the archbishop on 17 May he asked permission to allow the adjudicator to remain because he paid the rent with 'religious punctuality' and would even be prepared to pay more. In the interests of the convent Sra. Rayón's claim should not be accepted. After a prolonged correspondence in which the administrator defended the present tenant and referred to 'the sad circumstances of scarcity...the taxes and loans', the archbishop decided to compensate poor Sra. Rayón with a pension of twenty-five pesos a month for life. This was to be paid by the convent from the difference between the old rent and the new one, but the old woman probably had few years left to live. In return she was to renounce her claim to the tenancy. After doubling the rent the convent was still left with a little extra. The new contract stated that the tenant would have the right to buy the house should the convent decide to sell it. This was an important clause for it showed that the corporations were beginning to sell their properties.

In the second case agreement was not reached so easily.[2] The administrator was again A. M. Salonio and the convent Santa Teresa la Antigua, and the adjudicator, who had not been the tenant, was a government official. Problems arose from the beginning, for the adjudicator owed rent to the convent, presented it with an account for the cost of improvements and refused to vacate the house. In the end there was an agreement, and the adjudicator and the administrator concluded calling each other 'my very dear friend' and 'my very esteemed friend'.

Like any other institution the monasteries and convents had of course to bear in mind their own financial interests, and circumstances obliged them to desert their former tenants. It is noticeable that in both the above cases the tenants refused to vacate the house and the administrator re-

[1] AGN, PBN, leg. 125, '*Secretaría arzobispal, 1858. El señor mayordomo del convento de Santa Teresa la Antigua, consulta sobre la casa número 7 de la calle de este nombre, de que eran inquilinos las señoras Rayones*'.

[2] AGN, PBN, leg. 125, '*Secretaría arzobispal, 1858. El señor mayordomo del convento de Santa Teresa la Antigua, con relación a la casa número 4 del Puente de Dimas, que se adjudicó el señor Don José María Jarero*'.

ported that it was impossible to remove them. This confirms what has been previously said about the power of faits accomplis and vested interests. After all, it did not matter to the corporations who the tenants were. All that was important was that the rents were paid on time and wherever possible a higher rent than before was obtained. This was possible precisely from those wealthy individuals who had adjudicated and bought in auction several properties. Neither was it of any interest to Zuloaga that the former occupiers should recover their tenancy. He was only concerned that the Church should repossess its real estate so that it could be used as a mortgage for loans from the speculators.

CHURCH LOANS TO THE CONSERVATIVE
GOVERNMENT AND THEIR CONSEQUENCES

As early as 27 January the archbishop agreed to a loan to Zuloaga of 1,500,000 pesos.[1] On the next day the chapter decided to make an immediate payment on account of 150,000 pesos in cash, which 'would extricate the government from the urgent needs which it has at the present time'. How is the almost complete poverty of a government in possession of the wealthy capital of the country to be explained? Governments existed mainly on customs revenue, particularly during a revolution when merchants refused to pay taxes. Now the most important source of customs' dues, the port of Veracruz, was in the hands of the liberals, who of course decided to keep the revenue. Hence the desperate position of the conservative government. The Church felt that it was not possible to obtain the remainder of the loan, 1,350,000 pesos, from its normal income and, probably remembering the unfavourable experience of the years 1846–48, with the promissory notes, bills and bonds, it preferred to proceed with the alienation of some ecclesiastical real estate. Nevertheless, whether the properties were sold at a low price or whether it was hoped to retain them in case the conservatives should win the war, the traditional procedure was again adopted and on 8 April the Church delivered to the Minister of Hacienda three drafts amounting to 666,200 pesos and a fourth for 160,000 pesos. The total of the three amounts now handed over towards the 1,500,000 was 976,200 pesos, so that a little over 500,000 remained to complete the loan. Part of it was absorbed by the firm Barrón, Forbes and Co. International complications resulted from this transaction and information on it survived the disappearance of the

[1] Minutes of the metropolitan chapter of 27 and 28 January, 8 April, 24 and 25 June, and 29 and 30 July 1858, reproduced in Riva Palacio, *México a través de los siglos*, v, 308–10.

reactionary government and was reproduced in 1862 by Payno in *México y sus cuestiones financieras con la Inglaterra, la España y la Francia.*[1]

In March 1858 Barrón, Forbes and Co. loaned Zuloaga's government 320,000 pesos, the whole amount being guaranteed by the Church. 'As it was stipulated', Payno wrote, 'that Sr. Barrón was to be paid with part of the funds which the clergy had offered Zuloaga and the Church could not then raise the cash, Barrón's company finally had to accept payment at agreed prices in capital and property owned by the corporations, and we do not know at the moment what those prices were.'

In fact the financiers received twenty-two houses belonging to several convents, with a fiscal valuation of 309,078 pesos.[2] Labastida mentioned three other houses, without indicating their value, and part of the monastery of La Merced, again without a valuation. In all, Barrón received real estate worth approximately 350,000 pesos. The fiscal value, that is the one used for tax purposes, is taken from the aforementioned 1856 Account of the corporate holdings. The price at which the same twenty-two houses had been assigned amounted, according to Payno's data, to 229,124 pesos. Clearly the sale price had fallen 26%. Some of the houses had been adjudicated and others sold in auction to several well-known persons, who certainly cannot have been prepared to tolerate the 'Barrón operation' in the event of a liberal victory.

In addition to the properties, Barrón was granted a number of mortgages to the value of 47,710 pesos.[3] He received therefore total wealth worth 400,000 pesos approximately, this valuation of course being based on the assumption that the times were normal. The times were not normal, however, and in the event of a liberal victory it seemed certain that the transaction would be annulled in accordance with the circular of 29 January 1858, issued by Melchor Ocampo in Guanajuato, especially since the agreement between Barrón and Zuloaga had been reached in March, at a time when the previous adjudicators and buyers were only just returning the houses to the corporations. Clearly they must have resented the fact that the government was immediately handing them over to someone else. Secondly, it was not impossible that, should the conservatives be victorious, the Church would reclaim some of its holdings, alleging that it had been obliged by force to surrender them, which was no doubt true.

---

[1] Pp. 131–8.   [2] Labastida, 225–6.

[3] This information is from Labastida; Payno mentions 'some capitals' as part of a transaction, but he does not give the figures. The haste in which he had to write the work, during the French intervention, possibly caused him to forget them. The files must have existed in 1893 when Labastida consulted them.

The loan of 1,500,000 pesos was completed with the amount received from Barrón and several other sources which it is now impossible to ascertain. Following normal practice, the government placed the drafts among the main commercial firms at a discount which is likewise unknown. All these documents were secured by ecclesiastical real estate and mortgages. The amount of the loan was apportioned among the different corporations; for example, the metropolitan cathedral was allocated 60,000 pesos.[1]

On 27 April the French diplomatic representative wrote that 'only 80,000 of the clerical loan of 1,500,000 pesos is outstanding. The President told me the day before yesterday that this sum was payable in December and he had tried to negotiate it, only to find that nobody wanted less than three per cent a month.' In other words, the government sold the outstanding amount at 64% of the nominal value.[2] As Alexis de Gabriac had foreseen, Zuloaga was again soon in difficulties. Thus on 15 May he decreed a temporary extraordinary tax of 1% on capital and real estate, including mercantile capital.[3] With the encouragement of the United States Minister, Forsyth, all the foreigners refused to pay.[4] Faced with this failure, Zuloaga once again turned to the Church. The metropolitan chapter complained on 24 June 'that the government now frequently approaches the Church for assistance with its financial problems'. Furthermore, the Church had committed itself to the loan of 1,500,000 pesos in the hope that within a year, which was the agreed time to pay, peace would have been restored and the government consolidated. This had not been the case and the archbishop felt that, with things as they were, the Church could not fulfil its commitment. This was in fact what later happened. The Church had apparently reached the limit of its resources as a solvent institution. The hopes of the early months that Zuloaga would quickly defeat the liberals now vanished, and it was evident that the country faced a long war with an uncertain outcome.

The Church had no choice but to support the conservatives, and because of this it eventually gave in to their demands on 29 July:

the supreme government insists on the mortgage of free capital to the value of 1,000,000 pesos; the speculators only require the deeds to be endorsed for their own security, for Juárez has issued two decrees, one nationalizing all ecclesiastical possessions (a very premature rumour), and another revoking any contract arranged with them; but at the most, free capital will amount to 200,000 pesos.

[1] Riva Palacio, *México a través de los siglos*, V, 310.
[2] Díaz, *Versión francesa*, II, 14.
[3] MH 1870, p. 480.
[4] Díaz, *Versión francesa*, II, 23–5.

On the next day the archbishopric decided to lend 1,000,000 pesos in the following form: 200,000 in cash would be handed over immediately, although it was very unlikely that this sum could be collected; 300,000 would be given in loan contracts, which were not entailed and which were guaranteed by mortgages—these capitals were to be realized if the Church did not pay within a year; finally, all clerical properties were to be mortgaged for one year to the sum of 500,000 pesos. Apparently these conditions were not fulfilled because the Church was unable to raise the required cash. Faced with this situation, the government issued in August bonds to the value of 1,000,000 pesos.[1]

The government hoped to place these bonds among the capital's merchants, who were now faced with the knowledge that the loans would be annulled if the liberals were victorious, an outcome which no longer seemed impossible. The conservatives therefore had to resort to compulsion, and each merchant was assigned a certain sum, in exchange for which he was given an equivalent amount of the clerical mortgage.[2] In other circumstances they would have been competing to acquire a Church property or capital at a low price; now they all refused to co-operate. Since the capitalists were unwilling to pay—in order to avoid imprisonment, some fled and others went into hiding—their possessions were impounded to meet the sums assigned to them.[3] Capitalists known for their conservative connections were involved, but even they could not ignore the very high risk involved in accepting the clerical notes. It is not known how much the government managed to extract from them, although it seems to have been little since at the beginning of 1859 the treasury still had 700,000 pesos' worth of the notes.

Meanwhile Gabriac reported on 22 August that the Church had cashed, on the date due, notes to the value of 500,000 pesos—the first issued for the 1,500,000 loan—so punctually in fact 'that one could demand no better from a first class bank'.[4] To raise this amount the corporations had had to sell many of their properties. The second issue of notes was due in six months and many people were already preparing to buy.

The failure of the forced loan led the government to consider another means of meeting its needs. It was obvious that the Mexican capitalists would not co-operate and the management of their affairs by government employees would not produce the required money. Moreover it was dangerous to try to apply the forced loan to foreigners, particularly

---

[1] M. Payno, *La deuda interior de México* (Mexico, 1865), p. 29.
[2] Díaz, *Versión francesa*, II, 32–3.
[3] Ibid., II, 37.   [4] Ibid., II, 40.

the French and the British, for Zuloaga always tried to keep good relations with these two powers. So the conservative government devised a plan to raise funds abroad. The result of this was the loan by the Rothschild Company of 700,000 pesos in October 1858, which was negotiated by the company's permanent representative in Mexico, Nathaniel Davidson, and the respective contracts were signed by him as if the money was his own. It was for this reason that the loan is known in Mexico as the 'Davidson deal' or 'contract', never as the Rothschild. It was thus described by Payno in his *México y sus cuestiones financieras*[1] and by Labastida in his *Colección de leyes*.[2] The facts given by the latter differ from those of Payno, as they did in the case of the Barrón loan.

It seems that Davidson's own capital would not have been sufficient to lend the government the amount involved. In 1862, for the purpose of a percentage tax on the capital of the British, French and Spanish residents in the country, the assets of each company were estimated as follows: Eustaquio Barrón, then a British subject, 500,000 pesos; Pío Bermejillo, 350,000; Isidoro de la Torre, 330,000; Juan Antonio Béistegui, then a Spanish citizen, 1,200,000; and those of Davidson, only 205,000.[3] It was however not Nathaniel but Lionel Davidson who was involved in this assignment since the former was not in the capital at that time. He returned to it in June 1863 under the protection of the French occupation forces. It is possible that he had taken with him part of his capital assets, leaving the rest in the capital in the care of a relative. Whatever the case, the loan came from the Rothschild firm.[4]

The transaction of the 700,000 pesos loan from the company was as follows: Davidson offered to lend the government 475,000 in cash and 225,000 in bonds of the internal public debt, which then could be bought in the market at prices varying between 5% and 10% of their nominal value. These bonds were being amortized quickly at this time because all the buyers of clerical properties paid part of the price with them. Davidson, or rather Rothschild, had to pay more than 10% because of the increased demand. This is indicated in a letter which the firm in London sent to Davidson on 1 November 1858.[5] According to this the loan was negotiated at a price of 72%, that is Rothschild paid out 504,000 pesos—

---

[1] Pp. 117–30. [2] Pp. 218–25.

[3] The complete list was reproduced as an addendum to Payno's pamphlet, *Carta que sobre los asuntos de México dirige al señor Gen. Forey, comandante en jefe de las tropas francesas, el ciudadano Manuel Payno* (Mexico, 1862).

[4] C. Schefer, 'La grande pensée de Napoleon III, les origines de l'expédition du Mexique', *Revue d'Histoire Diplomatique*, no. 3 (1965), 41; G. Gille, 'Les capitaux français et l'expédition du Mexique', *Revue d'Histoire Diplomatique*, no. 3 (1965), 3; the author of the latter used the Rothschild archive. [5] Gille, ibid.

475,000 in cash to the government and 29,000 in cash to acquire the bonds—in exchange for notes worth 700,000 pesos. These notes consisted of deeds of the Church property. The delivery of the 475,000 was to be made in several payments and Davidson did not neglect to reserve the right to refuse to make payment, if by certain dates deeds of a determined value had not been handed over. Apparently what Davidson had anticipated did occur; owing to the numerous sales already effected in previous months, 'the agents appointed by the archbishop had considerable difficulty in handing over to Sr. Davidson some deeds, to be used towards payment of the 700,000 pesos; and not having obtained those which he considered good and payable, he accepted various properties situated in the capital.'[1] Certainly the Church was still very rich but more than half the national territory was involved in civil war or under the control of the liberals. As a result, Davidson could only accept the properties or mortgages in the capital or in a nearby region safe from enemy incursions. Most of the sales had been made in the capital, so that it was difficult to find any first-class houses or mortgages that remained.[2] Thus the payments by Davidson, which began on 2 October, were prolonged until the middle of August 1860.[3]

In total Davidson acquired, on behalf of the Rothschild firm, forty-six houses in the capital—assigned or auctioned and afterwards returned to the Church—for the fiscal valuation of 359,873 pesos. The adjudication price, however, had only amounted to 298,696, that is 17% less than the fiscal valuation. Judging solely on the discount obtained on the value of the properties, Barrón seems to have made a better deal. Davidson later received sixty mortgages with a nominal value of 289,697 pesos.[4] These were secured on houses in the capital and on haciendas, many of which belonged to prominent citizens. It can be assumed from this that the mortgages were among the best to be obtained. The total value of all the properties and capital bought by Davidson amounted to 649,570 pesos, and so the total of 700,000 was still not reached. The real value of the assets that he acquired, that is the price they would fetch at the time, could not have been very much more than he had paid for them. The Rothschild offices in London and Paris were rightly dissatisfied with the contract.[5]

In spite of the amounts handed over by Davidson in the last three months of the year towards the 475,000 pesos, the financial situation of

[1] Payno, *México y sus cuestiones financieras*, 117.
[2] Curiously, according to the registers there were few sales in Puebla.
[3] Payno, *México y sus cuestiones financieras*, 117.
[4] Labastida, 222; Payno gave a lower figure.   [5] Gille.

the government did not improve and the impact of the war caused a crisis in the conservative ranks. In January 1859 Miramón replaced Zuloaga as head of the conservative government. This was the occasion on which the 700,000 pesos' worth of bonds from the loan of 1,000,000 pesos were found in the treasury. According to Gabriac these were sold by General Robles Pezuela to various capitalists like Miguel Bringas, his brother-in-law, Manuel Escandón and Nathaniel Davidson, at a rate of 55% and a term of eight months, which corresponded to approximately 35% of their nominal value. This price represented a reduction, judging by the global product of the loan of 1,000,000 pesos, which yielded 460,000 pesos.[1] The Church's credit was declining because of the lack of punctuality with which it honoured the bills presented to it at maturity. As the Church itself had foreseen, the sum of 2,500,000 pesos was beyond its resources to meet. If it had paid the first loan of 1,500,000 pesos, then it was clearly unlikely to be able to meet the second of 1,000,000.[2] A liberal historian interpreted this in a different fashion: 'more than 1,500,000 pesos worth of notes were issued and placed in circulation under the signature of the clergy, but in spite of the sanctity of the character of the bishops who signed, when the time came for payment they refused to do so because of the way in which the revolution was going'.[3]

Barrón, Forbes and Co., and Rothschild or Davidson, were not the only ones to acquire clerical properties. As a result of the loans, capitalists, many of whom had connections with the conservatives, began to buy Church real estate. Some succeeded in persuading the former adjudicators to transfer their adjudication rights. This had been expressly forbidden by article 7 of the regulations of the Lerdo law, which stated that 'the right to adjudication conceded by the law to the tenants is personal, and

---

[1] Díaz, *Versión francesa*, II, 70; Payno, *La deuda interior*, 29.
[2] Díaz, ibid., p. 116; Payno, ibid.
[3] A. Toro, *La Iglesia y el Estado en México, estudio sobre los conflictos entre el clero católico y los gobiernos mexicanos desde la independencia hasta nuestros días* (Mexico, 1927), p. 265; according to Galarza, at that time the Church loaned the conservative government 4,658,000 pesos (E. Galarza, *The Roman Catholic Church as a factor in the political and social history of Mexico* (Sacramento, 1928, p. 112), but this is a mistake, the loans amounting to only 2,500,000 pesos. Galarza took the figure from M. Galindo y Galindo, *La gran década nacional, o relación histórica de la guerra de reforma, intervención extranjera y gobierno del archiduque Maximiliano, 1857–1867* (Mexico, 1904–6), vol. I, pp. 435–40; Galindo misunderstood the aforementioned minutes of the metropolitan chapter in which three notes for 666,200 pesos are cited. He assumed that these were three separate notes and multiplied the amount by three, arriving at a figure of 1,998,500 pesos; then he added the note for 160,000 pesos and 1,500,000 pesos, without realizing that both were on account of the total loan; finally he added 1,000,000 pesos from the second loan, giving an overall total of 4,658,000 pesos. W. H. Callcott, *Liberalism in Mexico, 1857–1929* (Stanford, 1931), p. 15, also used this incorrect figure.

they must in no way cede or sell it to other individuals, but only transfer it, legally with the tenancy, in the case of death'. Apparently someone in the capital thought that it would be a good idea, before buying a house from the Church, to acquire from the former adjudicator—usually the same person as the tenant—their rights under the Lerdo law. Hence in the event of a liberal victory the capitalists would be able to claim that they had obeyed the law and possibly keep their properties. Perhaps because of the frequency of these cases, the law of 5 February 1861 accepted such purchases as valid, subject to payment of a fine of 20% of the value of the house. For example, in making his numerous purchases Davidson had on several occasions acquired the adjudicatory rights. Those people who had thus sold their rights lost them in favour of the buyers.

Another case that arose even more often concerned the tenants, that is the adjudicators who had again become tenants, to whom the Church sold the same properties that they themselves had previously been assigned. The corporations needed funds with which to meet payment on the notes that were soon to mature. Nothing was simpler than to offer to sell the houses to the tenants on easy payment terms, but always provided some initial payment in cash was made. Only in a very few instances was the whole value paid in cash. One of these involved a high-ranking official in the Ministry of Hacienda, who had rented for almost thirty years a house in Vergara Street (at the present day Bolívar, between Tacuba and Madero) owned by the convent of Santa Clara, which had a number of properties in that double block (the 5 de Mayo Street had not yet been constructed).[1] The convent itself was on the corner of Bolívar and Tacuba and formed part of the block. In order to get the tenancy contract this official had to pay the cost of conveyance, and afterwards, as tenant, he made improvements to the house which were not credited against his rent. In August 1856 he was assigned it for 9,762 pesos,[2] which was a very high price considering that the fiscal valuation had only amounted to 3,000. After acquiring the house he had been paying interest to the convent. In January 1858 he resigned his post as senior official in the Ministry of Hacienda, probably because of his liberal convictions, and in March of the same year he had to return the title deeds to be officially cancelled. The convent, however, had to sell several properties to meet its quota of the cash loan. Thus in November 1858 the convent administrator con-

---

[1] *Representación que el Licenciado José María Urquidi dirige al Exmo. Sr. Ministro de Hacienda, pidiendo se sirva declarar que la casa de su propiedad, situada en la calle de Vergara, no. 4, no está comprendida en el artículo 11 de la ley de 5 de febrero de este año*, dated 10 February 1861.

[2] MH 1857, addenda, p. 174.

tacted the tenant who then bought the house 'to avoid the property being sold to someone else'. The tenants faced the same problem as two years before: they either acquired the house or risked its being bought by another person. The sale price is not known but the buyer did pay the whole amount in cash, which was no doubt welcomed by the convent in view of the general scarcity of money at the time. In order to raise the money the tenant mortgaged the house to a friend who, foreseeing the difficulties which might arise in the event of a liberal victory, lent him it only because the buyer was an adjudicator in full possession of his rights. Later, in 1859–60, the new owner spent 2,000 pesos on repairs. The deal was onerous for the adjudicator–buyer.

In other cases, which seem to form the majority, the buyers paid only a small part of the price in cash. The following is an account of one house owned by the convent of La Concepción.[1] In 1856 the house in question, originally valued at 30,000 pesos, was assigned to its tenant Mariano Rojo, a government official, for the sum of 37,500, which corresponded to an annual rent of 2,250. In March 1858 Rojo returned the house and the title deeds. This case turned out to be more complicated than the previous one. A French citizen, George E. Schoessling, apparently from Alsace, had a hardware business in the same house; he was therefore a subtenant of the adjudicator. Anticipating the possibility of a liberal victory, Schoessling persuaded the adjudicator to sell his rights to him: 'in order to make more certain the interests of my business, and believing Sr. Rojo's ownership to be valid, I bought the rights from him for 10,000 pesos'. This was a substantial amount for a house valued at 30,000 and assuming it was paid in cash. Schoessling gave these details in a letter to the Minister of Hacienda, dated 9 March 1861. Thus Rojo had ceded his rights of adjudication to the subtenant.

As in the previous case, the convent offered the house for sale and Schoessling hastened to buy it in December 1858, paying a price of 27,000 pesos, under the following conditions: 3,000 was paid in cash; the house was mortgaged to La Concepción for 17,000 and to a Sr. Rubin for 7,000. The convent therefore received 10,000 in cash, more or less one-third of the value, which was a highly satisfactory result. From the buyer's point of view it was not so favourable. Schoessling had paid 13,000 pesos in cash—10,000 for the adjudication rights and 3,000 to La Concepción—and he had arranged the private mortgage of 7,000. Moreover the con-

---

[1] *Manifestaciones que José Yves Limantour, en cumplimiento del decreto de 26 de febrero del presente año, ha dirigido al Exmo. Consejo de Estado, relativas a la casa núm. 6 de la calle de la Palma, y a la hacienda de Tenería, situada en la jurisdicción de Tenancingo* (Mexico, 1865).

vent, still in need of money, sold the mortgage to Pío Bermejillo, no doubt at a discount.[1]

Another case, concerning three houses owned by La Concepción, was found in the National Archive.[2] On 23 January 1858 the convent wrote to the archbishop complaining that the administrator had not presented his accounts. The reaction had just triumphed in the capital and it was now more probable that the administrator would take notice of the prior of La Concepción. The administrator then promptly presented his accounts, corresponding to the two years 1856–57 and these show that the revenue from rents amounted in 1856 to 42,370 pesos and in 1857 to 36,292, the drop probably being a result of the disentailment. The total for the two years was 78,708 (there is a small discrepancy in one addition); expenditure for the same period of 60,662, giving a surplus in cash of 18,046. This is certainly surprising in view of the alleged indigent situation in which the convents found themselves after the Lerdo law. La Concepción, however, was by far the richest convent and it was not alone in its problems with administrators, for many others made similar complaints in 1858, just when they urgently needed money.[3]

On 29 April the abbess sent the accounts to the archbishop, saying that the convent would not be able to pay the interest on the capital which it owed to certain pious works if it also had to pay the government its quota of 180,000 pesos, which was the 12% of the 1,500,000 loan. The size of the allocation indicates the wealth of La Concepción. On 22 December 1858 the diocesan accountancy office suggested that the request should be granted, for after all the pious works could wait, whereas the government, whose need increased day by day, could not. The sacrifice of the pious works was not enough and several properties had to be sold. Consequently, in 1859 Genaro Béistegui acquired three houses in Profesa Street—today, Madero. These three dwellings were valued at 74,000 pesos and they had been assigned in 1856 to three different individuals for 91,800.[4] Of course they were returned and then La Concepción sold them to Béistegui for 78,000; 64,000 in a mortgage held by the convent, and 14,000 in cash, to be handed over to the government immediately. As in the previous case the convent sold the mortgage to Pío Bermejillo.[5]

---

[1] *Ocurso que el doctor Don Antonio Fernández Monjardín presentó en 28 de abril de 1862 al juez 4º. de lo civil, Lic. D. Agustín Norma, reclamando el despojo que se le infirió en 24 de mayo de 1861 de una casa de su propiedad, de la que se dió posesión a D. José Yves Limantour* (Mexico, 1862).

[2] AGN, PBN, leg. 74, exp. unmarked.   [3] AGN, PBN, almost the whole of leg. 74.

[4] According to MH 1857, a French diplomat was mistaken on 10 August 1865 when he informed his government that Béistegui had adjudicated them; Díaz, *Versión francesa*, IV, 165.

[5] I. Reyes, *Rectificación de algunas especies vertidas en el cuaderno impreso de Don Joaquín Llaguno sobre el embargo de la hacienda de San Jacinto* (Mexico, 1862).

Two other cases have been taken from the notarial registers. In 1856 the countess del Valle, tenant of a house belonging to La Concepción, was assigned it for 27,800 pesos, which was less than the valuation figure of 35,000. In 1858 she retracted the adjudication and later transferred her right to it, together with the tenancy, to a Sr. Oceguera, in return for a cash payment of 6,000 pesos. Her profit was 4,500 and her declared costs 1,500, which seems an excessive amount, for even though the 5% tax was almost 1,500, only a part of it was paid in cash. Oceguera died and a Sr. Rivas, who was the estate's executor on behalf of the younger children, moved into the house as the tenant. He invested in several improvements the sum of 6,000 pesos. Then on 22 January 1859 La Concepción sold him the property for 30,000 pesos; 10,000 in cash and 20,000 on a nine-year mortgage at 6% per annum.[1] In this way the buyer had so far spent 16,000 pesos, approximately half the value of the house.

In the same year the monastery of Santo Domingo sold a house to the Swiss financier Jecker. The sale price of the property, originally valued at 10,000 pesos, was 6,825 pesos, giving the buyer a considerable discount. The price, however, was given 'to the buyer in part payment of a larger amount owed to him; and therefore, as if it was being handed over to him here and now, he declares that he has received it...'[2] Jecker had loaned an unknown amount to the monastery, no doubt to enable it to pay its quota of the loan to the government, and he was now being repaid in real estate. The notarial registers of F. Pérez de León for 1858–60 have not survived. Those of five other notaries for these years have been examined, and the sales registered in them of ecclesiastical property are very few, although it must be remembered of course that there were thirty-five notaries in Mexico City.

In Puebla the Church does not appear to have sold many properties in 1858–60, judging from the registers of the number five notary, which contain no such cases. One curious affair took place in Atlixco and perhaps ought to be mentioned here. On 6 August 1856 presbyter José A. Domínguez, the tenant since 1850 of a ranch belonging to the local Carmelite monastery, was assigned the property for 14,166 pesos, an amount corresponding to an annual rent of 850.[3] The buyer was to pay the interest, which was identical to the rent, 'for the time being and while the intervention of ecclesiastical goods lasted...to the Revenue Office...and after to the Carmelite monastery...' On 13 February the instrument was

---

[1] 1859 register of Antonio Ferreiro, book 1, fol. 11, ANM.
[2] Ibid., book 3, fol. 8.
[3] 1856 Atlixco register, fol. 147, ANP; see appendix III.

cancelled and consequently the ranch was returned to the community. Instead of taking the property away from the clerical adjudicator, the monastery was content to raise the rent by 100 pesos to 950 a year.[1] Important factors in this case seem to have been Domínguez's abilities as a farmer and merchant and the hope of the monks to increase their income. Questions of principle were less important. Yet these must have harmed the presbyter in the eyes of the faithful, for in 1860 a broadsheet appeared, signed by him, with these words on it: 'As it is my duty as a priest to avoid the sort of scandal which has been evoked in timid consciences by the adjudication which I improperly made of clerical properties, thereby contravening the diocesan orders, I renounce and return the said goods to their legitimate owners.'[2] The enterprising priest had waited two years to make this public confession of his error, an admission which was no doubt very laconic. Was he perhaps using the 1856 adjudication to defend the interests of the Church? The notarial records make no reference to this possibility, but in view of other cases already indicated it can be concluded that the bold priest acted like any other private citizen. If he had really been defending the Church there would have been no need to make a public retraction.

In urgent need of money, the ecclesiastical corporations in the capital not only sold their real estate after 1858, but they also tried to call in capital funds that were due, or at least the unpaid interest, but this was difficult because of the economic crisis. For example, in 1858 one person who was in debt to La Concepción could pay neither the interest nor the capital which was due, amounting to only 2,000 pesos, and he tried to extend the mortgage.[3] In the same year a merchant could not pay the capital he owed to a pious work.[4] In 1859 the convent of San Jerónimo wanted to increase from 5% to 6% the interest which Juan Goríbar owed it on a capital of 31,000 pesos. The parties finally agreed on $5\frac{3}{4}$% a year.[5] In a case similar to that of La Concepción, the convent of San Jerónimo had mortgaged various of its properties to several *capellanías* for 19,600 pesos, but it could not pay if it was to meet the amount allocated to it by the government.[6]

All these transactions were of course supervised not only by the highest ecclesiastical authority but also by the Minister of Justice in the conservative government, which feared that the Church might try to conceal its wealth under the guise of apparently legal dealings. Thus on 26 June

---

[1] 1858 Atlixco register, fol. 143 of 23 September.
[2] Ibid., page attached to the register.
[3] AGN, PBN, leg. 1708, exp. 4.   [4] AGN, PBN, leg. 1708, exp. 10.
[5] AGN, PBN. leg. 1708, exp. 12.   [6] AGN, PBN, leg. 1791, exp. 12.

1858 the Minister ordered that the corporations must first inform him when they wanted to sell a property.[1] This was in fact observed and the Ministry granted requests to alienate property and capital from the corporations which were trying to fulfil their share of the loan.[2] Perhaps at the request of the archbishop, the Ministry did order on 16 August of the same year that notaries were to execute the instruments of house sales and redemption of capitals belonging to the archdiocese, with only the permission of the prelate.[3]

The net result of the clerical loans to Zuloaga was correctly anticipated by Gabriac on 22 August 1858.[4] Noticing that several French adjudicators were again buying the same houses that they had returned to the Church, the diplomat commented:

In this way a large number of the adjudications are being regularized. At the same time the metropolitan chapter realizes that the moment has arrived to part with its goods amicably, and on advantageous terms, if it wants to avoid being completely deprived of them on the return of the radical liberals. Nevertheless this system of lending money to the government offers no guarantee to the clergy, for they will never be repaid by the debtor.

In spite of his conservative sympathies, Gabriac knew perfectly well that the so-called Church loan to Zuloaga was in fact a gift.

More than a year later, when he could already see the extent of the second massive transfer of property—the first having followed the Lerdo law—Gabriac assessed it on 12 October 1859 with these words: 'Little by little, Church properties are passing into the hands of the conservative party, in order to escape those of the demagogues.'[5] He was referring to the larger transactions which followed the placing of the loans among the capitalists. 'But', he concluded, 'these sales would provoke countless litigations on the day when the aspiring government at Veracruz does achieve its victory. There is a great number of foreigners in Veracruz, especially French, who have hastened to denounce Church possessions, thereby ancitipating those buyers who also intended to do the same thing here, according to the principles of civil law.' His prophecy was not exaggerated.

In one way or another, the Church was losing its wealth to private citizens. Even General Miramón, leader of the conservative government, understood the irreversible nature of this process, started as it was by the Lerdo law. In a message to the nation on 12 July 1859—issued, oddly

---

[1] AGN, JE, vol. 165, fols. 288 ff. [2] Ibid.
[3] AGN, JE, vol. 146, fol. 103. [4] Díaz, *Versión francesa*, II, 44.
[5] Ibid., p. 116.

enough, on the same day as the fundamental law of Reform by the liberal government in Veracruz—he declared that

it would be a foolish error not to recognize the powerful element inflaming the disastrous struggle which is ruining the republic; I speak of the considerable vested interests which arose as a consequence of the lamentable law of 25 June 1856. I recognize that this law is null and void. I swear on my honour the highest respect and the most certain guarantee I can give the interests of the Church. I swear on my honour that it will not be me who reduces their riches by a single centavo...but I am resolved to adopt the way which is most in accord with our beliefs...[1]

Nobody knows what Miramón meant by these last words. It can be assumed that the manifesto did not raise conservative morale but that it did give encouragement to the adjudicators and the buyers of clerical property.

NATIONALIZATION IN THE WEST OF MEXICO

Unlike the central region of the country, which broadly covered the states of Puebla, Querétaro and Mexico (which then included the present state of Morelos) in which Zuloaga had not only acquired power but also knew how to keep it, the western part of the nation did not find peace during the civil war. With the exception of Michoacán, which remained under liberal control, other states, particularly Jalisco, changed hands several times. As a result, the cruel and destructive character of the war increased and also the fiscal needs of the liberal armies which were active in these areas. The problem of supplying the armies had existed since the beginning of the war. Anticipating that two liberal groups would be active and to a certain extent independent of each other because of distance and the difficulty of communications during a war, President Juárez issued in Colima on 7 April 1858 a decree which was to be of vital importance for the future: he gave extraordinary powers in the matter of public revenue to Santos Degollado, Minister of War.[2] Degollado stayed in the west and Juárez left for Veracruz with the intention of establishing there the headquarters of the constitutional government.

The chaotic nature of the war and the obligation to satisfy the basic needs of their soldiers caused some liberal state governors and also some generals-in-chief to take the initiative in measures confiscating clerical property and capital. All these diverse decrees were legalized later by the law of 5 February 1861. For example, on 8 August 1858 Pedro Ogazón, governor of Jalisco, issued a decree ordering all those who owed money

---

[1] Riva Palacio, *México a través de los siglos*, v, 378.   [2] Labastida, 419–20.

to the ten rich educational institutions to redeem 10% of the amount they owed.[1] Those in debt to the other ecclesiastical corporations or pious works had to pay in advance one year's interest, at a discount of 25%, and the tenants of rural properties owned by the Church a year's rent at the same rate of discount. The stipulations were defined as a forced loan but neither the form nor date of payment was indicated. The decree declared null and void any payments which debtors made to 'the intrusive Guadalajara government'. The neutral citizen, the non-combatant, especially the merchant, faced the dilemma of a double payment. These decrees, which were always issued *ad terrorem*, were often toned down in practice when the liberal party took over a region which had been controlled until then by the conservatives. On the next day Ogazón hastened to add that the aforementioned annulment of the payments was valid 'even in the towns occupied by the reactionaries'. In addition he generalized the stipulation, declaring 'null and of no value all redemptions of ecclesiastical capital and payment of interest made by debtors to the *capellanía* fund, religious communities, brotherhoods, ecclesiastical corporations or any other association'.[2] In other words, the reactionary authorities adopted the same policy in Guadalajara.

After his capture of Guadalajara three months later, Ogazón incorporated both these previous decrees in another issued on 16 November.[3] This ordered all debtors, tenants, adjudicators and buyers to pay in advance one year's interest or rent, at a 25% discount. Only the capital and property belonging to hospitals, schools and certain *capellanías* were exempted. The siege had caused business activity to be paralysed and, recognizing this, Ogazón declared a moratorium on all mercantile payments, but at the same time he imposed a forced loan of 150,000 pesos on the city, which was not implemented because a short time later the liberals again abandoned it.[4] The danger that the conservatives might re-occupy Guadalajara made Ogazón follow the policy of establishing faits accomplis: more than two years before the same thing was done in the capital the governor began demolishing churches and convents to build new streets (see chapter 2). The measures taken by Ogazón were mild in comparison to that decreed by Santos Degollado on 7 December, again in Guadalajara. He revoked the previous decrees, as he was entitled to do, as the representative of the constitutional government at Veracruz, and

[1] The decree is given in M. Cambre, *La guerra de tres años en el estado de Jalisco* (Guadalajara, 1892), pp. 93–9.   [2] Ibid.
[3] Ibid., pp. 149–53. The decrees were possibly edited by Vallarta, nephew and secretary of the governor, González Navarro, *Vallarta y la Reforma*, p. ix.
[4] Pérez Verdía, *Historia de Jalisco*, III, 64–5.

therefore of higher authority than the various state governors. In fact his annulment was purely theoretical, for some days later both he and Ogazón, who seem to have had their differences of opinion, were forced to give up the city to the conservative forces.

The decree of 7 December still maintained the appearance of a forced loan for 2,500,000 pesos.[1] Degollado justified it on the grounds that by October the Church had loaned the reaction the sum of 2,500,000 pesos, and therefore it seemed logical to make it lend the same amount to the liberals. The figure was to go on increasing as the clergy lent more funds to the reaction (articles 1 and 2). But although it was just after October that the Church handed more funds over to Zuloaga from the 'Davidson transaction', Degollado, who perhaps did not know of this loan, was content for the time being with the 2,500,000 pesos.

The decree ordered that the capital sums which landowners owed to the Church, and the properties which had not yet been disentailed, were to be sold, with priority to purchase being given to the borrowers and the tenants (article 3). If they declined to buy, any other person could do so (article 5). Apart from his financial aim, Degollado based his approach on the Lerdo concept that a group of people had to be created who had a vested interest in the fate of the liberal party. From this time onwards not only could the tenants acquire the property they rented, but also borrowers could redeem the mortgage loans which encumbered their house or farm. As there was no central government in the western part of the country, which was dominated by the liberals, the decree declared that the sales would be made by the state governors or army leaders. This was an important stipulation, for it opened the way to regional variations in the implementation of the decree. The repayment of funds taken from the Church by way of the forced loan would be resolved once peace was re-established, for it was still not known if, for example, the clergy might assume an independent attitude in respect of the conservative government and in this way safeguard something of their wealth in a future liberal republic. This concern, or precaution, turned out in the end to be superfluous, for although it might have wanted to do so, the Church was no longer able to free itself from the conservatives. All it could do now was to continue handing over more and more of its possessions.

Degollado did not have time to enact the decree in Guadalajara. A few days later he left the city and headed for Morelia, which afforded a secure and permanent refuge for the liberals in the western region. It was from there that he issued on 11 January 1859 a set of regulations to govern the

---

[1] Dublán y Lozano, VIII, 658–61.

previous decree.[1] Urgently needing funds, he ordered the rapid and obligatory redemption of all capital due for repayment. Payment was to be made with 20% in cash and 80% in bonds and other credits (articles 1 and 2). Debtors had four days in which to pay the cash sum. After this time, those who refused to comply would have their property attached to the same value, that is a fifth of their mortgage debt to an ecclesiastical corporation. Six months were allowed for payment of the four-fifths in bonds or other 'papers' (article 3). These regulations made no mention of the properties which had not yet been disentailed and it may well have been that there was no such real estate left in Michoacán. All that remained were the many ecclesiastical capital funds invested in mortgage loans. Landowners were now to have the opportunity to redeem these debts by paying more or less only 25% of the nominal value, given that the public debt bonds could be acquired at 5–10%, and that there were six months before they had to be paid. The length of term tended to maintain their price at a low level.

Nevertheless the time to meet the cash payment was too short, for few hacendados had such a sum available. Apparently the farming interests of the Michoacán governors prevailed—both the governor, E. Huerta and his collaborator, P. García de León, were originally farmers—and Degollado moderated the conditions on 29 January.[2] It was thought that 'it would be harmful to agriculture to demand the redemption of capital that was due, when this might be done at the insistence of someone who had redeemed it by buying it from the government'; in other words, the capitals that were due, as almost all were, could be bought by a merchant who, unlike the farmers, had funds available and who could, as creditor, from then onwards be very severe with the debtor, an attitude which the corporations did not adopt. Declaring that 'given equal circumstances, it is just to give priority to the borrower over any other person who seeks to buy and redeem a capital', the new decree gave the landowners a term of one month, after which anybody could subrogate them (article 1). Although in a more simplified form, Degollado's decree anticipated the laws which were to be issued six months later in Veracruz in that not all ecclesiastical capital would be redeemed: some was to be devoted to the maintenance of educational and charitable institutions (article 3).

These two decrees were enacted especially in Morelia, partly because they were issued there and were in accord with social reality, and partly because Michoacán was throughout in liberal control. The notarial registers of Manuel Valdovinos were again examined because of this. The

---

[1] Ibid., p. 663.   [2] Ibid.

decree implied that within redeemable capitals, those which were owed to the corporations as a result of the Lerdo law were included. This meant that the adjudicators, purchasers and buyers in auction of clerical properties, mortgaged in favour of the Church because of the disentailment, now had the chance to redeem the purchase price. The corresponding annotations are to be found in the margin of the 1856 disentailment instruments. For example, the people who in 1856 bought urban houses belonging to the Augustinians by means of conventional sales now paid the purchase price to the government at a considerable discount.[1] Redemptions were made from July 1859, when the confiscation of clerical possessions was decreed by the constitutional government at Veracruz, but they were based on Degollado's decree. In some cases the government kept to the decree which demanded a 20% payment in cash, and in others it accepted 15 or only 10%, and for the bonds a term of a year instead of six months. The discounts conceded by the governors, in addition to those already granted by the decree, became so frequent that to regularize completed transactions they had to be made legal by the law of 5 February 1861.

Valdovinos' register for 1859 contains several examples in which capital was redeemed or bought from the government by people who were not the borrowers, either because they themselves could not or did not want to redeem it, because they considered it to belong to the Church.[2]

The information given in the registers is confirmed by the 1861 report of the same governor, Epitacio Huerta.[3] Commenting on the implementation of Degollado's measures, Huerta affirmed that while other governors or military leaders—in Jalisco, Zacatecas, Guanajuato and Veracruz—accepted even 5% of the value of the capital in cash, in Michoacán payment of 10% had been insisted on as a minimum.[4] It is not known if his first claim was true, but the second is confirmed by the notarial records in Morelia and also by the 1862 report of the Morelia Treasury Office in which the result of the Degollado decrees is calculated.[5] Table 11 is an extract of this; it shows that payment in cash of 10% of the capital was the norm and that 15% or 20% were exceptional cases.

[1] 1856 register, fols. 63–6, ANM.
[2] Ibid., fol. 73, and 1859 register, fols. 373, 388, 447, 448.
[3] *Memoria en que el C. General Epitacio Huerta dió cuenta al congreso del estado del uso que hizo de las facultades con que estuvo investido durante la administración dictatorial, que comenzó el 15 de marzo de 1858 y terminó en 10 de mayo de 1861* (Morelia, 1861). [4] Ibid., p. 41.
[5] *Jefatura de hacienda y tesorería general del estado de Michoacán de Ocampo. Su cuenta e informe por los ingresos y egresos habidos en ambas oficinas, desde 19 de marzo de 1858 hasta 6 de febrero de 1862 en la primera y 31 de enero del mismo año en la segunda.* Signed by Francisco Lerdo de Tejada and dated 31 October 1862.

TABLE 11. *Results of the Degollado decrees*

Capital to a total value of	1,077,231 pesos
produced in cash	120,173 (11% of value)
and in bonds and credits	957,058 (89% of value)
Of the bonds and credits worth	957,058
there were sold at 5% of face value	543,252 (product, 27,487)
Bonds owed were worth	152,033
Bonds and credits were amortized for	261,772

(Source: *Report of Treasury Office*, p. 4.
Note: Small differences in addition are
due to omission of centavos.)

Although at the beginning the Michoacán governor used the funds of
the College of San Nicolás Hidalgo de Morelia—a school much esteemed
in the country—to provide himself with funds, he subsequently carried
out the promise made in the Degollado decree to endow it with ecclesiastical capital. Similarly many confiscated capitals were given to the San
Juan de Dios hospital, which was the main institution of its type in the
state. Originally belonging to the monks of the order of San Juan de Dios,
the hospital was managed at the time of the Reform by the Michoacán
diocese. The state government considered it an ecclesiastical institution
and it was therefore secularized in a decree of 24 November 1858.[1] The
following year endowments began to be made with ecclesiastical funds.

In March 1858 the capital of the college amounted to 60,581 pesos and
produced, or rather should have produced, 3,425 pesos (between 5% and
6%). By April 1861 this capital sum had been reduced to 29,381 pesos,
but the school received new funds of 137,456 pesos, guaranteed mostly by
property mortgages. Hence its invested capital totalled 166,837 pesos.[2]
The secondary school at Pátzcuaro, originally directed by the priests of
San Vicente de Paul, also received funds to the amount of 77,941 pesos,
almost all of which were secured by hacienda mortgages. Finally, the
government had the excellent idea of founding a school of agriculture in
Zamora, which was endowed with 96,168 pesos in mortgages. In all,
therefore, the government gave these schools 312,467 pesos of the nationalized clerical capital.[3]

[1] *Memoria en que el C. General Epitacio Huerta...*, pp. 54–5.   [2] Ibid., addenda, pp. 66–72.
[3] *Tesorería general y jefatura de hacienda del estado de Michoacán de Ocampo. Su cuenta e informe
por los ingresos y egresos habidos en ambas oficinas, desde 18 de marzo de 1858 hasta 31 de enero de
1862 en la primera, y 6 de febrero del mismo año en la segunda* (Morelia, 1863); it is dated 31
October 1862 and signed by Francisco Lerdo de Tejada, apparently state treasurer and
jefe de hacienda at the same time. There is a slight difference in addition between this total,
which was almost certainly by mistake applied entirely to the San Nicolás college, and the
total of the three figures taken from Huerta's report.

The hospital received an endowment of 526,254 pesos.[1] Only 31,000 pesos remained from the capital previously held, the total amount of which is not indicated. The hospital also let properties with an approximate value of 60,000 pesos.[2] Its endowments at the time of the Reform were not substantial and it was probably financed by the diocese. The state government devoted to public education and charity a total of 838,721 pesos, which was a very large amount for a single state.

Many examples of these transactions are to be found in the registers for 1856–58, in the margin of disentailment instruments or resale deeds of disentailed property. For example, the merchant M. Cárdenas, who in 1856 had bought an hacienda belonging to the Augustinians, sold it on 28 December 1857 for the same price he had paid. He perhaps was afraid that the disentailment operations would be annulled. In the margin of this instrument there is a note, dated 19 November 1859, to the effect that the 30,000 pesos, which was the value of the hacienda, were to be applied to the civic hospital of San Juan de Dios, the most important in Morelia. This meant that the interest yielded by the capital would be given to the hospital.[3]

In the 1859 register there are no disentailment instruments but it does have mortgage contracts. For example, the Carrasquedo family had purchased an Augustinian hacienda and they were to owe its value by means of a redeemable mortgage at 3% annual interest, which was to be paid to the same hospital. The family could redeem the capital but it was probably more convenient to them to pay the low interest of 3%.[4] Such mortgage contracts are particularly numerous in the 1860 register.[5] The government directed the capitals not only to the hospital but also to the college of San Nicolás Hidalgo, for example the 4,000 pesos owed by Melchor Ocampo's hacienda Pomoca (Maravatío) to two *capellanías* were given to the school.[6]

THE CONSTITUTIONAL GOVERNMENT IN VERACRUZ

Juárez arrived at Veracruz on 4 May 1858 and he then established the headquarters of his government in the port.[7] The place had been well chosen because both the governor, Manuel Gutiérrez Zamora, and the

---

[1] Ibid., p. 30; there is a discrepancy between this figure and that given by Huerta, who states that the hospital had new capital of 523,909 pesos at 3% and 41,310 pesos at 5%.
[2] *Memoria en que el C. General Epitacio Huerta...*, addenda, p. 72.
[3] 1857 register, fol. 897, ANM.   [4] 1859 register, fol. 475, ANM.
[5] 1860 register, for example, fols. 130, 134, 135, 14–18 June, ANM.
[6] 1860 register, fol. 234, ANM.   [7] MH 1870, p. 1054.

The civil war, 1858–60

Veracruz merchants sympathized with the liberal cause. 'According to my reports', Gabriac wrote on 15 March, 'it is the German, Yankee and French merchants who sustain this last champion of radicalism', that is Gutiérrez Zamora. Gabriac then complained of 'the deplorable influence of a great French company, the chief of which is a very exalted democrat', although he did not give his name.[1] Many Frenchmen living in Mexico— among them there were refugees of 1848—were in sympathy with the liberal cause and thus they merited the scorn of the emperor's diplomats.

Gabriac was not concerned with the Mexican merchants in the port, who also supported the constitutional government. Gutiérrez Zamora did not confine himself to the role of state governor. When Miramón assumed power in the capital it was expected that the port would be besieged. Gutiérrez Zamora organized its defence—among other things he formed a national guard, composed of one thousand artisans and ordinary citizens—to the extent that Veracruz was converted into an impregnable fort, and during the siege he acted with outstanding heroism.[2] As the treasury revenue was insufficient to finance these defensive works, he provided funds from his family business's safe. As a result of this the business collapsed and his brother took his own life. A profound impression was caused by the suicide of José Gutiérrez Zamora but Veracruz was saved. In a critical moment the Veracruz bourgeoisie found a representative willing to sacrifice in the liberal cause not only his fortune but also his life and that of his family.

The constitutional government was fortunate to have at its disposal the maritime customs revenue, although this was reduced. Furthermore, it was also lucky in having weapons, almost from the beginning. A boat load of rifles, consigned to José Yves Limantour, arrived at the port. Limantour was a French citizen and belonged to the group of capitalists who were involved in transactions with the federal government. Already in 1850 he was one of the treasury's important creditors, for the government had assigned 160,000 pesos of the United States indemnity towards payment of his credits. This was undoubtedly a smaller amount than that assigned to Manning-Mackintosh (660,000), to Cayetano Rubio (238,000) and to Martínez del Río Brothers (760,000), but nevertheless it was greater than the sum allocated to the Church, which only amounted to 148,000 pesos.[3] On 12 June 1858 the constitutional government requisitioned 1,000 rifles from Limantour, and a week later 500 more. More shipments

[1] Ibid. [2] Mejía, *Memorias*, 30, 181.

[3] *Informes leídos en la cámara de diputados por el secretario de hacienda sobre el estado que guarda el erario público y sobre las últimas operaciones practicadas en la deuda exterior e interior de la república mexicana* (Mexico, 1852), pp. 41–2.

followed, so that the government received from him a total of 3,000 rifles, 2,700 large muskets (cavalry carbines), 2,000 carbines and 2,000 sabres.[1] These weapons, the last of which were received in the first days of March 1859 shortly before Miramón began the siege of Veracruz, undoubtedly saved the constitutional authorities.

The government did not have the cash to pay Limantour. Its income was consumed so rapidly that there was no time to formulate a proper system of public finance. In the words of Matías Romero who was to become the best-known Finance Minister of the nineteenth century, 'there was neither budgets nor accounts'.[2] Fortunately, both for Limantour and the liberal government, it was during those months that the citizens of the capital were returning adjudicated or auctioned properties to the Church. Many of them published in the newspapers statements to the effect that they had been forced by the Lerdo law to claim a property and now they were hastening to return it to the legitimate owner, the Church. The liberals must have compiled, by June–July 1858, quite a long list of properties returned in this way. The Veracruz government then resolved to sell them again. This is the meaning of the circular of 30 August 1858.[3] The circular first established that all rural and urban properties, which the adjudicators had returned voluntarily, were at the disposal of the constitutional government. Any sales of them made after 17 December 1857 would be considered void, 'being backdated for later measures to the state in which they were before the promulgation of the said law of 25 June'. In short, those who had given them back voluntarily lost all their rights. The properties could now be denounced to the constitutional government, in accordance with the same Lerdo law. The denouncers would replace, from then onwards, the adjudicators who had spontaneously returned them.

Consequently the government's creditors who were living in Veracruz could acquire the rights of adjudicators to houses situated in the capital. Under the Lerdo law the only payment required was the 5% tax on the price, as if the property had not been previously assigned. The purveyors of the government paid it in merchandise. In this way, in exchange for goods worth a relatively small amount some people in Veracruz were able to acquire rights to real estate in the capital worth twenty times as much. For example, in 1858 a number of rifles was bought from Limantour for 25,312 pesos, which was paid to him in January 1859 in exchange

---

[1] *Manifestaciones que José Yves Limantour...*   [2] MH 1870, p. 481.
[3] Labastida, 116; according to M. Ocampo, *Obras completas* (Mexico, 1900–01), vol. II, pp. 165–99, the circular was dated 20 August.

for the sales tax on properties denounced by him. 25,312 pesos equals 5% of 506,240 pesos, so that he must have acquired rights to real estate valued at half a million pesos.[1] He was not alone in making these deals; in particular Antoine Bonhomme,[2] whose transactions with the government took place after those of Limantour, was prominent.

Of course neither Limantour nor Bonhomme could take possession of the properties on which they had paid the transfer of ownership tax. In the event of a victory by the reactionaries they would lose their investment, and even with a liberal triumph it was not certain what would happen to it. They paid the sales tax in accordance with the Lerdo law but the future of Church possessions was still not known, although from August 1858 the far-sighted could perhaps foresee a total nationalization of ecclesiastical wealth. The degree of speculation was therefore quite high.

Limantour, Bonhomme and others paid the sales tax in merchandise or in cash, but not all the Frenchmen living in Veracruz in 1858–60 were wealthy. There were some who helped the liberal cause with their pens, not with money. One of the best known was Alfredo Bablot, who arrived in Mexico after the defeat of the 1848 revolution.[3] Together with others, Bablot was the target for the scorn of the French diplomats who, as members of the nobility, despised their plebeian compatriots' involvement with the Mexican liberal government. On 22 February 1859 Bablot asked the Veracruz government for permission to delay payment of the sales tax on properties which had been adjudicated to him in Chiapas and Tehuantepec, until after the constitutional government had been re-established for two months in the capital. The government, which was entering the most critical phase of its existence, had no difficulty in granting the request on the same day.[4]

At the end of the three years' war the Veracruz denouncers became a powerful pressure group, alongside the ordinary buyers, that is, those who had bought some property from the Church without acquiring the adjudication rights, and the adjudicators who had remained as tenants throughout the civil war without buying a Church property.

[1] *El Ministerio de Hacienda del 21 de enero al 6 de abril de 1861* (Mexico, 1862), p. 11; signed by Guillermo Prieto and José María Iglesias.
[2] Ibid., p. 22, and F. Mejía, *Memorias* (Mexico, 1958), p. 49.
[3] F. López Cámara, 'Los socialistas franceses en la Reforma Mexicana', *Historia Mexicana*, IX, 269–73.
[4] AGN, PBN, leg. 734.

THE NATIONALIZATION DECREED IN VERACRUZ

It has been seen in some examples that the military leaders and state governors implemented from 1858 onwards the confiscation of clerical goods and that they acted independently of one another. A federal law was required to make these measures uniform. It is probable that Juárez would have preferred not to issue this or, if it was possible, to postpone it until the end of the war, in part because of the reasons already given in discussing Degollado's decree. There were also other considerations, for example, it did not seem prudent to declare a total confiscation because this might well offend popular religious feeling and thus prolong the war.[1]

Nevertheless the law of 12 July 1859 was issued and its regulations published on the following day.[2] This declared the nationalization, without compensation, of Church capital and real estate. First, all monasteries— those of the regular orders—were suppressed. Their buildings were confiscated and the monks were converted by law into secular clergy, and they were forbidden to wear their habit or to live in community. As regards their churches, the government would decide if they were necessary for divine service 'previously and thoroughly assessing the need and utility of each one' (article 11 of 12 July law). Those churches which were considered superfluous would be sold, together with the monastery buildings (articles 5–10 of the regulations). Plans dividing the monasteries would first be drawn up, and then each of the sections would be valued separately. The reason for this division was that the monasteries were too big for any one person to buy the whole. Although they might not be easy to sell as buildings, in many instances the land they stood on was very valuable. The sections would be sold by public auction, at a reserve price of two-thirds of the valuation, thus following the precedent set for auctions in the Lerdo law. At least half the sale price was to be paid in cash and the other half in credits of the recognized public debt. Consequently the buyers could obtain a monastic building at 35–40% of its value, which was very similar to the terms prevailing in 1829. The government no doubt granted this discount in order to find prospective buyers as quickly as possible, and once vested interests had been created it would be more difficult for the monks to return to their former dwellings. To facilitate the sales even more it was ordered that, given the appropriate circumstances, instead of a cash payment the building or the section of it could be mortgaged to the government for a term of 5–9

---

[1] Sierra, *Juárez, su obra y su tiempo*, 155–63.   [2] Labastida, 137–44.

years at 6% annual interest. Considering that the monasteries were held as sacred in the popular mind, it was essential to encourage the maximum interest in their sale and, as far as possible, in their conversion or demolition.

Another procedure was adopted in respect, first, of the houses which had not yet been disentailed under the Lerdo law, although there can have been few of these left in the areas controlled by the liberals, and secondly, with ecclesiastical capital, whether this came from mortgages predating the law of 25 June 1856 or whether it was precisely a result of the law; in other words, the capital invested in a mortgage loan or a contract in favour of a *capellanía* or pious work, and the prices at which the properties had been adjudicated, sold or auctioned under the Lerdo law which the buyers owed to the ecclesiastical corporations. All such capital could be redeemed by the present debtors, property owners paying 60% in national debt bonds or credits and 40% in cash payable in forty monthly amounts (articles 11–20 of the regulations). Although the debtors received no discount on the capital or the property purchase price which they owed—unlike the buyers of the monastery buildings—they were allowed very favourable terms of payment. On redeeming a capital, for which the law granted one month, they had to hand over only the bonds, which were acquired at 5–10% of face value. In those places in which there was no trade in national debt bonds—that is everywhere, for the only real market in bonds was in Mexico City—the buyers were to be able to sign a promissory note to pay the bonds 'within a reasonable period', which depended on local circumstances. In practice the buyers were given six months, as in Degollado's decree. As for the payment in cash, the buyers were to pay, for forty months, 1% a month or 12% a year of the capital value of the property before its disentailment. As the rent had been capitalized at 6% a year it now meant that the buyer was to pay the government monthly double the amount of the original rent or double the interest which in theory he had been paying to the respective clerical corporation until the law of 13 July 1859. This measure must have evoked protests, for less than two months later, on 10 September, the constitutional government decided to allow monthly payments of half the amount, which meant that the 40% of the value of the capital had to be liquidated in eighty months, instead of the original forty.[1] After the publication of the law there were individuals prepared to pay the 40% in cash in one sum, which was certainly attractive to the government, which could thus acquire funds immediately instead of the monthly payments

[1] Ibid., pp. 191–2.

over three or six years. With regard to this Melchor Ocampo, then Minister of Hacienda, decided on 9 August to grant discounts, but he did not fix the amount.[1]

One very important measure for the future was as follows: to ensure the monthly payments the buyers were to sign promissory notes secured by the same mortgage of the capital they had redeemed. These notes would be payable to the bearer and hence the government could sell them and they could circulate.

If the borrowers renounced their right to redeem their debt—they had thirty days to do so—any other person could redeem it within the next ten days and on the same conditions as the borrowers. In the event that nobody appeared the capital was to be sold in public auction, again with the same minimum price. In addition a circular of 27 July 1859 gave those people in Veracruz who had denounced ecclesiastical real estate located in the capital, which had been returned to the Church, the right to redeem in advance the value of properties situated in a region still under the control of the reaction.[2] This was clearly a decision to the advantage both of the government and the denouncers in Veracruz.

The suppression of the monasteries and the sale of their buildings referred only to the male regular orders. The nunneries would continue to exist and follow their usual life (articles 14–20 of the law of 12 July). Naturally the nuns would have the right to leave the convents, in which case they were to receive the same amount that they had paid in the form of a dowry. The others could continue in the convents as before, but their dowry was to be converted into their private possession and it was to be contracted individually in favour of each nun. Each of the convents was to be left with capital large enough to yield sufficient interest to pay for repairs to buildings and churches, the celebration of their respective patron saints and the festivals of Christmas, Easter, Corpus Christi, Resurrection, and All Saints, as well as for the community's other costs.

The monks and the nuns were clearly treated differently. In spite of the fact that the nunneries were richer and therefore a potential source of considerable revenue to the treasury, they were respected. This could not have been a question of principle, for the convents were just as much ecclesiastical institutions as the monasteries, and their goods were utilized for the same Church aims as those of the monks.

The nationalization law began to be put into effect immediately in the city of Veracruz. As the disentailment under the Lerdo law had been practically completed in 1856, the only clerical property liable to be

---

[1] Ibid.   [2] Ibid., p. 190.

nationalized and sold was the four monastic buildings. Rivera Cambas wrote: 'It was in Veracruz that the government made the first alienations of goods which had belonged to the Church, one of the buildings sold being the monastery of San Francisco.'[1] A later notarial register shows that the monastery of La Merced was also sold, but the Dominican was still not sold in 1868 when the government let it for eight years but reserved the right to rescind the contract if a buyer was found.[2] These transactions involving the monasteries were insignificant compared with the redemption of capital. In the first place, the owners of urban dwellings owed the ecclesiastical corporations about 1,000,000 pesos as a result of the 1856 disentailment. They now had the opportunity to redeem their debts. The capital which resulted from the Lerdo law must be distinguished from the mortgages predating it. In the city of Veracruz, the latter in 1856 amounted to 576,795, according to the information provided during the intervention of ecclesiastical possessions in the Puebla diocese.[3] It can be classified, according to its owner, as in table 12. The debts of the various Veracruz corporations amounting to only 87,644 must be deducted from the total shown here, leaving a net ecclesiastical capital of 489,151 pesos.

It is again noticeable that the Puebla secular and regular clergy were much richer than their colleagues in Veracruz. Secondly, it is interesting to note that the capital of *capellanías* amounted to almost half the total. Certainly there is an apparent discrepancy in the figure of 258,633 pesos and that given by Lerdo in his book on Veracruz. He stated that there were 54 *capellanías* in the port, with a capital value of 110,341 pesos, but he was referring only to those foundations belonging to the parish, which were held by the city's clergy.[4] As already shown there were no more than ten of these. Perhaps this explains the difference.

Considering that clerical real estate in Veracruz was worth about 800,000 pesos and that it was sold for approximately 1,000,000 pesos, the result is that, in round figures, two-thirds of Church wealth in the city consisted of property and one-third of capital.

The abovementioned document enables the mortgaged properties to be

---

[1] M. Rivera Cambas, *Los gobernantes de México* (Mexico, 1872–73), vol. II, p. 598.

[2] 1868 register of José María Bello and Marcos María Castellanos, fols. 43, 72, Archivo de Notarías de Veracruz (cited hereinafter as ANV).

[3] AGN, JE, vol. 175, fol. 153, *Estado que manifiesta las fincas, capitales y fondos que existen en los departamentos de Veracruz, Jalapa y Jalacinco, pertenecientes a los bienes eclesiásticos intervenido por el que suscribe, en virtud del supremo decreto de 31 de marzo último, y que presentó con arreglo a la primera obligación impuesto en el artículo 2° de dicha ley y su 8a. prevención reglamentaria*, dated Veracruz, 8 May 1856; it includes only the city of Veracruz.

[4] Lerdo de Tejada, *Apuntes históricos*, III, 79.

TABLE 12. *Mortgages held by the Church in Veracruz, 1856*

Name of corporation	Its capital (in pesos)	Totals
Parish of Veracruz	6,350	—
Parish of Alvarado	7,300	—
Parish of Atlixco	2,000	—
Diocese, treasury and memorial fund of Puebla	33,864	—
Total for secular clergy	—	49,514
4 monasteries in Veracruz	53,344	—
Puebla convents and schools	150,028	—
Total for regular clergy	—	203,372
Brotherhoods in Veracruz	31,650	—
Brotherhoods in Puebla	2,300	—
Third Order	10,026	—
Total for associations	—	43,936
Capellanías in Veracruz	258,633	—
Pious works in Veracruz	20,000	—
Capellanías and pious works of Puebla	1,300	—
Total of *capellanías* and pious works	—	279,993
Total ecclesiastical capital	576,795[1]	—

identified. They belonged to different private owners, some of whom had several mortgages. From the comparison that has been made, it can be concluded that the houses were mortgaged for one-third and, at the most, one-half of their value. Taking into account the fact that there were about 800 privately owned houses in the city, worth 4,000,000 pesos, and that only approximately one-third of them—between 250 and 300—were mortgaged to the Church for 500,000 pesos, then the result is that only 12·5% of the total value of real estate was indebted to the clergy. The debt of private individuals to the Church was very small. Thus the Church in Veracruz was poor both in real estate and in capital.

This capital, including that which preceded the Lerdo law and that which resulted from it, was then sold. The 1868 register notes several of the sales. For example, in 1859 the owner of a house valued at 35,100 pesos requested permission to redeem a mortgage of 20,000 at 5% which had been invested in the house since 1810. In another case, on 15 August 1859, after the thirty-day term had passed, Pedro del Paso y Troncoso asked to be allowed to redeem several longstanding mortgages on properties which he himself did not own. There were also other cases of this type of

[1] It is incorrectly added in the document.

subrogation.[1] Melcher Ocampo, Minister of Hacienda on several occasions during the years 1858–60, referred to these transactions in the following note:

After thirty days had passed since the issue of the law there were some houses which had not been redeemed, and under the stipulations of the law, they were to be sold by public auction. I knew from unofficial sources that this was being done with malicious intent, so that they could be acquired at two-thirds of the value, and I tried to put a stop to this fraud.[2]

Ocampo was referring to previously assigned properties, the owners of which had allowed the term of thirty days to pass so that afterwards they could buy the mortgages at a lower price. Even though the law of 13 July 1859 had ordered that the properties were to be sold by public auction at least at the adjudication price, that is the mortgages were to be sold for their full value, it did not specify what was to be done if there were no offers. In this case it can be supposed that the government would have to sell at a lower price. The individuals in question ran the risk that a stranger might acquire the house by offering more, but judging by what happened elsewhere in the country there was virtually no competitive bidding in the auctions.

Quite substantial ecclesiastical possessions still remained in Veracruz in March of the following year. In fact it was not easy to sell all at once capital worth 1,500,000 pesos. On 11 February 1860 the constitutional government ordered that the owners of houses, which were outside the city limits and had been destroyed in the military operations, were to be compensated with ecclesiastical goods. Damage which could be proved would be set against the cash payment required in the redemptions. An analogous decree, relating to the properties within the city which had been damaged or destroyed by the bombardments, was issued on 25 March.[3] Though we cannot be certain, it is reasonable to suppose that, the most valuable capital having been sold in the first months, only those which were not easily saleable remained, and the government disposed of them in this way. Those who had suffered damage were given 'certificates of bombardment' which were later utilized in the purchase of capital funds, especially in Córdoba.

At the same time the law was applied throughout the state. Mejía, a treasury official and later Finance Minister, relates that he accompanied the liberal army to Orizaba where he ascertained from the notarial registers the mortgages invested in favour of the Church in private property. He

[1] Fols. 10, 101, 105, 106, 132.   [2] Ocampo, *Obras*, II, 197–8.
[3] Labastida, 294.

summoned the owners and obliged them to redeem all or part of the mortgage. He was thus able to raise, in a single day, 4,500 pesos, which he used to meet the expenses of the army for three days.[1] Mejía does not explain the form in which he made the landowners pay nor the discount that he allowed.

These transactions complemented, if they did not replace, the requisitions and forced loans, which could themselves be considerable. For example, during its temporary stay in Jalapa in 1859 the extraordinary revenue of the constitutionalist army was as follows: two forced loans on the city for 22,000 pesos, and in the surrounding area for 6,350 pesos; the seizure of horses from neighbouring haciendas, valued at 11,472 pesos and the same of cattle from diverse properties, worth 7,450 pesos; in addition, as it was customary to do in anticipation of the nationalization, the army collected 31,200 pesos from borrowers in the form of two years' payment in advance of the mortgage interest owed to the Church.[2] The sum corresponds to an approximate capital of 300,000 pesos (at 5%). This practice recalls the 1858 decrees of Ogazón, governor of Jalisco. The borrowers— the adjudicators and future buyers of clerical capital in the area of Veracruz liberated by the constitutionalist army—had to pay 10% of the capital in payment of interest and afterwards another 10–20% for the redemption of the capital. These and other costs tended to diminish the margin of their profit. Moreover, the law of 13 July 1859 stated in article 22 that unpaid interest which was nationalized in the same way as the capital would be condoned provided the capital debt was redeemed within thirty days. This concession was obviously very convenient for those who had not paid interest punctually to the Church or not at all during the years 1857–59. However, as this measure was somewhat demoralizing for those who had paid the interest punctually, Melchor Ocampo resolved in a circular of 27 July that the interest would only be condoned provided the borrowers redeemed the debt in cash within the thirty days.[3] The general meaning of the circular indicates that 40% of the capital had to be paid in cash, whereas it was normally payable over forty or eighty months. It is not known if discounts were granted in such cases.

THE END OF THE WAR

In the middle of 1860 the military situation changed decisively in favour of the liberal forces. All the sources of finance open to the conservative government had dried up. Now, nobody could or wanted to lend money

[1] Mejía, *Memorias*, 33–4.   [2] Trens, *Historia de Veracruz*, v, 233.   [3] Labastida, 190.

to Miramón. In the first place merchants were not prepared to make loans to him in exchange for clerical possessions, as such transactions would be annulled if the liberal government triumphed, which seemed more likely every day. Secondly, trade in the capital was more and more affected by the proximity of the military operations.

The most conclusive proof that the conservative exchequer was now receiving little or nothing by way of the loans secured with clerical goods is that in August 1860 Miramón decided to take the wrought silver contained in works of art and adornments in the cathedrals, excepting, naturally, the holy vessels, and also the jewels belonging to the Church. There could be no better illustration of the desperate plight of the conservatives.

The liberals had been practising this means of raising finance for some time. The best-known case was the confiscation of all the wrought silver from the Morelia cathedral which took place on 23 September 1858.[1] The events seem to have been as follows: on 31 December 1857 Santos Degollado, then governor of Michoacán, who was already preparing for the impending civil war, imposed a forced loan of 100,000 pesos on the clergy, an amount which was apparently paid. His successor, Epitacio Huerta, imposed another loan of 90,000 pesos on 17 September 1858, when the civil war was already being fought. The needs of the state treasury were very large, judging by the various forced loans imposed on business and on the city of Morelia and the extraordinary taxes and other means of extracting funds that were employed. On this occasion the Church only managed to raise 30,000 pesos. The governor responded by ordering the confiscation of the silver, gold, and jewels in the cathedral, which were estimated to have a total value of 500,000 pesos. Today it is impossible to establish the artistic value of all the silver articles adorning the interior of the cathedral and giving it a light and brilliance which it is now difficult to imagine. The value of the metal was much less, 162,820 ounces, worth 210,363 pesos.[2] In addition to the silver there was a relatively small quantity of gold. The value of the jewels is not known, but it can be assumed that it did not increase the aforementioned amount by very much. Probably the conservative writers inflated the total to make the confiscation hated by the public. 70,000 of the 210,000 pesos' worth of silver was secretly sent in bars by Huerta to the capital, where it was

[1] Riva Palacio, *México a través de los siglos*, v, 330; Bravo Ugarte, *Historia de Michoacán*, III, 101–4; Bravo Ugarte, *Historia de México*, III, book 1, 262; J. Romero Flores, *Historia de Michoacán* (Mexico, 1946), vol. II, pp. 166–7; Díaz, *Versión francesa*, II, 49.

[2] One ounce of gold was worth 20·67 pesos; silver was worth $\frac{1}{16}$ of gold, giving silver a value of 1·292 pesos per ounce; *Encyclopaedia Britannica* (1958), vol. XX, p. 683.

discovered by Zuloaga. As usually happens in such cases, little of the booty remained.

The conservatives therefore proceeded in 1860 to do the same thing, the only difference being in the method. On 21 August Miramón's government, with prior permission from the archbishop, established an office to receive the wrought silver and jewels from the ecclesiastical corporations. The silver was to be sent to the mint for coining, and the jewels, in which the gold was included—this seems to show that the Church did not have much of this metal—were to be pawned to people who lent cash to the government.[1] It can be assumed that, given the probable defeat of the conservatives, the merchants preferred to buy jewels rather than real estate. The conservative government hoped in this way to raise 300,000 pesos. The clergy in Guadalajara also sacrificed their silver and jewels to the conservative war effort.[2] The amounts obtained from these sources are unknown but they were probably insignificant. Without either credit or funds, Miramón confiscated on 17 November 660,000 pesos which had been entrusted to the British legation on behalf of the English bondholders.[3] But it was now too late, for the conservative government was about to disappear.

At the end of 1860 the Church was not exactly poor but its goods were perceptibly less than three years before. Both as a result of confiscations made by the liberals and of the forced loans imposed by the conservatives, the Church lost about 20,000,000 pesos during the three years' war.[4]

[1] Riva Palacio, *México a través de los siglos*, v, 431.
[2] Ibid.   [3] Ibid., p. 441.
[4] Pérez Hernández, *Estadística de la república*, pp. 205–7.

CHAPTER 5

NATIONALIZED PROPERTY IN THE CITY OF MEXICO: THE FINAL SETTLEMENT, 1861–63

In the last months of 1860, anticipating the liberal victory, many people wrote to Veracruz from areas still in conservative control with offers to buy ecclesiastical properties. For example, on 13 November Pedro Labat, a French merchant in the capital, asked permission to redeem the San Agustín monastery garden, which he had rented since 1828, and to buy the monastery building with a payment of 20,000 pesos in cash. On 15 November another of the capital's residents made an offer to buy a part of the Franciscan monastery, also paying part of the price in cash. On 22 November someone else in the capital offered a cash payment of 8,000 pesos towards the cost of the Dominican college of Porta Coeli.[1]

On 22 December Miramón lost at Calpulalpan the battle for possession of Mexico City, and three days later the liberal army entered. The constitutional government immediately set to work and in the Ministry of Hacienda during the first days of January 1861 the 'Special District Disentailment Office' was organized. Charged with the immense task of nationalizing and selling ecclesiastical possessions in the District of Mexico, the office began its work on 7 January. The result of its labours was collected in the *Memoria de las operaciones que han tenido lugar en la oficina especial de desamortización del distrito, desde el 7 de enero en que se abrió, hasta el 5 de diciembre de 1861, en que cesaron sus labores, para continuarlas la junta Superior de Hacienda, creada en virtud de la ley de 17 de julio del mismo año*, Mexico, Imp. de Ignacio Cumplido, 1862, 162 pp. This publication will henceforth be referred to as the 1862 Disentailment Report.

With the re-establishment of the constitutional government in the capital, the so-called Veracruz denouncers returned and now began to claim a considerable part of the city's real estate. This involved the properties in the possession of the earlier adjudicators-turned-buyers, the ordinary, straightforward buyers, those who had bought adjudication rights, and finally the houses remaining in the hands of the Church. When an ecclesiastical corporation still retained a house which had not

---

[1] All these documents are in AGN, PBN, leg. 734.

been denounced in Veracruz, then there was no problem. The property could be redeemed by the original tenant-adjudicator or, if it had not been assigned or auctioned in 1856–57, it was sold under the terms of the law of 13 July 1859.

However, when a house was in the hands of the Church through not having been sold in the three years between 1858 and 1860, but it had on the other hand been denounced in Veracruz, then difficulties arose from the beginning between the denouncers and the tenants. The latter might well be the original adjudicators, and probably were in most cases, and now they were willing to acquire the house under the nationalization law of 13 July 1859. If a house had been sold by the Church in 1858–60 and yet also denounced in Veracruz, even more complicated disputes arose. In principle, house sales made by the Church were considered void, because the constitutional government insisted on juridical continuity and there-fore on the uninterrupted validity of the Lerdo law from the time of its issue until 1861. Moreover, all conservative acts between 1858 and 1860 involving clerical possessions were null and void. Following these criteria, those people who had bought property in the capital during the years 1858–60 were considered as reactionaries who had helped the reaction by making purchases. In practice, however, it was soon realized that it was not possible simply to erase the three years of the conservative regime. Thus, as Zuloaga and Miramón had been obliged to compromise with some, perhaps many, adjudicators, so the constitutional government had also to recognize the existence of many adjudicators-turned-buyers and buyers-turned-adjudicators. Finally, when a house had been sold by the Church but not denounced in Veracruz the case was simple, for it was only a question of giving preference to the earlier adjudicator.

During its time in Veracruz, the liberal government became committed to a small number of the so-called denouncers—there was nothing defa-matory in the term, for they called themselves by it—to hand over the denounced properties, subject naturally to the prior redemption of the capital in accordance with the law. This handful of men now confronted the mass of different types of buyers and adjudicators who were not dis-posed to see themselves completely ignored. It was therefore essential to define the various categories of people, and as far as possible to reconcile their interests. In other words, the Lerdo law and the law of 13 July 1859 had to harmonize with the social and economic reality which the victorious liberals encountered when they liberated the nation's capital.

THE LAW OF 5 FEBRUARY AND ITS CONSEQUENCES

It was with this in mind that the new Minister of Hacienda, the poet Guillermo Prieto, issued on 5 February the so-called regulatory law.[1] The different groups were divided into adjudicators, buyers and denouncers. The law defined them in this order, probably on the basis of number, for undoubtedly the adjudicators were more numerous than the other categories and there were more buyers than denouncers.

According to the law, the legitimate adjudicators, that is those who had retained their rights to the houses, were in the first place 'those persons who had not returned the adjudication instrument nor collected the certificate of the return of the sales tax', which meant the ones who had not had the sales tax returned by the conservative government in 1858. It can be assumed that these cases were rare: to avoid returning the instrument, it was necessary to hide or to abandon the capital, and thus become a refugee, which few were prepared to do. Legitimate adjudicators were also those who had given back the instrument 'without any annotation' or 'with a note simply acknowledging the law of 28 January 1858, without any word denoting conformity or consent'. The corporations hoped that the people would act with humility but not all were submissive. The individuals who had given the deed back with an apology or any similar expression, in a word 'voluntarily', ceased to be adjudicators and therefore lost their claim to the property originally assigned to them. It is probable that the people who followed this course of action, either through conviction or convenience, were the same ones who confessed their guilt in the city's newspapers, which in turn were used by some Veracruz residents to denounce the returned properties. This stipulation was made precisely to avoid litigations between the two groups, and at the same time to honour the agreement with the denouncers and to punish the hostile or timid elements. Finally, legitimate adjudicators included those who had acquired the property from the original adjudicators, that is before the Lerdo law was annulled, as long as they had not subsequently lost their claim because of the type of conduct mentioned above.

As a means of protecting the more defenceless members of society, the gravely ill, spinsters, widows, orphans and persons under age, retained their status as adjudicators, even though they might have declared their

---

[1] The law is in Labastida, 144–56. To facilitate the work of its employees the Ministry of Hacienda published *Método para seguir la cuenta de redenciones de capitales que poseía el clero en las oficinas respectivas, expedido por el Ministerio de Hacienda y Crédito Público* (Mexico, 1861).

conformity with the return of the houses. The word auction buyer was not used in the law. By implication the adjudication instruments included those from auctions; the adjudicators under the law of 5 February 1861 included not only the normal ones from the Lerdo law but also the auction buyers.

As for the purchasers, the law began by declaring that 'every sale, either of property or anything else, contracted by the clergy without the express authorization of the constitutional authorities is null and of no value or effect' (article 10). Hence

those who in possession of deeds of adjudication, auction or conventional sale pre-dating 17 December 1857 [the date of the reactionary coup known as the Plan of Tacubaya], contracted purchases with the clergy of the same properties, thereby lost their rights as adjudicators...and they acquired none by contracts made with the clergy, nor retained rights to any return, nor indemnity, regardless of the amounts they might have given the clergy...

The legislator, however, was content with this threat, for a moment later the text reads: 'If today they wish to recover their earlier adjudication rights, the government is willing to concede them this favour on condition that the capital they owed by the adjudication is increased 20%' (article 11). The problem was resolved therefore by imposing a fine of 20% of the value of the property, so that these buyers would have to redeem 120% of the price. The buyers who were not the original adjudicators, 'those who bought from the clergy, acquiring possession at the same time of the adjudicators' rights', received the same concession as the adjudicator-buyers (article 12). Nevertheless, 'those who had bought from the clergy without obtaining the adjudicatory rights have no claim of any kind'. Consequently the adjudicators could take from them the houses acquired in 1858–60 (article 13). This measure was without any doubt the most severe, because not all the buyers had taken the precaution or seen the possibility of obtaining the adjudicatory right. It will be seen that it was on occasions impossible for the government to carry out this stipulation. In his exposition explaining the motives behind the law of 5 February, Guillermo Prieto branded as opportunists the adjudicators-turned-buyers. He thought that they had bought to cover themselves in case of a conservative victory, but it has already been explained that the adjudicators who were at the same time tenants had been obliged to buy the house. Prieto had spent the years of the civil war in Veracruz and he could not easily understand the people who had spent the same period in enemy territory.

The law specified that denouncers had to prove the denouncement and the payment of the sales tax. In those cases in which this could be done, the denouncers of properties voluntarily returned or of which the owners had had the sales tax repaid were legally subrogated in the place of the former adjudicators or buyers. The courts were to resolve any dispute between both parties. The legal recognition of these three divergent groups proved the cause of numerous lawsuits. A French newspaper in the capital described the situation in these words: 'Le beau temps pour les avocats! Que de travail pour les juges!'[1]

Having defined the most difficult part, the law continued with the form of payment. The law of 13 July 1859 had been quite clear, but force of circumstances soon obliged the government to concede discounts in exchange for payments in cash. Thus for example Ogazón, governor of Jalisco, decreed on 12 March 1860, during the campaign against the reaction which was then dominating Guadalajara, that mortgages could be redeemed by means of a 30% payment in cash and 60% in bonds, the government thereby sacrificing 10% of the total value. On these more advantageous conditions, many hacendados redeemed their debts.[2] The 30% in cash, instead of the 40% stipulated in the law, was payable by instalments.

As a result of the law of 13 July 1859, the federal government exchequer had begun to accumulate the promissory notes signed by the buyers. Then the government, always in urgent need of funds, began to sell them at a discount up to 50% of nominal value, that is, the 40% payable in instalments could be reduced to 20%. In this form, including also the real value of the bonds, it was possible to redeem the whole mortgage for 25% of its value.[3] The law of 5 February 1861 confirmed this practice with the following stipulation (article 38): 'Those who redeem in one payment all that they must pay in cash will be given an agreed discount in the District.' The law did not specify the size of the discount but, as will be shown later, the notes began to be sold at 30% of their nominal value; they represented 40% of the total value which could now be redeemed for 12% in cash—as the bonds used to redeem the 60% were obtainable at between 5% and 10% of face value, a property or a mortgage could be purchased at a discount of 80%. We have already seen in chapter 3 that the financiers made loans to the government at considerable discounts.

---

[1] *Le Trait d'Union*, 11 February 1861.
[2] Pérez Verdía, *Historia de Jalisco*, III, 112.
[3] On 26 October 1860 the Minister of Hacienda authorized treasury officials to sell promissory notes at a 50% discount; a month later only 33% discount was allowed, with the proviso that if this was not sufficient the Ministry should be consulted, which meant that in fact the higher rate must have continued; Dublán y Lozano, VIII, 717, 751.

Thus very large amounts of national debt bonds were accumulated by them and they were able to increase their holdings even further by buying bonds at 5–10% face value from other people. The liberal government faced the problem of extracting funds from these men, who were among the wealthiest in the capital. The problem was solved by offering them ecclesiastical possessions at the same discount which they were accustomed to receive in financial deals. Buyers thus paid for the deed of an ecclesiastical property about 20% of its value, for they considered that the government was in no position to guarantee that they would ever gain and retain possession of it. In view of the highly speculative nature of the transaction, the purchases became similar to the former loan contracts made with the government. It was only in this way that the latter was able to persuade the most prominent capitalists to buy nationalized goods. In the same manner, the capitalists themselves acquired an interest in the continuation of the liberal regime.

The laws of 12 and 13 July 1859—called the laws of Reform—had not dealt with the *capellanías* nor with institutions of social walfare or education. All these had considerable endowments which now attracted the attention of potential buyers. It was therefore necessary for the government to define its attitude to them.

The *capellanías* were divided into two categories: those which were hereditary and those which were not. The latter were foundations intended to maintain a *capellán* who would say masses for the soul of the founder.[1] The former were benefices restricted to the family or relatives of the founder. The Church was merely the trustee, not the owner of them. The example of the dowries belonging to nuns has already illustrated that the liberal legislators respected private property. Although the law of 12 July 1859 had nationalized 'all the properties managed by the secular and regular clergy, under diverse titles' (article 1), this same law exempted the dowries from the nationalization. It was therefore logical to apply the same criterion to the capital funds of the *capellanías*.

In addition to the *capellanías* mentioned above, the law of 5 February 1861 also dealt with those which were intended to maintain priests in the cathedrals, parishes or nunneries. The aim was to ensure religious services in the churches. The legislator declared that such capital could not be redeemed until such time that the government decided that the services of this type were not needed, in which case the funds would be disposed of by the civil authority.

The hereditary and other *capellanías* were declared redeemable but the

[1] Ocampo, *Obras*, II, 181.

redemption of the capital was different in either case. The hereditary ones, which were the great majority, as can be seen from the 1862 Disentailment Report, comprised 'only those in which the founder named as *capellanes* his relatives or those of another expressly designated person, and in which the present *capellán* is one of the named relatives. If these two circumstances are not met, the *capellanía* is not hereditary.' In spite of these conditions, which seemed difficult to meet, almost all *capellanías* were classified as hereditary. The capital fund of each had to be disentailed by the present *capellán* through payment of 10% of the capital. This meant that the person who was in receipt of the return on the capital could convert the latter into his own property by paying a 10% tax, which was what the payment in effect was. If the *capellán* did not pay within two months, the capital could be redeemed by the borrower, that is the person whose property was mortgaged with the capital, with a payment of 15%. The law justly gave preference to the founder's relatives.

The *capellanías* which were not hereditary, which were the ones in which the beneficiary was not a relative of the founder, could be redeemed within two months by the *capellanes*, like any other ecclesiastical capital, two-fifths of the payment being made in cash and three-fifths in bonds. Once the term allowed had transpired, the capital could be redeemed by the borrower or, should he not do so, by any other person. The non-hereditary *capellanías* were thus considered clerical possessions.

An exception was made in the redemption in respect of the possessions of the institutions of public welfare, such as hospitals, poor houses, asylums, orphanages, maternity homes and schools. Certainly these institutions were largely managed by the Church, but because of their public utility no attempt was made to sell their goods. On the contrary the intention was to preserve and, where possible, increase them. The government secularized them in a decree of 2 February, which created an Office of Public Welfare.[1] Their capital and real estate were to remain intact. The capital funds, invested both in assigned properties and in those which were originally privately owned, were to continue as before, without there being any obligation to redeem them. Indeed to redeem them a government permit would be required, and the capital would again be loaned with a mortgage of real estate as security. The law of 5 February declared that all these endowments were exempt from the effects of the law of 13 July 1859 (articles 64–68).

As regards the nunneries, the law of 4 February regulated the measures contained in the Reform laws regarding the dowries and capital funds.

[1] Labastida, 360.

The convents were to continue receiving the product from these (articles 69–78). Nevertheless, although the law of 12 July 1859 had said that 'the nunneries which at present exist are to continue', the new law ordered that within fifteen days the government would reduce the number to what it thought necessary. The convents which were considered unnecessary were to be vacated, the nuns going to the remaining ones and the buildings sold in auction. As already indicated, all the monastery buildings were to be sold. The money yielded from the sale of the suppressed convent buildings would be used for pensions for widows and orphans and for charity organizations. It was attempted at least to ensure that public welfare would receive the profits.

Finally, the law declared as null all the transactions made by the clergy with 'so-called ecclesiastical' possessions (article 86), but it approved definitively contracts and deals negotiated by military leaders and state governors (article 87). Prieto wrote in his explanation of the motives behind the law that the government 'has valued public peace more than the loss of some money, and it has not wanted vested interests created by officials to whom extraordinary powers were granted to remain unstable and uncertain'. This approval did not, or course, provoke any discontent but the attempt to annul faits accomplis in the capital stimulated immediate opposition.

A few days after 5 February, the eleven most important foreign buyers in the capital held a meeting, and on the 18th day of the same month they sent a protest to the president of the republic.[1] The firm of Barrón, Forbes and Co. and Antonio Escandón were among the signatories. Both Barrón and Escandón were Mexicans who had taken out foreign citizenship in order to protect their interests. Among the others were the Spaniards Pío Bermejillo and Isidoro de la Torre, the Swiss Jecker, and the Englishman Nathaniel Davidson. Barrón, Davidson and Jecker were mentioned in the previous chapter as persons who had loaned the conservative government large sums of money which were secured with clerical goods. Felipe Neri del Barrio was absent from the protestors. He was Guatemalan Minister and dean of the diplomatic corps, and he had been expelled from Mexico on 25 January, together with several other foreign representatives, because 'their actions in favour of the so-called reactionary government were a matter of public notoriety'.[2] It can be

[1] M. Payno (ed.), *Colección de las leyes, decretos, circulares y providencias relativas a la desamortización eclesiástica, a la nacionalización de los bienes de corporaciones, y a la reforma de la legislación civil que tenía relación con el culto y con la iglesia* (Mexico, 1861); the protest is in vol. II, pp. 377–91.
[2] Circular of the Ministry of Foreign Affairs, 25 January 1861, Colección Lafragua, vol. 396.

assumed that Barrio, a man of great wealth, could have helped the reaction more with money than with diplomatic aid, for Guatemala was not a powerful country; in other words, with loans in exchange for clerical property. He was perhaps not in Mexico on 18 February, although he does appear as a buyer of nationalized properties in the 1862 Disentailment Report, which registered the sales made in 1861. Probably represented by a relative, he redeemed mortgage debts of 96,000 pesos which his sugar plantation Temixco, near Cuernavaca, owed to various corporations.

The 1858–60 buyers began their protest in a tone of considerable self-confidence: 'Mr. President; the undersigned foreign subjects...' Their main argument was as follows: our governments 'recognized the legality of the defeated administration; it was also legal for us to negotiate onerous contracts with it'. Onerous for themselves, that is, unlike, according to them, the denouncers and adjudicators who had invested nothing and now expected to receive everything. The law of 5 February was confiscatory and therefore in need of reform. Altogether the protest was of less interest for its text than for the names of its signatories.

Encouraged by the foreigners' action, the Mexican buyers met and elected a committee which protested against the same law on 25 February.[1] The committee consisted of only three persons but many buyers were represented by it, judging from the fact that they had to meet in a theatre. In essence, the committee requested the annulment of the clause in the law relating to the so-called buyers because its implementation would lead to a monopoly of real estate by the foreign denouncers. The adjudicators had acquired the properties in 1856 'because of the imperious necessity of conserving their long held tenancies', in other words, not out of conviction. Afterwards, in 1858–60, they had bought from the clergy for the same reason. They had spent money on improving the houses in which they lived or had businesses or industries, and the clergy had offered them for sale. Adopting a polemical tone, the protest continued: 'It is said that the prices were given to foment, with the resources thus afforded the usurper, the civil war. Lies and more lies. Those prices were given to pay all or part of the value of the purchased properties.'[2] The pamphlet ended by asking that the purchases from the Church in 1858–60 should be declared valid.

---

[1] *Exposición que ha presentado al Exmo. Señor Presidente de la república la comisión nombrada por la reunión de compradores de fincas del clero, que tuvo lugar en el teatro principal y acordó representar contra las disposiciones del decreto de 5 de febrero de 1861* (Mexico, 1861); this was reproduced in Payno, *Colección de las leyes,* pp. 393–445.

[2] Ibid., p. 24.

The government remained firm in its support of the law and the denouncers, although in practice it did make concessions and settlements with various buyers. Only two agreements are known for certain, one with Davidson and the other with Barrón, who both succeeded in obtaining them because of their British citizenship.

The agreement between the Mexican government and Davidson was reached on 7 March 1861. It was formulated by the senior official in the Ministry of Hacienda, José María Iglesias, and signed by Guillermo Prieto.[1] Davidson undertook to hand over to the government 60,000 pesos in cash, 10,000 in bonds and 50,000 in mortgages in which the capital funds of dowries had been invested. The latter mortgages would help the government to fulfil its promise to return the nuns' dowries. In exchange for this the government recognized the purchases made by Davidson and undertook to ensure that he acquired possession of the properties. It would pay compensation to the adjudicators and denouncers who had acquired a claim and thus avoid litigation in the courts.

Later the government increased the sums that Davidson had to pay to 62,000 pesos in cash and 54,000 in dowries, in addition to the 10,000 in bonds. Considering that in 1858 he had disbursed 504,000 pesos in a loan of a nominal value of 700,000 pesos,[2] he now had to hand over various amounts totalling about 117,000 pesos, which equalled 20% of his original investment. This percentage recalls the fine imposed by the law on adjudicators-turned-buyers or vice versa. In total, he paid approximately 620,000 pesos for goods worth between 590,000 and 650,000 pesos. Hence he scarcely retrieved his investment, and of course did not increase the wealth of the firm he represented. It may be supposed that in view of the delicate international situation, the Mexican government calculated the transaction in such a way that the powerful Rothschild firm did not lose money.

Unfortunately, sufficient precise details are not available on the Barrón deal. It is not known if the 320,000 pesos was the nominal or real value of the loan. If it was the nominal value and Barrón had made the loan at the same discount as Davidson, then he had paid out in 1858 the sum of 230,000 pesos. On 6 May 1861 the government reached an agreement with him on the same basis as the one concluded with Davidson. Barrón, Forbes and Co. were to pay 30,000 pesos in cash, and 20,000 pesos in certain bonds pertaining to the national debt, the real value of which is not known.[3] In total he disbursed, therefore, between 260,000 and

---

[1] Payno, *México y sus cuestiones financieras*, 118–30.   [2] See chapter 4.
[3] Payno, *México y sus cuestiones financieras*, 132; Labastida, 225.

280,000 pesos. The value of the goods he acquired is uncertain because, apart from the capital funds for 48,000 pesos, there was real estate valued at 350,000 pesos but sold for 229,000 pesos. Taking the lowest value as the most likely, the company obtained goods worth 277,000 pesos, which was about what they had to pay. Hence this British banking firm likewise scarcely recovered its investment.

Barrón, Forbes and Co. had bought twenty-five houses and the government paid compensation to thirteen different adjudicators, auction buyers and denouncers to the total amount of 170,000 pesos.[1] Although in some cases the compensation was more than the value of the house which had been assigned and then sold to Barrón, it was not paid in cash but in nationalized promissory notes, which at the time were worth about a third of their face value. It is possible that the 40,000 or 50,000 pesos that the firm had to pay in 1861 to regularize its purchases equalled the cost of the compensation paid by the government. The latter perhaps accepted Barrón's purchases provided he paid the cost of the compensation. Although the exchequer probably lost nothing in this transaction, the adjudicators did suffer. Certainly there were some among them who had bought many clerical properties at a low price, so that his loss merely reduced their profit, but it seems that there were also others who were just ordinary adjudicators and people with little money. As was to be expected, the complicated nature of the Barrón and Davidson transaction caused many legal problems; for example, two buildings acquired by Barrón, Forbes and Co. had not been handed over by January 1862. Compensation to the value of 42,754 pesos was paid for twenty-five of the forty-six houses bought by Davidson and this amount was much less than what he had paid in cash in 1861.[2] Several people were given their compensation in cash, but only in very small sums. Therefore, of the forty-six houses assigned for approximately 300,000 pesos, compensation of only 42,000 was paid on twenty-five. The adjudicators were sacrificed for the sake of fiscal and political necessity. Those of six houses received no compensation because they had sold their rights directly to Davidson, who had thereby become the adjudicator in accordance with the law of 5 February. In all the other cases Davidson was apparently an ordinary buyer who had acted under the terms of the same law.

It is not known if the other important buyers of ecclesiastical possessions in the years 1858–60 came to any settlement with the government. In his book, written a year later and for which he had had access to the

---

[1] *L'Estafette*, 16 January 1862.
[2] Payno, *México y sus cuestiones financieras*, 129–30.

whole of the Ministry of Hacienda's archive, Payno only mentioned the agreements with Davidson and Barrón. This seems to indicate that these were the only cases and that the other buyers who protested on 18 February against the law of the 5th of that month must have suffered substantial losses. Nevertheless, at least some of them were able to make up for their losses in other lucrative deals with the government. For example, the brothers Manuel and Antonio Escandón, partners in several ventures, were able to establish such good relations with the government that as early as 5 April they received a concession to build a railway from Veracruz to Mexico.[1] The imaginative and rather inaccurate French diplomatic informant wrote on 17 July that Escandón was 'the soul of the new cabinet'.[2] Escandón had acquired a concession for the same railway from the liberal government in 1857. It was modified by the conservatives in 1859 and again by the liberals in 1861.[3] This illustrates the good relations which this entrepreneur was able to maintain with both the political parties. Needless to say, because of the circumstances of the time the construction of the line proceeded very slowly. Another transaction involving Escandón took place on 7 February 1862 when the so-called 'financing company' of the del Monte Mine, near Pachuca, was granted exemption from taxes because it had paid the government 300,000 pesos in cash.[4] The legal owner of these mines was in fact the Romero de Terreros family, but a joint stock company worked them.[5] It seems that Nicanor Béistegui was Escandón's partner in the financing company.[6] The biggest mining enterprise in the country clearly had to have connections with the party in power.

In 1861 the Escandón brothers redeemed mortgages to the value of 54,672 pesos, which had been invested by different corporations in their two sugar plantations and textile mill.[7] This indicates that they retained their good relations with the liberal government, whether or not they had reached an agreement over their purchases in 1858–60. The fact that neither Davidson nor Barrón appears in the 1862 Disentailment Report, which recorded all the purchases made in 1861, with one exception to be discussed later, signifies that the agreements made on the fringe of the law of 5 February were not included in it.

Isidoro de la Torre, another financier who made loans in 1858–60, redeemed clerical possessions in 1861 for 73,328 pesos.[8] If perhaps he lost what he had bought during the conservative regime, he was quickly

[1] Dublán y Lozano, IX, 131.
[2] Díaz, *Versión francesa*, II, 260.
[3] MH 1870, pp. 473, 501, 535–6.
[4] Dublán y Lozano, IX, 381.
[5] *Diccionario universal*, V, 350.
[6] Register of Mariano Vega, ANM.
[7] MD 1862, pp. 83, 133.
[8] Ibid.

re-established. His fortune cannot have suffered much, considering that after the defeat of Maximilian's empire in 1867 he owned two large sugar plantations in the Yautepec district.[1]

In contrast, Pío Bermejillo bought nothing in 1861, perhaps showing his non-conformity with the liberal government. It can be assumed that it was not for lack of money, for both in 1861 and in 1867–68 he owned several sugar plantations in the region of Cuernavaca.[2] In the previous chapter the sale of three houses by La Concepción to Genaro Béistegui was mentioned. The mortgage of 64,000 pesos which Béistegui owed was sold by the convent to Pío Bermejillo, probably at a considerable discount. After the promulgation of the law of 5 February, Béistegui redeemed the mortgage. Bermejillo defended himself in the courts but, to the advantage of Béistegui, no judgement was apparently given.[3] His redemptions of clerical possessions in 1861 amounted, according to the Disentailment Report, to exactly 74,000 pesos, which was the sum at which the three houses he had bought from the convent were valued. Unlike the 1857 report, the 1862 Disentailment Report has two separate lists, one of the redeemed goods and one of the buyers, so that it is impossible to determine from the data given which properties each one bought. Hence one of two buyers in the years 1858–60 won the case. Béistegui was perhaps also helped by his better relations with the government. He had not joined Bermejillo, Davidson and the others in their protest of 18 February, probably because he realized that his case was already won and that the law of 5 February was not prejudicial to him. This could mean simply that as a buyer during the years of the reaction he was already at the same time the owner of the adjudicatory rights on the three houses.

Another person who certainly lost in 1861 the properties he had acquired in 1858–60 was the banker, Jecker. During these years he had invested not only an unknown amount in buying clerical possessions but also approximately 1,500,000 pesos in bonds issued by the reactionary government. In 1861 the French representatives attempted to reach a settlement with the liberal government over the 'Jecker credit'.[4] For Jecker himself the recovery of at least a part of these funds was a matter of honour, because as a result of his loans to the reaction his bank had collapsed in 1860 and the savings of many French artisans had been lost.[5] The Jecker question was undoubtedly more difficult than the ones involving Davidson and Barrón, but it is equally certain that the constitutional government

[1] Maillefert, 291. [2] Ibid.
[3] Reyes, *Rectificación*. [4] Díaz, *Versión francesa*, II, 234.
[5] Ibid., p. 163.

had as much interest in retaining good relations with France as with Great Britain. Nevertheless there was no agreement and the Jecker credit served as a motive or a pretext for the French invasion.

The buyers were at one extreme of the capital's society. At the other there were the 'Veracruz denouncers' and in the middle of the two, the adjudicators. The latter were mingled with the buyers, some of whom had become adjudicators, and many adjudicators had turned buyers. It is clear from the notes in the margin of the 1856 and 1857 notarial registers that the great majority of the original adjudicators kept their houses in 1861. Some could have bought a house in 1858–60 but others could not; at any rate, they kept them. It can be concluded that this continuity significantly contributed towards stabilizing the situation following the liberal victory and towards creating a wide social basis for the government.

Apart from the Veracruz denouncers, the same names appear basically in the 1862 Disentailment Report as in the 1857 report. However, because of the presentation of the information in the 1862 document—the houses not being listed next to those who acquired them but in a separate list—it is not possible to deduce the continuity or its rupture by means of the transfer of the property from the hands of the original adjudicators to those of other people. In several instances, when the redemption value paid by one individual in 1861 is the same as the adjudication price of 1856, it is reasonable to suppose that the same property was concerned. This seems to have been the case of the senior official in the Ministry of Hacienda, mentioned in the previous chapter, who obtained a house in 1856 for 9,762 pesos. In 1861 he redeemed exactly the same amount, which indicates that the house was the same one on each occasion. It may well also have been that the government took into account the services which this longstanding official had rendered to the liberal cause and hence conceded him specially favourable conditions of payment.

The hypothesis of the continuity of possession of the clerical houses is confirmed by the various examples taken from the archival sources cited in chapter 4. For example, Lic. M. Navarro was assigned a house in 1856 for 18,000 pesos and in 1861 redeemed the same amount;[1] J. M. Jarero acquired a house in 1856 for 16,400 pesos and in 1862 redeemed 16,000 pesos, almost the same sum;[2] A. Alcérrega, adjudicator of a house for 7,400 pesos, redeemed the same amount in 1861.[3]

This continuity can also be seen in the conventional sales made in

[1] MD 1862, exp. 937.
[2] Ibid., exp. 1300; exp. 1301 registers the same person with 12,715 pesos but must refer to another matter.   [3] Ibid., exp. 720.

Nationalized property in the city of Mexico, 1861–63

1856. In September of that year J. M. Salas bought two houses from La Merced for 8,000 pesos, taking out a mortgage for the whole price. The sum was reduced in 1858 to 4,000 pesos. Then on 20 November 1860, a month before the liberal victory, a creditor appeared before the notary Negreiros. La Merced had owed him 13,900 pesos since 1852, although this had been reduced to 11,000 by payments on account. The prudent creditor succeeded in persuading the monastery to cede some mortgages to him because, as the nationalization of ecclesiastical wealth was enforced in the city, not only would assets be confiscated but also liabilities would disappear. The fact that the Reform laws were not to mention specifically the Church's debts to individuals may mean that the latter had insured themselves against the possibility of nationalization by acquiring clerical possessions in exchange for their loans to the corporations. One of the capitals ceded by La Merced to its creditor was the 4,000 pesos mortgage on Salas' house. In 1861 the liberal government resolved to respect not only the conventional sales of houses but also the mortgage conceded by the corporation to Salas. No doubt if the latter had loaned money to the Church during the three years' war, or if he had made loans to the government with the security of clerical possessions, then his credit or his acquisition would have been annulled. This case, however, concerned a loan made before the Reform. The liberal government had no wish to harm private interests or claims. Thus Salas was able to complete the mortgage by two payments to the creditor during 1861.[1] In another example, the conventional buyer of the three houses belonging to the Carmelites *del Desierto* redeemed the capital in 1861 like any other adjudicator.[2]

The continuity between 1856 and 1861 cannot be considered broken when an adjudicator transferred his right to another person, for this was a voluntary, mercantile transaction like, for example, the buying and selli ig of a house. There were adjudicators in 1856 who sold the house they acquired in 1857, and in these cases the buyers automatically became the adjudicators. Thus Sra. Mercado de Rivas, who had obtained the adjudicatory right from someone else, redeemed 27,460 pesos on 14 July 1862, which was almost the same as the 1856 adjudication price of 27,800 pesos.[3]

The adjudicators under the law of 5 February 1861 were not necessarily the original tenants or persons of few resources, as seems to have been

---

[1] *Dése conocimiento...*, AGN, PBN, leg. 1523, exp. 8, fols. 1–7.
[2] Register of José María Natera, 23 September 1856, ANM.
[3] 1859 register of A. Ferreiro, book 1, fol. 11, ANM; the redemption took place in 1862 and hence is not in the *Memoria* corresponding to 1861.

the case in the examples cited above. They could also be those individuals who in 1856 had bought a number of houses in auctions. The
addenda, number 11, reveals that Schiafino, the prominent auction
buyer in 1856, kept in 1861 almost all the houses he had acquired.

There is a very interesting example in the notary F. Pérez de León's
1857 register which, as indicated in chapter 3, contains in its first volume
details of the properties sold in auction to Manuel Morales Puente.
Attached to folio 7 there is a note from the Disentailment Office, dated
12 March 1861, according to which Morales Puente, representing and in
the name of Ignacio Loperena, redeemed eighty houses with a total value
of 505,477 pesos. The description of the houses reveals that they were the
ones originally bought in auction by Morales Puente and they appear as
such in the 1857 report. The form and conditions of payment are shown
in Table 13.

TABLE 13. *Form of payment (in pesos) for houses
redeemed by Morales Puente, 1861*

Obligation to pay in three months bonds for $\frac{3}{5}$ of the total		300,000
Money paid in cash immediately	30,000	
A draft payable in 30 days	10,000	
A draft payable in 60 days	10,000	
A draft payable in 90 days	10,000	
A credit in favour of J. Navarrete from 1857	90,000	
Discount agreed in special arrangement on 6 March 1861	50,000	
Total 'money' ('cash') ($\frac{2}{5}$)	200,000	200,000
		500,000

The 50,000 pesos discount, equalling 10% of the total, was perhaps
granted because of the cash payment of 60,000 pesos. It can be assumed
that the drafts were paid. The bonds were 'settled' more than six months
later by A. Labat, in the name of I. Loperena. This is shown in a note of the
Disentailment Office dated 2 November 1861. Considering that the credits
against the government and in favour of employees or suppliers could be
obtained at 20–30% of their nominal value,[1] the buyer paid approximately
100,000 pesos or 20% of the sale price of the properties. The auction and
legal costs have to be added to this, and the 1856–57 sales tax, which
together increase the amount paid to 25%. This excludes other possible
expenditure, for example, in litigation with the tenants-turned-buyers in

[1] Díaz, *Versión francesa*, III, 377.

1858–60. Such costs could increase the price actually paid by a significant amount.

Another note from the Disentailment Office, dated 11 May 1861, is appended to folio 14 of the same volume 1 for 1857. According to this, Loperena acquired more than twenty houses, auctioned in 1857, for 121,792 pesos. He paid 48,716 in cash immediately (two-fifths) and 73,075 (three-fifths) in credits. Finally, on 27 September 1861 more than twenty houses were redeemed, which had originally been auctioned in January 1857. The redemption price was 92,367 pesos; of this amount, 55,420 (three-fifths) was to be paid in bonds in three months and 36,946 (two-fifths) in promissory notes due in five years.[1] As far as the terms of payment were concerned the law was carried out. The total value of the three transactions was 719,636 pesos, which is the same figure given in the 1862 Report under the name of Ignacio Loperena.

In 1856 Loperena, together with Manuel Morales Puente and three other Mexican capitalists, was a member of a company formed to buy Church houses in the auctions.[2] When the partnership was liquidated in 1857 he was allotted houses worth 461,716 pesos, but now, in 1861, he redeemed property to the value of 719,636 pesos. The fact that his three capitalist partners do not appear by name in the 1862 Disentailment Report perhaps indicates that the group was again formed in 1861 for the purpose of redeeming the houses bought in 1856. If this was so, then other people also participated in the enormous sum of 719,636 pesos. It may also be said, therefore, that in the case of the large scale auction sales the 1856 disentailment was consolidated in 1861.

Apart from Loperena, Manuel Morales Puentes was the only one of the original partners who was prominent in 1861 on account of the large number of purchases he made. Nevertheless, whereas in 1857 he had obtained houses for 182,197 pesos, he only redeemed 120,600 pesos in 1861. It now turned out that this lawyer was in partnership with Antoine Bonhomme, the purveyor of the liberal government in Veracruz and the denouncer of houses voluntarily returned in the capital in 1858. The houses were bought in the name of Morales Puente.[3] Thus, according to a note from the Disentailment Office, dated 11 March 1861, Bonhomme redeemed several houses for 104,700 pesos.[4] Morales had already ceded these to him on 9 February of the same year.[5] He later ceded more worth 62,104 pesos and there were further transfers.[6] Finally, the Morales Puente–Bonhomme

[1] 1857 register of F. Pérez de León, vol. 1, fol. 41, ANM.
[2] See chapter 3.
[3] 1861 register of F. Pérez de León, vol. 1, fols. 80 ff. ANM.
[4] Ibid.   [5] Ibid., fol. 162.   [6] Ibid., fol. 181.

company was dissolved[1] and the latter retained a number of houses which he later redeemed, as shown in Disentailment Office document of 10 June 1861.[2] Bonhomme, who was defined in this document as the cessionary of Morales Puente and the denouncer of other houses, redeemed in total 371,490 pesos. The terms of payment were as follows: in six months, bonds for 222,894 pesos and 148,596 in cash. A discount of 35% or 52,086 pesos was allowed on the cash payment, leaving only 96,510 pesos. Adding 2,012 pesos in due interest, the amount to be paid in cash was 98,522 pesos, which Bonhomme 'paid under the agreed terms with the consent of the Minister of Hacienda' but the actual conditions are not given. This probably means that the government allowed Bonhomme a term of eighty months to pay the 98,522 pesos, as he had already been offered in Veracruz.[3] According to Mejía, an inflated price was charged by Bonhomme for the rifles which he sold the government during the civil war,[4] but it remained to be seen if the value of the real estate redeemed by him was not also too high. The discount of 52,086 pesos does not seem excessive in view of the service afforded the republic by those weapons. Mejía does not recall whether there were 5,000 or 8,000 rifles, so that it is impossible to calculate exactly how much the Frenchman had invested, nor the profit that he made. It can be estimated that in total his expenditure was approximately 100,000 pesos. Consequently he paid 25–30% of the redemption value of the real estate. As will be shown, the average sale price was 30% lower than the value. Therefore Bonhomme invested between 18% and 23% of the property value.

The bonds for 222,894 pesos (three-fifths) of the total were paid in November 1861, according to a note on the same deed. Bonhomme had not been the adjudicator nor the auction buyer in 1856. No doubt in 1861 he had to deprive many people of the property ownership to which they felt entitled, but who lost it as a result of the law of 5 February. Bonhomme did compensate a number of them—they were tenants now— by buying their adjudicatory rights.[5] Although he did not have to do it, the policy of respecting interests created by the Lerdo law was wise, and it might explain the absence of lawsuits connected with his name.

Bonhomme and Morales Puente's partnership was not the only one. For example, in 1861 the partnership between Manuel Cañizo and the widow of Francisco Iniestra was dissolved and the houses were shared.

---

[1] Ibid., fol. 162, 9 February 1861.
[2] 1857 register of F. Pérez de León, vol. 1, next to fol. 149, ANM.
[3] Mejía, *Memorias*, 49.
[4] Ibid.
[5] 1861 register of F. Pérez de León, passim, ANM.

She was the widow of one of the most important of the 1856 auction buyers. In 1861 another Veracruz firm of denouncers, Rayo and Co., redeemed a large number of houses that had been voluntarily returned.[1]

The most renowned example of an association of denouncers was that of Limantour and Co.[2] As a result of several vociferous court cases over the possession of properties, a quite abundant amount of information has survived, but even so, it seems almost impossible to clarify the matter.

Limantour denounced in Veracruz about sixty houses located in the capital, which had been voluntarily returned by the adjudicators or buyers. He did not become the owner of them all, however, for the government had decided to cede nine houses, worth 120,757 pesos, to other people. Among these was N. Davidson with four houses worth 28,757 pesos.[3] The remainder were given to other buyers, apparently people of scant resources, who presented a medical certificate declaring that they had returned their house 'in articulo mortis'.[4] Eventually Limantour was able to redeem in 1861 a total of forty-nine or fifty houses worth 525,528 pesos.[5] As stated in the 1857 report these properties had been disentailed for 587,410 pesos and therefore the treasury lost 61,882 pesos.[6] The difference is even greater if a comparison is made of the value of the thirty-nine houses which can be located in the 1856 Account, with the redemption value paid by Limantour. The valuation of these thirty-nine houses had been 615,848 pesos whereas Limantour had redeemed them for 438,635 pesos.

The 525,528 pesos were liquidated in the following manner. On 9 February 1861 the Minister of Hacienda accepted on account 202,500 pesos, as follows: 165,193 pesos as the value of the weapons and 37,306 pesos which Limantour had paid the army in cash.[7] The sum for weapons

---

[1] Ibid., fols. 342 ff.; communication from the Disentailment Office of 2 March 1861.

[2] In the pamphlets *Manifestaciones que José Yves Limantour...* of 1865, and *Représentation adressée à M. le Ministre de France à propos de la vente faite à M. Limantour par le gouvernement mexicain de diverses propriétés ayant appartenu aux corporations ecclésiastiques*, December 1863, there are copies of various instruments drawn up before notary Ignacio Torcida and signed by Francisco Mejía; Limantour appears in these only as the representative of the 'denouncing company known as Limantour & Co.'; the constitution of the company is not known.

[3] *Manifestaciones que José Yves Limantour...*, pp. 10–11.

[4] Mejía, *Memorias*, 49–50. Somewhat imprecisely, he speaks of the twelve or fifteen cases in which he was able to take houses from Limantour.

[5] *Manifestaciones que José Yves Limantour...*, pp. 48–9, and MD 1862, pp. 139, 141; the four expedientes of Limantour give the total of 533,078 pesos which perhaps includes the unpaid rent of the properties or the unpaid interest on the capital; in this work I have used the first figure because the pamphlet indicates the price of each of the houses.

[6] *Ocurso que el doctor D. A. Fernández Monjardín presentó el 28 de abril de 1862...*, p. 30.

[7] *El Ministerio de Hacienda del 21 de enero al 6 de abril de 1861*, p. 7; Limantour in *Manifestaciones* offers a different analysis.

corresponds more or less to the rifles handed over in 1858 and 1859, at 16 pesos a rifle, which according to Mejía was an excessive price. The 202,500 pesos equal almost two-fifths of the total 525,528 pesos.

The remaining three-fifths, amounting to 315,316 pesos, should have been paid in credits and they were liquidated as follows: Limantour paid immediately 63,063 pesos in bonds, and signed a note to deliver, in five years, bonds for 252,253 pesos.[1] To complete the total amount, there was still a balance of 3,054 pesos. He paid this with 1,832 pesos, having been granted a discount of 40%.[2]

Even admitting that the rifles were sold to the government at a high price—approximately double, according to Mejía—and totalling the various costs incurred by the bonds, varying between 5% and 10% of nominal value, the net result is that Limantour disbursed in total between 125,000 and 150,000 pesos. This equalled between 25% and 30% of the sale price of the properties. He had other costs, apart from these, which he listed in 1863 as follows: 86,712 pesos for rents in 1861–63 which he did not collect, for example a tenant refused to pay an annual rent of 1,450 pesos, which Limantour had raised from the original sum of 1,000 pesos; 52,550 pesos in taxes to the liberal government in 1861–63; and 31,531 pesos in lawyers' fees (this item seems credible, considering that Limantour apparently did not spend anything on compensation to former adjudicators); the total was 170,796 pesos.[3] The house which Schoessling had bought in 1858 was one of the properties redeemed by Limantour who finally succeeded in getting possession of it on 24 May 1861.[4] It was not all profit for the buyers of nationalized goods.

In general terms, the law of 5 February was carried out. The original adjudicators and the auction buyers regained possession of their houses or, if they had bought in 1858–60, they retained them. Basically, the 1861 redemption transactions consolidated the 1856–57 disentailment and thus stabilized the social base of the liberal regime. The continuity of the years 1856–61 gave the majority of the adjudicators confidence in the strength of the government. The country was being pacified when the French invasion took place.

Nevertheless, the social nucleus to which the real estate in the capital passed during 1861 was no longer exactly as it was five years earlier.

---

[1] *Manifestaciones que José Yves Limantour...*, pp. 11, 49.
[2] Ibid., p. 50.
[3] *Représentation adressée...*, p. 33; *Alegato de buena prueba presentado por la parte de la Señora Doña Loreto Bernal de Suárez en el juicio ejecutivo que contra ella sigue Don José Y. Limantour sobre arrendamientos de la casa número 19 de la calle de D. Juan Manuel* (Mexico, 1862).
[4] *Alegato de buena prueba que el Lic. D. Manuel Siliceo...*

The Veracruz denouncers, who had usually not been adjudicators in 1856, now occupied an important place. They replaced those who had voluntarily returned their properties. Another important group in 1861 was the 1858–60 buyers, some of whom were able to replace the adjudicators and even sometimes the denouncers.

The redemption prices of the houses were usually the same as those of the 1856 disentailment. The prices of the holdings of the seven corporations mentioned in chapter 3 are exactly the same in the 1862 Disentailment Report as they were in 1856. The value of the property which had been sold, therefore, continued depressed in comparison with privately owned property. The fall in value of these houses is also to be seen in the purchases made by Barrón in 1858; his twenty-two houses, valued at 309,078 pesos, were sold for 229,124 pesos, that is at a discount of 26%. The thirty-nine houses redeemed by Limantour and of which the price is known were valued at 615,848 pesos but were sold for 438,635 pesos, a fall of 29%. If these houses are added to those of the seven corporations, there is a total of 151 houses valued at 1,885,581 pesos but sold for 1,321,614 pesos, a fall of 30%. The fall in the value of the nationalized real estate, which is so often noted in the press and pamphlets of the time, can therefore be proved. It is surprising that the value did not decline even more as a result of the disappearance of the Church as a lending institution and the abolition of a maximum interest rate in 1861.

THE AMOUNT OF SALES AND THEIR FINANCIAL CONSEQUENCES

The result of the social transformation which occurred in Mexico City in 1861 can be investigated in the Disentailment Report, which recorded all the transactions from 7 January until 5 December 1861. The only omissions were the Davidson and Barrón, Forbes and Co. transactions, and it was logical to exclude these because they were on the fringe of the law, and the sales of the monastic buildings, probably due to the fact that these were processed by a different office. Details of these will be given later.

According to the Report, in 1861 properties were sold in the Disentailment Office of the Federal District for 16,256,036 pesos.[1] Of this total, 10,016,063 pesos pertained to 1,447 urban houses in the District (1,436 in the capital and 11 in the towns under the District's jurisdiction). Almost

---

[1] The result is summarized in MH 1870, pp. 559–60, with a few discrepancies; I have followed the original figures in MD 1862, pp. 1–105; unlike the MH 1857, the MD 1862 seems to have few errors.

all the capital resulting from the disentailment of clerical real estate in the city was redeemed, with the exception of the funds belonging to certain educational and public welfare institutions. These will be discussed later. Then in the capital twenty-one houses located in various states were sold for 107,051 pesos, and one house in Spain for 3,000 pesos. Four haciendas in the District were redeemed for 43,316 pesos and twelve haciendas and ranches in nearby states for 316,658 pesos. Finally 74 plots and 18 sites, gardens and other similar properties, almost all in the District, were redeemed for 258,601 pesos. The next item in the Report deals with capital funds, or by implication the mortgages predating the Lerdo Law. 520 mortgages on urban property were sold for 2,781,762 pesos, almost all in the District, and 225 mortgages on rural properties, mostly in nearby states, for 2,514,097. So far the total is 16,040,550 pesos. Finally, the product of 377 *capellanías* amounted to 215,485 pesos; seventeen non-hereditary *capellanías* were redeemed at nominal value for 58,593 pesos; 185 hereditary *capellanías* with a capital value of 679,189 pesos were disentailed at 10% of value, that is for a price of 67,918 pesos; and 175 hereditary *capellanías*, with principals amounting to 593,156 pesos, were disentailed at 15% of value, that is 88,973 pesos. Of the capital funds of the *capellanías*, 128 were invested in real estate in the capital and 249 in properties situated outside the city. The latter were mainly haciendas and ranches. The total for 1861 was therefore 16,256,036 pesos.[1]

Of this total, 13,414,033 pesos corresponded to real estate in the District, and a little less, 12,733,192, to the city.[2] Between three-quarters and four-fifths of the property sold in 1861 in the city of Mexico were houses in the capital and funds invested in them. The remainder comprised real estate located in other parts of the country, and the capital invested in it— certainly almost all these were in the states surrounding the District. Nevertheless, as the Disentailment Report does not list the buyers together with their property but in a separate section, it is impossible to ascertain whose purchases were within the city and whose were outside it, except in a very few cases revealed by other sources. Two other items need to be added to the 16,256,036 pesos which was the total value of houses and capital disposed of in Mexico City. These are the rents of the houses, the interest on mortgages and the surcharge on slow payers, until 5 December, when the Disentailment Office was closed. With these additional items the total rises to 16,553,147 pesos.[3] This sum produced or, in the significant

---

[1] The MD 1862 considers the product of the *capellanías*, not their value.
[2] The *capellanías* are included for their product, not their value.
[3] The third part of the MD 1862 deals with this, pp. 147–60; this part is summarized in the MH 1870, pp. 560–3.

expression of Matías Romero's 1870 report of hacienda, 'should have produced' 10,163,424 pesos (at 60% of the total, it should be 9,931,889 pesos) in bonds and in obligations to pay them within a stipulated term. in this way bonds of the internal debt of an approximate value of 10,000,000 pesos were amortized in the Federal District alone. If one considers that, according to the available data, the internal debt was reduced from 53,000,000 pesos in 1856 to 13,000,000 pesos in 1861, that is, 40,000,000 pesos' worth of bonds were amortized, then it could be concluded that goods to a value of 67,000,000 pesos were nationalized throughout the country. As will be shown later this figure is more or less correct. The 10,000,000 pesos includes notes for 156,892 pesos on account of 10% and 15% of the value of the disentailed *capellanías*, which were later given mainly to Vicente Escandón. It is not known how much he paid for these notes nor how much he managed to collect on them. By the end of 1861 bonds for 2,132,854 pesos, that is just over one-fifth, were outstanding.[1]

In cash the total produced 6,389,722 pesos (40% of 16,553,147 pesos should be 6,621,259 pesos). However, only 1,056,424 pesos were handed over by the buyers in real cash, that is in money; the remainder was paid in various credits and 4,416,691 in promissory notes payable monthly.[2] The 4,400,000 in promissory notes guaranteed by mortgages was a considerable amount, but it could not be realized immediately. The government needed funds for its own reorganization and to re-establish order in the country which was exhausted after three years of civil war, and so from the start it began to sell the notes at 30–37% of face value.[3] This discount does not seem excessive in view of the fact that they were payable in sixty to eighty monthly payments. The new Minister of Hacienda, however, ordered, at the end of April, that a weekly auction should be held with the notes offered in lots of 200,000 pesos each, with the result that they depreciated to 10–13% of nominal value.[4] Mata soon resigned on 2 May, the auctions were suspended and the government was able to continue selling them at 25–35%, or an average 30% of their value.[5] By 5 December only 803,407 pesos remained in promissory notes in the Disentailment Office. More than four-fifths of them had been disposed of in less than a year. Apparently the usual price of the notes one

---

[1] MD 1862, p. 160.
[2] There are differences between the figures of the MD 1862 and those of the MH 1870; those in the latter have been used.
[3] Prieto, *Lecciones elementales*, 727; the author was Minister of Hacienda from 20 January to 5 April 1861.
[4] Ibid.; Mejía, *Memorias*, 54–5; Prieto mentions 10–12% and Mejía 12–13%—neither was very exact.
[5] MH 1870, p. 562.

year later was exactly 30%. This was illustrated on 31 December 1862 when the administrator of municipal revenues allowed employees to be paid their salaries with disentailment promissory notes valued at 30% of par.[1] In 1861 the city council had received notes for approximately 300,000 pesos from the Ministry of Hacienda,[2] and the easiest way of disposing of them was to pay part of employees' salaries with them. The latter of course could sell them, probably at the same rate of discount. The 4,400,000 pesos in notes of this type was equivalent for the exchequer to revenue of 1,000,000 to 1,500,000 pesos, a relatively small and insignificant amount for the government which had high extraordinary expenses and very low ordinary revenue.

As early as 22 May 1861 the congress authorized the executive to raise 1,000,000 pesos by means of an extraordinary tax.[3] The regulations for this authorization were issued on 1 June. 250,000 pesos were to be collected in the state of Jalisco and the remaining 750,000 pesos were to be 'satisfied' by people whose names, together with the amounts corresponding to each, were added to the text.[4] The list, drawn up in a descending order of amounts from 48,000 pesos to 1,200 pesos, contained only Mexican citizens.[5] There were many buyers of Church possessions on it, which was to be expected as the buyers of large holdings were people of wealth, but there were also others who had not partaken in the Reform. It might be supposed that the list contained the richest Mexicans of the time but in fact only a few of these were large scale buyers of clerical property. The fiscal needs of the government were so urgent that a week later, on 8 June, each person's quota was reduced by a third, provided the remaining amount was paid within seven days.[6] The yield from the loan was not sufficient and consequently, on 21 August, a 1% tax on mercantile, industrial and mortage capital was established in the District.[7] On 26 December a general levy of 2% was imposed on capital.[8]

[1] Archivo del Ex-Ayuntamiento de México, Hacienda-Pagarés de Desamortización, vol. 2078. [2] MD 1862, pp. 150–3.
[3] Dublán y Lozano, IX, 218. [4] Ibid., pp. 224 ff.
[5] Díaz, *Versión francesa*, II, 245, report of 8 June; the diplomat succeeded in having Cayetano Rubio, who was to pay 12,000 pesos, exempted as if he were Spanish.
[6] Dublán y Lozano, IX, 231.
[7] Ibid., p. 293. [8] Ibid., p. 350.

THE BUYERS OF CHURCH WEALTH

The buyers appear in the 1862 Disentailment Report in the section entitled 'account of the persons who have come forward to redeem values and capitals or to disentail *capellanías*'.[1] They are listed according to the number of their liquidation: at the side of the progressive numeration—in total there were 2,007 liquidations, probably given in chronological order—are the name of the buyer and the value of the purchase. Many numbers are missing because some people failed at the last minute to complete the redemption, or because some liquidations were cancelled due to an error relating to the properties or the individuals concerned. The fact that there are about 2,000 files does not mean that as many people were involved. The number of buyers is much less because the name of some is repeated frequently. Most of the buyers probably redeemed only one house, but many liquidations incorporated more than one and in some instances as many as thirty and sixty houses.[2]

Both on account of the number of people—about 1,000—and of the total value of the sales—more than 16,000,000 pesos—the Disentailment Report provides a good basis for a social study of the buyers of Church wealth in Mexico City, on the understanding that, even though almost all the buyers, or at least those people who redeemed large amounts, seem to have been residents of the capital, not all the goods redeemed were located in the city. To obtain a number of people, whom it is possible to identify, an alphabetical list of persons each with total redemptions for 40,000 pesos or more has been compiled and is included as appendix XVI.

In all there are seventy-eight such individuals, who together redeemed goods for 6,927,639 pesos, or 43% of the total of 16,256,036. This was a very large amount in view of the fact that these people represented between $\frac{1}{2}$% and a maximum of 1% of all the buyers. It has not been possible to discover the occupation or nationality of eleven of them with purchases of 687,932 pesos. Hence an analysis can be made of only the remaining sixty-seven with acquisitions for 6,189,707 pesos. They can be classified by nationality as follows:

49 Mexicans with 4,235, 231 pesos, just over 68% of the 6,189,707 pesos
18 foreigners with 1,954,476 pesos, almost 32% of the 6,189,707 pesos

The eighteen foreigners can be divided between:

7 French with 1,230,951 pesos, 20% of the 6,189,707 pesos

---

[1] MD 1862, pp. 109–43.   [2] Figures mentioned in MH 1870, p. 560.

8 Spaniards with 556,073 pesos
3 various with 167,425 pesos $\Big\}$ 12% of the 6,189,707 pesos.

As almost all the foreigners were merchants, only the profession or occupation of the Mexican buyers has been considered, as follows:

29 public officials and professional people, especially lawyers, with 2,163,256 pesos

15 merchants, industrialists, bankers and miners-hacendados with 1,697,899 pesos

5 individuals who were both merchants and public officials with 374,076 pesos.

Of course if the total amount acquired by the foreign merchants is added to that of the Mexicans of the same occupation, who were almost as important from the point of view of their purchases, the result is that about two-thirds of the ecclesiastical possessions concerned were obtained by merchants and one-third by professional people and government officials. As for nationality, about two-thirds were acquired by Mexicans and the remainder by foreigners.

The list reveals the small group of Veracruz denouncers. Only the names of some of them are known, so that the whole group cannot be identified. The most important of the 1856 auction buyers, that is, adjudicators in terms of the law of 5 February 1861, basically retained their positions, above all considering that their guarantors in the auctions could be their partners and that in 1861 the former guarantors sometimes appear as buyers, and on other occasions both individuals are present. Thus from the former Morales Puente company the partners Ignacio Loperena and Morales Puente remain as prominent buyers in 1861. The auction buyer Francisco Iniestra and his guarantor Manuel Cañizo formed a partnership which was finally dissolved in 1861,[1] and in the 1861 list both M. Cañizo and Iniestra's widow appear. Two of Francisco Schiafino's guarantors in the property auctions, José de la Luz Moreno and Balbontín, are in the 1861 list, in addition to Schiafino himself. Other important auction buyers in 1856 were Marcelino Sánchez, Francisco Lazo Estrada and José María del Río, who each bought more than 40,000 pesos' worth of property in 1861. In only one case, the 1856 auction buyer Guillermo Wodon Sorinne was no longer present in 1861. He is replaced by his former guarantor, A. Bablot, to whom it seemed probable that Sorinne had ceded his claims. Finally, the list contains the names of the conservative buyers of 1858–60, like Bringas, del Barrio, Escandón,

---

[1] 1861 register of F. Pérez de León, index, ANM.

Béistegui and Goríbar, who did not appear in the 1856 disentailment but who perhaps bought adjudicatory rights in 1858–60. Without being able to define quantitively these three groups, that is the denouncers, the adjudicators and the buyers from 1858–60, the list does seem to confirm the conclusions already indicated, based on the study of pamphlets and archival sources.

The list is also significant for the proportion of purchases made by foreigners, in particular the French who, in spite of their small number, acquired a greater amount of goods than the more numerous Spaniards. The British made no redemptions.

The liberals always looked on the Spaniards as conservatives. Thus, for example, as early as July 1857 the Mexican and Spanish hacendados in the Cuernavaca and Cuautla districts protested against an accusation made by General Juan Alvárez that as Spaniards they were reactionaries. In reply to the term 'Spanish-hacendado' they defended themselves, saying that 'not even a fifth of the properties situated in both districts are owned by Spaniards'. The protest was signed by several well-known Spaniards such as Pío Bermejillo and Isidoro de la Torre, but mostly by Mexicans, for example Juan B. Alamán, Lucas Alamán's son, Ignacio Cortina Chávez, F. de Goríbar, Manuel Escandón and Felipe Neri del Barrio y Rengel, son of the Guatemalan Minister.[1] The Mexicans perhaps put up a joint front with the Spaniards because of the agrarian agitation in the region which, although disguised as an anti-Spanish campaign, in fact endangered both.

In the same month President Comonfort declared, according to the French diplomat, that 'all the Spaniards, or at least most of those who are in Mexico, are working for the reactionaries...so that I can see myself obliged to wage an internal as well as an external war'. At the end of the conversation, if Gabriac is to be believed, Comonfort spoke of an expulsion of the Spaniards.[2] This idea of the reactionary character of the Spaniards was commonly held by the Mexican liberals.

Later, during the three years' war, the Spanish merchants were, on several occasions and in various places, the target of persecution; for example, on 6 September 1858 the governor of Nuevo León, Vidaurri, ordered the expulsion of Spanish merchants from San Luis Potosí.[3] Hence it is not surprising that the Spaniards took a relatively small part in 1861 in the redemptions of clerical property and capital.

In contrast, the French residents in Mexico were from the beginning in sympathy with the liberal movement. Their two newspapers, pub-

---

[1] The protest was reproduced in Zamacois, XIV, 619.
[2] Díaz, *Versión francesa*, I, 424, report of 6 July 1857.   [3] Zamacois, XV, 31.

lished in the capital in 1856, *Le Trait d'Union* and *L'Indépendent*, were directed by refugees from the 1848 revolution,[1] and they were more radical than any of the Mexican press, campaigning since the Lerdo law for a complete nationalization of Church wealth. The French diplomat even claimed that the handful of French revolutionaries had a significant influence on the liberal party and was impelling it more and more towards increasingly hostile measures against the Church.[2] This is no doubt exaggerated but there might be a grain of truth in it, if it is remembered that the liberal party was directed by professional people, especially lawyers, who admired everything that was French. In 1861 these two French newspapers continued their radical campaign. *Le Trait d'Union* adopted a more radical platform than the Mexican government. For example, it criticized the law of 5 February for creating vested interests opposed to those which had resulted from the Lerdo law and for protecting persons loyal to the Church. In its view the nationalization should be a revolution.[3] The fact that both papers appeared daily implies that their readers were not only the few French residents but also the Mexican intellectuals.

The political ferment in France was still alive, and for the Paris revolutionaries, Mexico with its continuous internal wars was a place in which they thought they could put their ideas into practice. The opportunity arose after 1848. With the revolution defeated in France and central European countries, its adherents found refuge in Mexico where they were able to establish a relationship with their counterparts. In time many abandoned their radicalism, and of their once extreme ideas only liberalism remained.

The other Frenchmen also seemed inclined towards the liberal side. France had assimilated the confiscation of clerical wealth by the end of the eighteenth century, and for the young generation of the nineteenth century a relatively poor Church was usual. The French merchants in Mexico therefore had no difficulty in dealing by preference with the liberal party and governments. After all the latter were merely proposing to do what had been done in France two generations earlier.

Unlike the French, the British residents in Mexico did not take sides in the struggle between the liberals and the conservatives. Clearly, the protestant British were unlikely to sympathize with the Mexican Roman Catholic Church, but at the same time the Latin extremism of the liberals

---

[1] López Cámara, 'Los socialistas franceses...', pp. 269–73.
[2] Díaz, *Versión francesa*, I, 369; also pp. 268, 277, 309–13, 319, 351, 377.
[3] Zamacois, xv, 557 ff.; *Le Trait d'Union*, 11, 12 February 1861.

did not attract them. They seemed destined to a complete neutrality. Circumstances were such, however, that they slightly inclined towards the conservative cause. Many British went to Mexico as executives or representatives of the great mining companies based in London. They were not isolated individuals for they represented a concentrated economic power. Thus from the beginning they were accustomed to dealing with the higher levels of the government. The men who were involved in the mining-metallurgy of precious metals thereby acquired entry to the mint, they made loans to the government, they exported the silver and imported industrial goods from Great Britain. During the years 1830–55 they were thus connected with the conservative group. As a result, two British citizens, Davidson and Forbes, loaned more to Zuloaga in 1858 than anyone else.

Finally Spanish immigration to Mexico at that time was of an entirely routine nature. The violent liberal movements which were then jolting Spain do not seem to have affected the Spaniards of Mexico. As the Mexican liberal government of 1829 concentrated its attacks on them, and as in contrast the conservatives had adopted as their own the spiritual heritage of the mother country, the Spaniards in Mexico, devoted to hard work in trade and agriculture, formed tacit alliance with the conservative party, and they gave loans to Zuloaga and Miramón.

Not all the buyers registered in the 1862 Disentailment Report retained the property and capital they had redeemed. It has been shown that there were various companies which appear only by the name of the principal partner who redeemed real estate and capital. The goods were afterwards distributed. The buyers could also cede their claims for other motives or sell the house. In this respect the Disentailment Report states in the preamble:

As for the individuals who herein appear as new owners, there may be some alterations, for it must be noted that several properties have changed ownership due to cession of rights, subrogations etc., and although when one of these transactions has come to the notice of the office, the respective annotations have been made, indicating the new owner, this has not always happened, and in these cases where no notification of change has been received, the owner indicated is the one who first made the redemption. This seems appropriate in view of the fact that the promissory notes continue to circulate under the signature of the first owner and with a mortgage of the same property.[1]

The list of names in the Disentailment Report does not therefore give an exact picture of the buyers of Church wealth in 1861. The statistics given here as appendix xvi are only approximate. Nevertheless, as the words of the Report indicate, there were in fact few changes in ownership in 1861 (the Report was signed on 10 December 1861).

[1] MD 1862, p. vi of the text.

THE NATIONAL EMERGENCY OF 1862

Apparently the changes of ownership were rather more frequent in 1862 and 1863. The buyers were by nature optimists as far as their future prospects were concerned. Few had paid in cash. Most had signed promissory notes and the obligation to deliver the bonds within a specified term. When these matured, however, many people could not pay, probably partly because of the deterioration in the economic situation which itself reflected to some extent the unfavourable political circumstances. The government was having difficulty in pacifying the country, and after the end of 1861 it had to face the French invasion. Certainly Mexico repulsed the French at the battle of Puebla on 5 May 1862, but the invading army merely retired to Orizaba and the Mexican government was forced to mobilize all its resources. The nation could only be saved if it was prepared to make sacrifices.

The financial needs were reflected in the establishment on 27 June of an extraordinary tax of 100 pesos per person, which it was hoped would raise 800,000 pesos.[1] Foreign subjects were exempted from payment and on 2 July an alphabetical list of those who were liable was published.[2] Two months later an extraordinary tax on urban real estate in the Federal District was decreed.[3] On 12 September a 1% levy on both mortgage and mercantile capital was ordered and this was renewed on 9 December. On 2 December a war tax of 152,400 pesos was established and apportioned between approximately 250 people. The possessions of those who had not paid the taxes were offered for sale by public auction by the government but there were no bidders.[4] Finally, on 30 January 1863 a 1% tax on capital funds exceeding 1,000 pesos was ordered and on 28 April a 1% levy on capitals over 500 pesos.[5]

The situation which arose after 5 May 1862 was seen almost immediately in a number of measures designed to increase the revenue yielded by the sale of nationalized goods. It has already been stated that many buyers were unable to meet the matured promissory notes (also known as disentailment bonds). The people who held them then went to the government with their complaints. Finally on 23 May the government ordered that all the buyers of ecclesiastical wealth should take to the Ministry

[1] Dublán y Lozano, IX, 481.
[2] It can be assumed that all the buyers of large amounts of clerical possessions could pay 100 pesos; hence it can be inferred that those buyers who are not on the list were foreigners.
[3] Dublán y Lozano, IX, 520.
[4] Zamacois, XVI, 326–31, 1037–49.
[5] Dublán y Lozano, IX, 533, 558, 579, 610.

of Hacienda all the matured promissory notes signed by them which had now been settled. In other words, they had to prove that they had paid the value of the notes on time. If they failed to do so they would lose all rights to the properties or capital funds and the government would be completely free to dispose of them. The term of one month which had been granted was extended on 11 June by another month.[1] The government was thus enabled to resell the properties.

A different measure, but one of equal importance, was dictated on 13 August. Those persons who had signed an agreement to hand over bonds and who had not done so, even though the term of the agreement had expired, could redeem their obligation by paying in cash 4% of its total value. Until this decree the government had not been strict with the debtors and had not demanded punctual delivery of the bonds. These could be obtained in the market at 5%, 7% and sometimes perhaps at an even higher percentage of the par value, so that it was a definite advantage for the buyers to pay the government the 4% instead of the 5% or more in the open market. Also the decree stated that in those cases in which the agreement to deliver the bonds was not due, the buyer could redeem his obligation with a payment of 3% of the total debt. This was a logical concession to those who paid before the end of the contracted term. The 60% of the value of the house or capital fund, payable in bonds, was reduced to a payment of only 3% or 4% of the bonds and, therefore, to the payment of less than 3% of the value of the goods. It was characteristic of the government's urgent need that a term of eight days, dating from 13 August, was granted to the buyers whose agreements were due for settlement. After the period had transpired, all the matured notes were to be transferred by the government to persons of its choice. The exchequer claims on the goods would be transmitted to those who acquired them.[2]

The term of eight days probably turned out to be too harsh, for fifteen days later it was extended until 5 September. As far as is known, this was the only extension, and presumably after this date the decree was implemented.

There is one interesting case concerning the application of both laws.[3] The hacienda Tenería, in Tenancingo, state of Mexico and belonging to the Carmelitas Descalzos, had not been assigned in 1856. On 5 February 1861 Vicente Dardón, a Mexican-Guatemalan and a Veracruz denouncer,

---

[1] Labastida, 267.
[2] Ibid., p. 321.
[3] *Manifestaciones que José Yves Limantour...*, pp. 30–43.

redeemed it without paying anything, in the following manner: 61,750 pesos in bonds payable in three months, and 34,120 pesos in forty promissory notes of 853 pesos each; total, 95,870 pesos (the Disentailment Report gives the price as 95,000 pesos as can be seen in appendix XVI). A short time later, in March 1861, Dardón sold the hacienda to someone else, perhaps because he was unable to meet the commitments resulting from the redemption or because the buyer paid his costs, thus enabling him to make a small profit. The bonds due in three months were not paid and the government gave Dardón three days in which to hand them over, threatening to auction the hacienda if he failed to do so.[1] Judging from subsequent events, the bonds were never paid. The promissory notes signed by Dardón were put on the market and they were almost all bought by José Yves Limantour. By the beginning of 1863, two years after the redemption, most of them had matured but it seems that few were paid.

Then under the terms of the two decrees the government sold the hacienda on 10 January 1863 to Limantour on the following conditions: in cash, 1,852 pesos, which equalled 3% of the commitment in bonds (it should have been 4% because the credit had been due since 1861); Limantour handed over promissory notes to a nominal value of 23,884 pesos and finally he paid the government so that it could collect notes worth 3,147 pesos from other people. Considering that the real value of the notes was not more than 35% of their face value, Limantour disbursed in total approximately 11,000 pesos. Limantour defended himself against the accusation that this was an excessively low price by asking 'who would have wanted to buy hatred, abuse, sarcasm, persecution, excommunication, and even endanger one's own life?'. In fact there was a court case over possession of the hacienda and it is from the records of this that the above information is taken.

Limantour replaced Dardón in the list which is reproduced in appendix XVI. Judging from the frequency with which Mexican buyers in Puebla (see chapter 6) sold the assigned properties to foreigners, it seems likely that there were many similar cases in the capital. The proportion of foreigners in the total purchases was thus increased, although according to details given in a pamphlet this change was probably not large. This reports the total purchases made by 1863 in the Federal District, including the sites of the monasteries and convents, as being 24,822,321 pesos. Of this amount 9,020,131, that is 36% in place of the 32% resulting from 1861, corresponded to foreigners and the rest to Mexicans, divided between the conservatives who kept 10,300,150 pesos, and the liberals with

---

[1] *Le Trait d'Union*, 3 June 1861.

5,502,040 pesos.[1] It can be concluded that the statistical details of the 1861 buyers give an approximate idea of the social group which in the end acquired the Church wealth.

THE POSSESSIONS OF PUBLIC WELFARE ORGANIZATIONS

The 1857 report registers disentailment transactions in the District for approximately 13,000,000 pesos. The 1862 Disentailment Report, however, gives redemptions of property in the District for about 10,000,000 pesos. The disentailment was not completed in 1856, but nor was the redemption of the properties in 1861 although the impression is that in this year a larger proportion of clerical houses was involved. The discrepancy between the 1856 and the 1861 data is therefore even greater. It can be explained partly by the fact that the Lerdo law included the civil corporations which in 1859 and 1861 were omitted from the nationalization, and because in 1856 many of the properties belonging to hospitals and schools were disentailed, whereas they were exempt from the sale in 1861. In fact in the 1862 Report, with only a few exceptions, the hospital-owned properties do not appear. There were 100 houses belonging to hospitals and other institutions of public welfare, which in 1856 were valued at about 1,000,000 pesos. Approximately half were sold in that year, especially those belonging to the hospital of San Andrés, the main one in the capital, and those of the hospital of Jesus. It is not known if the remaining houses were disentailed in 1857. If this did happen the hospitals would still have possessed the mortgages for the price of their former holdings.

The secularization of the hospitals, decreed on 2 February 1861, only affected the institutions managed by the ecclesiastical authorities or corporations. It was subsequently confirmed that there was no need to secularize the Jesus hospital because the Church had no connection with it.[2] This hospital, renowned because it was founded by Hernán Cortés, continued as a private institution and thus it was able to save its endowments. It had only to dispose of one house, which had been disentailed in 1856 by the tenant, Miguel Lerdo de Tejada, for a price of 33,333 pesos. The former Minister of Hacienda died on 22 March 1861 and the govern-

---

[1] *Observaciones sobre la ley de 26 de febrero y sobre su reglamento* (Mexico, 1865); the informant must have had access to the archive of the Ministry of Hacienda; according to him, the number of files rose by May 1863 from 2,007 to 3,600.

[2] Labastida, 457; see also M. S. Macedo, 'El municipio. Los establecimientos penales. La asistencia pública', in J. Sierra (ed.), *México, su evolución social* (2nd ed., Mexico, 1902), vol. I, book 2, pp. 714–16.

ment resolved on 26 April to donate the house to his family, paying the hospital 30,000 pesos in disentailment promissory notes, which of course were circulating at a much lower price than their nominal value. The hospital's representatives refused to accept this, and on 8 August agreement was reached whereby it was given several mortgages worth an amount equivalent to the value of the house.[1] The general impression that the year 1861 was one of chaos in the capital is perhaps superficial. As far as possible the government respected private institutions and their property.

The weak point in the secularization of the public welfare organizations was that their endowments now belonged to the government which could, in case of need, appropriate them. This in fact happened after 5 May 1862. Two days later, 7 May, the government ordered that all those who owed mortgages of 8,000 pesos or more to these institutions, whether or not they resulted from the Lerdo law, had to redeem them within the obligatory term of three days, by means of an immediate payment of one-quarter in 'cash' and the delivery within two months of bonds for the remaining three-quarters. If they failed to comply with this, the government would declare them to have no title and subrogate their rights to a third person.[2] These terms meant a reduction of 15% from the customary 40% payment in 'cash'. The emergency compelled the government to sell at lower prices.

On 21 June the redemption of the mortgages belonging to the College of Agriculture was ordered, on the same terms as the previous decree.[3] These amounted to at least 200,000 pesos. According to the 1856 Account the school had twenty-two houses worth 230,000 pesos, of which about 150,000 pesos was disentailed in 1856. In 1861 the endowments of educational institutions were exempted from the sale, and in the national crisis of 1862 the only school affected was that of agriculture. Its endowments came from the Jesuit college of San Gregorio and the Hospital Real de los Naturales, both of which were abolished in 1822.[4]

Later, on 7 July, the 8,000 pesos or more which should have been redeemed was reduced to 4,000 pesos. Finally, on 30 August the Public Welfare Office was abolished and its funds passed into the control of the council.[5] The same decree ordered that all the convent buildings which

---

[1] *Documentos anexos a la Memoria de Hacienda de 1874, correspondientes a la sección sexta de la misma secretaría* (Mexico, 1875), p. 145.
[2] Labastida, 369.
[3] Ibid.
[4] *Documentos de la Memoria de Hacienda de 1874*, pp. 134, 140.
[5] Ibid., pp. 370–1.

for any reason were vacated must be sold and the product of the sales given to public welfare. This latter order was not implemented because of the war.[1]

The notarial registers of the city of Mexico reveal the fate of public welfare possessions as follows: in Francisco Pérez de León's 1862 register there are relatively few adjudications; those that there are mostly refer to the regular orders and the houses managed by the Public Welfare Office; these are not redemptions because the properties were mortgaged to the government office. Hence, in the first four months of the year the Public Welfare Office executed at least five adjudication instruments of houses;[2] the properties, some of which originally belonged to public welfare institutions, were mortgaged to the Office for nine years at 6% per year. Some of these instruments have a subsequent annotation in the margin to the effect that the mortgages were redeemed by payments of 25% in 'cash' and 75% in bonds.[3]

It seems that in 1862 there were many 'cessions of rights and claims' to the redeemed properties. One of these was connected with the public welfare funds.[4] Ignacio Loperena had bought two houses and in 1858 he appointed as his representative Alfonso Labat, and then he left the country. Now he was ceding the properties to another person for 5,570 pesos 'at the same price for which they were assigned to him...the capital not being redeemable...will be recognized by the assignee in favour of the public education funds for a term of nine years' at 6% a year. The reference to 'education' is here an error; it should have been public welfare. The guarantor is M. Morales Puente, and there is no indication that the seller received anything in exchange for the cession. Some time later, according to a Public Welfare Office document dated 29 November 1862, the buyer redeemed the capital, paying 25% in 'cash' and 75% in bonds.

The situation changed suddenly after May 1862. Thus in the second half of the year there were six subrogation instruments.[5] In four of them the French merchant Justo Carresse bought from the government mortgages worth 88,072 pesos, which were invested in fourteen different houses owned by the Public Welfare organization. Most probably the debtors did not have available the money needed to redeem the mortgage within three days, and the government, urgently in need of funds with

---

[1] *Memoria de Hacienda,* 1873–74, p. cclxxxv.
[2] Fols. 1, 17, 38, 46, 84.
[3] For example, fol. 84, note of 18 July 1862.
[4] 1862 register of F. Pérez de León, fol. 98, ANM.
[5] Ibid., fols. 22, 231, 235, 247, 256, 298.

which to organize the national defence, sold them to this capitalist. Carresse does not appear in the 1861 table, reproduced in appendix XVI, so that his purchase of the public welfare funds increases the proportion of French merchants in the redemptions for 1861–63.

Again, in F. Pérez de León's register for 1863 there are few adjudications. No doubt there were now not many ecclesiastical possessions left to be sold. There were on the other hand a number of subrogations. For example, on 21 January Cayetano Rubio bought a mortgage for 4,000 pesos invested in a house belonging to the Public Welfare Office. Rubio paid 300 pesos in cash and the remainder, 3,700 pesos, with a credit, dated 13 September 1862, with a nominal value of 56,428 pesos.[1] The conditions were not strictly in accordance with the decree.

As a result of these transactions, the San Andrés hospital had lost by 1863 capital of 881,848 pesos and had only 37,100 pesos left; San Juan de Dios had lost 187,169 pesos and was left with 22,193 pesos; and Divino Salvador 136,746 pesos, with only 28,232 left.[2] In spite of this, all three hospitals continued to exist.

Two former hospitals were also sold at this time. The first of these was the building of the Hospital Real de los Naturales, which had looked after the impoverished Indian people during the colonial period. After independence it was suppressed on 21 February 1822. During the Reform it housed the well-known printing business of Ignacio Cumplido. It was assigned to the printer for 60,000 pesos, with the price mortgaged in favour of the Public Welfare. With the advent of the crisis situation in 1862, the price was reduced to 33,240 pesos, 25% payable in cash and 75% in bonds.[3]

The second was the building of the Hospital de Terceros. Valued at 159,565 pesos, it was sold to Justo Carresse for 80,000 pesos[4] on the following terms: 27,853 pesos in credits against the exchequer, called Laguna Seca, and enjoying priority rating which thus gave them a higher price in the market; 22,146 pesos in cash; and finally 30,000 pesos in bonds which, costing 10% of par value, meant another 3,000 pesos in cash. The buyer was given the option of paying a total of 32,000 pesos in cash and for the rest, 48,000 pesos in credits of his choice.[5] This seems to show that the price of the Laguna Seca credits was not less than 30–35% of face value. It is not known which alternative the buyer chose.

[1] Fols. 35 ff.
[2] Muriel, *Hospitales de la Nueva España*, II, 303.
[3] *Documentos de la Memoria de Hacienda de 1874*, 140.
[4] Cossío, *Guía retrospectiva de la ciudad de México*, 41.
[5] *Documentos de la Memoria de Hacienda de 1874*, 140.

Nationalized property in the city of Mexico, 1861–63

PUBLIC EDUCATION ENDOWMENTS

At the beginning of January 1861 the following problem arose. In common with other ecclesiastical institutions the brotherhoods and archconfraternities were liable to the nationalization of their possessions, but many of them were engaged in a variety of works of charity. In particular the very rich brotherhood of Aranzazú, the members of which were Spanish merchants from Biscay, maintained the college of San Ignacio which at that time had 140 pupils.[1] Also, the 'archicofradía del Santísimo Sacramento en catedral' financed the college of Santa María de la Caridad, known simply as 'the girls' school', and this had 32 pupils.[2]

When the laws of Reform were put into effect in the capital, the endowments of these and other schools were in immediate danger of being sold. Then Melchor Ocampo intervened and, recalling that the directors of the Aranzazú brotherhood had defended the autonomy of the college against the interference of the ecclesiastical authorities, he declared on 6 January 1861 that the 'school of the Biscayans was a secular and non-ecclesiastical educational establishment, the patronage of which resided formerly in the king and now in the nation'. Consequently its endowments were exempted from the nationalization. The brotherhood was altered to a Management Committee, a name more in keeping with the time.[3] On 8 March the government likewise exempted from the nationalization the possessions of the girls' school.[4]

The Biscayan school was able to survive during the 1862 crisis, and it remains fulfilling its mission to the present day. The girls' school did not have the same fate. Under the pressure of financial necessity the school was closed in September 1862 and its pupils transferred to the Biscayan college. Its endowments were used to pay the salaries of government employees and to recompense various people for services to the nation. The school building itself was sold.[5] An engineer valued the property as follows:

---

[1] Labastida, 187; G. J. Obregón, *El Real Colegio de San Ignacio de México (Las Vizcaínas)* (Mexico, 1949).
[2] Labastida, 187.
[3] Ibid., p. 359.
[4] Ibid., p. 363.
[5] Three sources have been consulted on these transactions: *Documentos de la Memoria de Hacienda de 1874*; a pamphlet by M. de Icaza, *Exposición sobre la nulidad de las operaciones practicadas en los años 1861 y 1862 con los bienes pertenecientes al Colegio de Niñas y a la corporación que lo fundó* (Mexico, 1864); and the 1862 register of Crescencio Landgrave, fol. 194, 31 October, ANM. There are differences in the numbers; in these cases, the figures given in the notarial register have been used.

main building, 120,836 pesos; the church, 41,931 pesos; and the adjacent house occupied by the chaplain, 10,869 pesos; total, 173,636 pesos. The building was bought by the partnership Gargollo y Collado, well-known entrepreneurs, for payment of more than 77,000 pesos in bonds and 43,000 pesos in cash. Apparently the bonds were capitalized at 8% of par value and if the author of the pamphlet, hostile to the buyers, is correct, only part of the 43,000 pesos was actually paid in cash. Probably more reliable details from a notarial register refer to the purchase of the church. On 31 October 1862 Manuel Terreros and partners bought the church, including the organ and everything else in it, for the valuation price, but paying only 3,033 pesos in cash. The rest, 38,898 pesos, was paid in bonds, capitalized at 3%, that is 1,167 pesos in money, which was no doubt a very low price. The deed reveals, however, that the government only granted such favourable conditions to the buyers provided that the church was retained as a place of worship. If it was used for any other purpose, one-quarter of the price would have to be paid in cash and three-quarters in bonds, which were the terms under which the endowments belonging to public welfare bodies were then being sold. It seems that several pious individuals with resources available had joined to prevent the destruction of the church. It was saved and continued to serve its parishioners.[1] Another condition of the low price, according to the deed, was that Terreros should name the persons with whom he was associated in making the purchase. His reply was that 'at an appropriate moment he would state who were the persons connected with him in the purchase' but it is not known if he met this condition. The government adopted a benevolent attitude towards religion and the Roman Catholic faith, but it was no doubt interested to know who were the persons concerned to save the churches. It is not impossible that the main capitalist partner in this case was the buyer of the adjacent building, Manuel Gargollo, a Spaniard connected with the conservative governments which preceded the Reform.

Another girls' school which was undisturbed in 1861 was the college of San Miguel de Belem, known popularly as Belem 'de las mochas'. It had 106 pupils.[2] Maintained with the product of certain pious works, it had been administered by the archbishop and it is not difficult to imagine that it retained its clerical inclination in the midst of a general liberalization of the times. It was probably because of this that it fell a victim of the fiscal crisis of 1862. Like the 'girls' school', that of Belem was

[1] Labastida, list of churches open in the capital in 1887, pp. 502–3.
[2] Labastida, 187.

closed in September 1862 and its pupils transferred to the Biscayan college.[1] Its endowments were probably sold and the building was converted into a prison.

FATE OF THE MONASTERIES AND CONVENTS

In accordance with the law of 13 July 1859 the valuation and division into lots of the monasteries in the capital began early in 1861. The buildings of San Agustín, Santo Domingo and San Francisco were sold.[2] In 1862–63 the Carmelite monastery was divided between sixty-seven descendants of the heroes of independence and only a small part was sold. It was decided to demolish La Merced, though the demolition fortunately was only partly carried out and its beautiful cloister can still be admired to this day. The San Diego monastery had no building of its own.

The law of 5 February had ordered that some of the twenty nunneries could be suppressed, and there was not long to wait for the consequences of this measure. Within a few days it was decided to close half of them, and on 13 February the nuns in those affected were taken to the ten remaining ones. This action greatly disturbed the pious members of the population,[3] but the fiscal needs were inexorable and during 1861 about half of the convents were appropriated. Some were used to capitalize the pension funds of widows and orphans of civil and military employees, for example San Bernardo, providing sixty-five pensions with a total value of 92,447 pesos; La Concepción, ninety-one pensions; and Santa Inés, ten for 37,999 pesos. The government carried out, at least in part, the stipulations of the law of 5 February, but most of the convents were sold for financial gain.

The national emergency in 1862, which was becoming more and more serious each day, forced the government to decree on 26 February 1863 the extinction of all the nunneries in the republic.[4] The only exception was the Sisters of Mercy, who did not lead the communal life and were 'devoted to the service of suffering humanity'. All the convents were to be vacated within eight days of the law being issued and the government

---

[1] *Documentos de la Memoria de Hacienda de 1874*, 99; E. A. Chávez, 'La educación nacional', in Sierra, *México, su evolución social*, I, book 2, 514.

[2] The main source has been the *Documentos de la Memoria de Hacienda de 1874*, which on pp. 89–187 describes in alphabetical order the fate of the convents, monasteries, churches, chapels, educational and public welfare institutions in the federal district; in the complete *Memoria* (1873–74) the same text is on pp. 273 ff. of the addenda.

[3] Bravo Ugarte, *Historia de México*, III, 1, 264; *Le Trait d'Union*, 5 March 1861.

[4] Labastida, 404–5.

was to dispose of the buildings. For example the convent of Santa Brígida was sold on 1 May, a month before the constitutional government abandoned the capital. It may be suspected that the purpose in closing the remaining convents was not merely fiscal. The government was fighting in retreat against an invader, which from the military point of view was much more powerful. Moreover, the invader seemed to support the pretensions of the conservative party to re-establish the Church in possession of all its wealth. The policy of establishing faits accomplis made the realization of that programme more difficult, for even if the government was for the moment defeated the buyers of the convents would oppose the conservatives. The liberals would thus have a few more allies.

Three examples are sufficient to illustrate the sales of the monasteries and convents in 1861–62; those relating to San Agustín, San Francisco and Santa Clara. As quoted in the first paragraph of this chapter, Pedro Labat offered on 13 November 1860 to redeem the former San Agustín garden, which he had rented since 1828 for 2,544 pesos a year. He complained that in 1856 he had been denied the adjudication because the garden was considered a part of the monastery, even though the San Francisco garden had been assigned.[1] Labat bought it, therefore, for 42,901 pesos, a price corresponding to the capitalization of the rent at 6%, and he paid 17,461 pesos in cash and 25,440 pesos in bonds. Some time later, on 8 April 1861, he acquired the whole of the monastery and the church.[2] The building had been divided into ten lots and valued by the director of the Academia de San Carlos at 147,000 pesos. On signing the respective deed Labat paid 10,000 pesos in cash. He signed three drafts of 10,000 pesos each, payable on 1 May, 1 June and 1 July, giving a total of 30,000 pesos. The drafts were secured by a mortgage of the property. Finally, he signed a commitment to hand over 107,000 pesos in bonds of the national debt on 8 April 1862. A year passed and he could not honour the drafts nor the bonds commitment, and so on 10 April 1862 he requested an extension of six months, offering to pay 6% interest on the debt. His request was granted on the next day, but the national crisis after 5 May obliged the government to deprive him of four lots, including the church, the atrium and the sacristy, because of his failure to pay the 30,000 pesos.[3] The government intended to sell them to the conservative capitalist Vicente Escandón, who was interested in conserving the church as a place of worship. Hence on 27 December 1862

---

[1] AGN, PBN, leg. 734.
[2] Register of Remigio Mateos, fols. 15 ff., ANM; the other data is from the *Documentos de la Memoria de Hacienda de 1874.*
[3] This information is again from *Documentos de la Memoria de Hacienda de 1874.*

Escandón and unnamed partners bought the property for 40,000 pesos, paying 2,600 pesos in cash, 18,000 pesos in title deeds of Church capital (which had probably been acquired at discount in 1858–60 and which the government could now sell), and 19,400 pesos in bonds which were capitalized at 3%, equalling a sum of 600 pesos in cash. The transaction was quite advantageous for the government and the buyers yielded part of their peculium. The instrument specified that Escandón was authorized to allow the use of the Church as a place of worship.[1]

In another similar case, Antonio Escandón and partners paid 40,000 pesos on 5 June 1862 for the church of La Concepción, paying 10,000 pesos in cash and the rest in credits.[2] Apparently the preservation of several of the capital's churches was due to these conservative merchants. As for the convent itself, it can be assumed that Labat later paid the 3,000 or 4,000 pesos resulting from the capitalization of 107,000 pesos at 3% or 4%.

The largest monastery in the capital, that of San Francisco, was divided into fifteen lots, but its sale was prolonged until 1862 because of the reluctance of buyers. The total sale price was 441,881 pesos, but this amount yielded only 10% in cash. Nevertheless, if there is added to this more than 100,000 pesos in compensation for different credits against the government, the result is that about one-third was paid in money (always provided, of course, that these credits were not inflated).

On 16 April 1862 the convent of Santa Clara was sold for 100,000 pesos to two government officials. The price, which equalled the valuation, was on the following terms: 16,000 pesos in money and 9,700 pesos in a draft against the Treasury Office in Guanajuato—in other words, a quarter in cash; the rest in bonds, to be paid within six months.[3] Less than six months later, on 19 September, the three-quarters were capitalized at 4% in accordance with the decree of 13 August, but instead of paying cash they were settled with a credit held by one of the buyers against the exchequer, perhaps for unpaid salaries.

A total of eighteen ecclesiastical buildings may now be taken together, comprising twelve convents and monasteries, three schools and three hospitals.[4] They were all sold in 1861–63 for a total of 1,938,461 pesos, which yielded in cash 296,670 pesos. Two mortgages for 166,475 pesos

[1] 1862 register of Mariano Vega, no. 221, fol. 377, ANM; see also M. Romero de Terreros, *La iglesia y convento de San Agustín* (Mexico, 1951), p. 26.
[2] 1862 register of Mariano Vega, fol. 231, ANM.
[3] Ibid., instrument no. 91, fol. 132 and reverse.
[4] San Agustín, Balvanera, Sta. Brígida, Capuchinas, Carmen, Sta. Catalina de Sena, Sta. Clara, Sto. Domingo, S. Felipe Neri, S. Francisco, Sta. Isabel y S. Fernando; Betlemitas o Enseñanza Nueva, Enseñanza Antigua y Porta Coeli; Espíritu Santo, Hospital Real de los Naturales y Santísima.

need to be added to this last figure. One of these was reduced by a 25% payment in cash and the rest in bonds capitalized at 3%. Both mortgages produced approximately 50,000 pesos for the treasury. Thus the government received for the eighteen buildings about 20% of their value in money and 80% in various credits against the national debt, which in many cases were often capitalized. In total the buyers paid the equivalent of a quarter of the price of the properties. Judging from the examples previously given in this chapter, this seems to have been the average amount paid for clerical possessions in 1861–63. No doubt it was less than one-third of the valuation in cash and another third in national debt bonds equalling 35–40% of the value, which were the terms stipulated in the law of 13 July 1859. The low prices of the buildings can perhaps be explained by the fact that they were not really suitable for private purposes. Of course the land on which they stood was very valuable on account of its location.

The sales of the convent and monastery buildings were not included in the 1862 Disentailment Report. The names of those buyers whom it has been possible to identify indicate that they came from the same groups mentioned in the previous analysis of the Disentailment Report (sometimes they are the same people) and that the social picture would not basically change if these buyers and those of the endowments of public welfare and educational institutions were added.[1]

The Mexican liberals could be criticized for the sale of the convent and monastic buildings and the consequent destruction of a part of colonial art and architecture, a destruction begun long before by the adoption of the neo-classic style. They were men of their age who saw no beauty in it; the French and the English in the seventeenth and eighteenth centuries likewise did not appreciate the gothic style.

NUNS' DOWRIES

The capital funds redeemed in 1861 in the Special Disentailment Office of the Federal District only amounted to approximately 5,300,000 pesos, a small sum in comparison with the redeemed real estate valued at about 10,700,000 pesos. It must not be forgotten, however, that whereas all real estate goods were included in the nationalization, a part of the capital was exempted and therefore does not appear in the 1862 Disentailment Report. As we have seen, the capital belonging to public welfare and educational institutions and then the nun's dowries and funds used for

[1] *Documentos de la Memoria de Hacienda de 1874* has scarcely any names of buyers.

purposes of worship were not included. The dowries and these other capital funds amounted to approximately 2,000,000 pesos in the capital alone. Hence the 1862 Disentailment Report does not comprise the whole of the goods administered by the Church in the Federal District, but only a part of them.

In accordance with the Reform laws, the nuns were to receive a deed of ownership of their dowries and the convents were to be assigned sufficient funds to meet costs of worship. Even given the modest limits to be expected in the regular orders, it can be assumed that the amount must have been quite high considering the expensive nature of the Roman Catholic faith. The government was determined to carry out the law, even at the cost of a sacrifice by the exchequer. With this aim, the section 7 was created in the Ministry of Hacienda and two decrees were issued: that of 6 March 1861 ordered that the adjudicators and auction buyers could, if they wished, mortgage three-fifths of the value of a property in favour of the dowries and cost of worship, and pay the remaining two-fifths in bonds or acknowledged credits. The mortgage would be for a term of five to nine years and at 6% annual interest. Thus those buyers who lacked resources were offered the opportunity to redeem most of the value within a number of years. The aforementioned office was to execute the respective instruments for the nuns. Section 7 would terminate its work when mortgages for 1,980,000 pesos had been completed. This was the estimated sum of the dowries,[1] equalling an approximate average of 3,500 pesos for each nun, basing this on the fact that there were 542 nuns in the capital in 1859.[2]

It was not only assigned or auctioned properties which could be mortgaged to dowries and the costs of worship, but also privately owned property, that is houses mortgaged to a convent from the time before the Reform.[3] This decree of 6 March was later detailed in that of 8 April, the executive order of 15 April, the circular of 13 July and the executive order of 17 July.[4] The owners of these houses could redeem two-fifths of the mortgage in bonds and continue recognizing a mortgage for the rest in favour of dowries and the costs of worship. Any future redemption of capital belonging to the nunneries was strictly forbidden, because such funds pertained to dowries and costs of worship. It is clear that the government was concerned at the possibility that the capital would be entirely redeemed before the needs of the nuns had been met. Section 7

---

[1] Labastida, 195.

[2] Ibid., p. 184; the amount was very stable; in 1850 there were 541 nuns, according to the *Memoria de Justicia*, 1851.

[3] Labastida, 195.   [4] Ibid., pp. 400–1.

could also auction houses not yet sold, accepting payment for two-fifths of the value and a mortgage guarantee for the remainder.

The result of the work carried out by the new office in 1861 was reproduced in the *Memoria de las operaciones practicadas en la sección séptima del Ministerio de Hacienda, sobre reconocimiento de capitales en fincas de propiedad particular y en fincas adjudicadas y rematadas y a favor de las señoras religiosas y el culto, comprendiendo desde la creación de dicha sección hasta 15 de diciembre de 1861.* This Report, which consists of seven enormous tables, without a text, covers therefore approximately the same period as that of the Disentailment. Four Tables, arranged in chronological order of the mortgages, reveal that the properties 'of private ownership' were above all haciendas (judging from the value of the mortgages), almost all of which were in states near the capital. There were some well-known people and a number of foreigners among the owners. The nuns whose names are given—sometimes only the Christian name, and others both this and the surname—were almost all from convents in the capital. Of mortgages valued at 1,434,596 pesos, dowries of 422 nuns were assigned 1,268,810 pesos and 165,786 pesos was allotted for worship in the now impoverished convents. The assigned and auctioned properties, with which the three remaining tables are concerned, only involved houses situated in the capital. There were a few more foreigners among the proprietors. The mortgages totalled 741,605 pesos, and of this amount 685,940 pesos were to be used for 238 nuns and 55,665 pesos for the costs of worship. In total 1,954,750 pesos were assigned to 660 nuns and so the originally planned amount of 1,980,000 pesos was almost achieved. 221,451 pesos was given for the cost of worship, and thus the total for the year was 2,176,201 pesos.[1]

Of course the total of 660 nuns is not credible, for there were only 542 nuns in the capital. Some were included from Querétaro and Puebla, but there were scarcely a dozen, so that they need not be considered here. The explanation lies in the fact that many nuns received several amounts to complete the sum of 3,000 pesos which each was allocated. This was to be expected as the mortgages were at times of small amounts and several had to be put together to make up a dowry. Hence the name of many nuns is repeated.

This has been proved by examining the names of all the nuns in three convents in the capital, La Concepción, Jesús María and Regina Coeli. In the Report fifty-three names appear corresponding to La Concepción, but in fact they represent only thirty-two different nuns; Jesús María has

---

[1] MH 1870, based on these facts, nevertheless gave a slightly different figure on p. 564.

thirty-six names which in fact concern thirty nuns who received dowries; Regina Coeli has thirty-six names for twenty-seven nuns who received a dowry. In total, eighty-nine nuns of the three convents received their dowry in 1861. These examples serve to explain the discrepancy.

In 1859 La Concepción had thirty-four nuns, Regina Coeli thirty and Jesús María twenty-nine. Therefore in 1861 almost all the nuns of the first two convents acquired their dowry, and in the third there was one extra. At least in the case of these three important convents, the law was almost completely implemented in the first year of its operation. The nuns of the three convents received a total of 348,165 pesos, that is an average of 3,912 pesos each.

The financial pressures on the government in 1862 obliged it to sell certain goods until then exempt from the sale, but on the other hand the government did hasten to contract dowries for the remaining nuns who still lacked this protection of ownership of the dowry. The moment of the total closure of all the convents was approaching and the government, which had assumed responsibility for this, urgently needed the problem of dowries resolved.

Three examples will illustrate the procedure: the adjudicator of a house could not redeem 2,800 pesos in 1861; instead of selling the capital, the Minister of Hacienda decided on 26 April 1861 to preserve it as a mortgage on the property for nine years and at 6% annual interest.[1] On 6 September 1862 the house was mortgaged for the same amount to complete two dowries. In another similar case, the owner of an assigned house still owed the government in 1861 the sum of 786 pesos; on 6 September 1862 this amount was assigned to dowries and the cost of worship.[2] Finally, on 13 March 1861 the owner of an assigned house owed the government 5,600 pesos. On 15 September of the following year 4,000 pesos of this debt were used for a dowry and 1,600 pesos for worship in the convents.[3] Further transactions were made at the beginning of 1863.[4] Although the government had sold the greater part of the promissory notes, it still retained some owed by the buyers of the clerical possessions. In spite of its own desperate financial needs, it used them to meet the commitment to the nuns.

In the middle of a rapidly deteriorating military situation and consequently an ever more acute financial crisis, the total suppression of the nunneries was decreed on 26 February 1863. This measure had been

---

[1] There were printed forms for this; 1862 register of Remigio Mateos, fol. 90, ANM.
[2] Ibid., fol. 101.   [3] Ibid., fol. 95.
[4] For example, 1863 register of F. Pérez de León, fols. 41 ff., ANM; an assigned house was mortgaged for 6,000 pesos for two dowries.

preceded on 23 January by the decision to sell the capital funds assigned for the cost of worship in the convents. Prospective buyers could redeem them 'on the basis of a 50% payment in cash'.[1] The word 'basis' meant that discounts were conceded. In view of the fact that the endowments belonging to the public welfare organizations were sold for a 25% payment in money, it can be assumed that the quoted half was in practice reduced to a quarter. As in other similar cases, it was ordered that if the buyers did not redeem the mortgage within a very short term, in this instance three days, the government would transfer it to the person of its choice. With the convents closed and the nuns dispersed, the costs of worship in the churches and in the convent chapels were unnecessary.

A day after the decree abolishing the nunneries, the Minister of Hacienda ordered all nuns who were still without a dowry to go to the Ministry, or to treasury officials in the states, so that they could be given their capital fund 'or until this was possible, some assistance towards their maintenance'.[2] The available information indicates that this had little application in Mexico City, because by that time almost all the nuns had received their dowry.

The same order, dated 27 February, announced that a gratuitory dowry would be granted the Capuchine nuns, who were also known as 'poor Capuchines or Recollect Capuchines'. They lived on public charity. On 11 April 1863 the amount to be given them was specified:

the said nuns have been granted as a dowry, the capital of 3,000 pesos; various capitals have already been assigned for this purpose, and an attempt is being made to endow as quickly as possible not only the Capuchines, but also the other nuns who still are without dowries. For this object, section 6 of this Ministry has been ordered to assign to them all capital that has not been redeemed.[3]

A month and a half before abandoning the capital, the government tried to fulfil the law and its moral commitment with the nuns.

The law was carried out exactly. In the months of March to May donations from the government of 3,000 pesos per person were registered by only one notary on behalf of fourteen of the total of thirty-five Capuchine nuns that there were in the capital.[4] These funds were taken from various ecclesiastical funds. Even though in the middle of the nineteenth century the average for dowries was more than 3,000 pesos, this was considered the minimum sum needed to live. In the margin of the instruments the date was noted on which the attestations were given to the respective nuns, who apparently were willing to accept them.

---

[1] Labastida, 404.   [2] Ibid., pp. 405–6.
[3] Ibid., p. 408.   [4] 1863 register of José María Natera, ANM.

Nationalized property in the city of Mexico, 1861–63

Although the government was forced by circumstances in 1862–63 to sell certain funds which it had declared irredeemable and exempt from the sale in 1861, the nuns' dowries, which one might be tempted to include in Church wealth, were respected.[1]

[1] Other ecclesiastical goods confiscated in the capital in 1861 were several credits against the exchequer, especially bonds, worth about 4,000,000 pesos, which of course had little real value; these papers were partly found in various clerical buildings and partly handed over by the convent administrators (MH 1870, p. 564). The wrought silver, gold, and jewels of the cathedral and other churches in the capital were likewise acquired (ibid., p. 563); it can be assumed that the metropolitan cathedral was richer than that of Morelia, although it must be remembered that the latter had handed over part of its silver to Miramón in 1860. From this amount, about 200,000 pesos were minted by August, almost all in silver coin (MD 1862, p. vi and MH 1870, p. 564); the figures given by the latter are less but only go as far as April.

CHAPTER 6

NATIONALIZED PROPERTY IN THE PROVINCES: THE FINAL SETTLEMENT, 1861–63

Unlike the capital, which enjoyed peace during the two years 1861–2, the civil war continued in the states, although on a reduced scale. The activities of the conservative guerrillas hindered the work of the constitutional government, but they did not succeed in gaining possession of the country's important cities. Thus it was possible to implement the Reform in Puebla, Orizaba, Córdoba, Jalapa, San Luis Potosí, Morelia, and Guadalajara.

PUEBLA

The city of Puebla surrendered to the liberal army some days after the city of Mexico, when General Chacón's representatives arrived on 28 December offering his allegiance to the constitutional government.[1] Those who had acquired a property in 1856–57 and had returned it in 1858 now hastened to claim it. The Puebla notarial registers that have been examined reveal that almost all the buyers under the Lerdo law, whether adjudicators, conventional buyers or successful bidders in auctions, recovered their houses in 1861–62. This conclusion is based on the annotations made in the margin of the instruments. Not all are annotated, and in such cases it is not known who redeemed the property in 1861. In the appendices I, II and V, which contain an extract of the registers which were consulted, it can be seen that most of the adjudication instruments—which are the predominant type—have the respective note. According to these notes the adjudicators again became owners of the same house as before. The available information on the conventional sales and the auctions also leads to the conclusion that most categories of buyers regained possession of their property in 1861. The buyers did not always redeem the value of the house; according to the registers, in some instances the value was mortgaged to dowries or the costs of worship. What is important is the fact that the buyers in 1861–62 were the same as in 1856–57, with one exception which will be discussed later.

[1] Bravo Ugarte, *Historia de México*, III, I, 260.

Apparently the change of owner in Puebla in 1861 and 1862 was more or less automatic, in the same way as the return of the properties had been in 1858. Those who had given them back retrieved them three years later without difficulty. This is partly due to the lack of claims to houses in Puebla from the Veracruz denouncers. Not a single example of such a claim has been found. Secondly, the Church in Puebla does not seem to have sold many properties during the three years' war. For example, the notarial register number 5, which is so rich in information, recorded no sale of clerical property during the years 1858–60. It is not known why the refugees resident in Veracruz showed no interest in the valuable Puebla real estate, nor why the ecclesiastical corporations in the city did not sell many of their houses. It may have been that in Puebla the Church was able to pay its allotted quotas to the reactionary governments from its ordinary revenue and therefore it did not need to sell its houses.

Whatever the case, the nationalization and sale of clerical wealth were peacefully effected in Puebla without the triangular struggle between adjudicators, buyers and denouncers which had so confused the situation in the capital. There was none of the competitive element between the different pressure groups; generally the original buyers were the definitive ones. Only one example has been discovered, and this seems to have been exceptional, in which three adjudicators lost their right to a house, probably because they had 'voluntarily' returned it to the reactionary government.[1] Cases in which the 20% fine on the value of the property was imposed, payable by the adjudicators, have likewise not been found, probably because there were very few of them.

There were many redemptions in 1861. From 7 January to 31 May ecclesiastical possessions worth 3,037,387 pesos were redeemed in Puebla.[2] Since in 1856 the value of clerical real estate was calculated to be 5,000,000 pesos, and Church properties were very often sold for prices lower than the valuation, it can be said that a large part of Church wealth was disposed of during the first five months of 1861.

It has already been stated that the original buyers in Puebla were almost always the definitive ones. The cases involving transfer of ownership by means of sale are, of course, exceptions to this. Such transactions also took place in Mexico City in 1861 but the available information indicates that there were relatively few. Apparently the residents in the capital had enough with the numerous transfers of property effected between the adjudicators, the buyers in 1858–60 and the denouncers. In contrast the

---

[1] 1862 register of notary 7, ANP.
[2] *Observaciones sobre la ley de 26 de febrero y sobre su reglamento.*

people of Puebla, who did not have these problems, began immediately to resell the nationalized properties.

The first example of a resale in Puebla was registered by notary number 5 as early as December 1857. On the 19th of that month President Comonfort had accepted the reactionary plan of Tacubaya, proclaimed two days before, thus making politically aware people realize the possibility of the future repeal of the Lerdo law, which of course did happen a few weeks later. Thus on 21 December 1857 the public official Santiago Vicario sold to the German merchant Edward Heit four houses that he had acquired in 1856 by conventional sales and an adjudication. The houses were sold for the same price at which they had been disentailed (they were mortgaged for their entire value to the corporations), with the result that the seller, far from making a profit, lost the disentailment sales tax which he had paid. No doubt he sold as a precautionary measure, for it was reasonable to be afraid that when the Lerdo law was annulled, the reactionary government would punish the adjudicators or the buyers of assigned houses. This fear was in fact unfounded, for Zuloaga merely cancelled all transactions made under the Lerdo law and imposed no fines on the participants in the disentailment. Heit sold one of the houses two weeks later, before Zuloaga's coup. The final buyer redeemed it in 1862.[1]

At the beginning of 1861 the notarial register number 5 registered another type of resale. Several auction buyers of 1857 transferred their rights to the German merchant Jorge Berkenbuch, in exchange for a cash payment of 150 pesos per house 'for the sales tax and other costs'. As each house cost approximately 2,000 pesos, the sales tax could not have been more than about 50 pesos (half of 5% of the price). Hence the resellers made a profit of nearly 100 pesos per house. The buyer paid 7.5% more, but the houses had usually been auctioned at two-thirds of their value. One of these houses was again sold for the same price on 22 May 1861.[2]

Few resales were registered by notary number 5. In contrast, notary Francisco de Paula Fuentes, number 2, recorded in 1861 at least sixty-two cases of resale by the original buyers to a few individuals.[3] In almost every transaction the houses had been bought in auction in 1857 by different people who were now transferring their rights to others. All the instruments are dated in January and most of the sales were made on 15 January 1861. The deeds contain the following text: the seller '...using his legal

---

[1] Register of notary 5, fols. 593, 595, 596, ANP.
[2] Ibid., fols. 96, 104, 107, 188.
[3] Register of notary 2, fols. 24–288, ANP.

rights, sold some time ago to Sr...the claim pertaining to him to that adjudication...in exchange for only the reimbursement of his costs, which was complied with'. Apparently the buyers had sold their adjudication rights during the three years' war and now the instruments were legalizing the sale. The amount of the 'costs', which is only mentioned in a few instances in the register, was approximately 10% of the auction price. Of this percentage, about one-quarter was spent on the disentailment sales tax.

The auction buyers-sellers were, it seems, Mexicans, among whom the Puebla industrialist, Mariano Caballero de Carranza can be identified. He had been an important adjudicator in 1856.[1] The buyers were almost all foreign merchants living in Puebla. During the civil war, especially the early months, the auction buyers had probably thought it expedient to sell their rights at a profit. For their part, the new buyers had acquired the claim, perhaps thinking that their foreign nationality made them less vulnerable. Hence whoever won the war, their claims would have to be taken into account when the final arrangements over the properties were decided. The protest made by Turnbull in 1858 against Zuloaga's law—no similar protest has been found in the notarial registers in Mexico City— implies that the foreign merchants had more influence in Puebla than in the capital, and that therefore their hopes did not appear exaggerated.

Whatever the factors influencing the seller and the buyer of the adjudication right, four persons, E. Turnbull, J. Berkenbuch, E. Heit and F. Becker, acquired in this way 54 houses worth in total 131,279 pesos.[2] The four merchants, the first British and the others probably German, were prominent in 1856 as buyers of corporately owned property.[3] Among the many foreign merchants, these four specialized, as it were, in dealings involving nationalized goods. Needless to say, in 1861 they not only bought the houses but also redeemed the corresponding capital by making the required payment in promissory notes and bonds. One question arises from the fact that Mariano Caballero de Carranza often sold to Berkenbuch, the biggest buyer, and less often to Turnbull. Were the 1857 auction buyers independent operators or merely agents acting on behalf of the final buyers? In the case of Carranza, it does not seem likely that he would act for other people, for he himself was wealthy. It seems more feasible that, like so many others, he had bought the properties in the auctions because they were cheaper, and that he sold his rights to them,

[1] See appendix VI.
[2] Other persons bought the eight remaining properties for 34,646 pesos, with the result that the total resales in January before notary number 2 amounted to 161,925 pesos.
[3] See appendix VI.

not for economic motives but because he thought the liberal cause was lost. The names of the other resellers do not always appear associated with the same buyers. When they are repeated, they sell each time to a different person. For this reason it is improbable that they were acting on behalf of other people.

Naturally, if the purchases made by these four are added to the general picture, the proportion pertaining to the foreign element would be increased for it replaced the amount acquired by Mexicans. Using different means to those employed in the capital, the foreign merchants in Puebla were able to increase in 1861 their percentage in the social and national groups which bought clerical wealth. In the absence of an official publication dealing with the 1861 sales in the city, we must rely on the statistics based on the 1857 Report of Hacienda. It can only be assumed that, as happened in Mexico City, the proportion of foreign buyers increased from approximately one-quarter in 1856 to one-third in 1861. It must not be forgotten that all the sales involved houses. According to the reasonably full data in Paula Fuentes' registers, no Mexican-owned hacienda or ranch passed into foreign hands.

Examples of resales are also to be found in the registers of other notaries. For example, according to that of number 10, in December 1861 J. Berkenbuch bought two houses assigned for 1,212 pesos to Miguel de las Piedras on 5 October 1857.[1] He paid the seller 150 pesos for his rights, redeeming two-fifths of the capital with forty promissory notes and three-fifths with bonds. Berkenbuch displayed the most activity in this field and therefore his name is immediately noticed in the registers but, as has been shown, he was not the only one.

Apart from the resales, adjudications were negotiated in 1861–63 and, above all, the 'conventional sales' of properties which had not been disentailed in 1856–57. For example, six transactions of this type were registered before notary number 5 in 1861, fourteen in 1862 and four in 1863. The individuals who acquired them were not the same persons as the resellers but rather the same Mexicans—lawyers were particularly prominent among them—whose names already appeared in the 1857 report. Although the reappearance of the same buyers in 1861 gives the impression of continuity between the transactions of 1856 and those undertaken five years later, it seems that the number of resales was greater than the sales of properties not yet disentailed, and this changes the result of the nationalization in the sense that the foreign buyer played a greater part.

[1] Years 1861–63 in one volume.

Hence properties which were already disentailed, and those which had not been affected by the Lerdo law, were sold in Puebla in 1861 and their capital value legally redeemed. Clerical mortgages predating the Reform were also redeemed. For example, Salomon Simonsfeld, a German merchant in the capital and a partner in the firm of Simonsfeld, Taussig and Co., made a number of purchases.[1] At the beginning of 1861 the federal government owed this company 202,743 pesos for ships and gunpowder which Carlos Butterfield had contracted to supply during Santa Anna's administration.[2] The Minister of Hacienda credited him with 101,371 pesos in the Special Disentailment Office, and also in the same year the government paid him disentailment promissory notes for a larger amount.[3] Simonsfeld subsequently presented on 8 November 1861, in Puebla, a request for permission to redeem ecclesiastical capital, basing his petition on his 'distinguished services rendered to the constitutionalist cause'. It seems possible therefore that, being a merchant—perhaps a refugee from one of the central European revolutions of 1848 in which case he would be sympathetic to the liberals—Simonsfeld made loans to the constitutional government during the three years' war. A short time afterwards he redeemed eight ecclesiastical capitals, secured by mortgages of several privately owned properties, for 30,500 pesos.[4] He paid two-fifths of the price in forty promissory notes and the other three-fifths in bonds which he was committed to hand over within six months. The instrument specified the 'former mortgage deeds were to be cancelled' and that 'an order would be issued to the borrowers of those capital funds, to the effect that, when the term fixed by law had ended, they were to be repaid to Simonsfeld, and in the meantime annual interest of 6% was to be paid to him'. At the same time Simonsfeld gave the power of attorney to Berkenbuch who, as a resident of Puebla, would be able to represent him in these transactions. The affair later encountered a complication; according to a page attached to the register and dated 5 February 1863, four of the capitals worth 10,200 pesos 'have been found to be worthless'. This was quite a frequent occurrence because of a partial destruction of the property or because it was not of sufficient value to support so many mortgages with the result that these depreciated. Simonsfeld was then compen-

[1] Galván Rivera, *Guía*, 289.
[2] Iglesias y Prieto, *El Ministerio de Hacienda del 21 de enero al 6 de abril de 1861*, 9; apparently, Simonsfeld was only the representative of the creditor. In 1856 he was owed 145,649 pesos, which must have increased during the five subsequent years; *Memoria de Hacienda*, 1856, pp. 41–2.
[3] MD 1862, pp. 150–3.
[4] Register of notary 7, 27 December 1861, ANP.

sated with two capital funds worth 15,000 pesos, thus gaining 4,800 pesos by the change.

It was not only the foreigners who made a large number of deals in Puebla in 1861–62. For example, the local official, Santiago Vicario, who had already bought several houses in 1856, acquired six more worth 17,100 pesos on 1 March 1862.[1] The first three had not been disentailed. In the case of the others, the adjudicators had lost their rights, apparently an exceptional phenomenon in Puebla. He bought more houses on 24 April of the same year.[2]

There was also in Atlixco in 1861 a number of cases of the resale of houses auctioned in 1857.[3] In general the original adjudicators in this town likewise seem to have reacquired their properties on the arrival of the liberal army and they redeemed the corresponding values.[4] Even the presbyter Domínguez, buyer in 1856 of an ecclesiastical property in Atlixco, probably obtained it again in 1861. A person with the same surname but a different Christan name is recorded as a buyer, perhaps his brother.[5]

The data available for the state of Puebla indicates that the transactions effected in 1861 and 1862 consolidated and completed the disentailment of the years 1856 and 1857.

The national emergency of 1862 affected Puebla more than the capital of the republic. On 21 September of that year, Marshal Forey arrived at Veracruz to lead the second French campaign.[6] The Mexican reaction was immediate: two days later General Jesús González Ortega, chief of the army in the east, was given wide powers in the states of Puebla, Tlaxcala and Veracruz.[7] From this date onwards Puebla became the centre of resistance against the invasion. The defence preparations could not be paid for out of normal revenues and the general-in-chief was faced with two possibilities: first, raise the funds needed by extraordinary taxes; or secondly, sell at any price what was left of the ecclesiastical wealth. General Ortega chose the second course of action and it was for this purpose that he issued on 23 October a resolution concerning the redemption of the capital funds and the sale of certain properties. The desperate financial situation is reflected in the preamble:

As rules and requirements established for normal, peaceful times must be sacrificed for the salvation of the fatherland, and as it is unjust for a government to disturb

---

[1] Ibid., notary 7, 1862, ANP.   [2] Ibid.
[3] 1861 register of J. A. Ochoterena, fol. 18, 18 March, ANP.
[4] 1857 register of J. A. Ochoterena, notes on fols. 128, 289, ANP.
[5] 1856 register of J. A. Ochoterena, fol. 147, ANP.   [6] Zamacois, XVI, 281.
[7] Labastida, 423.

society with more taxes when there are other resources remaining available to it, you will order that there are displayed in public places lists of capital funds belonging to the extinguished 'dead hand' which have not yet been redeemed...[1]

The resolution allowed any interested parties, resident in Puebla, a term of three days to redeem the mortgages by means of a cash payment of 8% of the value. The term allowed for those who did not live in the city was one week. In the event that the owners, whose properties were encumbered with a mortgage in favour of the Church, did not redeem the debt within the specified time, the mortgages were to be auctioned on the following day with 8% of the value as a minimum price. If there were no bidders within three days, the mortgaged properties were to be seized and auctioned three days later. Nevertheless, in spite of the obvious urgency shown by the terms allowed, the resolution exempted from sale the endowments belonging to public welfare and educational institutions. Only two buildings which housed clerical colleges were to be sold, by a minimum cash payment of 5% of the valuation price. Even though other types of real estate were not mentioned, this latter stipulation was taken as a precedent for the sale of several convents at 5% of their valuation price. The sale of the capital funds at 8% and of the real estate at 5% —much lower percentages than those employed in Mexico City—is to be explained as follows: in addition to the general risk that the transactions would not be recognized by the invaders, there was also the fact that Puebla was being converted into a fortress, prepared to withstand a long siege, during which nationalized houses might well be destroyed.[2] The capitalists were ready to pay only for the site and this at a fraction of its value because the advance of the French army increased the probability that the sales would be annulled, especially those of the convent buildings which for many people were sacred.

Five days later on 28 October, General González Ortega ordered the redemption of the capital funds used towards the cost of worship at 8% of their value, as if they were like any other clerical capital included in the above-cited resolution. Puebla thus anticipated Mexico City where a similar measure was not decreed until 21 January 1863. The law in Puebla also declared that dowries were irredeemable.[3] On 10 December Ortega ordered that five convents, still in being at the time, should be vacated so that they could be used for troops and the storage of artillery and munitions, for the buildings were 'more extensive, higher and of stronger

---

[1] Ibid.
[2] Zamacois, xvi, 320.
[3] Colección Lafragua, vol. 426.

construction...¹ It may perhaps be inevitable, because it is thus required by the hostilities or some divers fate, that the very buildings be reduced to ruins, either by combatant friends or enemies.' These words referred to the possibility that the buildings might have to be demolished. This fate of the convent buildings clearly helped to depress their value, for whether they had been sold or not they could still be utilized by the army.

Perhaps unaware of the above decree, the federal government ordered on 10 December that the Puebla convents were to be converted into military hospitals.² Two weeks later, on 26 December, 'in view of the fact that the measure dictated on the 10th of the month in respect of the vacating of the monasteries has not been sufficient to meet the ever-increasing exigencies of the situation', González Ortega ordered that the now unoccupied convents were to be sold at 5% of their value, the nunneries were to be dissolved and the nuns' dowries formally registered by deed.³ Necessity thus forced the closure of the convents in Puebla two months earlier than in Mexico City.

Two days after the resolution of 23 October, the Puebla government auctioned several parts of the San Agustín and Santo Domingo monasteries, of the San Felipe Neri congregation and the convents of Santa Teresa and Santa Mónica.⁴ The latter had apparently been suppressed as a result of the law of 5 February 1861 and the monasteries had also been closed since the beginning of that year. Perhaps due to the conservative views of the Puebla bourgeoisie, most of the convents remained unsold in October 1862. Only one sale before this date has been found in the notarial registers, that of a section of the convent of Santa Inés, which was bought by Pablo María de Zamacona.⁵

The transactions resulting from the resolution of 23 October were so numerous that special forms had to be printed. These are attached to the notarial registers and their text is as follows:

Treasury Office, No...Liquidation of the capital of...owed to...and which is redeemed by Don...under the terms of the order of 23 October 1862. Capital... 8% which he pays in cash to this Office. This liquidation serves as title of ownership to the buyer, both for the cancellation of the contract in the case of the borrower redeeming the debt, and so that the buyer may collect the capital from him should the redemption be made by another person.

---

¹ Zamacois, XVI, 306–8; other convents had already been closed, probably in 1861 as a result of the law of 5 February; the monasteries of course no longer existed.
² Labastida, 416.
³ Zamacois, XVI, 310; see also Colección Lafragua, vol. 426.
⁴ Addenda to *Memoria de Hacienda*, 1874, pp. 76–7.
⁵ Register of J. M. Tello, fol. 131, 5 June 1862, and of J. Nazario Díaz, fol. 19, 16 January 1863, ANP.

The following examples will illustrate the transactions that were effected. In November 1862 Julio Ziegler, a French merchant in Puebla, made a proposal to the state government to the effect that he would buy for 60,000 pesos the clerical colleges of San Juan, San Pedro and San Pablo.[1] He also offered to purchase various mortgages totalling 160,000 pesos. He would pay for the colleges 5% of their value, that is 3,000 pesos, and for the capital funds 8%, equivalent to 12,800 pesos, giving a total of 15,800 pesos. As often happened, however, insufficient mortgages were found to make up the 160,000 pesos, and so instead of these Ziegler suggested that he take five lots of the convent of Santísima Trinidad for 78,662 pesos, and in addition thirty-nine capital funds worth 110,836 pesos. Sixteen of the latter were invested in rural properties, mostly haciendas, some of which were in other states. At 5% the price of the convent lots was 3,933 pesos, and 8% of the capital was 8,866 pesos. This gave 12,800 pesos which was the cost of the mortgages worth 160,000 pesos. On 24 November he paid the 3,000 pesos as the price of the colleges, in the words of the instrument, 'even though they were valued at 60,000 pesos; but if the value is even greater, the smaller or larger excess is given to Julio Ziegler...as an absolute and irrevocable gift...' He later paid the remaining amounts. Ziegler's second transaction was begun on 28 January 1863 with his offer to buy the convent of Santa Clara. This had an area of approximately 10,000 square metres (according to a plan attached to the register) and it was valued at 75,000 pesos, giving a corresponding sale price of 3,750 pesos. Santa Clara was one of the nunneries vacated as a result of the decree of 10 December and offered for sale on the 26th of the same month.[2] Three days later the state government accepted Ziegler's proposal 'in view of the urgent need of revenue to prosecute the war, and because the war has as its aim the salvation of the honour, dignity and independence of Mexico, before which all else is insignificant...' Ziegler paid on 3 February 1863 and the contract was drawn up on the 9th. In all, he acquired goods worth 326,506 pesos, in exchange for only 19,550 in money.

The sales made to William Corwin provide another example of the type of transactions undertaken as a result of the emergency laws.[3] On 28 November 1862 Marcus Otterburg bought a part of the convent of Santa Mónica, the whole of the convent of Santa Teresa, four lots of the

---

[1] All the history of this case is in the register of notary number 7, José Antonio Ochoterena, 1863, fols. 28 ff., 36 ff., 66 ff., 76 ff., ANP.

[2] Only one of the four other convents was sold in 1863, according to the addenda of the *Memoria de Hacienda*, 1874.

[3] 1862 register of notary number 2, Nazario Ortíz, fols. 254–8 and 1863, fols. 47–52, ANP.

monastery of San Agustín, one of Santo Domingo and two of Belem. The valuation price was approximately 135,384 pesos and he paid 6,764 pesos, equivalent to 5% of the valuation.[1] The printed forms indicated 8%, but in this instance the number 8 was crossed out in ink and replaced by the number 5. This was in accordance with the decree which stated that the mortgages were to be liquidated at 8% and real estate at 5% of valuation. On the next day the buyer commissioned the German merchant Agustín Bertheau, a resident of Puebla, to take possession of the buildings in his name. Nevertheless, the buyer was not satisfied with three of the lots which he returned on 7 February 1863, receiving others in exchange. On this occasion, it was revealed that Otterburg[2] was acting on behalf of William Corwin, son of Thomas Corwin, the United States Minister in Mexico.[3]

The two lots remaining from the four into which the Belem monastery had been divided were acquired on 26 December 1862 by Gabor Naphegy. They were valued at 7,628 pesos and he paid 5%. He was a doctor and the owner of the gas lighting company in the capital, and was perhaps a refugee from the 1848 Hungarian revolution.[4] A number of residents in Puebla redeemed clerical properties located in the capital,[5] and of course some people from the metropolis did the same in Puebla and other cities. This was logical for the transactions involved commercial dealings, investment of capital in mortgages and real estate, and the capital merchants' business affairs extended to several parts of the country.

Moreover, it was not only foreigners who acquired nationalized goods in Puebla at the end of 1862. On 29 December of that year Manuel García Teruel, a native of Veracruz who lived in Puebla and had business interests in the port and in Jalapa,[6] bought 'on behalf of and to be divided with' Jorge Berkenbuch, a block of houses belonging to the convent of Santa Rosa. They were valued at 12,000 pesos and he paid 12% on the same day.[7] In addition, García Teruel bought the college of San Pantaleón, worth 30,000 pesos and the small Franciscan monastery in Totimehuacán, near Puebla, valued at 6,000 pesos, both for 5% of the valuation price. Finally he redeemed various mortgages at 8% of their nominal value. A native of Jalapa, he thus finally managed to establish himself in Puebla,

[1] The information from the notary is completed in the addenda to *Memoria de Hacienda*, 1874, pp. 76–7.
[2] Also written as Otterbourgh; in 1867 he was U.S.A. Minister in Mexico.
[3] Minister in Mexico from 1861 to 1864.
[4] 1862 register of Nazario Ortíz, fol. 229, ANP.
[5] For example, Santiago Vicario; see appendix XVI.
[6] See chapter 2.
[7] 1862 register of Nazario Ortíz, fol. 302, ANP.

providing an example of a gradual migration of the sons, or in general the descendants, of Spaniards from the port of Veracruz to Puebla, via Jalapa, or Córdoba-Orizaba. This case also illustrates how Mexican merchants were associated with foreigners for these and certainly other business pursuits. After all they were themselves descended from foreigners.

At the end of 1862 and the beginning of 1863 the Puebla government also disposed of the nationalized mortgages which remained unsold. Thus the Puebla merchant Mariano Oropeza, probably Mexican, for the instruments do not indicate to the contrary, redeemed six mortgages on 2 January 1863. Three were invested in rural properties. The valuation price was 10,375 pesos, which he covered with an 8% payment in cash. He undertook the deal on behalf of the Belgian, Eduardo Strybos (Strybas?), using 'funds from the Santa Inés transaction, in which he is partnered by Eduardo Turnbull'.[1] Oropeza, who had already disentailed clerical properties in 1856,[2] was therefore part of the same small group of Mexican and foreign merchants who specialized in these concerns.

On the same day Santiago Vicario, a Mexican and public official, redeemed nine mortgages worth 34,656 pesos, paying 8% of the nominal value. The biggest of these was for 21,000 pesos and was invested in a mill and the rest, with one exception, in several houses in Puebla.[3] Finally he bought six clerical houses worth 11,200 pesos which he paid for as follows: 8,700 pesos at 8% and 2,500 pesos in promissory notes and bonds. The laws were not always strictly obeyed. Exceptions were made, sometimes more, and others less, favourable to the client, depending on the case. However, contrary to the general impression which has prevailed to date, the law was generally observed.

The result of all these transactions was that a large sum of money entered the state government's coffers, considering that the goods were sold at a fraction of their real value. It is not known if pious members of the industrial and merchant classes in Puebla protested against the sales, particularly those of the convents and churches which to them must have seemed sacrilegious. If they did not complain, this might have been because the sales saved themselves from having to contribute to forced loans. In one way or another, it was due to the revenue yielded by the redemptions that the army was able to store a large amount of munitions and supplies in Puebla, and these enabled the city's defenders to withstand the French siege for sixty-two days, from 16 March to 17 May. Although

[1] 1863 register of José Antonio Ochoterena, fol. 4, ANP.
[2] See appendix VI.
[3] 1863 register of José Antonio Ochoterena, fols. 8, 19, ANP.

the final dealings in ecclesiastical possessions in Puebla did not prevent the French occupation of the country, the defence of the city, made possible by the funds from the transactions, did show the world that Mexico was opposing the foreign invasion and that the spirit of resistance was alive. It was this that in the end was more important than all the French military victories.

The social group in Puebla which benefited from the sales effected at the end of 1862 and the beginning of 1863 was no longer as numerous nor as Mexican as that of 1861–62, and even less so than in 1856. The reasons for this are obvious. In 1856 the great majority of tenants, mostly Mexicans, were converted into proprietors. In 1861–62 they paid the government for the houses. However, unlike in 1856, as a result of the three years' war the government in 1861 was openly anti-clerical and it may be supposed that many wealthy Mexicans refrained from redeeming clerical possessions because of this. Therefore among the buyers there were more French, central European and English speaking persons, all of whom originated from countries in which liberalism in matters of religion was an accepted practice. Of course, this restriction in the demand, and also an increase in the supply because of mounting fiscal difficulties, caused a drop in the sale prices. This tendency was even more pronounced in the crisis of the last months of 1862. Naturally, towards the end there were few buyers because the government, pressed for time, hastened to reach agreement with a few individuals over the sale of the remaining property and capital. As a result of all that has been described, the overall group now having a vested interest in the fate of the Reform was no longer the same in 1863 as in 1856. The composition of the group changed both in Mexico City and in Puebla.

During the fiscal crisis at the end of 1862 the Puebla government decided to carry out the law relating to dowries. The capital funds of the dowries had been invested in property mortgages for many years. For example, in 1856 Juan Thévenard had disentailed a house rented from the Cathedral Treasury Office. The sum involved was 13,334 pesos, equalling an annual rent of 800 pesos capitalized at 6%.[1] In April 1861 the house was redeemed by someone else[2] but on 28 October 1862 the chief treasury official ordered the notary to cancel the redemption because the property was in fact mortgaged for 12,000 pesos to three dowries. Thévenard owed the other 1,333 pesos to the church of San Jerónimo and he redeemed this amount on 6 November 1862, paying 8% in accordance with the decree

---

[1] 1856 register of Gregorio Sandoval, fols. 262–3, ANP.
[2] Ibid., notes in the margin of the register.

of 28 October. In examining the statistics for the 1856 buyers in Puebla, in which Thévenard is naturally included, it must be remembered that not all the adjudicators paid for their property in 1861. As will be shown later, many kept their mortgages for years.

Even a few days before the decree of 26 December 1862, which ordered that the nuns be assured of their dowries, these funds began to be formally registered before notary number 5. The aim was clear: to hand them over to the nuns before the war, with its inevitable destruction and disorder, made this impossible. Thus between 17 and 31 December forty-two 'nuns' deeds' were registered before this notary, and a further twenty-five between 2 January and 6 March. The total value of these was 408,050 pesos.[1] There were special printed forms for this in which the owner of the assigned house or one mortgaged to the Church before 1856 acknowledged a capital in favour of a nun (or, in some cases, several capitals to various nuns) for a term of five years at 6% annual interest, payable three times a year in advance. If he failed to pay, 'the term of the investment would be considered as completed and the borrower obliged to redeem the capital immediately...' The fund belonging to the nun was therefore well secured from the legal point of view, but not in the financial sense, for the available information indicates that the mortgage debt was usually equal to the value of the security, that is the house.

Even though none of the sixty-seven deeds was signed by the beneficiary, it would be wrong to conclude that the nuns were not willing to accept the capital. Apart from the fact that no case of a nun renouncing her rights as a form of protest has been found, there is evidence in the notes contained in the margin of the register that they did receive the funds. For example, the first dowry registered on 17 December was for 4,000 pesos and this was invested in a mortgage which was extended several years later and finally redeemed in 1882. The second instrument was for two dowries of 3,000 pesos each. The first was paid back in 1873 (to the nun or her heirs) and the other continued invested. The mortgage detailed in the fourth instrument corresponded to Thévenard and it was extended for nine years. The fate of the mortgages is described in more detail in the 'Books of mortgage contracts'.[2] The following five examples are taken from the latter and they were all recorded in the notarial register 5. A mortgage of two dowries totalling 6,000 pesos was extended many

---

[1] 1862 register of notary 5, fols. 407–48, and 1863, fols. 98–123, ANP.
[2] Registro Público de la Propiedad (cited hereinafter as RPP), Puebla, libro de censos 50, December 1862–66, fols. 29–32.

times until it was finally cancelled in 1920. Another of 1,000 pesos, part of a dowry, was paid to the nun exactly five years later, at the beginning of 1868. One was of 10,000 pesos, incorporating three dowries, and the term of 4,000 pesos of this sum was extended in 1868 for nine years and afterwards cancelled. A mortgage of 6,000 pesos included one dowry and part of another, and in 1885, 4,000 pesos of this sum was extended for seven years in favour of the heir, and the term of the other 2,000 pesos was likewise lengthened. Finally, a mortgage of 12,000 pesos belonging to four dowries was extended at the end of 1867 for a further seven years. No cases have been found in which persons other than the interested parties appropriated the capital. All the indications are that not only did the government fulfil its obligations, but also the nuns or their heirs, contrary to what is at times believed, enjoyed the product of their invested capital.

As far as the mortgage borrowers were concerned, who for the most part were the former adjudicators, the transactions were not so good. Even though they were now owners, they could not redeem the debt at a low price like those with greater resources had been able to do. Instead they had to continue paying the nun the same amount that they were previously paying to the corporation as rent. Furthermore, they now had to meet all the obligations of a houseowner.

In two and a half months 408,050 pesos belonging to dowries were invested in property mortgages. Taking a dowry to be 3,000 pesos, 135 nuns were provided with a capital fund before notary 5, but accepting that a dowry amounted to 4,000 pesos on average not only in the capital but also in Puebla, then only 100 nuns benefited. The average in Puebla was probably less than in Mexico City, perhaps 3,500 pesos. Using the estimate that there were 261 nuns in Puebla in 1851,[1] this means that almost half of them received a capital fund before a single notary.

Even supposing that dowries were not formally registered before other notaries—in fact such instruments have not been found in the other registers—it can be concluded that the terms of the law could not have been better implemented, especially given the pressure of the time factor, for several days after the last instrument the French siege of Puebla began.

[1] *Memoria de Justicia*, 1851.

CÓRDOBA

In Córdoba the nationalized goods began to be sold at the end of 1860. First, it may be assumed that the capital funds resulting from the disentailment in 1856 were redeemed by the respective adjudicators. Secondly, the mortgages predating the Lerdo law were sold. According to the document already cited in chapter 2,[1] the total of ecclesiastical property and capital in Córdoba amounted in 1856 to more than 200,000 pesos. If, as it appears, the value of real estate was less than 50,000 pesos, then the capital funds reached more than 150,000 pesos. The brotherhoods seem to have been the wealthiest of the various corporations, for their capital was almost 70,000 pesos (that of Santísimo was 21,000 pesos and that of Animas 41,000 pesos). The *capellanías* had 55,000 pesos, pious works 15,000 pesos, and the 'girls' school' 62,000 pesos.

The list is incomplete because the following are omitted: vacant *capellanías* in which the interest on the benefices was collected by the tithe collection district office; the monastery of San Diego, the only one in Córdoba, which in 1843 had capital worth 11,475 pesos;[2] finally, certain capital funds belonging to the hospital of Santísima Trinidad which was managed by the council.[3] On the other hand, the nominal capital of the girls' school, which was directed by the Church, seemed to have been reduced almost to nothing:[4]

the hacienda of Guadalupe, insolvent although it owes 41,932 pesos. This capital has depreciated to such an extent because of the freedom of slaves that the Supreme Government accepted responsibility, and to date it is not known how much has been lost, nor how much remains...The hacienda of San Francisco, in which a capital of 2,214 pesos was invested, pays nothing and has not done so for many years, because it is completely ruined. That of San Joaquín, in which 1,000 pesos are invested, owes up to last year the sum of 4,500 pesos in interest. The Consolidation treasury has 4,000 pesos and owes up to last year 9,400 pesos in interest...The San Antonio inn (owned by the council) has 4,000 pesos invested in it and its account is unliquidated ...The house...embargoed, with 1,000 pesos invested in it, on which no interest is paid.

Another house mortgaged for 3,000 pesos was embargoed by the school, but it was in such a lamentable condition 'that it has cost and is costing considerable sums to repair, after many years' interest had not been paid, to the notable detriment of the school...' Only two debtors owing

---

[1] *Estado que manifiesta las fincas, capitales y fondos eclesiásticos...*, 3 May 1856, AGN, JE, vol. 175, fols. 141–8.   [2] *Memoria de Justicia*, 1844, table.

[3] *BSMGE*, vol. IV, 1854, pp. 73 ff.: *Estadística del partido de Córdoba*, formed in 1840.

[4] *Estado que manifiesta las fincas, capitales y fondos eclesiásticos...*, 3 May 1856, AGN, JE, vol. 175, fols. 141–8, p. 8.

5,000 pesos were up to date with their interest payments. The nominal capital of 62,147 pesos, therefore, was in fact reduced by more than 90%, either because it was impossible to retrieve it, or because the real estate security was ruined. This is an illustration of a socially useful institution which was originally rich but which had been declining since the war of independence. Even if the capital holdings of the other clerical organizations in Córdoba seem real—the Account provides the figures without comment—this example of the girls' school reveals the difficulty, if not the impossibility, of calculating the true size of clerical wealth before the Reform. The case of the Córdoba girls' school was not the only one. In this, and in other similar instances, the traditional accounting system of the corporations retained figures which no longer corresponded to reality.

For details of the sales of nationalized goods in Córdoba, the 1860 and 1861 registers of the notary José Fructuoso Corona were examined.[1] In the first transaction, dated 23 December 1860, Agustín Legrand, a merchant and industrialist in Córdoba and Orizaba, redeemed a mortgage valued at 3,181 pesos. He did so in the name of the firm Messrs. Legrand & Co. He undertook to pay 1,908 pesos in bonds (three-fifths), two months after the capital of the country had returned to liberal control. He met the remaining 1,272 pesos with a 'Veracruz bombardment certificate'. As stated in chapter 4, these credits were admitted in the laws of 11 February and 25 March 1860 in place of cash payments. Thus those who had them, whether they were the ones who suffered the damage or their assignees, could pay 40% of the price of nationalized goods with a certificate, giving them clearly a considerable advantage. According to the next instrument, dated the same day, Legrand redeemed 1,500 pesos, committing himself to pay 900 pesos in bonds (three-fifths) and paying 600 pesos with a bombardment certificate worth that amount. Legrand later punctually handed over the bonds, as is noted in the margin of the register.

On 23 March 1861 the notary began to register, in Legrand's favour, a large number of mortgages of different amounts, all of which were in part redeemed with the bombardment certificates. The capital funds involved predated the Lerdo law and belonged to several clerical corporations to which the houses in the city and surrounding areas were mortgaged. The owners had not redeemed their debts within the stipulated term of thirty days allowed them by the law of 13 July 1859, and so Legrand then redeemed them before the end of 1860. In this way he was

---

[1] In the possession of notary number 13, Lic. Salvador D. Zamudio; from the 1860 register of 163 fols., fols. 155 ff. are quoted; from that of 1861 of 106 fols., fols. 44–80 are used.

able to buy a total of thirty-four mortgages with a total value of 71,647 pesos.[1] One important fact was revealed in the first instrument, dated 23 March, and this was that Legrand was acting 'on behalf of his partner, Manuel Escandón'. A native of Orizaba and the owner of the Cocolapam factory in the city, Escandón had probably decided to buy a large number of mortgages in Córdoba with the aim of strengthening his economic control along the route of the future Mexico–Veracruz railway. As far as it is known, neither Escandón nor Legrand owned important real estate in the port of Veracruz. Hence they must have bought the bombardment certificates, presumably at a low price, from the people who had suffered damage to their property.

The Account of 26 June 1862 is incomplete. According to it the mortgages which were sold (those predating the Lerdo law) amounted to 152,594 pesos, but this is 100,000 pesos less than the figure given in 1866 (see chapter 7). Nevertheless, although it is not complete, the Account does give reasonably exact information on the disposal of the mortgages. It shows that, with the exception of Legrand's purchases, the mortgage borrowers usually redeemed what they owed previously to the Church. Apparently Legrand intervened to acquire them wholesale, only in those instances in which the owners of the property did not have the money to redeem the mortgage or refused to do so on grounds of conscience.

The owners who redeemed their debt in 1861 were almost all Mexicans. Among them professional people and public officials were prominent, for example Mariano Antuñez, the Ceballos brothers, Francisco Hernández y Hernández, the de la Llave brothers and Francisco Talavera. Both they and the rest did what any sensible person would have done in their place. Also J. B. Sisos, the only foreigner to appear in the list, redeemed the mortgage on his house.

ORIZABA AND JALAPA

The total value of possessions sold in Orizaba is taken from two documents of 1861–62.[2] According to the first, dated 19 August 1861, goods to a total value of 330,000 pesos were sold. The second, which is undated

---

[1] *Noticia de los capitales pertenecientes a bienes eclesiásticos y otras corporaciones que han sido redimidos por las personas que se expresan, así como las adjudicaciones, sacadas de los únicos datos que en la actualidad existen*, dated Córdoba, 26 June 1862, when the city was already occupied by the invading army; the manuscript is in AGN, PBN, leg. 734.

[2] *Noticia de los capitales y fincas que fueron del clero y se han enajenado en esta oficina con arreglo a las disposiciones de la ley de 13 de julio de 1859*, dated Orizaba, 19 August 1861, AGN, PBN, leg. 734; and *Noticia de las fincas y capitales del clero, enajenados en esta*, undated, AGN, PBN, leg. 734.

and could well be a little later, gives the sum as 360,000 pesos, in round figures. In 1865–66 sales in Orizaba were shown as for 433,000 pesos (see chapter 7).

The notarial registers indicate that the first transaction registered took place on 8 October 1860.[1] In this several people redeemed the mortgages on various houses belonging to other individuals. As had happened in Córboba, there were house owners in Orizaba who allowed the term for redeeming their mortgage to expire, with the result that it was redeemed by someone else. For example, a mill owner had owed 3,000 pesos to *capellanías* since 1853. This debt was redeemed by another person, who now 'spontaneously ceded the credit to the original borrower'. In another similar case, dated 13 February 1861, Francisco de P. Carrillo, a liberal journalist, redeemed mortgages on several houses worth 8,900 pesos.[2] These belonged to L. Iturriaga 'who did not come within the correct time to register formally the respective redemption contract, and so Dr. F. de P. Carrillo was subrogated in place of the exchequer'. Iturriaga now paid the capital to Carrillo and the mortgage was cancelled. He may perhaps have had to pay the doctor's costs. There are a number of other similar cases.[3]

As for the original adjudicators, they almost always redeemed in 1860–61 the corresponding capital, except in those cases in which they had meanwhile sold the property to someone else. This is concluded from the few available data (appendix VIII).

Professional people and liberal officials also seem to have been prominent buyers in Orizaba. Nevertheless, it must not be forgotten that the names of the professional people and public officials of the time are quite well known, whereas the same cannot be said of the merchants in Orizaba. It is possible, therefore, that among the people who redeemed Church possessions and whose occupation is unknown, there were some merchants. If a complete account of the occupation of all the buyers could be compiled, it would perhaps reveal that the number of purchases made by the merchants was no less important than that of the professional classes.

The Account of the capital, properties and other funds belonging to the clergy in the department of Jalapa, cited in chapter 2,[4] shows that in 1856 the Church owned in the Jalapa region urban real estate worth

[1] 1860 register, vol. II, fol. 70, Biblioteca de la Universidad Veracruzana.
[2] 1861 register, vol. I, fol. 41, ibid.
[3] Seven instruments from 1860 were examined, twelve from 1861 and one from 1862.
[4] *Estado demonstrativo de los capitales, propiedades y otros fondos pertenecientes al clero en el departamento de Jalapa, formado en cumplimiento del supremo decreto de 31 de marzo próximo pasado,* 1856, AGN, JE, vol. 175, fol. 107.

58,000 pesos, invested capital in urban houses of 125,880 pesos, and 148,763 pesos invested in rural properties. The creditors were primarily several brotherhoods and then the *capellanías*. Unlike the Accounts for Orizaba and Córdoba, that of Jalapa indicates in detail each mortgaged house with the name of the owner and its mortgage creditor. This information reveals that to have one's house mortgaged was not a sign of poverty, for the two rich Jalapa residents mentioned in chapter 2, Sáyago and García Teruel, had mortgaged not only their houses but also their hacienda and mill to the *capellanías* and to the local San Francisco monastery. Nor were the amounts involved small, being 10,000 pesos approximately to the former and 20,000 pesos to the latter.

The registers of the notary Antonio C. de Hoyos prove that many of these mortgages were redeemed in the last months of 1860 and during 1861. In addition, the debts owed on assigned properties from 1856–57 were redeemed. As in Orizaba, the adjudicators in Jalapa usually freed their own house from its mortgage commitment (see appendix IX). There was only one case found in the 1856–57 registers in which another person liquidated the value of the promissory notes signed by the adjudicator. In one transaction found in the 1861 register, a person replaced the adjudicator and redeemed 2,200 pesos invested in a house in favour of two clerical corporations; a mortgage of 600 pesos in favour of a school continued valid in accordance with the decrees issued to protect educational institutions. These cases were, however, exceptional. The state of Veracruz, therefore, also saw a continuity between the disentailment of 1856–57 and the nationalization of 1860–61. Finally, in 1861 a number of properties were assigned which had not been disentailed five years earlier.[1]

SAN LUIS POTOSÍ

The liberals took possession of the city of San Luis Potosí on 3 April 1859, and in the following months of August and September they implemented the law of 13 July concerning the nationalization and sale of Church wealth. The conservatives, however, re-entered the city on 24 November and interrupted the operations. Finally the liberals regained control on 30 April 1860 and the redemptions were confirmed during the early months of 1861.[2]

---

[1] 1860 register of Antonio C. de Hoyos, fols. 326, 328, 329 of 10 November; 1861 register of the same notary, fol. 11 of 22 January, fol. 33 of 8 February, fol. 53 of 27 February, fol. 76 of 20 March, fol. 113 of 22 April and fol. 122 of 25 April; all the latter are in Biblioteca de la Universidad Veracruzana.

[2] *Noticias de la jefatura superior de hacienda de San Luis Potosí*, cited in Betancourt, *San Luis Potosí*, 364–71.

Nationalized property in the provinces, 1861–63

Throughout the whole state of San Luis Potosí, ecclesiastical possessions worth 706,559 pesos were redeemed in 1861.[1] This amount includes both the redemption of the houses disentailed in 1856–57 and the mortgages predating the Lerdo law. The total redemptions amounted in round figures to 1,000,000 pesos, according to data of 1866 (see chapter 7).

In the first place, properties already disentailed earlier were redeemed. It is of interest to know if the adjudicators, buyers and auction buyers of 1856–57 kept their houses in 1861 or if ownership of these was transferred to other people. As in other places, the information for this had to be sought in the notes in the margin of the registers. The extract of the 1856 and 1857 registers of the notary Isidro Calvillo, reproduced in appendices XII, XIII and XIV, indicates that only in a few cases was there information on this question. The majority of the instruments of sale, adjudication and auction do not have any annotations in the margin. It would be erroneous to deduce from this that the goods were not therefore redeemed in 1861, 1862 or 1863. If the great fiscal requirements of those years are remembered, it is easy to imagine that the government sold at the time all the saleable capital at almost any price except, as we have seen, the funds devoted to the dowries. This was certainly done not only in the big cities like Mexico and Puebla, in which the 1856 and 1857 registers note in the margins the fate of disentailed property, but also in the provincial cities like Atlixco, Jalapa, Orizaba and San Luis Potosí, where the registers for those years do not give the same information. The absence of these annotations may perhaps be attributed to the carelessness of the notaries who, when they effected a redemption of clerical capital in 1861–62, neglected to make the corresponding note in the margin of the 1856 or 1857 register. Such an omission did not invalidate the redemption. Both in Mexico and in Puebla the 1856 and 1857 registers contain details of certain disentailed properties and in those of the years 1861 or 1862 the same properties appear as redeemed, but the corresponding marginal notes were not put in the 1856 or 1857 instruments. Hence the absence of such notes does not mean that there were no redemptions.

The few annotations in the margin of the 1856 and 1857 registers in San Luis Potosí indicate that, with only one exception, the original adjudicators cancelled the mortgage on their property in subsequent years. The exception involved the sale by the adjudicator of his rights to another person, who later redeemed the capital. As regards the rest of the properties, about which there are no notes in the margins of the

---

[1] MH 1870, p. 565; the state of San Luis Potosí is used as an example; the MH 1870 does not have data on other states.

instruments, the impression is that they were redeemed by the original buyers. Outside the capital the redemption of a property by the adjudicator, auction buyer or original buyer was, as we have seen in the case of Puebla, something quite normal and routine. Redemption by a stranger was rather unusual and perhaps justified greater attention by the notary. Thus it is likely that in these cases, the latter would not forget to note in the earlier registers such an anomalous event. The few available data indicate that in San Luis Potosí also there was continuity between the disentailment and the subsequent nationalization.

For details of the sales of nationalized goods the register of Isidro Calvillo has been consulted. He was one of several notaries of the time and consequently the sales which he registered represent only a small part of the total number. The following are intended as an illustrative sample. In September 1859 there was a sale derived from a denouncement; in December 1860 there were two redemptions; in 1861 twelve redemption deeds of clerical capital were recorded; in 1862 only four; and in 1863 only two.[1] In general, the picture which arises is very similar to that observed in other states, with a local variant recalling some of the cases already mentioned in respect of Orizaba. Thus Francisco Bustamante, a deputy in 1862 and governor of San Luis Potosí in 1877, had acquired two clerical mortgages on properties owned by another person. The latter came to an agreement with Bustamante on 30 January 1861 whereby he committed himself to redeem the capital owed within the next five years. In another similar case the debtor, who apparently had few resources, provided a quarter of the money needed for the redemption. The remaining three-quarters were furnished by someone else who then negotiated a special agreement with the debtor whereby they would be repaid to him at a future date. There was at least one other case involving the transfer of capital.[2] In this way the mortgage debtors found a way of redeeming their debt and persons with money were able to make an investment.

Not all the recently acquired properties were redeemed. Those which belonged to the schools formerly administered by the clergy were now mortgaged to the public education fund.[3] As early as 4 August 1859 the state governor wrote to the constitutional government at Veracruz to ask if a community of pious women established in the San Nicolás girls' school should be considered as a convent under the law of 12 July (these were women known as *beatas* and were the teachers in the school—they

---

[1] 1859 register of I. Calvillo, fol. 86; 1860, fols. 326, 338; 1861, fols. 42–283; 1862, fols. 32, 130, 166, 446; 1863, fols. 71, 108, ANSLP.

[2] 1861 register of I. Calvillo, fols. 53, 120, 189, ANSLP.

[3] *Noticias de la jefatura de hacienda*, Betancourt, *San Luis Potosí*, 366.

were not really nuns). The latter law had not mentioned such communities which were not constituted with all the formalities of a convent. The Minister of Justice replied on 10 September that 'as a general rule, it must be observed that every establishment of public welfare or education... should be retained and improved, even though it may be, or may have been, under the immediate supervision of the clergy. It must be taken from the ownership, administration and direction of the latter and be entirely subject to the civil authority.'[1] This communication already outlined the policy which the federal government was to follow in 1861, namely to secularize such institutions but at the same time preserving their endowments. The old community and its possessions were, therefore, basically retained.

Only the amount of real estate owned in 1856 by the public welfare and educational organizations of San Luis Potosí is known, and these were the figures summarized in chapter 3. The amount of their mortgages, which could be obtained if detailed information on all the redemption transactions of 1861–63 were available, is not known. Hence it is not possible to ascertain to what extent the 1861 laws and 1862 measures were implemented. What is certain is that the capital funds belonging to public welfare organizations survived the national emergency of 1862–63 and the foreign occupation. This is proved by the fact that in 1873 the mortgages belonging to the former San Juan hospital and the poor house (the latter was established in 1851 and had no real estate in 1856) amounted to approximately 59,000 pesos. These mortgages, at 5% and 6% annual interest, were on properties owned by various proprietors in San Luis Potosí, for example P. Verástegui, F. Bustamante and J. M. Coca. The capital belonging to primary education amounted in the same year to 18,500 pesos, and that of secondary level, to 78,000 pesos. These mortgages were likewise held on various properties and yielded 5% and 6% annual interest. In one case, involving a capital of 3,000 pesos, the interest rate was 12% a year.[2] It is not known if these funds were greater ten years earlier.

The facts available on the several nationalization operations make it possible to reconstruct broadly the picture of the social group which acquired the ecclesiastical wealth. The information given in chapter 3 on the occupation or profession of some of the residents of San Luis Potosí is of some help in this. Among the buyers the following were prominent: Francisco Antonio Aguirre, owner of a silver mine; José

[1] Labastida, 359.
[2] *Memoria de Hacienda*, 1873–74, pp. ccxxxiv, ccxxxv, ccxxxix.

Antonio Barragán, hacendado and public official; the aforementioned Bustamante; E. Domínguez, miner and financier (financing miners); C. M. Escobar, lawyer and public official; the Gordoa and the Verástegui families, lawyers, hacendados and public officials, already noted in chapter 3. All the above were Mexican. There were scarcely any foreigners among the buyers; indeed, outside the Mexico-Veracruz route there were few foreigners in the country. This is the first important difference between the result of the nationalization in Mexico, Puebla and Veracruz on the one hand, and in San Luis Potosí on the other. Nevertheless the names of the merchants are not known. If they were, perhaps merchants as well as miners, professional people and hacendados would be among the buyers.

MORELIA

As stated in chapter 4, the state of Michoacán remained within the liberal orbit during the three years' war, with the result that the disentailment was gradually transformed into the nationalization without being broken. The sale of nationalized goods continued in the state in the years 1861–63. The capital, Morelia, was occupied by the invading French army on 30 November 1863.[1] Thus the operations involving nationalized goods in Morelia during those three years will be considered here.

There is not as much information available on Morelia as there was about San Luis Potosí. Therefore the sources used have been almost exclusively the registers of the notary Manuel Valdovinos and the already cited 1862 reports of the state Treasury Office and the general treasury. According to the registers, the redemptions effected under the laws of Reform (which were later than Degollado's decrees) took place mainly in the years 1860–61, especially in the latter.[2] The financial results are shown in table 14.

The ecclesiastical capital in Michoacán, which was affected by the Reform laws to January 1862, amounted to nearly 2,000,000 pesos. Adding to this sum the goods nationalized as a result of Degollado's decrees which, as shown in chapter 4, amounted to 1,000,000 pesos, we obtain the approximate total of 3,000,000 pesos for ecclesiastical wealth in Michoacán, including the capital funds of both before and after the Lerdo law. This total would be increased even further if the transactions of 1862–63 were included but their value is not known. According to the 1866 data, the total goods sold in the state were worth about 4,500,000 pesos.[3]

---

[1] Bravo Ugarte, *Historia de Michoacán*, III, 109.
[2] Lerdo de Tejada, *Jefatura de hacienda...*, pp. 4–6.   [3] See chapter 7.

TABLE 14. *Results of the sale of nationalized goods in Michoacán, 1860–61*

	Pesos	Product in cash
Clerical capital of	1,283,867	519,612 (nearly 40%)
Capital belonging to public education of	111,826	33,840 (less than 40%)
Capital belonging to public welfare of	323,040	98,740 (less than 40%)
Capital belonging to councils of	97,693	43,931
Clerical capital sold in district offices of the state; amount unknown	—	117,880
Capellanías	—	20,171
Other capital	—	8,303
10% and 15% of disentailment	—	7,406
Total capital (approx.)	2,000,000	849,887

The item corresponding to the cash payments of capital belonging to public welfare and educational organizations was reduced by a quarter, in accordance with article 38 of the law of 5 February 1861 which ordered that in the states a discount of 25% would be granted to those who redeemed in one payment the total amount they were required to meet in cash.[1] It must not be thought that the so-called cash total was always in fact received in coinage. As in the capital of the republic, the greater part of the so-called cash probably consisted of promissory notes, credits and other documents. The same Report indicates that the 60% corresponding to the bonds produced a total of 1,186,712 pesos; of this, by 1862 bonds worth 736,391 pesos were received and amortized, leaving commitments to hand over bonds of 450,331 pesos. From the viewpoint of the accounts, the operations in Morelia did not differ much from those in the capital. Both coincided in at least one respect: neither produced much real money.

Like the federal government, each of the state administrations experienced a fiscal crisis. The deterioration of the civil war, perhaps a consequence of the assassination of Melchor Ocampo by the reaction on 3 June 1861, may have led to the Michoacán government order of 3 October which declared that all public welfare and educational funds were to be redeemed. The local administration thus anticipated the federal decree of 7 May 1862.[2] We have seen in chapter 4 that the government had gone to considerable trouble to assign capital to these socially useful institutions.

[1] Labastida, 148.
[2] This order has not been found but it is invariably cited in the respective instruments.

Hence public education received an endowment of 312,467 pesos, and the hospital 526,254 pesos, both amounts being taken from ecclesiastical funds.[1] The public education funds decreased by 111,826 pesos, so that 200,641 pesos remained in 1862. Those of public welfare were only 203,214 pesos in 1862, having been reduced by 323,040 pesos. Little more than half of these funds disappeared.

This development is reflected in the notarial register of Manuel Valdovinos. A hacienda was mortgaged to public education for 36,000 pesos but this was redeemed by the owner on 4 November 1861.[2] Another hacienda owed the hospital 4,000 pesos which were likewise redeemed by the owner on 28 December 1861. On 23 October 1861 a houseowner redeemed 20,900 pesos invested in his property by the hospital.[3] In view of such substantial amounts it is not surprising that the capital funds should have been so quickly reduced by almost half.

Under the terms of the order of 3 October 1861 Melchor Ocampo's heirs should have redeemed 4,000 pesos, for which their hacienda was mortgaged to the San Nicholás school, but in an act of generosity a decree was issued on 19 November 1861 annulling the capital.[4]

The reports of the state Treasury Office and the General Treasury Office cover up to the beginning of 1862. The question thus arises as to whether the public welfare and educational funds still subsisting in Michoacán on this last date were not redeemed subsequently in 1862 and 1863. The registers for these years contain very few cases of such redemptions. One example: on 18 November 1863 Gregorio Patiño redeemed 11,000 pesos owed by another person who had mortgaged his property for that amount to the hospital.[5] The fact that this took place only twelve days before the invading troops entered Morelia possibly means that Patiño was anxious to buy at a good price while the constitutionalist government was still in control. The purchase was not in any way endangered in view of Forey's manifesto of 12 June, which essentially recognized the nationalization. The case however was exceptional. Therefore the public welfare and educational endowments did not suffer much loss in the critical two years from 1862–63, as far as can be known from the available data. After an initial loss during the last months of 1861, these Funds were apparently respected.

Details have been given in chapter 4 of the adjudicators who redeemed

---

1 Lerdo de Tejada, *Tesorería general y jefatura...*, p. 30.
2 1856 register of Manuel Valdovinos, fol. 105, ANM.
3 Ibid., 1860, fols. 134, 135.
4 Ibid., 234.
5 1856 register of Manuel Valdovinos, fol. 53, ANM.

their mortgages in 1859 and 1860 under the Degollado decrees. We have seen above that at the end of 1861 the adjudicators redeemed mortgages invested in their properties in favour of public welfare and educational institutions. Nevertheless not everybody succeeded in redeeming their debts, as the following examples will show. On 27 October 1860 the governor, Epitacio Huerta, had been assigned the hacienda Chucándiro, situated near Cuitzeo, for the sum of 75,000 pesos. Of this amount, 1,000 pesos was in the form of a mortgage owed to a *capellanía*.[1] As the property had not been previously disentailed, article 28 of the law of 13 July 1859 was applied, by which the adjudication was to be made on the basis of the value declared for tax purposes, or if this was not available, on the value corresponding to the rent currently paid.[2] In this instance the law improved the terms of payment: 70% of the price could be met in bonds and 30% in promissory notes. Yet the buyer did not take advantage of this. 44,400 pesos, exactly 60%, was to be paid in national debt bonds within six months, and 29,600 pesos in forty monthly promissory notes. Huerta probably was unable to meet even the first of these notes, for on 18 June 1861, less than nine months later, another person, F. López, redeemed the 29,600 pesos, no doubt having bought the notes from Huerta's own government. By this date the adjudicator had still not handed over the bonds for the 44,400 pesos. The hacienda was therefore mortgaged for its full value. A year later the governor decided to resign to join the army then fighting the foreign invader. It was probably for this reason that on 22 October 1862 he let the hacienda for five years at a rent amounting to 5% of the purchase price, which had been 75,000 pesos. The rent was payable yearly in advance.[3] The governor left on 10 November.[4] To that moment the transaction had not been very satisfactory for him as the hacienda owner, because almost all the rent would go to the creditor. Of course eventually the promissory notes would be amortized and then the owner would begin to receive the whole of the rent.

Above all in 1862 and 1863, many redemptions were made by people other than the original adjudicators who had become owners of the properties. Thus one individual redeemed 1,500 pesos, the value of a mortgage on a house owned by someone else. He then sold his claim to F. López to whom the capital was assigned on 24 February 1862.[5] On

[1] 1860 register of Manuel Valdovinos, fol. 259, ANM.
[2] Labastida, 143.
[3] 1862 register of Manuel Valdovinos, fol. 154, ANM.
[4] Bravo Ugarte, *Historia de Michoacán*, III, 105.
[5] 1862 register of Manuel Valdovinos, fol. 30, ANM.

Nationalized property in the provinces, 1861–63

12 June 1862 the state Treasury Office assigned to Porfirio García de León, an hacendado and liberal official, the hacienda of Santa Rosalía, which had been originally bought by the merchant A. Luna for 24,000 pesos from the San Agustín monastery (see chapter 3). Luna had been able to meet only one of the payments of 2,000 pesos to which he was committed, and so García de León redeemed the capital in accordance with the decree of 11 January 1859, which had offered very favourable conditions to the buyers, and hence he acquired the hacienda.[1] He obtained the hacienda of Guaparateo in a similar way.[2] In 1863 he also made several purchases for large amounts. The instruments reveal that the federal treasury owed him 256,000 pesos and to liquidate this account the Minister of Hacienda issued an order on 22 September 1862 to the effect that nationalized property and capital were to be given to him to the amount of the debt.[3] Hence the San Agustín inn, valued at 40,586 pesos,[4] was transferred to him and also several other properties in the state of Michoacán. The purchase of the inn was effected on 7 November 1863, about three weeks before the invading army entered Morelia.

Although the index to M. Valdovinos' registers does show that there were foreigners among the buyers of nationalized goods, for example Guillermo Wodon Sorinne, who in 1856 bought many corporately owned houses in auctions in the capital,[5] the general impression is that there were not many, simply because few foreigners lived in Morelia. Due to its geographical location, the population of Morelia was even more Mexican than that of San Luis Potosí. It was inevitable therefore that Mexicans, the professional classes as well as public officials and merchants, should predominate among the buyers of nationalized goods.

The fate of the convents and monasteries was the same in Morelia as in the other cities already described. Some were demolished to make way for streets, others were divided and sold, and finally, a few were converted into government offices. Pedro Gutiérrez,[6] owner of a large shop in the city, bought the monastery of San Agustín, and he also acquired the convents of Santa Teresa la Nueva and Santa Catarina in Pátzcuaro.[7] Unlike Puebla, where the most valuable monastic buildings were acquired by foreign merchants, in Morelia it was the Mexicans who obtained them.

[1] Ibid., fol. 115.
[2] Ibid., 2 December 1862, fol. 181.
[3] Cited in the 1863 register, fol. 326.
[4] Ibid.
[5] 1863 register, 20 May, fol. 253, ANM.
[6] Maillefert, 297.
[7] *Memoria de Hacienda*, 1873–74, addenda, pp. 73, 74.

Of course it is possible that the buyers were Spaniards but this is unlikely in view of what has already been explained in the previous chapters about the political associations of Spaniards in Mexico.

P. Gutiérrez, in common with buyers of some of the other convents and monasteries in Morelia, mortgaged the part of the payment required in cash to the nuns' dowries, that is 40% of the sale price of the properties. Thus El Carmen, San Agustín, Santa Catarina—the most valuable of the monasteries in the city—the Carmelite community, and that of Santa Catarina in Pátzcuaro were mortgaged to the sum of 30,000 pesos.[1] There were about 100 nuns in Morelia,[2] and as the dowries there were probably less than in Mexico City, it can be concluded that at least ten nuns were endowed with the sale of the five buildings.

GUADALAJARA

After a month-long siege, Guadalajara was liberated by the constitutionalist forces on 2 November 1860. The transactions involving the nationalized goods began immediately and lasted until the end of 1863. The invading French army occupied the city on 6 January 1864.

As in the other cities, the buyers, adjudicators and original auction buyers hastened to redeem the mortgages, both those predating 1856 and those resulting from the disentailment. This fact is evident from the registers of the notary Jesús Durán for 1857 and that of Juan Riestra for 1856. Twelve instruments were examined in the former, pertaining to the auction and purchase, as a result of a denouncement, of ecclesiastic properties. These deeds were cancelled, that is declared null and void, in 1858. Nine of them have notes in the margin, dated 1861, which indicate the redemption of the properties by the adjudicators (auction buyers). In only one of these the note about the redemption seems to have been annulled and the signatures obliterated. The redemption of a capital fund was a little more complicated: on 16 January 1861 the auction buyer Nicanor Reyes redeemed only the 40% corresponding to the cash payment but he left owing the bonds which he finally paid much later, during the Empire.[3] Three of the twelve instruments do not have notes in the margin.

Twenty-seven instruments of conventional sales were examined in the 1856 register of Juan Riestra (there are more than this). None of these sales, spontaneously effected by the various corporations, was annulled in 1858.

[1] Ibid. [2] *Memoria de Justicia*, 1851, table.
[3] 1857 register of Jesús Durán, fol. 9, ANG.

When the Reform laws were put into force in Guadalajara, the capital owed formerly to the Church and now to the nation had to be redeemed. Of the twenty-seven instruments fourteen, or approximately half, have a note in the margin relating to the redemption of the mortgage. These notes are very interesting because they reveal a great variety of solutions that were adopted.[1] In three cases the buyers had already freed their property of the mortgage in 1857, paying the corporation 'capital and interest'. Such redemptions, which have not been found in the registers in other cities and therefore were presumably rare, were carried out under the terms of the Lerdo law and consequently were not affected by the later laws and decrees.[2] In a single instance the capital was 'totally paid', according to a note dated 1 September 1858,[3] which probably implies that the last payment was made before that date. Even though the payments made during Zuloaga's government were declared void, this one was perhaps discharged before the conservative occupation of the city and thus the redemption was accepted in 1861. Two redemptions were made in 1859 to the reactionary authorities.[4] In the first, the buyer had to pay on 28 May 1863 the sum he had already liquidated in 1859 and now had to hand over 40% in promissory notes or cash under the terms of the existing laws. The second case in 1859 is not very clear. Another redemption was made at the end of 1860.[5] In three cases the original buyers redeemed their mortgages in 1863.[6] Also in that year, one buyer redeemed part of a mortgage and refunded the remainder in favour of a dowry.[7] In 1861 another original buyer redeemed only 280 pesos of a 10,000 pesos mortgage and subsequently, in 1863, he mortgaged his house for the remaining 9,720 pesos in favour of four dowries.[8] In only two cases were the capitals redeemed by other prople, but in at least one of these there is evidence that the original buyer continued to own the house, because the person who had effected the redemption simply became the mortgage creditor.[9] As long as the debtor, that is the house owner, paid the interest to the new creditor, he was in no danger of losing his home. These examples clearly confirm once again the continuity between 1856 and 1861, which must have given the liberals a wide social basis.

The 1861 register of Jesús Durán contains a few examples of adjudicators losing their rights because they had voluntarily returned the

---

[1] Appendix xv of this work.
[2] 1856 register of Juan Riestra, fols. 372, 486, 491, ANG.
[3] Ibid., fol. 418. [4] Ibid., fols. 335, 361.
[5] Ibid., fol. 302. [6] Ibid., fols. 306, 351, 383.
[7] Ibid., fol. 342. [8] Ibid., fol. 352.
[9] Ibid., fols. 357, 395.

properties during the administration of the reactionary government. For example, on 17 January 1861 the chief treasury official sold to various people twelve nationalized properties for the sum of 14,150 pesos. There were other prospective buyers, but the government gave priority to those who had requested permission to acquire them from 1860. It was noted that the original adjudicators lost their rights because they had voluntarily returned them during the reaction. The obvious interest in obtaining clerical real estate, which arose in Guadalajara after the liberal triumph, perhaps resulted in the rigorous application of the law of 5 February 1861, for there was no danger, due to the demand, that the houses would remain unsold. Also it must be remembered that these and other instruments were collective, that is each one involved several properties being sold for a relatively high sum. Although these examples of the loss of rights were apparently more common in Guadalajara than in Puebla, San Luis Potosí or the towns in Veracruz, they were on the other hand certainly more frequent in the capital, where many original adjudicators lost their claims in 1861 to the group of Veracruz denouncers. The latter were not successful in Guadalajara. As far as is known, Alfredo Bablot was the only person in 1858 to denounce from Veracruz a large number of houses located in Guadalajara but the houses were sold to other people after the liberal victory. Bablot thus lost the amount he had paid in the sales tax. The absence of denouncers may perhaps be explained by the marked independence which the city usually showed in managing its own affairs, a characteristic which may well have been strengthened during the three years' war. During the Empire, Bablot asked the government for more than 2,000,000 pesos in compensation for the properties he had denounced.[2]

Most of the transactions in Durán's register for 1861 and 1862 confirm the previously made disentailments. In addition a number of properties not yet disentailed were sold, showing that the Lerdo law was not completed in 1856–57.

The Guadalajara convents and monasteries suffered the same fate as those of the other cities, except that the state governor, Pedro Ogazón, displayed rather more activity than some of his colleagues in opening new streets, which of course involved the demolition of the monastic buildings. It was in this way that those of Santo Domingo, Santa María de Gracia and a community of *beatas* were totally or partially destroyed as a result of the decree of 1 November 1858. The same thing happened to the

[1] 1861 register of Jesús Durán, fol. 5, ANG.
[2] Díaz, *Versión francesa*, IV, 391; Payno, *Cuentas*, p. iii following p. 756.

Franciscan monastery in Cocula, again on the orders of the governor.[1]
The El Carmen building was also included in the decree, but apparently
Santos Degollado issued another order on 6 December of the same year
to the effect that the property and all other goods belonging to El Carmen
were to be assigned to public welfare and education. Finally, after 1860
part of the building was sold and another part used for an artillery regi-
ment's barracks.[2]

The absence, in the states that have been described, of a pressure group
similar to that of the so-called Veracruz denouncers in the capital, and
the very few sales realized in the provinces by the Church during the three
years' war, meant that there was no formation of groups of buyers. Consequently, in the five states relatively few disputes arose between those
competing for the Church properties and capital.

In the nation's capital the denouncers had eliminated in many cases
not only the buyers of the Zuloaga and Miramón administrations but
also the original adjudicators. Moreover in two cases, exceptional but
important because of the size of the transactions involved, the 1858–60
buyers dispossessed both the original adjudicators and the denouncers.
It is certain, however, that these transactions were not typical in the capital,
and much less so in the states. The great majority of the adjudicators,
due to their vested interests, supported the liberal cause during the three
years' war. If in 1861 they had been abandoned in favour of a handful of
denouncers and buyers, then it seems indisputable that they would have
naturally turned against the constitutional government. The fact that
Juárez was eventually able to defeat the foreign invasion in spite of his
very limited resources may have been due to the support of the nation
which to a large extent consisted precisely of the 1856–57 adjudicators.
The nation appreciated that the concessions which the government made
to the Veracruz denouncers had been the price of the liberals' military
victory in 1860,[3] and that the sales of Church wealth made in 1861–63,
which were of little profit to the exchequer, had been necessary, first
to consolidate the government, and later to finance the resistance against
the foreign occupation.

The Veracruz denouncers, among whom foreigners apparently predominated, were able, together with other numerically small groups,
to acquire possession of a substantial part of the real estate in Mexico City.
Also in Puebla, a small group of merchants, again containing many
foreigners, obtained through purchase much of the city's property. The

---

[1] *Memoria de Hacienda*, 1874, addenda, p. 72.
[2] Ibid. [3] Prieto, *Economía política*, 720–2.

same phenomenon, on a reduced scale, has been seen in Córdoba. In Orizaba and Jalapa the situation was not so clear. In San Luis Potosí, Morelia and Guadalajara the business sector was equally important in the purchases, but in these cities there were relatively few foreigners and so the merchant buyers were mainly Mexican. Taking the country as a whole, the proportion of foreign merchants involved in the purchase of urban real estate is notable. This is simply due to the fact that they were outside the conflict which the nation was experiencing.

The situation was very different with regard to rural property. Unlike the urban areas, the Church had few rural properties. With the advent of the Reform these passed largely into the hands of their tenants, both Mexican and Spanish. The latter, by tradition, easily became hacendados. The other foreigners, however, seemed to shun agriculture, so that few owned haciendas, and their number did not increase by very much during the years 1856–63. The rural areas remained solidly in Mexican hands, and since the nation's centre of gravity was not yet in the cities, it can be concluded that, as a whole, it would be wrong to think as some have stated, that the Reform handed Mexico over to the foreigners.

CHAPTER 7

THE FOREIGN OCCUPATION AND THE LIBERAL REPUBLIC, 1863–75

The conservatives in Mexico promoted the French invasion with the aim of re-establishing the power and wealth of the Church. They did not achieve their objective. On 12 June 1863, two days after his entry in the capital, General Forey, commander-in-chief of the invading forces, published a manifesto to the Mexican nation, in which he basically recognized the validity of the nationalization and sale of Church wealth. He declared that 'the owners of nationalized goods which have been properly and legally acquired will in no way be molested; only fraudulent sales will be revised'. He ended with the latter, presumably to satisfy the demands of the clergy who alleged that the transaction was of a scandalous nature.[1] This statement disillusioned the conservatives, but at the same time the threat of a revision caused much concern to the buyers, many of whom of course were liberals. Nevertheless the position was now clear and it was evident that the occupiers were inclined to accept faits accomplis.

The conservatives were not prepared to see themselves obliterated. Many tenants of assigned houses stopped paying rent to the owners, and some proprietors refused to liquidate the promissory notes which were due and were guaranteed by the mortgage of their property. It is reasonable to suppose that in the final days before its forced evacuation of the city, the liberal government disposed of all the promissory notes in a last attempt to raise funds, and therefore several million pesos' worth of the notes must have been in circulation. Of course many had been settled by that time but the majority were probably still valid. For example, in 1861–63 one buyer had signed on average sixty notes, due month by month, so that the last would mature five years after the date of signing. Those from 1861 must for the most part have been in circulation two years later.

It is possible, however, that many were redeemed by the debtors, who were perhaps given considerable reductions by creditors who feared that the notes would be declared invalid. In 1864 the real value of those

[1] Riva Palacio, *México a través de los siglos*, v, 588.

that were in circulation in Mexico City was 500,000 or 600,000 pesos, equivalent to an approximate nominal value of at least 1,500,000 pesos.[1]

The confused situation that existed had to be resolved and on 15 October, with this in mind, Marshal Bazaine, the new head of the French expeditionary army, asked the Regency—the Mexican conservative government —to approve the circulation of the disentailment notes. Rumour had it that he himself had acquired a large number at a low price and that he was hoping that the issue of such a decree would result in an appreciation of their value.[2] The truth of such reports, which were very common in similar cases, was as difficult to refute as to prove. It may be that he also wanted to protect the French citizens who had acquired so many of the clerical possessions. The most likely explanation, however, is that he was merely obeying his government's instructions. The archbishop of Mexico, Labastida, protested on 20 October, claiming that 'to enable the promissory notes to be paid, the solution of the problem of rents owed by adjudicators, the continuation of works begun on Church property...only serve...to discourage the solitary friends which the intervention has had'.[3] He undoubtedly spoke the truth when he continued that 'the legalized circulation of the promissory notes recognizes the illegitimate values which, on his departure, were forced on the country by Benito Juárez; the lifting of the suspension relating to rents is a recognition of the ownership of those who retain clerical properties'.[4] Bazaine ignored the prelate and persuaded the Regency to order the courts to admit cases concerning the payment of the promissory notes and demands against people who refused to pay rents on assigned houses.[5] This order was issued on 9 November.

Although liable to revision, the sale transactions were in fact approved. Apparently the French residents in Mexico had had some influence in these decisions. On 14 July 1863 the newspaper *L'Estafette*, which had consistently defended the nationalization of Church wealth in the preceding years, wrote that 'nothing would make a greater contribution to the ending of the civil war...than the legal sanction of the legitimate sales of clerical properties'.[6] No doubt the French and the other foreigners in the country, always well aware of their own interests, formed a powerful pressure group from the time of the Lerdo law in 1856. In this sense they contributed to the recognition of the Reform laws by the occupiers.[7]

[1] See the *Informe* by Binel in Díaz, *Versión francesa*, III, 376.
[2] Zamacois, XVI, 818.
[3] Ibid., p. 823.   [4] Ibid., p. 826.
[5] Ibid., p. 832.   [6] Ibid., p. 845.
[7] P. Parra, *Sociología de la Reforma* (Mexico, 1967), p. 221.

At first the Church pressed the government to return its possessions, as had happened in 1858. Labastida had even prepared a plan according to which the adjudicators would be classified into three groups: those who had acquired clerical properties solely in order to conserve them and return them to the Church, those who bought without intending to make a profit, and finally, the speculators. He hoped that the first group would spontaneously return the properties. An agreement could be reached gradually with the second, and the third was to be punished by the law.[1] The archbishop's project differed from Zuloaga's decree in that it tried to separate the ordinary buyers from those who made large-scale purchases. In practice it would clearly be difficult to distinguish one from the other. With their efforts in this direction frustrated, the conservatives placed their hopes on archduke Maximilian,[2] but as early as 10 April 1864, in Miramar, he had committed himself to support the French policy concerning the nationalization,[3] and he kept his promise during his regime.

The fact that the events of 1858–60 in respect of the fate of clerical wealth were not repeated in the years 1863–67 is to be explained not only by the decisions of the French government or by the aggressive propaganda of the French colony in Mexico, but also by the substantial purchases made in 1861 by Mexican capitalists. In 1856 few of the latter had acquired Church properties. Thus, when Zuloaga annulled the Lerdo law the capitalists did not suffer in any way and they were able to give him financial support, at least as long as the conservative government seemed a good risk. In contrast, in 1861, the Mexican capitalists considered the market in clerical properties to be sufficiently attractive to invest large amounts in it. Béistegui, Bringas, del Barrio, the Escandón brothers, Goríbar, Portilla and others were all soon involved, even though some of them may have bought the real estate only to retain it for the Church.[4] But this latter factor cannot have been decisive because during the foreign occupation they do not seem to have supported the Church in it. attempts to retrieve its wealth. On the contrary, far from antagonizing the French invaders or Maximilian, some of them accepted posts in the government and others had business dealings with it.

For example, Felipe Neri del Barrio, having returned from exile in 1863, became the emperor's chamberlain,[5] thereby achieving the highest office to which a liberal capitalist-turned-conservative, and also the husband

---

[1] Bravo Ugarte, *Historia de México*, III, 291.
[2] Ibid., p. 292.
[3] *Historia documental de México* (Mexico, 1964), vol. II, pp. 324–6.
[4] See appendix xv.
[5] Valle, *El viajero en México*, 723–38.

of a marchioness, could aspire. One of his sons was a canon of the collegiate church of Guadalupe, which is perhaps the best indication of the former liberal's reconciliation with the Church.[1] Del Barrio died in 1870, three years after the republican victory. A palace occupied by Cayetano Rubio was ceded by him to General Forey, although it in fact belonged to Jorge Pérez Gálvez, a descendant of the count of Valenciana. Marshal Bazaine later lived in the house. The government bought it in 1864, apparently for 125,000 pesos and it was mortgaged to Barrón, Forbes and Co. for 60,000 pesos at 6% annual interest. The Empire paid the unencumbered part in cash and the mortgage was liquidated at the end of February 1866 with bills on the maritime customs at San Blas.[2] This example illustrates the collaboration of three capitalists, one of whom was descended from the colonial nobility, with the invader. Apart from fleeing the occupied territory and thus sacrificing entirely their interests, they had no choice but to enter into business deals with the governments in control of the nation. On 8 September 1863 Antonio Escandón concluded an agreement with the French authorities for the construction of a section of the Mexico–Veracruz railway, and he received a considerable subsidy.[3] The respective contract, which slightly modified that of 5 April 1861, was signed on 23 January 1865.[4] Meanwhile, on 20 August 1864 Escandón had transferred the concession to British interests and he remained a partner in the new company.[5] Finally Davidson, a British citizen although representing Paris bankers, undertook to sell the bills drawn by the government on funds from the loans granted the Empire by France.[6]

The recognition of the purchases of clerical possessions by the occupation authorities is perhaps to be explained less by the influence of the vociferous French group than by the financial power of the Mexican capitalists, and perhaps even more so by the presence of the great number of Mexican adjudicators, including liberals, conservatives, merchants, lawyers and public officials. From the beginning of the French occupation of the capital, this large group had representation in the so-called *Junta de Notables*, which was something like a parliament, installed on 8 July 1863. At least four of the 'distinguished citizens' on this committee

---

[1] 1864 register of Mariano Vega, fol. 424, ANM; Rafaela Rengel, last marchioness del Apartado, died; the prebendary José María del Barrio renounced the title in favour of his brother, Felipe Neri del Barrio y Rengel.
[2] Payno, *Cuentas*, 382–9.
[3] MH 1870, p. 646.
[4] Ibid., p. 663.
[5] A. Tischendorf, *Great Britain and Mexico in the era of Porfirio Díaz* (Durham, N.C., 1961), p. 31.
[6] Díaz, *Versión francesa*, IV, 248; Payno, *Cuentas*, 802.

had spent more than 40,000 pesos each on clerical goods in 1861, and about another eight of its members seem to have been close relatives or descendants of other important buyers in the capital.[1] As in so many other cases, history could not be undone.

STUDIES FOR THE REVISION

The announcement of a revision of the transactions involving Church properties, made by Forey on 12 June, was not simply shelved. Even though the stated official motives for such a revision were to adjust the sales in accordance with the law, it can be assumed that the real reasons were fiscal. The French diplomatic report, dated 27 February 1864, indicates this, for it stated that the enormous amounts which Mexico owed France for military expenditure could only be raised by way of extraordinary revenues.[2] These could consist mainly of the product yielded by a revision of the sales of nationalized goods. With this aim in mind, the French Minister appointed a French lawyer, L. Binel, to make a detailed study of the matter. He presented his report on 17 March 1864 and three days later the Minister sent it to Paris, together with a summary and his conclusions.[3]

Binel naturally had access to the archive of the Ministry of Hacienda. Nevertheless he apparently found very little there. For the years 1856–57 he had at his disposal only the Report of Hacienda, corresponding to 1856, and he could not even discover which transactions—all included in the Report—had been adjudications and which conventional sales. He found nothing on the disentailments of 1857, and he saw no documents relating to the sales effected by the constitutionalist government in 1859–60 in Veracruz, which were presumably taken from the port to the capital in 1861.[4] For the transactions which took place in 1861–63 he consulted the Disentailment Report corresponding to 1861. The only thing he did find in the Ministerial archives was an incomplete register of the sales made in 1861. Apart from the information published in the Report, this contained nothing more than fragmentary facts on the form and terms of payment, that is the way in which the three-fifths of the price payable in bonds and the two-fifths in cash were settled, and a few details on the discounts granted to the buyers who wanted to pay in cash. He found nothing about

---

[1] A list of the *notables* is given in Riva Palacio, *México a través de los siglos*, v, 590.
[2] Díaz, *Versión francesa*, III, 334.
[3] Both documents are in *Versión francesa*, III, 341–80.
[4] According to Suárez Navarro, the archive arrived in May 1861: cited in Buenrostro, *Historia del primero y segundo congresos constitucionales*, vol. I, part 2, pp. 31–2.

the transactions of 1862 and January–May 1863. He did not examine the records of the archives of other Ministries, one of which, that of Justice and Public Education, had formerly been responsible for relations between the Church and the State. Nor did he look in the notarial depositories. In summary, with one exception, his sources were the two Reports, which any private individual could acquire.

In explaining the almost total absence of the relevant documents in the Ministry of Hacienda, a scholar wrote in 1893 that the constitutional government had taken with it to the north at the end of May 1863 'an incredible number of promissory notes and bond commitments... together with the corresponding files. Nothing more has been heard of these documents, and one imagines they were lost or destroyed during the defeats at San Luis and Chihuahua.'[1] It scarcely seems likely that the government would have kept, until May 1863, many of the promissory notes. In view of all that has been described in chapters 5 and 6, it is more probable that most were sold at any price.[2] It is, nevertheless, logical that the government would have taken the files on the sale of Church wealth, not so much to prove the promissory notes which did not need it because they were secured by property mortgages, but rather because it was feared that once in possession of the government offices, the conservatives would destroy all the documents as the first step towards the return of the nationalized wealth to the Church. The day the liberal government returned to the capital, the files might be needed to prove ownership of the properties and the mortgages. It was not safe to rely entirely on the notarial registers, for these could be burned during military operations.

On the basis of the register of the sale transactions of the nationalized goods, Binel reached the conclusion that a large number of the sales had been effected in contravention of the laws. The criteria used by the lawyer were very narrow because, for example, he considered to be illegal the discounts granted on the price of the goods that were sold, and also any term longer than the forty months stipulated for payment of the two-fifths of the price because these items had not been included in the law of 13 July 1859. He paid no attention to the numerous and diverse decrees which were issued later to modify the law and thus facilitate and dispatch the transactions more quickly. The document which he cited no longer exists, and so it is impossible to ascertain whether he extracted the data

---

[1] Labastida, p. xxvii.
[2] In 1867 the government published a list of 92 persons, among them Limantour, Labat, Naphegy and other important buyers of 1861, asking them to pay what they owed according to the promissory notes in the hands of the government; nevertheless neither amounts nor redemption dates were indicated; *Diario Oficial*, 9 October 1861.

correctly, or was mistaken in his interpretation or inaccurate in his calculations. The main purpose of his enquiry must not be forgotten, however, for he was fundamentally asked to prove the irregularity of almost all the sales. The treasury needed to impose a fine on the buyers.

Although the figures given by Binel cannot now be confirmed nor refuted, some of his commentaries or opinions are of interest. He was surprised at the efficient way in which the Lerdo law had been implemented, especially in the capital, in spite of the existing difficulties. He thought that Zuloaga's decree 'incited to a high decree the resentment of the real buyers' who were thus driven to support the confiscation of Church wealth. He understood Mexican politics as far as clerical wealth was concerned.

As a result of his calculations, Binel recommended a method by which the government could obtain immediately between 4,000,000 and 5,000,000 pesos from the buyers in the District of Mexico. Finally, inflating even further the figures given by Mora of the total value of Church wealth in the country, he concluded that enormous amounts of goods still remained to be nationalized and sold.

The government's action in respect of the revision of the sales was halted because of the expected acceptance of the imperial crown by archduke Maximilian. This in fact took place in Miramar on 10 April. The entry of the emperor into the city of Mexico on 12 June did not improve the fiscal situation. Until that time the French army, financed from France, had been paying the Mexican troops. Maximilian soon discovered that he could not assume the costs of the national army and on 1 July he asked Bazaine to continue supplying funds to his government.[1] Of course this system increased Mexico's debt to France, but there was no alternative solution. On the contrary, as the French diplomatic representative wrote on 28 January 1865, the occupiers would be exposed 'to an inevitable catastrophe if they suddenly refused the Mexican exchequer the daily advances which are indispensable to it'.[2] In this situation the product of a revision of the sales of nationalized goods could contribute a little towards diminishing the deficit.

[1] Díaz, *Versión francesa*, v, 5.
[2] Ibid., p. 81.

THE REVISION OF THE SALES OF NATIONALIZED GOODS

It was against this background that the imperial authorities on 26 February 1865 issued a decree in which Forey's manifesto of 12 June 1863 was implemented. The new decree declared that all the nationalization and disentailment operations, except Davidson's acquisitions, were to be revised by the Council of State.[1] Legitimate transactions would be confirmed but others would be regularized by means of a fine, payable in cash, of 25% of the value of the property or mortgage. A special office called 'administration of nationalized goods' was established to implement the decree. In an attempt to coerce buyers into declaring their acquisitions to the new office, it was ordered that any redemptions of capital which were not presented for revision within two months would be considered null and void. Gathering all the information required more than threats against the buyers. The notaries were told to present an account, based on their registers, of all the sale instruments of nationalized goods, and they were warned that failure to do so would result in their dismissal. The punishments were therefore strong. Finally, nationalized properties which had not yet been alienated, and those resulting from the revision, were to be sold in auction to the highest bidder. The purchase price could be mortgaged at 6% annual interest, with the capital being liquidated by eighteen annual payments.

In spite of the fact that the decree recognized the nationalization and on the same day the emperor decreed freedom of religion, thus giving a clear indication of the anti-clerical tendency of his regime, the buyers nevertheless were disturbed. Not without reason, for it was to be expected that most of them would have to pay a very considerable fine, and moreover, the dividing line between irregular transactions and fraudulent ones was not well defined. The buyers had the impression that they were being confronted with an attempt at extortion by the government. One sign of their discontent was the pamphlet, *Observaciones sobre la ley de 26 de febrero y sobre su reglamento*.[2] Its anonymous author was apparently a liberal and he described as beneficial the social transformation which the country had undergone since 1855. He then tried to demonstrate that because of the enormous number of files involved, some 20,000, the attempt to carry out the decree would produce upheaval, and it was therefore doubtful that the measure was even practical. He attacked the

[1] J. S. Segura (ed.), *Boletín de las leyes del imperio mexicano* (Mexico, 1863–65), vol. IV, p. 198; the decree was summarized in the MH 1870, p. 640. Davidson's properties were exempted on 11 May; ibid., p. 641.
[2] Published in 1865, Imprenta Ignacio Cumplido, 37 pp.

conservatives who alleged that the nationalization had only favoured the speculators. Nevertheless, he continued, neither Juárez, Lerdo nor Ocampo had prospered from the whole operation. Turning to the frequent statements about the excessively low price at which the goods were sold, he recalled that the depreciation had been foreseen by Mora, Lerdo and Ocampo, and that only by selling cheaply could the timidity of the buyers be overcome. The laws of the Reform must be worth something, in view of the fact that Maximilian's government had adopted them. Finally, an enormous number of vested interests would have to be upset if any attempt was made to modify the results of the nationalization. Solely in the country's capital, there were 3,600 files pertaining to sales of ecclesiastical possessions up to the end of May 1863 (to the end of 1861 there were only 2,007). Not without irony, he pointed out that the properties, mortgages and monastic buildings that had been sold in the District of Mexico to May 1863 had been worth 24,822,321 pesos, but of this amount 10,300,150 pesos went to Mexican conservatives, 5,502,040 pesos to Mexican liberals and 9,020,131 pesos to foreigners. Of course it is not possible now to verify the accuracy of these figures but the approximate proportions were probably right and correspond in general terms to the result of the enquiries described in the preceding chapters of this work. Undoubtedly the pamphlet was symptomatic of the general feeling of the buyers, both foreigners or Mexicans, liberals or conservatives. These people now formed, if not the majority of the nation, at least an articulate and influential minority. It was perhaps a result of opposition by this group that the decree of 26 February was not fully carried out. At any rate, the liberal buyers and most of the foreign ones were encouraged in their opposition by a decree issued by the republican government. This was published in Chihuahua on 11 May 1865 and it declared that all the transactions involving nationalized goods which had been approved at the time by the government, were irrevocably valid, even though there might be some irregularity in them.[1] Anybody who was deprived of the ownership of nationalized goods would have the right to compensation from those who took over the said goods.

In Paris, the revision was considered of sufficient importance for the Minister of Hacienda, Achille Fould, to put various questions about it in the summer of 1865 to the head of the French financial mission in Mexico.[2] He wanted to know the nature of the revision, the size, the product of the transactions so far revised and its estimated duration. According to the French diplomatic report of 10 August, the revision was in general reduced

---

[1] MH 1870, p. 641; Labastida, 157–60.   [2] Díaz, *Versión francesa*, IV, 165.

to collecting the difference between the price of the property as fixed by the law based on the valuation or rent, and the redemption price. In some instances, the variation in the two values was substantial and could be a source of considerable revenue to the treasury. As an illustration, the diplomat cited three houses in San Francisco Street, disentailed in 1856 for 91,800 pesos but redeemed in 1861 by Genaro Béistegui for 74,000 pesos.[1] There was, therefore, a difference of 17,800 pesos which the government could collect. The houses had been valued at only 74,000 pesos. It is not known why they were disentailed at the higher price, but it can be assumed that the capitalization of the rent raised the figure to 91,800 pesos. The three houses thus had two values, one derived from the valuation and the other from the rent. Hence the right of the government to demand the difference from the buyer was debatable.

The diplomatic report alleged that the number of files presented for revision by the beginning of August amounted to 10,000 and that the 1,900 already revised confirmed sales of goods worth about 22,000,000 pesos. The public exchequer expected to recuperate about 2,000,000 pesos from these. Approximately one-tenth of the value of the goods sold was to be paid into the treasury. The 2,000,000 pesos had not at that moment been handed over in cash—the amount was secured with mortgages of the properties. Finally, it was calculated that the revision would be concluded at the end of 1867.

The official records which survived the fall of the Empire indicate that the number of files revised or to be revised by September 1865 only amounted to about 3,000 and their value to almost 24,000,000 pesos. In April 1866, when the revision was almost at an end, the 7,000 files covered goods sold for a total of 62,365,516 pesos.[2] According to another source, a total of 37,000 declarations was presented.[3]

The occupying authorities hoped to recover through the revision between approximately 10% and 15% of the value of the goods sold, that is between 6,000,000 pesos and 10,000,000 pesos in cash.[4] They no longer thought in terms of the sum envisaged by Binel but merely of an additional revenue for the public treasury. Nevertheless the product was a disappointment to the imperial exchequer. After the defeat of the imperial administration in June 1867, Payno found various details in the office managing the nationalized goods in the capital, and he published them in the following year. According to these, the total revenue reaching the office from March 1865 to June 1867 amounted to 2,550,000 pesos; 1,000,000 pesos

---

[1] See the history of the three houses in chapters 4 and 5.   [2] Payno, *Cuentas*, 411.
[3] Labastida, p. xxvii.   [4] Ibid., p. 921.

in mortgages in favour of the exchequer—which here can be taken as at nominal value—500,000 pesos in promissory notes, 900,000 pesos in bonds and amortized credits, and only 150,000 pesos in cash.[1] The government demanded that the buyers should pay the difference in prices, but as was the traditional practice, debts were paid almost entirely in credits, which were worth only a fraction of their face value. The revenue did not consist solely of price differentials. Part of it was in bonds which buyers owed to the government and which to all intents and purposes they would have paid.[2] In the final months of the Empire, the amount yielded by the revision was not even enough to pay the salaries of the persons employed to implement it.[3] The annual salary bill for the administration of nationalized goods in the capital had been fixed in March 1865 at 24,000 pesos, and for the offices established in May 1865 in eight of the states, at almost 20,000 pesos.[4] Thus in just over two years of its operation the office expended on employees' salaries approximately 100,000 pesos. If other costs paid in cash are estimated at 50,000 pesos, the result is that the product of the revision in terms of cash was hardly enough to cover the administrative expenditure.

The total revenue of the administrative office probably also includes the product of the sales of ecclesiastical wealth made in 1865–67, although the information available indicates that there were few of these.[5] Thus the revision of the transactions of a total of more than 62,000,000 pesos produced in round figures an equivalent of 1,500,000 pesos, that is about 2·5% of the total value of the goods revealed for the purposes of the revision. This operation can be considered as virtually ended in April 1866 when the Empire began to disintegrate. Hence very little can have reached the treasury between April 1866 and June 1867. From the fiscal viewpoint, the revision was a failure.

Even though the hopes of the invading authorities, who had direct control over the Ministry of Hacienda, were exaggerated, the product of the revision was nonetheless excessively low, and this in spite of the fact, as is admitted, that almost all the purchases of clerical possessions had been declared to the imperial government.[6] Payno gave an explanation of the low return when praising the director of the nationalized goods'

[1] Ibid., p. 415.
[2] Ibid., p. 920.
[3] Ibid.
[4] MH 1870, pp. 640–1.
[5] For example, no sale of nationalized goods by the government was registered in 1865 by notary G. Sandoval; in a single case, the Third Order of San Francisco of Jalapa sold a house with the approval of the office administering nationalized goods in Puebla.
[6] Labastida, p. xxvi; MH 1870, p. 641.

office, Juan Suárez Navarro, a conservative politician who had suggested the revision as early as 1861.[1] Payno said that the latter

stated that he had accepted the post because he believed that by doing so he could render a possible service to the many interested parties and persons of liberal opinions who would have been significantly harmed by the presence of a hostile director... In the cause of truth and justice, it must be said that without him a great number of people would have been deprived of their properties, even though later they would have been able to regain their rights on the return of the constitutional government.[2]

It is significant that a liberal politician like Payno should have recognized the merit of a imperial official less than a year after the death of Maximilian, at a time when republican resentment against the Empire was still strong and the government was trying to erase everything that had happened in the previous four years. Another protector of the buyers had been the president of the Council of State, José María Lacunza, a poet and lawyer connected with the liberals. In January 1861 he had succeeded in obtaining exemption from the nationalization for the college of San Ignacio and now he repaid the liberals for that favour. Payno himself offered a more profound explanation for the attitude of the imperial officials when he wrote that the main beneficiaries of the Reform had been the conservative landowners whose haciendas had been mortgaged to the Church long before 1856 and who five years later were able to redeem the debts at a very low price.[3] Among these landowners there must be included the Mexican capitalists such as the Escandón and Barrio families who, as we have seen in chapter 5, redeemed mortgages on their haciendas. This generalization is subject to one limitation, namely, not all the hacendados, some of whom were genuine farmers, had the resources needed to redeem their debts. Although some landowners were able to clear their mortgages, others could not and so lost their properties to other people. Payno only showed one side of the coin.

In spite of the difference in their origin, for 1865–66 the buyers, liberals or conservatives, hacendados, merchants or public officials, Mexicans or foreigners, formed a united front against which the attempts of the occupiers to extract large sums from them failed. Those of the Mexican or foreign merchants and landowners who had suffered losses in 1861–62 as a result of their purchases from the Church in 1858–60, and who therefore felt their own interests to be identified with those of the Church, did not succeed in exercising any significant influence during the Empire. The reason for this is that the main conservative capitalists had bought

---

[1] Buenrostro, *Historia del primero y segundo congresos*, I, 83.
[2] Payno, *Cuentas*, 410.   [3] Ibid., p. 921.

substantial amounts in 1861–62. As conservatives these people automatically assumed a distinguished place in the imperial society, but as capitalist-buyers they at the same time blocked the Church's attempt to recover its wealth.

When the Empire was defeated in June 1867, the archive of the office, together with the files and declarations, fell into the hands of the republican government. A new administration of nationalized goods was then established and it was ordered on 12 August 1867 that the files should be examined with a view to utilizing the information which they contained.[1] Payno reported the next year that the work had not been carried out because of lack of time and personnel, and that moreover the archive was incomplete and in complete disorder.[2] This archive no longer exists at the present day and therefore it is not possible to unravel the operations undertaken by the imperial office of nationalized goods.

The 1856–57 registers of the notary F. Pérez de León contain, from time to time, annotations in the margins or attached certificates of the Council of State, signed by J. M. Lacunza. These cover the years 1865–66 and they declare subsistent or valid the particular purchase of clerical property.[3] The registers reveal proportionately very few declarations of invalidity of transactions with nationalized goods. This of course accords entirely with Payno's conclusion about the scant product from the office of nationalized goods. Purchases declared invalid could be revalidated by means of a payment of a fine of 25% of their value. If the director of the office concerned with administering the nationalized goods and the president of the Council of State had been hostile to the nationalization, then the proportion between the valid and invalid sales would certainly have been the inverse, and thus the product of the revision much greater. Only a minority of the instruments have a note for 1865–66 or a respective certificate attached. Most of them are not annotated. This does not mean that the corresponding sales were not revealed to the office. Rather it could imply that these transactions were not revised, or if they were, the appropriate certificate was not appended to the register. A similar situation has been found in the registers of other notaries, both in the capital and in the provinces. In summary, it was an exceptional case when a buyer paid a fine. If the sum of the fines and other payments by the buyers to the government which amounted to 1,500,000 pesos is averaged between the total of the goods sold, for 62,000,000 pesos, the result is that each

[1] Labastida, p. xxvii.   [2] Payno, *Cuentas*, 410.

[3] From this it can be seen that many houses bought originally by Manuel Morales Puente no longer belonged to him in 1865, although there was still a large number in the name of M. Morales Puente & Co.

buyer paid the government something like 2·5% of the value of his acquisition. Thus, provided Payno's figures are correct, it can be said that the buyers did not suffer significant losses during the Empire. Certainly it was rumoured that the office had received 3,000,000 pesos' worth of mortgage deeds alone, that is three times the amount indicated in the archives.[1] Nevertheless, if the revenue had been three times as much, then it would not have been necessary to supplement the employees' salaries. Nor would the revision have been ended as too expensive.

An example will demonstrate how unproductive the revision was. When Otterbourgh, in the name of Corwin, presented for revision the purchase of the Puebla convents,[2] made for more than 135,000 pesos, he demanded at the same time that the Empire should pay damages for his half-destroyed ex-convents.[3] He assessed these costs at 45,928 pesos, plus an amount for rents which he had not been able to collect. The office of nationalized goods decided that Corwin should have paid 60% of the value in bonds and 40% in cash, in accordance with the Reform laws, instead of the 5% actually paid by the buyer under the emergency decree of González Ortega. The difference was so great that Corwin preferred to sell the properties to the government. With the accounts finalized, Maximilian accepted an agreement on 27 August 1866 whereby for the convents Corwin would be paid immediately 5,000 pesos and in fifty days another 5,000 pesos, and in addition he was granted a licence to export merchandise worth 600,000 pesos without paying the 8% customs duty on the value. It is doubtful if the Empire, which was now rapidly collapsing, could have kept these terms. Corwin perhaps did no more than recover his original investment and the interest due since 1862. The case of such properties being sold to the government was exceptional. The buyers usually preferred to pay a small sum to the office of nationalized goods, hoping that the properties would appreciate in value once the republican government returned to power.

FACTS OF THE REVISION

Although the revision did not yield large amounts for the treasury, it did on the other hand produce something very important for Mexico, namely a quantitive account of the transactions with Church wealth in 1856–63, which was reproduced as document number 19 in the Report

---

[1] Payno, *Cuentas*, 411. [2] See chapter 6.
[3] The details of this case were given in *Diario oficial del gobierno supremo de la república*, 4–9 January 1868.

of Hacienda of 1872–73. The account shows the value of the operations presented for revision up to March 1866 and it is set out by states. The sales are classified into property and capital, and the former in turn subdivided into rural and urban real estate, and capital, belonging to the various corporations and *capellanías*. The list can be considered to be reasonably complete even though it omits the states of Chiapas, Chihuahua, Guerrero, Sonora, Tabasco and Tamaulipas. Church wealth in these territories was relatively very small.

In total, purchases worth 62,429,127 pesos were presented for revision.[1] Of this amount, 29,408,737 pesos corresponded to real estate, including of course the conventual and monastic buildings and the churches that had been sold. 33,020,390 pesos corresponded to mortgages. The Church apparently maintained a balance between both types of goods. Taking into account the six states that were omitted, the concealed goods, the possibility that some nationalized goods still to be sold were not included and that, in spite of the heavy punishment threatened, not all the transactions were presented for revision, the sum of 70–80,000,000 pesos can be estimated as the amount of the sale price or value of Church wealth, consisting of real estate and mortgages. In 1870 the value of real estate throughout the republic was calculated to be a little less than 340,000,000 pesos.[2] Thus Church riches formed approximately a quarter to a fifth of the total national wealth, as regards real estate. The statement that the Church until the Reform possessed half or more of the national wealth therefore seems very exaggerated. The clerical proportion is reduced even more if the mining, mercantile and industrial resources, all belonging to private citizens, are included. On the other hand, the Church had great quantities of precious metals in works of art. It is impossible to calculate the value of these, and so it is preferable to limit discussion to real estate.

Of the clerical real estate sold for over 29,000,000 pesos, 23,636,627 pesos was in urban and only 5,722,109 in rural holdings. The 1843 figures on the holdings of the monastic orders illustrate this difference more precisely.[3] The monks owned 201 rural properties, both haciendas and ranches, valued at 2,460,000 pesos, that is more than 10,000 pesos each. The nuns, who had no rural holdings, had 2,174 houses valued at 12,526,400 pesos. The corresponding figure for the monks was 1,740 houses valued at

---

[1] Yucatán is listed as having 523,000 pesos; this sum appears to be correct since at the beginning of 1861 ecclesiastical goods in the state were calculated to total 500,000 pesos; J. Suárez y Navarro, *Informe sobre las causas y carácter de los frecuentes cambios políticos ocurridos en el estado de Yucatán* (Mexico, 1861), pp. 45–56.

[2] MH 1870, p. 995.

[3] The information for 1855 is incomplete.

3,385,920 pesos. In total, the regular orders owned in 1843 urban houses valued at 15,902,320 pesos. Thus their houses were worth approximately six times as much as their haciendas and ranches. Of course the 1866 amounts include not only the property of the regular orders but also that of the other branches of the Church, apart from the fact that the value of clerical property apparently increased in 1843–56. The value of haciendas and ranches that were nationalized and sold did not reach 6,000,000 pesos, which was a small percentage of the 173,000,000 pesos estimated in 1870 as the value of all rural real estate.[1] The Church was relatively poor in rural holdings and it was proportionately richer in urban property.

The figure of 33,000,000 pesos, corresponding to mortgage capital, is subdivided into 26,000,000 pesos in round figures belonging to mortgages in favour of 'corporations and various bodies', and 7,000,000 pesos in favour of *capellanías*. The latter amount seems too small but the form in which the data was classified is not known. Certainly the 33,000,000 pesos did not represent the larger part of national capital wealth, for money in circulation in 1856 amounted to 100,000,000 pesos and bills of exchange to 30–40,000,000 pesos.[2]

The same account states that sales in the District of Mexico totalled 19,744,420 pesos. According to other sources already cited, the latter transactions amounted to 24,000,000 pesos, but the discrepancy is to be explained by the assumption that the higher figure included sales made in the capital of properties that were located outside of the city. This was done in the 1862 Disentailment Report. The operations in Jalisco amounted to 4,606,732 pesos, in Michoacán to 4,511,842 pesos, in Puebla to 10,658,111 pesos, in San Luis Potosí to 1,010,475 pesos and in Veracruz to 2,318,350 pesos. The figures relating to the value of ecclesiastical wealth in these regions are higher but this means that usually the goods were sold at lower prices. In total, the possessions sold in the six federal regions with which this study has been concerned, amounted to 42,000,000 pesos, that is approximately two-thirds of the total ecclesiastical wealth of which the purchase was revealed to the imperial authorities.

END OF THE EMPIRE

Compared with the reactionary and liberal governments of 1858–60 and the constitutional administration of 1861–62, the de facto authorities established in Mexico City from June 1863 did not suffer for any length of time from real financial need. The deficits were covered by foreign loans,

[1] MH 1870, p. 995. [2] Lerdo de Tejada, *Cuadro sinóptico*, 44.

advances and subventions. This fiscal idyll ended on 22 January 1866 when Napoleon III announced his decision to withdraw the French troops from Mexico.[1] As a logical consequence of this, Fould ordered the Mexican government account to be closed and all payments to the Mexican army to be suspended.[2]

The fiscal crisis resulting from the French decisions came to a head in July 1866. Deprived of the convenient foreign aid, Maximilian was obliged to turn to the country's internal resources. Apart from an increase in some taxes,[3] it was planned to derogate the revision of the sales of nationalized goods, which was costing more than it produced, and in place of this to impose a tax on the value of the goods sold, payable by all the buyers. The clergy were to receive one-third of the yield, provided they advanced the government 500,000 pesos a month,[4] which was the sum France had refused to furnish.[5] Abandoned by France and impelled more and more into the arms of the Church by the increasing military victories of the republicans, Maximilian tried to adopt the financial methods employed by Zuloaga. It was obvious that with the evacuation of French troops, begun in July, the Empire was condemned to collapse. In these circumstances Maximilian could not expect capitalists resident in the country to help him and his only hope was the Church to which the Empire represented a lesser evil than Juárez. It was now too late.

The decree of 23 August 1866 ordered that transactions not yet revised were ratified definitively. The revision was abolished and in its place a 15% tax was imposed on the sale price of a property and on the nominal value of a clerical mortgage.[6] The 15% was approximately the same percentage that the French authorities had sought to obtain from the revision. Payment of the tax was equivalent to recognition by the government of the validity of the purchase. All those who acquired goods, including the purchases already approved by the Empire, had to pay the levy. In other words, the tax affected equally the transactions that had been revised and those which had not. It was probably thought that the office of nationalized goods had unduly favoured the buyer.

The Ministry of Hacienda then compiled lists of people liable to the

[1] Bravo Ugarte, *Historia de México*, III, 329.
[2] Nevertheless, the French continued for some time to subsidize the economy of the country; thus, for example, at the end of June Bazaine authorized the French army's treasury department to discount 200,000 pesos' worth of notes on the Veracruz customs, handed over by the government to the Mexico–Veracruz railway company as a result of the aforementioned contract (Díaz, *Versión francesa*, IV, 337, 340). In their own interest the French wanted certain sections of this line completed.
[3] Payno, *Cuentas*, 856.
[4] Díaz, *Versión francesa*, IV, 368.
[5] Bravo Ugarte, *Historia de México*, III, 332.
[6] MH 1870, p. 702.

tax and the amounts which each should pay.[1] The first seventy-three individuals in Mexico City had to pay 1,362,014 pesos, equalling approximately 15% of 9,000,000 pesos. These figures recall the statistics of the 1861 buyers in the capital (addenda 16). In 1861 seventy-nine people had acquired property worth 7,000,000 pesos. Five years later seventy-three people had 9,000,000 pesos' worth, which seems to confirm what has already been said about the 1862–63 sales and the concentration of property. All the other buyers in the District of Mexico were to pay 2,248,000 pesos, which equal 15% of 15,000,000 pesos. According to these figures, the sales in the District amounted to 24,000,000 pesos, a sum approximately equal to that given in the pamphlet against the decree of 26 February 1865. Finally, the states in which the government still retained sufficient control to apply the law were to provide 1,500,000 pesos. On 5 September it was resolved that the 15% tax would be collected during the first ten days of October.[2]

The military situation of the Empire was growing daily worse. Not only the entire northern part of the country but also some places in the central area were already in the hands of the republicans. As far as the buyers were concerned, it suited them to wait and meanwhile to refuse to pay the tax.[3] It is not surprising, therefore, that the levy should have produced by the middle of October only 43,153 pesos instead of 5,000,000 pesos. Even of this yield only 19,119 pesos was paid in cash.[4] The tax was annulled two weeks later,[5] and the second attempt by the imperial authorities to finance themselves at the expense of the buyers collapsed against their determined resistance.

During the early months of 1867 the now staggering Empire imposed various forced loans in the capital, which were apportioned among the rich residents.[6] There were naturally among them many buyers of clerical possessions. The quotas were assigned according to the capital or the resources of each person or company, so that buyers paid on account of their wealth, not because they were purchasers of ecclesiastical wealth. From 1 January to 19 June 1867 almost 1,000,000 pesos were paid into the imperial treasury as a result of these loans.[7]

---

[1] Payno, *Cuentas*, 856.
[2] MH 1870, p. 702.
[3] Díaz, *Versión francesa*, IV, 391–9 reproduces the protest of the French buyers in Mexico and of those in Veracruz, both being dated 20 September.
[4] Payno, *Cuentas*, 857.
[5] Díaz, *Versión francesa*, IV, 412.
[6] Payno, *Cuentas*, 876 ff. gives the names of the people, their quotas and the amounts really paid.
[7] Ibid., p. 866.

In the same period the office of nationalized goods reported revenue of 263,707 pesos, a sum which Payno said did not consist of cash but 'papers', the generic term applied to any document.[1] At first sight an income of this nature seems inexplicable, for neither the revision nor the 15% tax on the value of the sales of nationalized goods now existed. Payno gave the key for the explanation of this phenomenon when he asserted that in the last days of its existence, the imperial government paid for merchandise from several suppliers with clerical mortgages at 30%, 40% and as a maximum 50% of their nominal value.[2] It may seem strange for a capitalist to accept a discount of only 50–70% when the fall of the Empire was already undisputed, and it seemed certain that the republican government would annul the transaction. The only explanation lies in the supposition that the capitalist was a creditor of the Empire from some previous occasion, and now in June 1867 he had to accept a scarcely advantageous payment, because the only alternative was to receive nothing at all. This possibility seems confirmed by the following: Cayetano Rubio was a creditor of the Empire for 84,243 pesos,[3] perhaps on account of military uniforms, for he had one of the biggest textile factories in the country. This debt was repaid to him on 12 June 1867, a week before the liberation of the capital, by way of ecclesiastical mortgages worth 223,648 pesos. Hence, Rubio paid in effect 38% of their nominal value. The figures agree with those given by Payno. They imply that Rubio was not the only supplier paid with ecclesiastical wealth, but he certainly took the biggest amount.

THE FINANCES OF THE REPUBLICAN GOVERNMENT

While in the second half of 1863 a discussion was taking place in the capital over the recognition of the sales of ecclesiastical wealth by the occupation authorities, the constitutional government continued quietly in San Luis Potosí to sell the few clerical properties which remained in its power.[4] There were not many transactions[5] but they helped to sustain the government. Only three cases involving clerical funds, which were arranged during the republican government's stay in San Luis Potosí, have been found in the notary Isidro Calvillo's register. On 15 April 1863 a hereditary *capellanía* of 4,000 pesos was disentailed at 10%

---

[1] Ibid., p. 859. [2] Ibid., p. 412.
[3] *Diario oficial*, 25 March 1868, pp. 2–3.
[4] The exact itinerary of the '*República nómada*' in 1863–67 is given in F. A. Knapp, Jr., *The Life of Sebastián Lerdo de Tejada, 1823–1889: a study of influence and obscurity* (Austin, 1951), pp. 80–1. [5] Prieto, *Economía política*, 732–3.

of its value, that is with a payment of 400 pesos. Three months later the operation was annulled because it was discovered that the beneficiary was married and so could not be the *capellán*. Another person redeemed the capital of 4,000 pesos by paying 1,000 pesos in cash. Under financial pressure the government enforced the law. In the second transaction an hacienda belonging to the Carmelites of Puebla was sold to a Spanish denouncer, and in the third a few mortgages were realized.[1]

In the early months of 1863 an attempt had been made to safeguard Puebla and Mexico from the foreign occupation and because of this effort many nationalized goods had been sold at low prices. Now, however, the strategy no longer consisted in defending at any cost a determined piece of territory. Consequently governmental costs were relatively modest. Thus the goods belonging to public welfare and educational organizations in San Luis Potosí were in general respected by the 'nomad republic'. Indeed an attempt was even made to increase them. On its return to San Luis Potosí, the republican government ceded to the state in March 1867, two months before the final defeat of the Empire, the San Nicolás girls' school for use as a library and a music conservatory. In the same way the Juárez administration ceded the state the former cemetery of San Agustín, the site of which was to be used for the construction of a school.[2]

The republican government stayed in the state of Chihuahua from October 1864 to December 1866. There were few ecclesiastical possessions there and by 1864 they had probably all been sold. With the aim of raising funds, the government dictated a measure on 12 November 1864 concerning the revalidation of the sales of clerical property and clerical capital.[3] Their alienations, made previously in contravention of the general laws, were to be recognized as definitively valid, without need of further revision, provided a cash payment of 4% of the value of the sale was made. Although the payment involved only those transactions made in contravention of the law, three days later it was extended to all adjudicators.[4] This was logical, because to decide if a transaction adhered strictly to the law it would be necessary to revise it. To avoid a revision it was ordered that everybody should pay what was in effect a tax.

The only transactions to be revised were those against which protests or objections had been raised, and the government would decide the justice of each case. Several days later a list of the contested adjudications was published.[5] These involved the purchase of eight mortgages worth a

---

[1] 1863 register of I. Calvillo, fols. 108, 216, 345, ANSLP.   [2] Dublán y Lozano, x, 7.
[3] Labastida, 485.   [4] Ibid., p. 486.   [5] Ibid., p. 487.

total of 24,000 pesos and that of two haciendas the price of which was not given. The decision of the government is not known but, judging from other similar cases, it can be assumed that an agreement was reached over most, with the government recognizing the acquisitions in exchange for the payment of a percentage higher than the 4%. The republican government, because of fiscal necessity, carried out in its territory what was in fact a revision of the sales of clerical possessions, and levied a fixed tax on them.

In view of the poverty of Chihuahua in Church goods, the revenue to the treasury from this source cannot have been very high. Perhaps to complete the needed income, the government had recourse to confiscations of the possessions of enemies of the republic.[1] This so-called sequestration of goods was originally introduced by the invaders in Puebla in their decree of 21 May 1863, which was directed against the enemies of the French occupation.[2] Afterwards in San Luis Potosí, Juárez's government established in the circular of 18 July and the law of 16 August 1863 the crime of treason and the corresponding penalties.[3] The amount collected in Chihuahua from this source is likewise unknown.

INDEPENDENCE RECONQUERED

The city of Mexico was liberated, this time permanently, by the republican army on 21 June 1867. The government was faced with two tasks, that of ending the nationalization and sale of Church wealth, interrupted by the invasion and foreign occupation, and that of applying the law of sequestration of the goods owned by those who had made deals with the Empire. Among the latter there were buyers of clerical property and capital, and thus some of the former clerical possessions were confiscated in 1867. Although unintentionally, the government had favoured a group of capitalists selling clerical possessions to it at low prices. It could logically be argued that these goods were still national property and that the nation could dispose of them again, above all because the buyers had collaborated with the enemy government.

In this way, four lots of the San Agustín monastery, which in 1862 had been sold for 40,000 pesos to Vicente Escandón and partners[4]—perhaps Antonio and Manuel Escandón—were confiscated in 1867 and used for

---

[1] Prieto, *Economía política*, 737; also on 21 October 1864 a forced loan of 10,000 pesos and another of 100,000 pesos were decreed but the amount collected is not known; J. Fuentes Mares,... *Y México se refugió en el desierto: Luis Terrazas: historia y destino* (Mexico, 1954), p. 94. [2] MH 1870, p. 587.
[3] Ibid.. p. 596. [4] Chapter 5 of this work.

the national library which persists to this day.[1] Under the same law of 16 August 1863 the sale of the convent of Enseñanza Antigua for 169,956 pesos was annulled.[2] Another case involved the annulment of the clerical mortgages ceded by the imperial government to Cayetano Rubio (see above). In this instance the law on treason was not invoked but instead the decree of 11 May 1865 which counteracted the imperial revision.[3] It would perhaps have been more correct to base the measure on the decree of 13 December 1862, which declared null and void all the acts of the invading or collaborationist authorities as well as all the contracts made with them.[4]

Nevertheless these cases were apparently exceptional. In the first place, once re-established in the capital, the government had no wish to continue applying the measures issued during the war.[5] The order of the day was a national reconciliation. Secondly, in practice it proved difficult to punish those who had dealt with the Empire because usually the persons involved were capitalists, and given the absence of foreign loans, the government was to some extent dependent on such individuals. It was for these reasons that on 12 August 1867 a law was issued commuting the confiscation, in general, to fines. In some very serious cases the fines amounted to four-fifths of the possessions of the person found guilty, but of course it was difficult, if not impossible, to ascertain an individual's private fortune.[6] The government preferred to reach an agreement with the capitalists. For instance, in the law of 27 November 1867 the Veracruz railway company was pardoned the sentence of caducity which it had incurred through its collaboration with the occupiers. The government granted the company a concession which was almost identical to that of 1861.[7] In practice it turned out to be impossible to annul the vested interests created during the Empire, just as the imperial authorities had been unable to destroy those created in 1861-63. In fact the same interests had influenced events in Mexico since much earlier times. There was also an agreement reached in the case of the buyer of the convent of Enseñanza Antigua. Four years later, in 1871, the government ceded him the former convent of Regina Coeli, which was valued at 46,000 pesos. He was thus compensated for the loss of Enseñanza Antigua which had cost him approximately the same in cash.[8] It is also possible that the government came to an arrangement with Cayetano Rubio. The mortgages which he had acquired,

[1] *Memoria de Hacienda*, 1874, addenda, p. 93.   [2] Ibid., p. 125.
[3] *Diario oficial*, 25 March 1868, pp. 2–3.   [4] Labastida, 485.
[5] *Memoria de Hacienda*, 20 February 1868, pp. 49–53.   [6] Ibid.
[7] MH 1870, p. 743.
[8] *Memoria de Hacienda*, 1874, addenda, p. 161.

worth 222,947 pesos, were put up for sale on 17 March 1868, prospective buyers being given a term of fifteen days to make their bids.[1] Almost six months later, on 13 October, the Ministry of Hacienda summoned another sale of the instruments taken from Cayetano Rubio, but this time only for the amount of 142,338 pesos.[2] It is possible that mortgages worth 80,000 pesos had been disposed of in the first sale, but it is equally likely that nothing had been sold on the first occasion and that Rubio had subsequently been given back deeds for 80,000 pesos. This was approximately the sum owed to him by the Empire, and so the only part confiscated from him would be the profit he had made. The public did not want or could not take part in the auction sales. For example, two houses confiscated in 1867 could not fetch their real value in three separate sales. Eventually the price was reduced by one-third but it is not known if they were finally sold.[3] It is not really known if C. Rubio lost or saved his investment.

As regards the nationalization, the constitutional government took two forceful measures on its return to the capital. On 21 June it was ordered that the religious communities which had been installed in the city under the protection of the occupying army and the Empire should be vacated and the buildings handed over to the civil authorities within two days.[4] On the same day a decree was issued to the effect that those people who had been deprived of their goods as a result of the revision were to have them restored immediately.[5] The official criterion of the continuity between the republic preceding the foreign invasion and that which followed it was in this way imposed. As there were few cases in which a confiscation had taken place because of the revision, it was not difficult to implement the new law. If they had been frequent, and if the Empire had sold the confiscated properties to influential people, then the republic would not have been able to destroy so easily the vested interests thereby created. It would probably have had to reach agreement with them, just as it had done in 1861 with the 1858–60 buyers.

A decree of 12 August 1867 established a new 'administration of national goods'[6] and a week later a law was issued announcing the redemption of nationalized goods that had not yet been sold, but on conditions which were more difficult than those specified in the 1859–61 laws.[7] Whereas the 40% of the value of a property could be paid according to the earlier laws in bills payable monthly, the new measure stipulated that the amount

---

[1] *Diario oficial*, 25 March 1868, pp. 2–3.
[2] Labastida, 213.
[3] *Diario oficial*, 3 January 1868, p. 4.
[4] Labastida, 183.
[5] Ibid., p. 487.
[6] Ibid., p. 304.
[7] Ibid., p. 161.

was to be settled in cash. The government perhaps thought that now that the country was finally pacified and the liberal regime firmly in power, the vested interests would consider what was in fact an increase in price to be compensated by a lesser risk. Nevertheless, the anticipated full payment in cash did not materialize and the government found itself obliged in general to accept payment in credits—national debt bonds— for at least part of the 40%.[1]

Finally, on 10 December another law reduced the cash payment from 40% to $33\frac{1}{3}$%.[2] Even this no longer had to be paid immediately in cash but over twenty monthly payments. On 15 September 1870 the author of the law, Minister of Hacienda, Matías Romero, observed with satisfaction a renewed activity in the market of nationalized goods.[3] The law, however, no longer seemed to him to be of any use to the country:

Having now seen the greater part of the goods alienated and believing that the transfer of those still remaining in the nation's control should be effected as quickly as possible, and above all that an end should be made to the causes of alarm and constant insecurity of the buyers of those goods, who feel themselves exposed to a deprivation of their ownership by administrative decision, a baseless denouncement or some other reason, it is now apparent that Congress should consider the convenience and even the necessity of quickly ending the nationalization. This could be done by adopting two measures. The first would be to authorize the alienation of nationalized goods which still remain in the power of the exchequer, accepting in payment of their value those national debt credits which in the market are at a lower price. Secondly, the administrative operations concerning the nationalization should be declared irrevocably terminated, with no recourse other than the judicial left open. Both these measures seem to be a real public need.[4]

Romero thus suggested that even better terms should be offered to the buyers so that the sales could be effected as quickly as possible. Finally, he recommended the adoption of a period of one year, after which the nationalization and redemption would be finally concluded.

A year later Romero again insisted on the same thing. Few goods remained to be sold but in spite of this and the law of 10 December 1869, the nationalization was still not ended. Again he suggested that Congress should declare it as concluded, for it was a question of giving guarantees to the citizens which, once received, would result in an appreciation of the value of their properties—thus the people who had helped the government in difficult moments would be rewarded.[5] In May 1872 Romero was

[1] MH 1870, p. 802.
[2] Labastida, 163–5.
[3] MH 1870, p. 982.
[4] Ibid.
[5] MH 1870–71, reproduced in *Diario oficial*; the part pertaining to the nationalization was published on 28 September 1871.

replaced by Francisco Mejía, director of the Disentailment Office in the District in 1861. A short time later Sebastián Lerdo de Tejada, president of Mexico and brother of the former Minister of Hacienda, took the opposite way to that advised by Romero.

There is no doubt that the real clerical possessions were now in private hands. The only ones that remained were some belonging to public welfare organizations which had survived the fiscal pressures of 1862–63, and above all the mortgage capital owned by education institutions. These latter funds were still almost intact, and in the already cited laws of 1867 and 1869 they had been declared irredeemable. It must be remembered that since 1861 the schools had been lay institutions and the Church had had nothing to do with them. Their endowments consisted of mortgages which had replaced the previously held properties under the disentailment law. Nevertheless, related to an increasing anti-clerical campaign, the law of 14 December 1872 ordered that all capital funds belonging to public education establishments in the Federal District were to be alienated in favour of the borrowers. In those cases in which the mortgages were for an indefinite term, they were to be redeemed by a 40% payment in cash and 60% in national debt credits.[1] The proportions would vary if the term was specified but not completed, or if it was matured. The money and credits were to be paid in six monthly amounts. For the purposes of the redemption, the laws of 1859 and 1861 were basically followed. What is strange is that the law was only valid in the Federal District.

In December 1872 school funds in the Federal District amounted to 625,702 pesos.[2] By 30 June 1873 they had been reduced to 223,475 pesos, which meant that in approximately six months mortgages worth 402,227 pesos had been redeemed. The people who had disentailed the schools' properties in 1856, and to the end of 1872 had been paying in interest what they had formerly paid in rent, now considered it convenient to redeem the mortgage at 35% or 50% of the nominal value. Two examples will illustrate the transactions. In 1856 Macedonio Ibáñez had disentailed a number of houses belonging to the college of San Ildefonso, of which the rector at that time was Sebastián Lerdo de Tejada. Of the properties disentailed by Ibáñez for 96,000 pesos, mortgages worth 57,500 pesos (including interest, 64,119 pesos) remained invested in houses owned by him at the end of 1872. On 14 January 1873 he redeemed them by

---

[1] Labastida, 395.

[2] *Estado que manifiesta las operaciones hechas conforme a la ley de 14 de diciembre de 1872*, document no. 8, following p. 41 of the addenda to the *Memoria de Hacienda*, 1872–73.

paying in cash only 24,191 pesos, a little over one-third. He paid part of the rest in credits, owed another part and was excused another. In the second case Leonardo Fortuño, a Mexican hacendado who had signed the protest against the accusation of General Alvarez[1] and whose name had been included in the 1861 tax, held mortgages worth 43,173 pesos. On 4 April 1873 he redeemed them by paying 21,550 pesos in cash and the rest in credits. Very little was redeemed in the next two fiscal years, from 30 June 1873 to 30 June 1875.[2] The Biscayan college again had the good fortune to avoid losing its endowments, for it was not a public education institution but a private school. The Porfirio Díaz revolt of 1876 marked the end of this last and quite curious outburst of disentailment passion.

The denouncements of ecclesiastical property that had been concealed continued, however, for it was believed that such actions were a necessary support for the republic against the repossession of its wealth by the Church. The laws of nationalization became a source of insecurity for landowners, many of whom were unable to prove, because of lack of original documents, that as adjudicators they had liquidated the price of their property. In other cases, under the pretext of denouncing a hidden clerical property, proprietors were challenged to prove that they had paid, many years previously, certain taxes, and of course this was very difficult to do.[3] On 29 May 1892 Matías Romero assumed for the last time the post of Minister of Hacienda and he was finally able to realize what he had proposed twenty-two years earlier. The result was the law of 8 November 1892, drawn up by Romero and the chief official in the Ministry, José Yves Limantour, son of the so-often mentioned buyer of Church wealth. Under the new measure the landowners were to receive, in exchange for payment of a moderate tax, a certificate from the Ministry of Hacienda to the effect that their properties were free for ever of all responsibilities stemming from the laws of nationalization, and from all taxes so far incurred.[4] Limantour, who succeeded Romero in the Hacienda post from February 1893,[5] put the law into effect, and as a result the landowners were no longer troubled by denouncers. Thus after thirty years the buyers or their heirs were finally rewarded. The final step was taken in the law of 16 November 1900 which declared the nationalization of Church wealth as definitively concluded.[6]

[1] See chapter 5.
[2] *Memoria de Hacienda*, 1873–74, document no. 15, p. 117 of the addenda, and *Memoria de Hacienda*, 1874–75, pp. 147–9.
[3] Macedo, 488.   [4] Ibid.; Labastida, 170.
[5] Macedo, 454.   [6] Ibid., p. 488.

THE BUYERS' PROFITS

Finally an attempt must be made to answer the question of whether the buyers or their descendants derived any profit from the transactions with nationalized goods. In order to ascertain this, it is necessary to know first the movement in rents of the ex-ecclesiastical properties and the costs which the proprietors incurred, and secondly the increase in value, if any took place.

The sources that have been studied do not give any clear and precise information as to whether there was an increase in rents, or if there were, to what extent, as a result of the nationalization. Certainly the protection afforded the tenants by the Lerdo law had expired in 1861 and the new owners could raise rents. Nevertheless, we have seen that some tenants put up a tenacious defence against increases, even though the rent was now considered the result of a contract freely entered into by two private citizens, in which the state should have only the minimum right of intervention.[1] In addition there are indications that the vacating of so many monasteries and convents tended to lead to lower rents.[2] The sources do not have any details of the costs—various taxes, repairs, improvements—invested in the properties by the new owners.

The figures relating to rents and costs are relatively abundant up to 1856, due to the accountancy system employed by the regular orders. Many of their accounts came into the possession of the government at the beginning of 1861 and those of the monasteries and convents in the capital were placed in the Archivo General de la Nación. To find out the same details for the ex-clerical properties during the years 1861–1900, it would be necessary to consult the accounts of the buyers or their descendants, as far as their holdings of nationalized properties were concerned. Unfortunately these have not been preserved, or if they have, have not been available.

As for the value of the former ecclesiastical possessions, the general details available imply that this was for a long time lower than that of the 'privately owned property'. In 1872–73, that is at least ten years after their sale, the value of the clerical property was still lower than that of other comparable real estate.[3] The explanation of this consists partly in the persistent anathema of the Church against the buyers and the tenants, for clearly the pious members of the public refused to buy or rent the properties. This therefore depressed their price.[4] Another reason was the

---

[1] Buenrostro, *Historia*, I, 146.
[2] *Le Trait d'Union*, 13 April 1861.
[3] *Memoria de Hacienda*, 1872–73, pp. 147–67.
[4] Leicht, *Las calles de Puebla*, 198.

fact that many buyers had not been able to amortize the promissory notes they had signed in their purchases—the notes were secured with a mortgage of the property either because they were not presented by their holders or because they were lost. It may be assumed that the value of these properties did rise because the value of real estate in general appreciated. Thus in the capital, property in 1870–72 was worth between 40,000,000 and 43,000,000 pesos, that is about 30% more valuable than in 1856 when the valuation of 1836–38 was employed.[1] Values increased even more during the Porfirio Díaz regime, with the result that in 1892 the valuation reached 100,000,000 pesos, producing an annual rent of 10,000,000 pesos.[2]

Such a general comment cannot be very useful. To know how much the value of nationalized and privately owned property appreciated in 1870–1900, a study must be made not only of the notarial records for those years but especially the Public Registers of Property, which were established by law in 1870. Because of the magnitude of the task, this study was considered outside the scope of the present monograph.

Consequently it is not known, for the moment, if the buyers in general earned more than they would have done during the same period if they had invested in other ventures. As long as this remains unknown, the problem cannot be resolved of whether a part of the dominant class during the Porfirian era owed their fortune to the purchases they made of nationalized goods, or whether they acquired their wealth in other ways.[3]

The following are only a few examples taken from the notarial records which have been consulted. They may serve as a point of departure for a future investigation. Mention has been made more than once of Juan Thévenard, who in 1856 disentailed a house in Puebla for 13,334 pesos. The house was later mortgaged to dowries for 12,000 pesos, the owner having redeemed the difference. In 1874 Thévenard sold it for 12,000 pesos, with the same mortgage. In other words he made no profit. The only thing he saved, for eighteen years, was payment of an annual rent of 800 pesos, but throughout that time he had to pay interest of about the same amount, first to the clerical corporation and afterwards to the nuns. It is true that the amount of interest was slightly less than the rent because he had redeemed 1,334 pesos, but on the other hand he was not

---

[1] MH 1870, p. 995; *Memoria de Hacienda*, 1872–73, p. 41; *Memoria de Fomento*, 1873, pp. 883–939.

[2] J. C. Valadés, *El porfirismo, historia de un régimen* (Mexico, 1941, 1948), vol. II (1948), *El crecimiento, 1876–1884*, p. 98; see also L. Pombo, *México, 1876–1892* (Mexico, 1893), p. 75.

[3] The difficulties of such a study can be seen in the article of A. V. M. Bogue, 'Profits and the frontier land speculator', *Journal of Economic History* (March 1957), 1–9.

even able to sell it for the same amount at which it had been disentailed. The costs incurred with the property during the years 1856–74 are not known. It seems therefore that in the first years, or even decades, after the Lerdo law, the adjudicators did not make large profits. In some cases, such as the latter, they suffered losses. This is more or less in accord with what is known about the 1861 resales of houses assigned in 1856. We have seen that, at least in Puebla, the sellers were content with a relatively small profit.

The buyers who acquired monastic or conventual buildings at only 5% of their values made much bigger profits over the same period. At the beginning of 1863 Julio Ziegler bought the Puebla convent of La Santísima, valued at almost 80,000 pesos and divided into five lots. He paid approximately 4,000 pesos. In 1873 he sold the first lot, in turn divided into two parts, for 4,800 pesos. The property did not attract taxation 'because it was non-productive', an allusion probably to the deterioration caused by the war. The second lot was sold in 1871—always through José Leyssens, his representative since 2 August 1856—for 2,000 pesos. Lot three was sold in 1872 for 1,900 pesos and this likewise was not taxable for the same reason. In 1871 part of lot four was sold for 1,000 pesos, not for immediate payment in cash like the other transactions but over a term of one year.[1] It is not known what happened to the other part of lot four, nor to lot five.[2] As the government sometimes included the convent and the church together, lot five could have been the church of La Santísima. If this was the case, then Ziegler made no profit from it because it is known that he chose not to claim it, probably out of respect for religion.[3] Even so the information is not clear. Assuming that the church was not included in the five lots, Ziegler made at the most 15,000 pesos from them because the four incomplete lots brought him nearly 10,000 pesos. Thus in eight to ten years Ziegler had tripled or quadrupled his investment, although it must not be forgotten that during this time the properties produced no rent; on the other hand there seem to have been no costs. Taking into account the fact that at that time it was possible to double one's capital in a few years by making mercantile loans at 12–24% or in some cases as much as 36% annual interest, it can be concluded that Ziegler earned as much profit as he would have done in this other type

[1] 1871 register of Angel Genaro Figueroa, fol. 27 of 9 January and fol. 964 of 2 December; 1872, fol. 241 of 24 April; 1873, fol. 186 of 5 April, and fol. 192 of the same date, ANP; during the French occupation Ziegler asked for compensation for the damage done to the convent during the siege; Payno, *Cuentas*, p. xxxvi.
[2] Nothing was found in the registers of this notary for 1867–70 and 1874.
[3] *Memoria de Hacienda*, 1874, addenda, p. 77.

of commercial transaction. The sale price amounted in this case to a maximum of 20% of the value of the property; therefore if Ziegler had expended 20% of the value, as was done for other clerical properties, he would have earned nothing.

His second transaction was more complicated. He had bought three schools in Puebla for 3,000 pesos and he sold these in 1871 to the state government for 15,000 pesos.[1] He received 1,000 pesos in cash and the state agreed to settle the remaining 14,000 pesos in fourteen monthly payments. The properties were mortgaged to secure the latter commitment. If the debt was not paid it was to carry an interest of 8% a month. The sale price only amounted to a quarter of the sum at which the properties had been valued, namely 60,000 pesos, but it was five times the size of his investment. In less than ten years the seller hoped to earn more than he would have done in loans to commerce. The buildings had not produced any income because they were occupied from 2 April 1867 when the republicans entered Puebla by the government, which paid no rent during those four years to the date of sale. On the other hand, there cannot have been any repair or improvement costs. The government, however, could not meet even the first of the monthly payments, and by 1873 a new agreement was reached.[2] The government would return to the seller the two schools of San Pablo and San Pedro, retaining only that of San Juan for 12,000 pesos, not including the 1,000 pesos already paid. A further 4,000 pesos was to be paid the seller in compensation for the loss of eight years' rents from the three schools. In fact the properties were apparently occupied in 1865 by the imperial authorities, which probably means they were empty—thus they had produced no rent for ten years. The government was to pay the 16,000 pesos in certificates of tax payable by cotton industrialists in Puebla (this was a special tax proportional to the number of spindles). Payment was secured by mortgaging the building of the San Juan school. It was also stipulated that as long as the two other schools were not returned, the state would pay 120 pesos a month. There is no doubt that this agreement was much more favourable to Ziegler than the first one, but it is impossible to estimate his profits because the subsequent fate of the returned schools is not known and neither is the real value of the tax certificates. If it had been easy to collect the tax, then the government would presumably have paid Ziegler in cash, and so it is to be suspected that the current price of the

[1] RPP, Puebla, libro de censos 52, fol. 300, and 1871 register of Martiniano Porras, fol. 141, 8 May.
[2] 1873 register of Angel Genaro Figueroa, fol. 449, 28 July, ANP.

certificates was low. The instrument was finally cancelled in 1891 because Ziegler had received payment. In these two cases the former ecclesiastical possessions were sold ten years later at 20–30% of their value; thus it can be tentatively concluded that most buyers who invested precisely 20–30% made no profit during these years.

His third transaction was more straightforward although equally obscure. It involved the purchase for 3,750 pesos of the convent of Santa Clara, which had been valued at 75,000 pesos. In 1864–69 he built ten houses on the site and years later, in 1891, they were valued at approximately 100,000 pesos.[1] Considering that thirty years earlier the same site had been valued at 75,000 pesos, the increase was very small. In addition the cost of construction has to be taken into account. However, allowing for the fact that he only disbursed in cash 3,750 pesos, his margin of profit was clearly substantial.

Thus Ziegler retired to live in France where he died in 1905.[2] He was perhaps one of the few buyers of Church wealth in Mexico who was able to enjoy his profits, for not many lived to the last years of the century when the effects of the 1892 law, which was beneficial to them, must have been felt.

If Ziegler had bought the property at 20–30% of value, that is for approximately 15,000–25,000 pesos in cash, the fact that this investment increased fivefold in a term of thirty years does not imply that he made a fortune, especially taking into account construction costs and the 25% depreciation in the value of the peso by 1891. In Puebla the value of real estate seems to have increased very little over the same years. In contrast, in Mexico City it seems that real estate values increased during these years approximately threefold; in other words, a property valued in 1861 at 33,000 pesos was worth 100,000 pesos in 1892. If a person bought a nationalized property at 20–30% of value, that is for 6,000–10,000 pesos, as most buyers did, then he increased his investment between ten and twenty times over in the course of one generation. Nevertheless this profit margin again decreases if one takes into account the two cost factors mentioned above.

[1] RPP, Puebla, vol. 21, fol. 11.   [2] Ibid., vol. 52, fol. 478.

CONCLUSION

The disentailment in Mexico from 1856 to 1863 has often been interpreted as a revolution which achieved the transformation of the country from a feudal to a capitalist society; the Church was a feudal institution in economic, social and political matters, and the destruction of its power made way for capitalist developments in the economy and bourgeois interests in the social and political spheres. One example of this type of interpretation runs as follows: 'Agricultural lands belonging to the clergy specialized in the production of goods for self-consumption and they were substituted by latifundia agriculture, which began to be market orientated.'[1] The traditional image of a monastic economy as isolated and inward-looking is inaccurate. The real situation was very different. In the middle of the last century the Church's rural properties were rented both to farmers and city merchants. Haciendas owned by the Church produced for the market to the same extent as those owned privately, that is, part of the produce was destined for self-consumption and part for the market. The proportions in turn depended on the quality of the lands, the proximity to markets, given the state of communications, and on other factors. In economic matters an ecclesiastical hacienda was similar to a private one. With the disentailment and nationalization, the economy of the lands changed in so far as the tenant who became the owner of an hacienda began to make improvements which he had previously been unwilling to do. Thus a base was created on which agriculture could later evolve, as a consequence of the establishment of a stable government, an increase in the population, the introduction of railways and modern industries and the growth of the market. However, only a thorough investigation can reveal if the buyers really invested in production as a direct and immediate result of their acquisitions.

As regards the cities, to quote a common conclusion, 'the purchase-sale of urban property freed by the nationalization enabled an accumulation of capital', which was subsequently invested in the industrialization of the country, or in other words the buyers employed the profits of their

[1] L. Solís, 'Hacia un análisis general a largo plazo del desarrollo económico de México', *Demografía y Economía* (1967), no. 1, p. 4; R. Vernon, *The dilemma of Mexico's development* (Cambridge, 1963), pp. 31, 36. See also Akademia nauk SSSR, *Ocherki novoi i noveichei istorii Meksiki, 1810–1945* (Moscow, 1960), pp. 162, 187, where the nationalization is defined as the early accumulation of capital; at the same time this work does not ignore the fact that the Church usually rented its haciendas.

Conclusion

speculation in productive investment. In fact the buyers were to a large extent merchants who had already accumulated capital in a variety of mercantile activities. This capital was consumed; it was amortized in real estate which the merchants aspired to own. This is the case as far as the immediate effects of the nationalization and sale are concerned.

The more long-term effects raise the possibility that because of the increase in the value of former clerical properties, the buyers might have accumulated large amounts of capital and that, by selling or mortgaging them, they were able to place the funds in new industries. Nevertheless, the possibility that some great fortunes were amassed as a result of the increase in the value of the former clerical real estate does not automatically mean that the productive investments of the Díaz era were stimulated by them. It seems more likely that these private fortunes, instead of being converted into another type of wealth, remained immobilized in real estate. The second generation of the purchasing group had acquired an aristocratic way of life, and to maintain this it was essential to retain their possession of the land, whether in the city or in the country. Rents from property were usually likewise not used for investment but for ordinary living expenses. In the years immediately following the disentailment the ownership of many properties changed, but the situation was soon stabilized and the final buyers entered the landowning class. Real estate was again amortized. The liberal programme did result in the short term in a considerable increase in the circulation of property but in the long term it failed.

Certainly about 1880 there were several well-known buyers of nationalized goods, or their descendants, among the textile manufacturers.[1] Almost all these men, however, had been industrialists already in 1856 and some in 1843–45.[2] Thus in general the buyers did not become industrialists. Towards 1890 many textile manufacturers sold their factories to French entrepreneurs. Although the textile industry towards the end of the nineteenth century was controlled by Frenchmen, they were not the same individuals, or their descendants, who had been active in the market of nationalized goods. Some of the main industrial ventures such as the tobacco firm El Buen Tono, the brewery Cervecería Moctezuma, the Compañía Industrial de Orizaba (cotton textiles), San Ildefonso (woollen textiles), the paper mill San Rafael and others, were financed partly by French residents of Mexico who had made money in business

---

[1] Busto, *Estadística*, I, table no. 2, 'Cuadro estadístico de la industria de tejidos de lana y algodón en la república mexicana'.

[2] *Memoria de Fomento*, 1857; *Memoria de la Dirección General de Industria*, 1843, 1844, 1845, tables.

and partly by Franco-Swiss capital channelled through the Société Financière pour l'Industrie au Mexique.[1]

The great foreign investments in Mexico were made possible not only by the existence of a relatively stable government but also because the government in a way defended liberalism in the economic and social spheres. In other words, the Mexican Reform facilitated the penetration of industrial capitalism and thus led to the growth of the economy during the Díaz era. This does not necessarily imply, however, that industrial capitalism would have been implanted in Mexico, even in part, by the buyers of nationalized goods or with the profits derived from the increase in the value of those goods.

On the contrary the buyers or their descendants quickly adapted to the traditional way of life of Mexican landowners. In this way the social system and the possession of the land existing on the eve of the Reform was consolidated. The hacendados and other conservative elements survived the various projects for dividing the latifundia and they probably came out of the Reform stronger than they were before it, partly perhaps because the counterweight of the Church as an independent institution was lacking, and partly because the landowning class was rejuvenated with the assimilation of more modern elements coming in from the merchant and professional groups. The descendants of some foreign buyers were also incorporated. Although some of the latter resold their properties and returned to their country of origin, others were attracted by the generous attitude of Mexico and stayed in the country. As in other places, the possession of land was a powerful vehicle of assimilation. The result of the fusion of these different groups was a compact class of hacendados and urban proprietors, united to the apparently monolithic regime personified in General Porfirio Díaz.

Until the Reform the Church had a large number of houses in the cities. At least part of these passed into the hands of relatively poor people. In the rural areas the situation was different. Instead of many small rural properties, the Church as a general rule had few but large haciendas. These became the possessions of a small number of people. The dream of the liberals of creating a rural middle class by the division and sale in parts of the clerical haciendas was not realized.

If the disentailment and the nationalization had taken place in an atmosphere of internal and external peace, and if in turn the exchequer

[1] A. Génin, *Les français au Mexique du XVIe siècle a nos jours* (Paris, 1933), p. 246; D. Cosío Villegas (ed.), *Historia moderna de México*, vol. VII, *El porfiriato. La vida económica* (Mexico, 1965).

Conclusion

had not had to meet extraordinary costs, then the nationalized goods would have been sold slowly, in parts and on conditions of payment favourable to those in need of land and at high prices to the capitalists. In this way, not only an agrarian reform would have been achieved, with social peace as a result, but also the public finances would have been put in order and the subsequent foreign debt avoided. Even further, with the budget surpluses the State would have been able to foment the national economy and thus avoid the excessive foreign investment of the Díaz era. No doubt this programme, envisaged by at least some of the liberals, was both logical and possible.

It did not happen, however, for the war and then the foreign invasion did not allow a moment's respite to the liberal government which was forced to sell the confiscated goods as quickly as possible, at any price and to anybody. As a result the democratic ideal did not become a reality. Only economic progress within an enormous social inequality remained from liberalism.

In the introduction we have examined the experience of several European countries which undertook the confiscation of Church wealth, especially Spain, France and England. Since the confiscation was also effected in those nations during a period of crisis, the State was obliged to sell the properties and capital to those people who had the means to pay for them. As a result the Church possessions were to a large extent acquired by the nobility and the bourgeoisie, and these groups were later consolidated into a landowning aristocracy. Although the nationalization may in some cases have led to economic progress, it was not effective as a social reform. We must conclude therefore that the Mexican experience did not differ much from that in Europe. What happened in Mexico recalls above all the disentailment in Spain, perhaps because of the whole heritage common to both countries.

Today the Reform belongs to history. This history, which treated ideals with such severity, is shared by Mexico with other countries which also at one time or another nationalized Church wealth.

Chronological list of adjudications in Puebla in 1856, taken from the register of notary number 5, Gregorio Sandoval

All the adjudicators are tenants; those cases in which the adjudicator was not the only tenant are noted, and in these the rents of all the tenants are totalled.

Except where indicated, all sale prices equal rent capitalized at 6%.

All properties were redeemed by their adjudicators, except where indicated.

Register		MH 1857		Annual rent (pesos)	Sale price (pesos)	Redemption date	Observations
fol.	Date	Page	Line				
127	23 July	441	2	120	2,000	1861	
132	23 July	441	3	306	5,107	1861	MH incorrectly gives 9,775
139	23 July	441	4	406	6,779	1861	MH incorrectly gives 6,779; adjudicator was main tenant
156	24 July	441	5	586	9,775	1861	
149	24 July	441	6	264	4,400	1861	
160	25 July	441	7	396	6,600	1862	
165	25 July	441	8	1,536	25,600	1862	
169	25 July	441	9	438	7,300	1862	6 December at 8% less 25%
176	25 July	441	10	846	14,100	1862	6 December at 8% less 25%
186	28 July	444	11	192	3,200	1861	
192	28 July	444	12	288	4,800	1862	
197	29 July	444	13	656	10,940	1861	
202	29 July	444	13–14	900	15,000	1861	Term for bonds was 8 months but paid before
211	29 July	444	15	516	8,600	1861	
214	29 July	444	16	396	6,600	1861	(1863 redeemed 2,600 owed to culto)
219	30 July	444	17	420	7,000	1861	
221	30 July	444	18	168	2,800	1861	
225	31 July	444	19	—	—	—	Emphyteusis
233	1 Aug.	444	20	300	5,000	1861	
237	2 Aug.	444	21	153	2,550	not given	
242	2 Aug.	444	22	288	4,800	1861	
247	2 Aug.	444	23	420	7,000	—	1862 mortgaged to dowries
253	2 Aug.	444	24	360	6,000	?	
256	2 Aug.	444	25	570	9,500	—	1862 mortgaged to dowries

| Register | | MH 1857 | | Annual rent (pesos) | Sale price (pesos) | Redemption date (pesos) | Observations |
fol.	Date	Page	Line				
263	4 Aug.	445	14	800	13,333	1862	Only 1,333 at 8%; 12,000 mortgaged to dowries
264	4 Aug.	445	15	1,320	22,000	1863	By another person to whom house sold in 1861; adjudicator was main tenant
269	4 Aug.	445	16	384	6,400	1862	By another person
277	4 Aug.	445	17	360	6,000	1861	Subtenant; adjudicated as result of tenant's renouncement
292	4 Aug.	445	18	270	4,500	not given	
296	8 Aug.	445	19	480	8,000	1861	
302	8 Aug.	445	20	54	900	1861	
310	9 Aug.	445	21	1,400	23,333	—	
315	11 Aug.	448	19	150	2,500	1861	
321	11 Aug.	448	20	360	6,000	—	1862 mortgaged to dowries
328	12 Aug.	448	21	700	11,667	1861	
333	12 Aug.	448	22	306	5,100	1861	
335	12 Aug.	448	23	366	6,100	1861	Redeemed by M. M. Bello
342	12 Aug.	448	24	495	8,250	—	1862 mortgaged to dowries
347	13 Aug.	448	25	780	13,000	1861	
349	13 Aug.	448	26	540	9,000	1863	By Julio Ziegler
356	13 Aug.	449	1	120	2,000	—	
363	13 Aug.	449	2	607	10,125	1861	
366	13 Aug.	449	3	600	10,000	1862	
375	25 Aug.	450	7 below	570	9,500	1861	MH incorrectly gives 2,500
414	12 Sept.	453	9	60	1,000	—	1861 mortgaged to *culto*
429	20 Sept.	455	6 below	97	1,625	1862	Redeemed by Eufemio M. Rojas
438	22 Sept.	456	1 below	72	1,200	1861	Redeemed by Manuel Sevilla; 1856, court case over adjudication with J. Tamborrel. Adjudicator was main tenant
478	8 Oct.	467	12	414	6,900	1861	
504	10 Oct.	467	15	432	7,200	—	
506	10 Oct.	467	16-17	480	8,000	—	
539	13 Oct.	not given					

APPENDIX II.

Chronological list of conventional sales in Puebla in 1856, taken from the register of notary number 5, Gregorio Sandoval

In column headed 'Tenant', it is indicated if the buyer was the tenant. In the column of 'Observations', the subsequent fate of the property is given; and it is noted when the property was redeemed by someone other than the original buyer.

Register		MH 1857		Tenant	Annual rent (pesos)	Capitalized at 6% (pesos)	Cadastral value (pesos)	Sale price (pesos)	Observations
fol.	Date	Page	Line						
418	13 Sept.	453	10	No	597	9,950	9,000	6,200	Resold 21 December 1857
433	20 Sept.	455	5[1]	Yes[2]	778	12,966	3,000	2,200	This adjudication seems like a conventional sale. Resold 21 December 1857
441	22 Sept.	457	1-2	Yes	—	—	8,500	5,667	Redeemed in 1861
452	6 Oct.	467	8	—	—	—	5,000	4,000	Empty house
460	6 Oct.	467	9	Yes	144	2,400	1,200	1,200	
467	7 Oct.	467	10	Yes[2]	1,068	17,800	11,500	7,666	Bought for C. Saulnier
473	8 Oct.	467	11	?	—	—	10,000	6,667	Appears to be concealed sale
485	8 Oct.	467	13	Yes[2]	—	—	9,750	6,500	MH incorrectly states 5,500; redeemed 1861
491	9 Oct.	467	14	Yes	1,080	18,000	16,000	11,000	Redeemed 1861
510	11 Oct.	467	18	—	—	—	16,500	12,375	
511	11 Oct.	467	19	Yes (?)	—	9,600	8,000	6,000	Redeemed 1861
524	11 Oct.	467	20	—	—	—	8,000	5,333	Redeemed 1862
526	13 Oct.	464	10[1]	Yes	96	1,600	1,200	833	Redeemed 1862 by J. Berkenbuch
531	13 Oct.	464	9[1]	Empty house	—	—	12,000	8,000	Redeemed 1862
538	13 Oct.	464	7-8[1]	Yes[2]	330	5,500	4,800	3,200	Resold 21 December 1857
541	13 Oct.	not given		—	508	8,474	—	4,170	Resold 21 December 1857
544	16 Oct.	464	6[1]	—	—	—	20,000	13,333	Redeemed 1861
549	16 Oct.	464	5[1]	No	—	—	2,000	1,340	

[1] Below. [2] Main tenant.

Register of the Atlixco notary in 1856. Disentailment instruments.[1]
(The Lerdo law was published in Atlixco on 9 July 1856.)

Register		MH 1857 (page)	Property	Tenant	Rent capitalized at 6% (pesos)	Observations (in the register, the redemptions are not given.)
Date	Fol.					
5 Aug.	138	446	Urban	Yes	1,200	Sales tax, 30 pesos in cash
6 Aug.	147	446	Rural	Yes	14,166	Redeemed by relative, 1860
6 Aug.	150	446	Urban	Yes	3,400	Redeemed by relative, 1860
6 Aug.	156	446	Rural	Yes	13,000	
6 Aug.	167	446	Urban	Yes	1,000	
8 Aug.	173	446	Urban	Yes	4,800	
8 Aug.	173	446	Urban	Yes	100	
8 Aug.	192	446	Urban	Yes	134	
8 Aug.	182	446	Urban	Yes	100	
8 Aug.	194	446	Urban	Yes	2,500	
8 Aug.	203	446	Urban	Yes	2,500	
8 Aug.	209	446	Urban	Yes	1,600	
8 Aug.	216	446	Urban	Yes	5,000	
8 Aug.	228	446	Urban	Yes	834	
9 Aug.	236	446	Urban	Yes	3,300	
9 Aug.	243	447	Urban	Yes	100[2]	
9 Aug.	245	447	Urban	Yes	834[2]	
	263	454	Urban	Auction	256	
	271	454	Urban	Tenant	400	
	276	454	Urban	Tenant	2,500	
	280	454	Urban	Tenant	100	
	284	451	Town of Calpam	—	3,833	

[1] There are 22 more instruments, mostly relating to Calpam.   [2] The MH incorrectly gives the city of Puebla instead of Atlixco.

APPENDIX IV.

Adjudications and conventional sales in Puebla in 1857, taken from the register of notary number 5[1]

Register		Adjudication or sale	Buyer	Annual rent (pesos)	Capitalized at 6% (pesos)	Sale price (pesos)	Sales tax
Date	Fol.						
16 July	131	Conventional sale	Tenant	132	2,200	2,025	—
23 July	138	Adjudication	Tenant	96	1,600	1,600	—
1 Aug.	156	Adjudication	Denouncer	120	2,000	2,000	100 pesos in cash
1 Aug.	161	Adjudication	Tenant	144	2,400	2,400	½ in cash, ½ in certificates
3 Aug.	168	Adjudication	Denouncer	252	4,200	4,200	—

[1] There are 21 other transactions.

Sales as a result of the auction of houses which were not adjudicated or sold in Puebla in 1857, taken from the register of notary number 5

Register		Properties		Sale price (pesos)	Redemption by successful bidder[1]	Sales tax (pesos)
Date	Fol.	No.	Value (pesos)			
29 Aug.	198	1	8,500	5,666	1861	—
21 Sept.	270	1	4,650	3,100	1861	—
21 Sept.	276	1	1,000	666	1861	—
21 Sept.	282	2	—	2,800	1861	—
22 Sept.	293	1	2,500	1,766	—	—
2 Oct.	369	1	4,500	3,105	—	—
5 Oct.	397	2	2,000 / 1,200	1,333	1861 (by Turnbull)	—
6 Oct.	408	1	2,000	799	1861	—
6 Oct.	415	4	1,736 / 1,736 / 1,736 / 5,500	1,156 / 1,156 / 1,156 / 3,666	—	—
12 Oct.	448	1	2,600	2,939	Resold 1861	101: ½ in cash and ½ in bonds
17 Oct.	498	3	3,000	2,000	Resold 1861	100: ½ in cash and ½ in bonds
17 Oct.	506	1	3,000	2,000	Resold 1861	100: ½ in cash and ½ in bonds
17 Oct.	512	1	1,900	1,266	—	—

There are 11 more auctions. (There were no auctions in 1856, at least according to notary number 5.)
Sale prices normally amounted to two-thirds of the cadastral value or the valuation.

[1] If redeemed by another person, the name of the latter is given.

APPENDIX VI.

Alphabetical list of the buyers of corporate goods in the state of Puebla, for 10,000 pesos or more per family

The names in italics indicate that the data in columns (2) and (3) refer to that person. In column (6) the town is indicated when it is not Puebla, and the property when this is not urban.

Name (1)	Nationality (2)	Occupation or profession (3)	No. of properties (4)	Sale price (pesos) (5)	Town and property (6)
Abadio, Dolores	—	—	2	12,400	
Alarcón, Ciriaco	—	—	1	13,333	
Alatriste, *Miguel Cástulo* and Joaquín	M	PO	6	25,600	
Almendaro, José Pablo	M	PO and I	1	22,250	
Alvarez, Ignacio	—	M	1	11,000	
Amador, José Ignacio	M	PO	1	13,583	
Arrioja, Diego, Macedonio and *Juan*	M	M and I	4	31,620	
Arrioja, Francisco	M	PO	3	15,333	
Banuet, *Francisco* and Luis G.	M	PO	2	11,466	
Barroso, Pedro L. and Mariano	M	M	2	21,375	
Berkenbuch, Jorge	F	M	1	18,333	
Caballero de Carranza, J. Mariano	M	I	5	36,400	
Cabrera (José Domingo Rito) and José Luis Bello (Co.)	M	M and I	3	22,225	
Calderón, Joaquín and Juan	—	M	2	24,200	
Camacho, José M.	—	—	1	16,666	Atlixco
Campero, José	M?	M	1	13,333	
Carreto, José M.	M	M	1	10,000	
Caro, Gabriel		F	1	15,000	hacienda
Casarin, Miguel	M	PO	1	18,125	
Castillo Quintero, José María del	M	PO	2	13,466	
Cisneros, Manuel	—	—	1	12,600	
Consalvi, Camilo	—	—	1	14,340	
Cortés (J.), Miguel		M and F	1	25,600	
Díaz, Francisco	M	M and F	2	12,500	
Domínguez, José A.	M	F and Cleric	2	17,576	ranch
Echeverría, Joaquín and Pedro	M	Owner	2	20,533	

Name (1)	Nationality (2)	Occupation or profession (3)	No. of properties (4)	Sale price (*pesos*) (5)	Town and property (6)
Fernández, Francisco	—	M	3	22,883	
Furlong, Cosme	M	M and I	2	15,900	
García, Agustín and Eusebio	—	M	2	12,733	
García, Bringas Manuel	M	M	1	22,000	
Garcilazo de la Vega, Juan	—	M	2	14,100	
Guerra, Manzanares Ignacio	M	PO	2	11,533	
Hacho, Ramón (Acho)	M?	M	3	26,866	
Heit, Eduardo and Becker, Felipe (Heit and Pauce Carlos Co.)	F?	M	6	52,967	
Howard, Manuel	F	M?	1	66,000	Atlixco: hacienda
Inchaurregui, Luis	F?	M	1	11,000	
Isunza, Agustín, Felipe and Rafael	M	PO	3	27,249	
Lama, Vicente	—	—	3	15,200	
Lara, Pascual	—	—	1	10,843	
Leiva, Feliciano and Luz	—	—	2	10,000	
Limón, Miguel	M	M	1	12,666	
Lisaola, Manuel (J.)	M	M	1	11,667	
López, Antonio	—	M	3	16,850	
Lora, Rafael	—	—	1	10,000	
Marrón, Ciriaco	F	M and I	1	58,333	hacienda
Mier, Bernardo (Sebastián)	M	I	1	20,833	
Millán, Manuel G.	M	M?	1	12,000	
Morillas, Rafaela	—	—	1	10,000	
Múgica (y Pardo) Osorio, Juan	M	PO and I	1	12,100	
Nieto, Andrés José	M	PO	1	10,112	
Oropeza, Mariano	M?	M	1	13,000	
Pérez (de Leon?), Francisco	M	PO	3	16,516	
Priani, Antonio María (Priano?)	—	M	1	14,200	
Rangel, José Pablo	—	M	2	20,925	
Rivadeneira, D. (J.M. o M.M.?)	M?	PO	1	15,000	Tlatzalan: house and 2 ranches
Romero Vargas, *Ignacio* and Domingo	M	PO	2	12,600	
Rosas, José M.	—	M	1	11,000	

Name (1)	Nationality (2)	Occupation or profession (3)	No. of properties (4)	Sale price (*pesos*) (5)	Town and property (6)
Ruiz, *Alejandro, José Manuel* and Feliciano	M	PO	3	19,282	
Salazar, Laureano and María Soledad	M	I	2	15,500	
Sánchez, José María	—	M	1	14,100	
Sauhnier, Carlos	F	Engineer and M	4	27,200	
Saviñón, Gumesindo	M	I	1	10,940	
Soriano, Miguel	—	M	1	23,333	Tecamachalco: hacienda
Thévenard, Juan	F	M?	1	13,334	
Tisado, Manuel (Tirado?)	—	—	1	15,100	
Torreblanca, José M.	M	F	1	23,324	Nopalucan: hacienda
Torre, Rafael M. (Martínez de la)	M	PO	1	60,000	Tehuacan: hacienda
Torres, Andrés	—	M and I	3	27,000	
Trepino, Antonio (Treviño?)	—	—	1	22,915	
Turnbull, Eduardo	F	M, F and I	2	23,600	Atlixco: house, ranch
Vargas, Santiago and Victoriano	—	I	2	19,667	
Vicario, Santiago	M	PO	3	11,600	
Villaseñor, Práxedis	—	—	1	10,700	
Zamacona, Manuel María de, Micaela M. (Ant. M. and J. J.)	M	PO	4	41,230	3 houses and a ranch
Zambrano y Vicinay, Miguel	—	—	2	15,600	
			Total	1,460,368	

Alphabetical list of the buyers of corporate goods in the city of Veracruz
for 6,000 pesos or more each one

Name	Nationality	Occupation or profession	No. of properties	Value (pesos)
Antuñano Co.	M	M	3	29,000
Arechavaleta, José	M	PO	1	8,200
Argüelles y Panes, Dolores	F	—	1	13,600
Bailleres, D. Juan		M	12	36,350
Ballesteros, Juan		M	3	8,220
Bárcena, Sebastián A.	M	PO	1	14,000
Blanco, José María	M	M and PO	1	11,000
Bobadilla, Juan F.	M	PO	1	20,000
Boig, Juan		—	1	6,500
Bureau, Domingo	M	M and PO	5	10,860
Calderón, Manuel S.		M	3	20,200
Campos, Pablo		M	2	20,500
Cano, Francisco		M	1	8,400
Celarayn, Mariano	M	PO	1	7,600
Cortinez, Diego		M	1	7,000
Cueto, Antonio		—	4	9,288
Dehesa, Carlos		M(?)	2	7,120
Díaz, Mirón Manuel	M	PO and M	5	21,410
Eizaguirre, Felipe (J. Felipe) (Elizaguirre)	M	M and PO	4	27,600
Esteva, Sebastián A.	M	M	2	9,000
Fernández, Alonso (José?)	M	PO	2	8,450
Ferrer, Lorenzo	M	M	1	8,670
Fitzmaurice, Guillermo	F	PO and M	1	14,000

Name	Nationality	Occupation or profession	No. of properties	Value (*pesos*)
Font, Juan	F	M	2	10,000
Galainena, Juan & Co.	—	M	1	14,025
Galatoire, José	F	M	1	14,200
García, Martín	—	M	2	20,100
Garrido, Torres	—	—	1	9,000
Gassos, Mariano	F(?)	M	4	26,600
Geaves, Graham	F	M	1	31,000
Gómez y Gómez, Joaquín	—	M	4	35,800
González, Clemente	—	M	1	12,000
Grinda, Helena Pujol de (Ramón G. ?)	—	M	1	13,320
Gutiérrez Zamora, José	M	M	2	16,400
Hernández, Ignacia	—	—	1	12,000
Jaime, Mariano (Jaymes)	M	PO	1	15,000
Leisegui, Luciano	—	M	1	7,000
León, Joaquín	—	M	2	10,225
Luelmo, Pedro	M	PO	5	9,750
Magarola, Antonio P.	—	—	1	12,000
Martínez, José R. (Ramón)	M	M	1	7,200
Montero Vidal, Ignacio	M	—	1	10,000
Muntada, Serafín	—	M	1	25,000
Ontañón, Juan	—	M	2	29,000
Palacios y Cosío (Palacios Miguel)	M	PO	1	7,505
Pasquel, Fernando	M	M	8	39,950
Pérez, Ana	—	—	2	6,600
Pérez del Molino, Manuel	—	M	12	31,368
Ramos, José Ma.	M	PO and M	1	8,050
Rivera, Lorenzo	—	M	6	15,635

APPENDIX VII (*cont.*).

Name	Nationality	Occupation or profession	No. of properties	Value (*pesos*)
Rocha, Francisco	—	—	1	6,500
Rodríguez, Hermenegildo	—	—	5	18,950
Rodríguez, Miguel	M	M and PO	2	9,200
Romaní, Bros.	—	M	2	22,400
Romero, Soledad	—	—	1	17,200
Rueda, José	—	M	1	7,000
Ruíz, Gregorio	—	M	1	6,000
Sánchez, Ramón	—	—	8	20,322
Saulnier, Carlos	F	M	4	22,767
Sevilla, Juan M. (Manuel de)	F	M	5	26,400
Sierra, Pedro de la	M	M	1	8,800
Trigo(s), José Antonio	M	PO	2	8,715
Troncoso, Alejandro	M	—	7	77,810
Valenzuela, Miguel M.	M	PO	8	63,865
Velarde, Higinio D. (Díaz ?)	—	M	2	28,000
Velasco, Dionisio (José de)	M	PO and M	5	13,260
Velez, Angel M. (María)	M	PO	1	9,200
Vidal, Ignacia M. de (y Alarcón?)	—	M	1	10,000
Wittenes, Julio	F	M	1	14,000
Zayas, Rafael	M	PO	6	22,825

ABBREVIATIONS: Nationality: M = Mexican; F = Foreigner. Occupation or profession: M = Merchant; PO = Public Official.

APPENDIX VIII.

Register of the Orizaba notary in 1856, vol. II. Chronological list of
some adjudication or auction instruments

Date	Instrument no.	Fol.	MH 1857 page	Buyer	Type of purchase	Price (pesos)	Redeemed (date and person)
8 Aug.	106	236	483	Denouncer	Adjudication	4,000	1861, someone else
8 Aug.	107	241	483	Denouncer	Adjudication	4,000	1860, same
8 Aug.	108	246	483	Tenant	Adjudication	3,750	End of 1860, same
9 Aug.	109	251	483	Tenant	Conventional sale	1,500	
5 Sept.	120	281	484	Tenant	Adjudication	1,200	
6 Sept.	121	292	484	Denouncer	Adjudication	5,000	Sold December 1860 to Ign. Llave
6 Oct.	134	326	494	Tenant	Adjudication	4,166	
7 Oct.	136	332	494	Tenant	Adjudication	2,000	
7 Oct.	137	335	495	Tenant	Adjudication	225	1870, same
9 Oct.	138	344	495	Tenant	Adjudication	125	
20 Oct.	145	364	510	Tenant	Adjudication	16,666	
22 Oct.	153	418	Not in MH	Auction buyer	Auction	3,528	
22 Nov.	155	429	510	Auction buyer	Auction	20,500	

Other instruments for small amounts follow.

Jalapa. Notary, Antonio C. de Hoyos. Some adjudication instruments, 1856–57

Date of instrument	Fol.	MH 1857 page	Buyer	Type of purchase	Price (pesos)	Redeemed (date and person)
3 Sept. 1856	355	484	Tenant	Adjudication	6%—6,000	17 October 1860 Tenant
6 Oct. 1856	398	493	Tenant	Adjudication	6%—3,000	17 October 1860 Tenant
17 Oct. 1856	421	498	Denouncer	Adjudication	6%—2,500	10 February 1861 Denouncer
18 Oct. 1856	422	498	Denouncer	Adjudication	6%—1,400	17 October 1860 Denouncer
27 Oct. 1856	436	519	Denouncer	Adjudication	6%—2,400	30 May 1862 P. Luelmo
27 Oct. 1856	439	519	Denouncer	Adjudication	6%—1,200	Not given
14 Jan. 1857	15	519	Auction buyer	Auction	fiscal value —6,000 new valuation —3,500: $\frac{2}{3}$ = 2,333	8 October 1860 Auction buyer
21 Jan. 1857	26	519	Auction buyer	Auction	valuation —1,800: $\frac{2}{3}$ = 1,200	26 April 1861 Auction buyer
21 April 1857	170	—	Auction buyer	Auction	valuation —3,000: $\frac{2}{3}$ = 2,000	11 October 1860 Auction buyer

APPENDIX X.

Chronological list of adjudications in Mexico, D.F., in 1856.
Notary, Francisco Pérez de León, 1856, vol. I, to 26 September

Register		MH 1857 page	Main or only tenant	Annual rent capitalized at 6% (pesos)	Redemption date	Redeemed by adjudicator	Observations
Date	Fol.						
21 Aug.	81	172	Yes	10,000	Not given	Note	Cession of tenancy before 25 June to Eternod
22 Aug.	87	172	Yes	23,200	Not given	Note	
26 Aug.	93	174	Yes	4,400	Not given	Note	
26 Aug.	97	174	Yes	14,000	1861	Yes	
27 Aug.	101	174	Yes	14,000	—	Yes	Note of 1865
1 Sept.	105	176	Yes	18,333	1861	Yes	
3 Sept.	112	176	Yes	2,400	1861	Yes	
(Adjudications of rural lands follow in the register)							
11 Sept.	138	179	Yes	10,833	1861	By Justino Fernández as it was voluntarily returned	
11 Sept.	140	179	Yes	15,800	1861	By another person, Davidson having ceded his rights	
11 Sept.	147	179	Yes	5,400	1861	Yes	
12 Sept.	149	179	Yes	8,666	1861	Yes	Apparently by someone else
12 Sept.	157	179	Yes	5,000	1861	By someone else	
12 Sept.	160	179	Yes	8,800	1861	Yes	
13 Sept.	169	179	Yes	40,000	1861	Zozaya replaced by Davidson	
13 Sept.	171	179	Yes	5,000	1861	Yes	
15 Sept.	182	207	Yes	3,000	?	?	

The instruments which follow could not be located in the MH 1857.

APPENDIX XI.

Auctions: Notary, Francisco Pérez de León, *vol. II*, *1856 from 27 September*

Register date	Fol.	MH 1857 page	Tenant	Valuation (pesos)	Auction price (pesos)	Redemption price in 1861	Redeemed by the adjudicator
17 Nov.	505	?	Subtenant	Subrogation	7,000		M. M. Puente
28 Nov	581	275	art. 10[1]	16,000	10,700	10,700	Yes
2 Dec.	607	274	art. 10	28,000	28,060	—	Yes
9 Dec.	697	275	art. 10	16,000	10,700	Sold in 1857, not redeemed in 1862	—
3 Dec.	608	276	art. 5	13,000	8,670	8,670	Yes
3 Dec.	614	275	art. 10	12,600	8,500	8,500	Yes
3 Dec.	618	276	art. 10	12,600 (two houses)	4,235	—	—
3 Dec.	619	276	art. 10	3,500	2,350	2,350	Yes, in the name of R. Mateos
3 Dec.	625	276	art. 10	10,250	6,834	6,834	Yes
3 Dec.	629	276	art. 10	16,100 (two houses)	6,670	—	—
3 Dec.	630	276	art. 10	?	10,325	10,000 in Veracruz by someone else (sale)	—
3 Dec.	632	275	art. 10	13,200	8,800	8,800	Yes
3 Dec.	634	276	art. 10	?	6,670	6,670	By someone else
3 Dec.	638	276	art. 10	?	4,000	—	—
3 Dec.	640	276	art. 10	10,250	4,070	Enkelbart? cession?	—
3 Dec.	641	276	art. 10	36,000	25,334	—	Yes
3 Dec.	643	276	art. 10	10,000	6,675	6,675	—
3 Dec.	647	276	art. 10	12,000	8,000	—	Sold 1857
18 Dec.	758	283	art. 10	21,676	17,550	New owner	Sale 1861
18 Dec.	763	282	art. 10	20,600	12,600	12,600	Yes
18 Dec.	768	282	art. 10	20,142	20,300	20,300	Yes
18 Dec.	775	283	art. 10	5,150	9,300	9,300	Yes
18 Dec.	765	282	art. 10	—	9,900	—	—
18 Dec.	762	284	art. 10	5,000	8,010	8,010	Yes

(Rows Fol. 608–630 are bracketed under the name "Schiafino" in the Tenant column.)

APPENDIX XII.

Adjudications to tenants in San Luis Potosí. Notary, Isidro Calvillo, 1856

Date	Fol.	MH 1857 page	Annual rent (pesos)	Value (pesos)	Sales tax (pesos)	Redemption
July	94	472	6.50 at 6%	108.17		
July	95–7	472				
July	98	472				
July	98	472				No information given
Aug.	102	472	(common lands)			
Aug.	105	472				
Aug.	107	473				
Aug.	116	472				
Aug.	118	473				
Aug. (28)	121	473	144	2,400	Cash 80 / Bonds 40 / 120	The same person, 1862
Aug.	122	473	—	—	—	—
Aug.	132	473	—	—	—	—
Aug.	134	473	—	—	—	—
Sept.	138	473	—	—	—	—
Sept.	141	473	—	—	—	—
Sept.	142	473	—	—	—	—
Sept.	142	473	—	—	—	—

APPENDIX XII (*cont.*).

(Many adjudications of municipal lands follow in the register.)

Date	Fol.	MH 1857 page	Annual rent (*pesos*)	Value (*pesos*)	Sales tax (*pesos*)	Redemption
23 Sept.	167	474	168	2,800	Cash 105 / Bonds 35 / 140	The same person; approved 14 February 1866
23 Sept.	168	474	9	—	—	—
26 Sept.	180	474	120	2,000	Cash 75 / Bonds 25 / 100	Not given
27 Sept.	184	474	600	10,000	Cash 375 / Bonds 125 / 500	The same person, 13 October 1861 (only 6,000; 4,000 not redeemed)
29 Sept.	185	—	192	3,200	Cash 120 / Bonds 40 / 160	Sold to someone else; redeemed (illegible)

Conventional sales by San Agustín in San Luis Potosí. Register of I. Calvillo, 1856

The buyers are tenants unless otherwise indicated. All the sales were cancelled on 5 January 1859, as a result of the private agreement of October 1856.

Date	Fol.	MH 1857 page	Tenant and annual rent (pesos)	Sale price (pesos)	Valuation (pesos)	Redemption
30 Sept.	192	479	—	900	—	—
30 Sept.	197	479	72	1,000	360	1865 sale approved by the Empire
30 Sept.	203	479	—	1,400	850	The same person
30 Sept.	205	479	—	500	208	—
30 Sept.	211	479	—	300	145	—
1 Oct.	213	479	—	300	63	The same person
1 Oct.	218	479	—	200	110	—
1 Oct.	222	479	—	400	260	—
2 Oct.	225	479	—	300	145	—
2 Oct.	227	479	18	360	84	—
18 Oct.	278	—	No (tenant renounced)	200	125	—
18 Oct.	291	—	No, 96 (tenant renounced)	600	240	The same person
20 Oct.	299	—	84	1,000	360	—
20 Oct.	304	—	—	700	365	Redeemed by Jesús Sáenz
25 Oct.	308	—	No (tenant renounced)	600	216	The same person

APPENDIX XIV.

Auctions in San Luis Potosí. Register of I. Calvillo, 1857

Date	Fol.	Sale price (pesos)	Valuation (pesos)	Redemption
10 March	10	351	—	Not given
10 March	11	861	—	Not given
11 March	13	580	—	Not given
11 March	14	11,000[1]	—	Same person, 20 July 1861 for 13,205
11 March	15	426	—	Not given
11 March	16	209	—	Not given
11 March	18	1,217[2]	1,825	Not given
12 March	19	1,081	2,950?	Not given
12 March	20	505	640	Not given
12 March	21	1,057	1,500	Not given
17 March	24	415	475	Not given
17 March	26	425	640	Not given
28 March	28	489	600	Not given
30 March	29	207	310	Not given
31 March	31	—	—	—
31 March	32	365	494	Same person, 21 Dec. 1862
6 April	34	172	250	Not given
		179	250	Not given

Date	Fol.	Sale price (*pesos*)	Valuation (*pesos*)	Redemption
7 April	35	350	—	Not given
7 April	37	535	—	—
14 April	38	{ 245 { 251	—	—
16 April	39	213[2] 208[2]	310 310	—
21 April	43	570	—	—
23 April	47	200	—	—
23 April	49	1,750	3,750	Requested valuation because of fire which ruined the house
9 May	55	1,077	—	—
15 May	58	—	—	—
15 May	59	—	—	—
20 May	61	—	—	—
23 May	64	—	—	Same person; included in the 13,205 (fol. 14)

[1] Bought by tenant; annual rent 660 pesos.　　[2] ⅔ of valuation.

Chronological list of conventional sales in Guadalajara in 1856, taken
from the register of notary Juan Riestra

All the buyers are tenants. The rent is not given. Unless otherwise indicated, all the houses were redeemed by their original buyers.

Register Date	Fol.	MH 1857 page	Selling corporation	Name and occupation of buyer	Sale price (pesos)	Conditions	Redemption
26 July	302	—	Belem	Palomar (merchant)	1,200	Mortgage at 5%	1860
27 July	306	—	Poor House	Prieto	60,000	At 5%	1863
7 Aug.	318	315	Carmen	Berrueco (merchant)	1,800	1,000; then 800 in a year	—
9 Aug.	320	314	Carmen	Tapia	95,000	5% for 15 years	1859 ⎱ double
25 Aug.	335	—	Carmen	Iguiñez	2,000	1,000; same sum owing	1863 ⎰ payment
29 Aug.	342	315	Jesús María	Cevallos	2,400	1,000; 1,400 owing	1863 to dowries 400 redeemed
30 Aug.	344	315	Capellanías	Camarena (lawyer)	25,000	Annual payments of 1,000	—
30 Aug.	351	315	Carmen	P. Sánchez	2,000	At 5%	1863
30 Aug.	352	315	Sta Teresa	R. González	10,000	At 5%	1863 to dowries
30 Aug.	357	315	Jesús María	Arredondo	8,670	At 5%	1862 by someone else
30 Aug.	361	315	San Juan de Dios	Plancarte (merchant)	12,000	At 5%	1859, part only
30 Aug.	372	315	Jesús María	Villa	10,000	At 5%	1857
6 Sept.	383	317	Colegio Guad.	Prieto	8,000	At 5%	1863
15 Sept.	395	318	Sta Teresa	Navarro (lawyer)	8,000	1,500; then 6,500 at 5%	1863 by someone else

APPENDIX XV (*cont.*).

Register		MH 1857 page	Selling corporation	Name and occupation of buyer	Sale price (*pesos*)	Conditions	Redemption
Date	Fol.						
24 Sept.	418	319	Jesús María	Ortigosa	8,000	Owed	1858
24 Sept.	420	319	Sta Mónica	Berni	3,840	—	—
(The above are followed by conventional sales, particularly by El Carmen.)							
30 Sept.	443	319	S. Agustín	Castro	4,300	Immediate payment	—
25 Oct.	486	320	S. Agustín	Martínez (merchant)	13,000	Owed	1857
25 Oct.	491	321	S. Agustín	Ortiz	10,000	Owed	1857
25 Oct.	495	320	S. Agustín	Berrueco (merchant)	9,000	At 5%	—
25 Oct.	504	321	S. Agustín	Martínez (merchant)	8,000	To be paid with merchandise	—
27 Oct.	508	—	S. Agustín	González (merchant)	12,800	5%—to be paid with merchandise	—
27 Oct.	511	322	S. Agustín	Cogordat (merchant)	2,000	—	—
27 Oct.	515	—	S. Agustín	Mendiola (merchant)	5,000	5%—to be paid with merchandise	—
27 Oct.	518	—	S Agustín	Asencio (merchant)	8,000	5%—to be paid with merchandise	—
27 Oct.	522	322	S. Agustín	de Pacheco (merchant)	3,600	5%—to be paid with merchandise	—
27 Oct.	525	322	S. Agustín	Cortés (merchant)	7,200	To be paid with merchandise	—

Alphabetical list of the buyers of ecclesiastical goods in the city of Mexico in 1861
for 40,000 pesos or more each one

Name	Nationality	Occupation or profession	Value (pesos)
Alvarez del Lazo, Manuel	M	—	43,500
Argumedo, Juan (Balbontín Co.)	M	M and PO	52,400
Arrangoiz, Agustín	—	—	112,400
Arriaga, Pedro	S	M	66,666
Arriojâ, Miguel	M	L and PO	42,016
Bablot, Alfredo	F	Journalist	66,362
Barreda, Antonio	M	L and PO	52,917
Béistegui, Genaro	M	Miner	74,000
Berdusco, Francisco (Verduzco)	M	PO	88,386
Bigarz Linder	Ge	I	72,046
Bonhomme, Antonio	F	M	371,490
Bringas, Miguel	M	M	40,000
Buenrostro, Miguel (Felipe)	M	L and PO	50,560
Cano, Guadalupe	S?	M	41,500
Cañizo, Manuel	S?	M	115,631
Carbajal, Antonio	M	PO	116,859
Ceballos, Lorenzo	M	PO	101,928
Cuevas, Leandro	M	PO	52,646
Dardón, Vicente	M (G)[1]	L and PO	95,000
De la Tijera, Mateo	S	M	67,674
De la Torre, Isidoro	S	M, I, H	72,328
Del Barrio, Felipe Neri	M (G)[1]	I, H, B	96,000
Del Río, José María	M	L and PO	54,370
Desfontaines, Eduardo	F	Schoolteacher	103,400
Díaz, José	S?	M	43,800
Escandón, Manuel and Antonio (Bros.)	M	M, I, H, Miner	66,472
Flores de Trujillo, Teresa	—	—	50,000
Flores, Luis	S?	M	48,906
Flores, Ma. del Carmen	—	—	42,500

[1] The two Guatemalans were in effect Mexicans and therefore are considered as such.

Name	Nationality	Occupation or profession	Value (pesos)
García Granados, Joaquín	M	PO	69,408
García Munive, Miguel	M	PO	48,468
Gargollo, Manuel Casimiro, Collado	S	M	48,525
Gil Flores, José and Joaquín F. cessionary of Estanislao Flores	M	M	93,000
Goribar, Juan	M	M	89,200
Iglesias, Ramón	M	PO	53,100
Iniestra, Francisco	M	M and PO	131,225
Labat, Pedro and Alfonso	F	M and Broker	52,900
Lascurain, Luisa (Angel)	M	M	57,567
Lazo Estrada, Francisco	M	L and PO	70,507
Legarreta, Manuel and José Luis	S	M	78,587
Lezama, Darío	—	—	134,470
Limantour, J. Y.	F	M and B	533,078
Loperena, Ignacio	M	M and B	719,636
Madrigal, Manuel	—	—	42,275
Mendieta, Aquilino	S	I	95,328
Micheaud, J. Agustín	F	M	42,500
Morales, Agustín	S	M	70,965
Morales Puente, Manuel	M	L and PO	120,600
Moreno, José de la Luz	M	PO	71,208
Naphegy, Gabor	H	M, Doctor	54,301
Ontiveros, Francisco	M	M	51,355
Ordeniana, Antonio	I	M?	41,105
Pavón, Francisco	M	PO	53,715
Pérez de Tagle, Mariano	M	PO	60,050
Piña y Cuevas, Manuel (Piña y Saviñón)	M	L and PO	64,991
Pontones, Fernando	M	PO and M	52,000
Portilla, Francisco de Paula	M	M and B	40,000
Prado, Cornelio	M	L	50,563
Quintana, Benito	M	PO and M	77,340
Ramírez, José Ma.	M	Notary	40,001
Rayo, José & Co. (Del Rayo)	M	PO	110,995
Rincón, Pedro	M	M	60,000

Name	Nationality	Occupation or profession	Value (*pesos*)
Robalo, Agustín (Robelo)	S?	M	62,000
Rosas, Joaquín José	M	M	58,195
Rosas Landa, Vicente (Ricoy Carlos)	M	PO	50,907
Sánchez, Marcelino	M	M	140,904
Sánchez Tagle, Agustín	M	PO	46,236
Saviñón, Bartolomé	M	L	55,425
Schiafino, Francisco	M	PO	274,885
Schoessling, Jorge $\left[\begin{array}{l}\text{C. Nieth, 29,361} \\ \text{A. Wagner, 31,860}\end{array}\right]$ [1]	F	M	61,221
Somera, Francisco	M	Engineer, PO and M	52,544
Terreros, Manuel	M	PO	52,700
Torres Adalid, Ign. and Javier	M	L, Councillor, M	60,967
Traconis, B. Juan	M	PO	110,066
Uscola, Ambrosio	M	M	59,170
Vera, Juan N.	—	—	44,450
Vicario, Santiago	M	PO	61,249
Zamora, Romualdo	S	M	56,000
		Total	6,927,639

[1] According to the Manifestaciones of Limantour, Nieth and Wagner were employees of Schoessling and bought in his name.

ABBREVIATIONS: Nationality: M = Mexican; F = French; S = Spanish; G = Guatemalan; Ge = German; H = Hungarian; I = Italian. Occupation or profession: B = Banker; H = Hacendado; I = Industrialist; L = Lawyer; M = Merchant; PO = Public Official.

LIST OF SOURCES AND WORKS CITED

MANUSCRIPT SOURCES

The following archives and collections have been used:

Archivo de Notarías, Guadalajara
Archivo de Notarías, Mexico City
Archivo de Notarías, Morelia
Archivo de Notarías, Orizaba and Jalapa, housed in the Biblioteca de la Universidad Veracruzana, Jalapa
Archivo de Notarías, Puebla
Archivo de Notarías, San Luis Potosí
Archivo de la Notaría de Córdoba, in the possession of notary Salvador D. Zamudio
Archivo de la Notaría de Leandro Rivero, Veracruz
Archivo del Ayuntamiento de Puebla
Archivo del Ex-Ayuntamiento de México, Mexico City
Archivo General de la Nación, Mexico City: particularly two sections:
  Papeles de Bienes Nacionales
  Justicia Eclesiástica
Archivo Histórico del Instituto Nacional de Antropología e Historia
Archivo Parroquial de Río Verde, microfilm collection, housed in the Biblioteca de la Universidad de San Luis Potosí
Colección Lafragua, Biblioteca Nacional, Mexico City
Latin American Collection, University of Texas
Registro Público de la Propiedad, libros de censos, Puebla

WORKS CITED

Akademia nauk SSSR. *Ocherki novoi i noveichei istorii Meksiki, 1810–1945*. Moscow, 1960.
Alamán, L. *Historia de México desde los primeros movimientos que prepararon su independencia en el año de 1808 hasta la época presente*. 5 vols., 4th ed., Mexico, 1942.
  Obras. 13 vols., Mexico, 1942–48.
  Documentos diversos (inéditos y muy raros). 4 vols., Mexico, 1945–47.
Alegato de buena prueba presentado por la parte de la Señora Doña Loreto Bernal de Suárez en el juicio ejecutivo que contra ella sigue Don José Y. Limantour sobre arrendamientos de la casa número 19 de la calle de D. Juan Manuel. Mexico, 1862.
Alegato de buena prueba que el Licenciado D. Manuel Siliceo, patrono y apoderado del Dr. D. Antonio Fernández Monjardín, ha hecho en el juicio posesorio promovido contra D. José Y. Limantour, reclamando el despojo de la casa no. 6 de la calle de la Palma, ante el juez de lo civil, Licenciado D. Antonio Aguado. Mexico, 1863.
Almonte, J. N. *Guía de forasteros de la ciudad de México*. Mexico, 1852.

Sources and works cited

Antuñano, E. de. *Economía política en México. Insurrección industrial. Documentos básicos para la historia de la industria moderna.* Puebla, 1846.

Arróniz, J. J. *Ensayo de una historia de Orizaba.* Orizaba, 1867.

Bancroft, H. H. *History of California.* 7 vols., San Francisco, 1886.

Banda, L. *Estadística de Jalisco, formada con vista de los mejores datos oficiales y noticias ministrados por sujetos idóneos, en los años de 1854 a 1863.* Guadalajara, 1873.

Bazant, J. 'Estudio sobre la productividad de la industria algodonera mexicana en 1843–45', *Industria nacional y comercio exterior (1842–1851).* Mexico, vol. VII of the *Colección de documentos para la historia del comercio exterior,* 1962.

'Evolution of the textile industry of Puebla, 1544–1845', *Comparative Studies in Society and History,* vol. VII, no. 1, 1964.

'Industria algodonera poblana de 1800–1843 en números', *Historia Mexicana,* vol. XIV, no. 1, 1964.

'La desamortización de los bienes corporativos de 1856', *Historia Mexicana,* vol. XVI, no. 2, 1966.

Historia de la deuda exterior de México (1823–1946). Mexico, 1968.

Berry, C. R. 'The fiction and fact of the Reform: the case of the central district of Oaxaca, 1856–67', *The Americas,* vol. XXVI, January 1970.

Betancourt, J. *San Luis Potosí, sus plazas y calles.* San Luis Potosí, 1921.

Bogue, A. y M. 'Profits and the frontier land speculator', *Journal of Economic History,* March 1957.

Boletín de la Sociedad Mexicana de Geografía y Estadística. Mexico, 1859.

Bouthonnier, P. 'The role of the peasants in the revolution', *Essays on the French revolution.* Ed. T. A. Jackson, London, 1945.

Bravo Ugarte, J. *Historia de México.* 3 vols., Mexico, 1944.

Historia sucinta de Michoacán. 3 vols., Mexico, 1964.

Brentano, L. *Eine Geschichte der wirtschaftlichen Entwicklung Englands.* Jena, 1927.

Buenrostro, F. *Historia del primero y segundo congresos constitucionales de la república mexicana.* 9 vols., Mexico, 1874–82.

Bulnes, F. *Juárez y las revoluciones de Ayutla y de la Reforma.* Mexico, 1905.

Busto, E. *Estadística de la república mexicana.* 3 vols., Mexico, 1880.

Callcott, W. H. *Church and State in Mexico, 1822–1857.* Durham, 1926.

Liberalism in Mexico, 1857–1929. Stanford, 1931.

Santa Anna. Norman, 1936.

Cambre, M. *La guerra de tres años en el estado de Jalisco.* Guadalajara, 1892.

Carrión, A. *Historia de la ciudad de la Puebla de los Angeles.* Puebla, 1896–97.

Castillo, R. del. *Cuadro sinóptico del estado de San Luis Potosí, con varios datos históricos, geográficos, estadísticos y administrativos.* San Luis Potosí, 1878.

Chávez Orozco, L. (ed.). *El banco de Avío y el fomento de la industria nacional.* Mexico, 1966.

Constant, G. *The reformation in England.* 2 vols., London, 1934.

Corral, J. J. del. *Breve reseña sobre el estado de la hacienda y del que se llama crédito público, o sea exposición de los males y ruina de la república, a que han llevado y siguen conduciendo las maniobras de los agiotistas y de los malos empleados.* Mexico, 1848.

Sources and works cited

Cosío Villegas, D. (ed.). *Historia moderna de México*. Vol. VII: *El porfiriato. La vida económica*. 2 vols., Mexico, 1965.

Cossío, J. L. *¿Cómo y por quiénes se ha monopolizado la propiedad rústica en México?* Mexico, 1911.

Avalúo de los terrenos de la ciudad, publicado en la Memoria del Ayuntamiento de 1830, y de las casas de la misma. Mexico, 1937.

Guía retrospectiva de la ciudad de México. Mexico, 1941.

El gran despojo nacional o de manos muertas a manos vivas. Mexico, 1945.

Costeloe, M. P. 'Church–State financial negotiations in Mexico during the American war, 1846–1847', *Revista de Historia de América*, no. 60, July–December 1965.

'The Mexican Church and the rebellion of the Polkos', *Hispanic American Historical Review*, vol. XLVI, May 1966.

'The administration, collection and distribution of tithes in the archbishopric of Mexico, 1800–1860', *The Americas*, vol. XXIII, July 1966.

Church wealth in Mexico. A study of the 'juzgado de capellanías' in the archbishopric of Mexico, 1800–1856. Cambridge, 1967.

'Guadalupe Victoria and a personal loan from the Church in independent Mexico', *The Americas*, vol. XXV, January 1969.

Cumplido, I. *Noveno calendario*. Mexico, 1844.

Denis, E. *La Bohême après la Montagne Blanche*. Published in Czech as *Cechy po Bílé Hore*. 2 vols., Prague, 1904.

Despojo de los bienes eclesiásticos, apuntes interesantes para la historia de la iglesia mexicana. Mexico, 1947.

Diario oficial del Gobierno Supremo de la república. 1868.

Díaz, L. (ed.). *Versión francesa de México. Informes diplomáticos, 1853–1867*. 4 vols., 1963–67.

Diccionario Porrúa de historia, biografía y geografía de México. Mexico, 1964.

Diccionario universal de historia y geografía. 7 vols. and 3 appendices, Mexico, 1853–56.

Documentos anexos a la Memoria de Hacienda de 1874, correspondientes a la sección sexta de la misma Secretaría. Mexico, 1875.

Dublán, M. y Lozano, J. M. (eds.). *Legislación mexicana o colección completa de las disposiciones legislativas expedidas desde la independencia de la república*. 58 vols., Mexico, 1876–1912.

Estadísticas del estado libre y soberano de Veracruz. Jalapa, 1831.

Estado de las fincas rústicas y urbanas respectivas a las temporalidades de los ex-jesuitas y Ordenes Hospitalarias y Monacales suprimidas. Mexico, 1823.

Estado de las fincas urbanas y rústicas respectivas a las temporalidades de los ex-jesuitas y Monacales suprimidos, con expresión de sus valores, gravámenes que reportan, y renta anual. Mexico, 1829.

Estado general que manifiesta todos los bienes y créditos que poseía el extinguido Tribunal de la Inquisición. Mexico, 1823.

Estado que manifiesta todos los bienes y créditos pertenecientes al extinguido Tribunal de la Inquisición de México, excluídos los correspondientes a los ramos que tenía sólo en administración, según se hallan en la presente fecha. Mexico, 1829.

Sources and works cited

L'Estafette des deux mondes. Journal français. Mexico, 1861, 1862.

Exposición que el provincial del Carmen hizo al Supremo Gobierno sobre las ventas de fincas que celebraron algunos conventos de su orden. Mexico, 1834.

Exposición que ha presentado al Exmo. Señor Presidente de la república la comisión nombrada por la reunión de compradores de fincas del clero, que tuvo lugar en el teatro principal, y acordó representar contra las disposiciones del decreto de 5 de febrero de 1861. Mexico, 1861.

Fisher, H. A. L. *The history of England from the accession of Henry VII to the death of Henry VIII (1485–1547). The political history of England,* vol. v, London, 1906.

Flores, R. *La contrarevolución en la independencia. Los españoles en la vida política, social y económica de México, 1804–1838.* Mexico, 1969.

Fuentes Mares, J. . . *Y México se refugió en el desierto: Luis Terrazas: historia y destino.* Mexico, 1954.

Galarza, E. *The Roman Catholic Church as a factor in the political and social history of Mexico.* Sacramento, 1928.

Galindo y Galindo, M. *La gran década nacional, o relación histórica de la guerra de reforma, intervención extranjera y gobierno del archiduque Maximiliano, 1857–1867.* 3 vols., Mexico, 1904–06.

Galván, M. *Colección de ordenes y decretos de la soberana junta provisional gubernativa y soberanos congresos generales de la nación mexicana.* 4 vols., Mexico, 1829.

Galván Rivera, M. *Guía de forasteros de la ciudad de México para el año de 1854.* Mexico, 1854.

García Cubas, A. *Noticias geográficas y estadísticas de la república mexicana.* Mexico, 1857.

Génin, A. *Les français au Méxique de XVIe siècle à nos jours.* Paris, 1933.

Gille, G. 'Les capitaux français et l'expédition de Méxique', *Revue d'Histoire Diplomatique,* no. 3, 1965.

González de Cossío, F. *Xalapa. Breve reseña histórica.* Mexico, 1957.

González Navarro, M. (ed.). *Vallarta en la Reforma.* Mexico, 1956.

González y González, L. 'La situación social de Jalisco en vísperas de la Reforma', *La Reforma en Jalisco y el Bajío.* Guadalajara, 1959.

Goodwin, M. C. *The Papal conflict with Josephinism.* New York, 1938.

Habakkuk, H. J. 'The market for monastic property, 1593–1603', *The Economic History Review,* April 1958.

Hanser, A. S. *Church and State in Bavaria, 1799–1806; an absolutist reform in the age of revolution.* Dissertation of the University of Chicago, 1964.

Historia documental de México, 2 vols., Mexico, 1964.

Icaza, M. de. *Exposición sobre la nulidad de las operaciones practicadas en los años 1861 y 62 con los bienes pertenecientes al Colegio de Niñas y a la corporación que lo fundó.* Mexico, 1864.

Iglesias, José M. and Prieto, G. *El Ministerio de Hacienda del 21 de enero al 6 de abril de 1861.* Mexico, 1862.

Inclán, L. G. *Astucia.* 3 vols., 2nd ed., Mexico, 1946.

Informe presentado al Exmo. Sr. Presidente de los Estados Unidos Mexicanos por el contador mayor, jefe de la oficina de rezagos, Juan Antonio de Unzueta, en cumplimiento de la

Sources and works cited

comisión que le confirió S.E. para que manifieste el manejo y el estado que guardó la hacienda pública en los años de 1830, 1831, y 1832. Mexico, 1833.

Informes leídos en la cámara de diputados por el Secretario de Hacienda sobre el estado que guarda el erario público y sobre las últimas operaciones practicadas en la deuda exterior e interior de la república mexicana. Mexico, 1852.

Jaurès, J. *Histoire socialiste de la révolution française.* 8 vols., Paris, 1927.

Kaminsky, J. 'Chiliasm and the Hussite revolution', *Change in medieval society.* Ed. S. L. Thrupp, New York, 1964.

Knapp, F. A., Jr. *The life of Sebastián Lerdo de Tejada, 1823–1889: a study of influence and obscurity.* Austin, 1951.

Knowles, D. *The religious orders in England.* vol. III, *The Tudor age*, Cambridge, 1959.

Knowlton, R. J. 'Clerical response to the Mexican Reform, 1855–1875', *The Catholic Historical Review*, vol. L, January 1965.

'Some practical effects of clerical opposition to the Mexican Reform, 1856–1860', *Hispanic American Historical Review*, vol. XLV, no. 2, 1965.

'Chaplaincies and the Mexican Reform', *Hispanic American Historical Review*, vol. XLVIII, August 1968.

'Expropriation of Church property in nineteenth-century Mexico and Colombia: a comparison', *The Americas*, vol. XXV, April 1969.

'La Iglesia mexicana y la Reforma: respuesta y resultados', *Historia Mexicana*, vol. XVIII, April–June 1969.

Labastida, L. G. *Colección de leyes, decretos, reglamentos, circulares, órdenes y acuerdos relativos a la desamortización de los bienes de corporaciones civiles y religiosas y a la nacionalización de los que administraron las últimas.* Mexico, 1893.

Lancaster-Jones, R. 'Bienes del convento agustino de Guadalajara', *Historia Mexicana*, vol. XIII, April–June 1964.

Latreille, A. *L'Eglise Catholique et la révolution française.* 2 vols., Paris, 1946.

Lavrín, A. 'The role of the nunneries in the economy of New Spain in the eighteenth century', *Hispanic American Historical Review*, vol. XLVI, November 1966.

Lefèbvre, G. 'La vente des biens nationaux.' Reproduced in G. Lefèbvre, *Etudes sur la révolution française.* Paris, 1963.

Leicht, H. *Las calles de Puebla.* Puebla, 1934.

Lerdo de Tejada, F. *Jefatura de hacienda y tesorería general del estado de Michoacán de Ocampo. Su cuenta e informe por los ingresos y egresos habidos en ambas oficinas, desde 19 de marzo de 1858 hasta 6 de febrero de 1862 en la primera y 31 de enero del mismo año en la segunda.* Morelia, 1862.

Tesorería general y jefatura de hacienda del estado de Michoacán de Ocampo. Su cuenta e informe por los ingresos y egresos habidos en ambas oficinas, desde 18 de marzo de 1858 hasta 31 de enero de 1862 en la primera y 6 de febrero del mismo año en la segunda. Morelia, 1963.

Lerdo de Tejada, M. M. *Cuadro sinóptico de la república mexicana en 1856 formado en vista de los últimos datos oficiales y otras noticias fidedignas.* Mexico, 1856.

Memoria presentada el Excmo. Sr. Presidente Sustituto de la república por el C. Miguel

Sources and works cited

Lerdo de Tejada, *dando cuenta de la marcha que han seguido los negocios de la hacienda pública, en el tiempo que tuvo a su cargo la secretaría de este ramo.* Mexico, 1857.

Apuntes históricos de la h. ciudad de Veracruz. 3 vols.; vols. 1 and 2, 2nd ed., Mexico, 1945; vol. 3, 1857.

Liljegren, S. B. *The fall of the monasteries and social changes in England leading up to the great revolution.* Lund, 1924.

Limantour, J. Y. *Représentation adressée a M. le Ministre de France à propos de la vente faite à M. Limantour par le gouvernement mexicain de diverses propriétés avant appartenu aux corporations ecclésiastiques.* Mexico, 1863.

López Cámara, F. 'Los socialistas franceses en la Reforma mexicana', *Historia Mexicana*, vol. IX, no. 3, 1960.

Macedo, P. *La evolución mercantil. Comunicaciones y obras públicas. La hacienda pública. Tres monografías que dan idea de una parte de la evolución económica de México.* Mexico, 1905.

Maillefert, E. *Gran almanaque mexicano y directorio del comercio de la república mexicana para el año de 1869.* Mexico, 1869.

Manifestaciones que José Yves Limantour, en cumplimiento del decreto de 26 de febrero del presente año, ha dirigido al Exmo. Consejo de Estado, relativas a la casa núm. 6 de la calle de la Palma, y a la hacienda de Tenería, situada en jurisdicción de Tenancingo. Mexico, 1865.

Marroqui, J. M. *La ciudad de México.* 3 vols., Mexico, 1900–3.

Mejía, F. *Memorias.* Mexico, 1958.

Memoria de Hacienda y Crédito Público. Mexico, 1823, 1830, 1856, 1857, 1868, 1870, 1872, 1873, 1874 and 1875.

Memoria de la Dirección General de Industria, 1843, 1844, 1845.

Memoria de la Secretaría de Relaciones Exteriores de 1930–31. Mexico, 1930–31.

Memoria de las operaciones practicadas en la sección séptima del Ministerio de Hacienda, sobre reconocimiento de capitales en fincas de propiedad particular y en fincas adjudicadas y rematadas y a favor de las señoras religiosas y el culto, comprendiendo desde la creación de dicha sección hasta 15 de diciembre de 1861. Mexico, 1861.

Memoria de las operaciones que han tenido lugar en la oficina especial de desamortización del distrito, desde el 7 de enero en que se abrió, hasta el 5 de diciembre de 1861, en que cesaron sus labores, para continuarlas la Junta Superior de Hacienda. Mexico, 1862.

Memoria del gobierno del estado de San Luis Potosí. San Luis Potosí, 1868–69.

Memoria del Ministerio de Fomento. Mexico, 1857, 1873.

Memoria del Ministerio de Justicia. Mexico, 1833, 1844 and 1851.

Memoria en que el C. General Epitacio Huerta dió cuenta al congreso del estado del uso que hizo de las facultades con que estuvo investido durante su administración dictatorial, que comenzó en 15 de marzo de 1858 y terminó en lo. de mayo de 1861. Morelia, 1861.

Método para seguir la cuenta de redenciones de capitales que poseía el clero en las oficinas respectivas, expedido por el Ministerio de Hacienda y Crédito Público. Mexico, 1861.

Mora, J. M. L. *México y sus revoluciones.* 3 vols., 2nd ed., Mexico, 1950.

Obras sueltas. 2nd ed., Mexico, 1963.

Sources and works cited

Muriel, J. *Conventos de Monjas en la Nueva España*. Mexico, 1946.

Hospitales de la Nueva España. 2 vols., Mexico, 1960.

Naredo, J. M. *Estudio geográfico, histórico y estadístico del cantón y de la ciudad de Orizaba*. Orizaba, 1898.

Nef, J. U. 'Prices and industrial capitalism in France and England, 1540–1640', *Essays in economic history*. Ed. E. M. Carus-Wilson, London, 1954.

Noticia de las fincas pertenecientes a corporaciones civiles y eclesiásticas del distrito de México. Mexico, 1856.

'Noticia de los conventos del arzobispado de México. Año de 1826', *Boletín del Archivo General de la Nación*, no. 3, 1953.

Obregón, G. J. *El Real Colegio de San Ignacio de México (Las Vizcaínas)*. Mexico, 1949.

Observaciones que los actuales poseedores de los bienes que pertenecieron al fondo piadoso de Californias, hacen a los señores diputados y senadores. Mexico, 1845.

Observaciones sobre la ley de 26 de febrero y sobre su reglamento. Mexico, 1865.

Observaciones sobre los términos del decreto que el senado acaba de pasar sobre la revisión de los contratos en que se enagenaron dichos bienes. Mexico, 1845.

Ocampo, M. *Obras completas*. 3 vols., Mexico, 1900–1.

Ocurso que el doctor Don Antonio Fernández Monjardín presentó en 28 de abril de 1862 al juez 40. de lo civil, Lic. D. Agustín Norma, reclamando el despojo que se le infirió en 24 de mayo de 1861 de una casa de su propiedad, de la que se dio posesión a D. Jose Yves Limantour. Mexico, 1862.

Odlozilik, O. *The Hussite king; Bohemia in European affairs, 1440–1471*. Rutgers University Press, 1965.

Ortega y Pérez Gallardo, R. *Historia genealógica de las familias más antiguas de México*. 3 vols., Mexico, 1908–10.

Parra, P. *Sociología de la Reforma*. 2nd ed., Mexico, 1967.

Payno, M. *Carta que sobre los asuntos de México dirige al señor Gen. Forey, comandante en jefe de las tropas francesas, el cuidadano Manuel Payno*. Mexico, 1862.

México y sus cuestiones financieras con la Inglaterra, la España y la Francia. Mexico, 1862.

La deuda interior de México. Mexico, 1865.

Cuentas, gastos, acreedores y otros asuntos del tiempo de la intervención francesa y del imperio. De 1861 a 1867. Mexico, 1868.

Los bandidos de Río Frío. 5 vols., Mexico, 1889–91.

La reforma social en España y México. 2nd ed., Mexico, 1958.

Payno, M. (ed.). *Colección de las leyes, decretos, circulares y providencias relativas a la desamortización eclesiástica, a la nacionalización de los bienes de corporaciones, y a la reforma de la legislación civil que tenía relación con el culto y con la iglesia*. 2 vols., Mexico, 1861.

Pérez Hernández, J. M. *Estadística de la república mexicana, territorio, población, antigüedades, monumentos, establecimientos públicos, reino vegetal y agricultura, reino animal, reino mineral, industria fabril y manufactura, artes mecánicas y liberales, comercio, navegación, gobierno, hacienda y crédito público, ejército, marina, clero, justicia, instrucción pública, colonias militares y civiles*. Guadalajara, 1862.

Sources and works cited

Pérez Verdía, L. *Historia particular del estado de Jalisco, desde los primeros tiempos de que hay noticia hasta nuestros días*. 3 vols., 2nd. ed., Guadalajara, 1952.

Pombo, L. *México, 1876–1892*. Mexico, 1893.

Portilla, A. de la. *México en 1856 y 1857. Gobierno del General Comonfort*. New York, 1858.

Prieto, G. *Lecciones elementales de economía política*. 2nd ed., Mexico, 1876.

Quintana, M. A. *Estevan de Antuñano*. 2 vols., Mexico, 1957.

Reflexiones sobre la ley de 17 de mayo del corriente año, que declara irredimible los capitales pertenecientes a corporaciones y obras pías; en respuesta al monitor republicano de 23 del mismo. Mexico, 1847.

Report of the Committee of Mexican Bondholders (29 April 1861). London, 1861.

Representación que el Licenciado José María Urquidi dirige al Exmo. Sr. Ministro de Hacienda, pidiendo se sirva declarar que la casa de su propiedad, situada en la calle de Vergara no. 4, no está comprendida en el artículo 11 de la ley de 5 de febrero de este año. Mexico, 1861.

Representación que hacen al congreso constituyente varios dueños de propiedades territoriales contra algunos artículos de los proyectos fundamentales que se discuten actualmente. Mexico, 1856.

Representaciones que hacen al congreso constituyente varios dueños de fincas rústicas y urbanas, en Michoacán, Guanajuato, Guerrero y Puebla, secundando la que los propietarios, residentes en la capital de la república, dirigieron al mismo congreso el 10 de julio del presente año, contra algunos artículos de los proyectos de leyes fundamentales que se están discutiendo. Mexico, 1856.

Représentation adressée à M. le Ministre de France à propos de la vente faite à M. Limantour par le gouvernement mexicain de diverses propriétés ayant appartenu aux corporations ecclésiastiques. Mexico, 1863.

Reyes, I. *Rectificación de algunas especies vertidas en el cuaderno impreso de Don Joaquín Llaguno sobre el embargo de la hacienda de San Jacinto*. Mexico, 1862.

Ríos, E. M. de los. *Liberales ilustres mexicanos de la Reforma y la intervención*. Mexico, 1890.

Riva Palacio, V. (ed.). *Mexico a través de los siglos*. 5 vols., Mexico, n.d.

Rivera Cambas, M. *Historia antigua y moderna de Jalapa y de las revoluciones en el estado de Veracruz*. 3 vols., Mexico, 1870.

Los gobernantes de México. 2 vols., Mexico, 1872–73.

Rodríguez de San Miguel, J. *La república mexicana en 1846, o sea directorio general de los supremos poderes, y de las principales autoridades, corporaciones y oficinas de la nación*. Mexico, 1845.

Romero, J. G. *Noticias para formar la estadística del obispado de Michoacán*, Mexico, 1862.

Romero de Terreros, M. *La iglesia y convento de San Agustín*. Mexico, 1951.

Antiguas haciendas de México. Mexico, 1956.

Romero Flores, J. *Historia de Michoacán*. 2 vols., Mexico, 1946.

Sánchez, J. M. *Reform and reaction: the politico-religious background of the Spanish civil war*. Chapel Hill, University of North Carolina Press, 1964.

Sources and works cited

Savine, A. *English monasteries on the eve of the dissolution.* Oxford, 1909.

Schefer, C. 'La grande pensée de Napoleon III, les origines de l'expédition du Méxique', *Revue d'Histoire Diplomatique*, no. 3, 1965.

Scholes, W. V. *Mexican politics during the Juárez regime, 1855–1872.* Columbia, 1957.

Segunda exposición que el comercio de la capital del departamento de Morelia hace al soberano congreso, manifestándole la justicia y necesidad de derogar la ley de 26 de noviembre de 1839 que aumentó los derechos de consumo a los efectos extranjeros en las aduanas interiores. Mexico, 1840.

Segura, F. S. 'La desamortización de 1855', *Economía Financiera Española*, XIX–XX, Madrid, 1968.

Contribución al estudio de la desamortización en España. La desamortización de Mendizábal en la provincia de Gerona. Madrid, 1969.

Contribución al estudio de la desamortización en España. La desamortización de Mendizábal en la provincia de Madrid. Madrid, 1969.

Segura, J. S. (ed.). *Boletín de la leyes del imperio mexicano, o sea código de la restauración. Colección completa de las leyes y demás disposiciones dictadas por la intervención francesa, por el supremo poder ejecutivo provisional, y por el imperio mexicano, con un apéndice de los documentos oficiales más notables y curiosos de la época.* 4 vols., Mexico, 1863–65.

Semanario de la industria mexicana, que se publica bajo la protección de la junta de industria de esta capital. Mexico, 1842.

Sesión del honorable congreso de Veracruz, en que se discutió y aprobó el decreto que declara de la pertenencia del estado algunos conventos y sus propiedades. Veracruz, 1833.

Sierra, J. *Juárez, su obra y su tiempo.* 2nd ed., Mexico, 1948.

Evolución política del pueblo mexicano. 3rd ed., Mexico, 1950.

Sierra, J. (ed.). *Mexico, su evolución social.* 3 vols., 2nd ed., Mexico, 1902.

El Siglo Diez y Nueve, 1856.

Solís, L. 'Hacia un análisis general a largo plazo del desarrollo económico de México', *Demografía y Economía*, no. 1, 1967.

Suárez y Navarro, J. *Informe sobre las causas y carácter de los frecuentes cambios políticos ocurridos en el estado de Yucatán.* Mexico, 1861.

Tawney, R. H. 'The rise of the gentry', *Essays in economic history.* Ed. E. M. Carus-Wilson, London, 1954.

Tesorería general y jefatura de hacienda del estado de Michoacán de Ocampo. Su cuenta e informe por los ingresos y egresos habidos en ambas oficinas, desde 18 de marzo de 1858 hasta 31 de enero de 1862 en la primera, y 6 de febrero del mismo año en la segunda. Morelia, 1863.

El Tiempo, 1857.

Tischendorf, A. *Great Britain and Mexico in the era of Porfirio Díaz.* Durham, 1961.

Toro, A. *La Iglesia y el Estado en México, estudio sobre los conflictos entre el clero católico y los gobiernos mexicanos desde la independencia hasta nuestros días.* Mexico, 1927.

Torres, M. de J. *Historia civil y eclesiástica de Michoacán desde los tiempos antiguos hasta nuestros días.* Morelia, 1914.

Sources and works cited

Le Trait d'Union; Journal français universel. Mexico, 1861, 1862.

Trens, M. B. Historia de la h. ciudad de Veracruz y de su ayuntamiento. 6 vols., Jalapa, 1949–55.

Trevelyan, G. M. Illustrated English social history. 4 vols., London, 1954.

Turlington, E. Mexico and her foreign creditors. New York, 1930.

Valadés, J. C. Alamán. Estadista e historiador. Mexico, 1938.

El porfirismo, historia de un régimen. Vol. 1: El nacimiento, 1876–1884; vol. 11: El crecimiento. Mexico, 1941, 1948.

Valle, J. N. del. Guía de forasteros de la capital de Puebla. Puebla, 1852.

El viajero en México. Mexico, 1859, 1864.

Velázquez, P. F. Historia de San Luis Potosí. 4 vols., Mexico, 1947.

Vernon, R. The dilemma of Mexico's development. Cambridge, 1963.

Vigil, J. M. La reforma. Vol. v: México a través de los siglos. Ed. V. Riva Palacio, Mexico, n.d.

Woodward, G. W. O. 'A speculation in monastic lands', The English Historical Review, October 1964.

Zamacois, N. de. Historia de México desde sus tiempos más remotos hasta nuestros días. 20 vols., Barcelona, 1876–82.

Zavala, L. de. Ensayo histórico de las revoluciones de México, desde 1808 hasta 1830. Vol. 1, Paris, 1831; vol. 11, New York, 1832.

INDEX

Index

Index

Index

Index

Navarro, M., 189
Neri del Barrio, Felipe, 21-2, 24, 28, 88-9, 183-4, 201-2, 258-9
New York, 69
Nueva Holanda, ranch, 104
Nuevo León, 133, 202

Oaxaca, 10, 131
Ocampo, Melchor, 122, 145, 163, 169, 172-3, 212, 247-8, 264
Ogazón, Pedro, 128, 157-8, 175, 180, 253
Olazagarre, Prieto and Co., 127, 129
Omealco, hacienda, 77
Orizaba, 70, 72-3; *see also under* Buyers of corporate property, Church wealth, Disentailment, Nationalization
Oropeza, Mariano, 234
Otterburg, Marcus, 232-3, 269

Pacheco, M. de, 130
Pachuca, 187
Palomar, José, 127
Páramo, Francisco, 122
Páramo, Norberto, 122
Paredes y Arrillaga, Mariano, 29
Paris, 93, 149, 203, 259-60, 264
Paso y Troncoso, Pedro del, 72, 75, 171
Patiño, Gregorio, 248
Patiño, J. R., 122
Pátzcuaro, 162
Pérez Gálvez, Jorge, 259
Pezuela, Robles, 150
Piedras, Miguel de la, 227
Pious Fund of the Californias, 14-15, 22-4, 27-8
Pomoca, hacienda, 122, 163
Porta Coeli, college, 10, 176
Portilla, Francisco de Paula, 86, 258
Prieto, Guillermo, 178-9, 183, 185
Prieto, Pedro J., 129
Property values, 98, 108, 217, 286
  as result of nationalization, 1, 196-7, 264, 282-3
  by capitalization of rent, 29, 53-5, 58-61, 63-4, 130
Public education endowments, 212-14
Public welfare organizations, their possessions, 208-12
Puebla
  economy and society, 42-6
  intervention in, 47-52
  see also under Buyers of corporate property,

Church wealth, Disentailment, Nationalization

Querétaro, 9, 42, 69, 86, 132-3, 157, 219

Ramírez, Ignacio, 96
Rascón, José Domingo, 27
Rayo and Co., 194
Rayón, Sra., 143
Regina Coeli, convent of, 31, 37, 113, 219-20. 277
Regular clergy
  number of, 9, 39
  property of, 8-9, 32-9
  property of in Córdoba, 77-8; in Jalapa, 78-9; in Jalisco, 128-31; in Mexico City, 93-5, 214-17; in Michoacán, 128-31; in Orizaba, 76-7; in Puebla, 46-52; in San Luis Potosí, 117-18; in Veracruz, 75-6
Rengel y Fagoaga, Rafaela, 89
Revision of sales, *see under* Nationalization
Reyes, Nicanor, 251
Río, José María del, 201
Río Verde, 115-16, 121
Rodríguez de San Miguel, Juan, 27
Rojo, Mariano, 152
Rome, 2, 46
Romero, Matías, 165, 279-81
Rothschilds, 85, 148-50, 185
Rubio, Cayetano, 24, 88, 92, 108, 164, 211, 259, 274, 277-8
Rubio, Francisco, 24
Ruíz, Manuel, 103

Salas, José María, 140, 190
Salas, Mariano, 29-30
Salonio, Antonio María, 143
San Agustín, monastery of, *see also under* Augustinians, Regular clergy
San Andrés, hospital, 94, 111, 208, 211
San Angel, college of, 10, 25
San Bernardo, convent of, 113, 214
San Camilo, order of, 7
San Diego
  monastery of, 78, 238
  order of, 9, 123
San Felipe Neri, congregation of, 7, 76, 231
San Francisco, hospital, 35
San Francisco, monastery of, *see under* Franciscans, Regular orders
San Francisco, Third Order of, 35-6, 75, 77

Index

Index